SOFTWARE QUALITY

Concepts and Plans

Robert H. Dunn
Systems for Quality Software
Management Consultants

PRENTICE HALL
Englewood Cliffs, N.J. 07632

Library of Congress Cataloging-in-Publication Data

Dunn, Robert H.
    Software quality : concepts and plans/Robert H. Dunn.
       p. cm.
    Bibliography
    Includes index.
    ISBN 0-13-820283-4
    1. Computer software—Quality control. I. Title.
QA76.76.Q35D86   1990
005—dc20   89-35696
                                 CIP

Cover photo courtesy of the Port
of New York Authority.

Editorial/production supervision and
    interior design: Fred Dahl
Cover design: Ben Santora
Manufacturing buyer: Ray Sintel

©1990 by Prentice-Hall, Inc.
A Division of Simon & Schuster
Englewood Cliffs, New Jersey 07632

This book can be made available to businesses
and organizations at a special discount when
ordered in large quantities. For more information
contact:

    Prentice-Hall, Inc.
    Special Sales and Markets
    College Division
    Englewood Cliffs, N.J. 07632

Printed in the United States of America
10 9 8 7 6 5 4 3

ISBN 0-13-820283-4

Prentice-Hall International (UK) Limited, *London*
Prentice-Hall of Australia Pty. Limited, *Sydney*
Prentice-Hall Canada Inc., *Toronto*
Prentice-Hall Hispanoamericana, S.A., *Mexico*
Prentice-Hall of India Private Limited, *New Delhi*
Prentice-Hall of Japan, Inc., *Tokyo*
Simon & Schuster Asia Pte. Ltd., *Singapore*
Editora Prentice-Hall do Brasil, Ltda., *Rio de Janeiro*

Contents

PART 2. QUALITY ESSENTIALS

PART 3. QUALITY CONSTRUCTION

Preface

Supposedly, Haydn got the idea for the opening theme of one of his quartets from the singing of a lovesick lark. We have all heard that a falling apple inspired Newton's work on gravitation. As viewed by either producers or consumers, a few software successes have happened without anyone giving much thought to quality. All of which demonstrate that serendipity does work every now and again.

This book is written for those who cannot depend on accident, but need a deliberate path to software quality. To this end, the book deals with planning the measures one can take in the interests of software quality. Part V, in fact, is given to formal software quality plans, Parts I through IV deal with basic concepts that should lie beneath quality plans, not least of which is the business of defining what we mean by software quality. (Section 1.5 of the first chapter amplifies this skimpy outline.)

Let us identify the people who demand constructive approaches to software. Certainly, software managers, but also programmers who aspire to management. Another group of people consists of the ever-increasing number of systems engineers and managers attacking—or attacked by—software-intensive projects. An obvious audience for the book is made up of quality control (or quality assurance) managers involved with software-intensive systems or concerned about the quality of the software their companies depend on. We need to include one more category, the one that lies at the intersection of quality assurance and software engineering: software quality engineers.

These are the people the book addresses. (Well, also, my mother-in-law, because she loyally reads everything I write.) Despite the diversity of the intended audience, I have tried to accommodate all its parts. The one prerequisite is some exposure to development or maintenance projects: Terms such as "defect" and "manageable" first appear pages or chapters before their meaning is clarified within the context of software quality.

Admittedly, readers who are not software professionals may find some of the going difficult, especially in Chapter 4, which discusses various software technology issues with respect to the influence of technology on quality or project control. Still, such readers need not give up: The summaries at the end of each chapter provide enough background to permit the reader to skip ahead to more familiar ground.

I should like to thank John Musa, Amrit Goel, and the anonymous reviewers rounded up by Prentice Hall, from whom I received a great many useful suggestions. I should also like to thank my perennial first reader, Steve Dunn, for his usual meticulous criticism of the manuscript.

ROBERT H. DUNN
Buck Hill Road
Easton, Connecticut

CHAPTER 1

The View from Above

Gather a group of computer scientists or software engineers and ask them to discuss any issues that they care to. Start a stopwatch. In the interval between 7 minutes 30 seconds and 9 minutes 15 seconds (my contribution to the science of software metrics)—after such topics as professional sports, new automobile models, and expectations of interest rate movements have been disposed of—the subject will invariably turn to programmer productivity and software quality.

Gather a group from the ranks of senior management concerned with the development or maintenance of software, and it will take considerably less time to get around to the issues of productivity and quality. They who pay the bills, have to confront disgruntled customers or boards of directors, or have to assume the ultimate risks, tend to get to the bottom line with little delay.

Their risk can be considerable. My last six months as a salaried employee were spent on a project that burned corporate funds at the rate of about $100 million a year in an attempt to adapt a software-intensive line of telecommunications equipment to new markets. The problems faced by the several hundred engineers and programmers were diverse, but nearly all were related to the software of the system. I was only one of many who were convinced that the project was in such disarray that there was no practical way of completing it without spending at least another $250 million, and then only by scrapping much of the work accomplished and starting anew. It takes a while for the conclusions of senior technical management to percolate to the level of senior

1

corporate management, but to the surprise of few the project was finally (and properly) terminated. The writeoff was reckoned in the hundreds of millions.

The essential precept of this book is that the issues attending the quality of software are those that lie at the heart of risk, cost, and schedule containment. Oh yes, and these issues have also to do with producing software that people are pleased with. After all, people ought to get something for their millions.

1.1 THE SIZE OF THE SOFTWARE PROBLEM

Millions? Try billions, about $40 billion for the United States alone. The cost of data processing has been quadrupling every ten years or so. Initially, hardware represented most of the cost, but few of us are old enough to remember those days. The cost of computer hardware performance has been decreasing by orders of magnitude each decade, sowing the field for ever larger, ever more ambitious software projects. To take a small-scale example, at one time I had a personal computer furnished with 256K of internal memory and two floppy disk drives, each capable of handling 360 kilobytes of data. For little more than this system had cost 18 months earlier, I replaced it with a new desktop with 640 kilobytes of internal memory and a processing speed roughly four times as fast. Also, instead of two floppy drives, the new system had one floppy and a 20 megabyte hard disk. Within two years, I had added a math coprocessor to increase speed and graphics to use newly available software. More telling, I was spending unproductive time at the tasks of conserving both RAM and disk space.

As cheaper hardware creates an insatiable demand for more software, we become more aware of the cost of that software—as software productivity has not in the least kept pace with hardware cost/performance ratios. Indeed, despite the introduction of structured programming, structured design, design tools, modern programming languages, and all the other shibboleths by which software engineers recognize each other, the most optimistic rate at which programmer productivity is increasing is about 5% per year. Five percent is scarcely enough. Quoting an eminent computer scientist, "A conservative estimate indicates a tenfold increase in the demand for software each decade."[1] Looking at the most voracious consumer of software development effort, the DoD, it is estimated that software costs will account for 10% of the defense budget by 1990.*

Cost is not the only concern. Where will all the programmers who are going to generate the new software come from? In the United States, we now have a half million or so, depending on the labor classifications one wants to include under the word "programmer." Without closing the gap between supply and demand, the number of people entering the software business is monotonically increasing. As reported in the *New York Times* March 23, 1986, basic data of the U.S. Department of Labor forecasts that the number of computer programmers will, by 1995, increase by 72% to a total of 586,000. During the same interval, the category the department calls "computer-analysts, data processors" is forecast to increase by 69% to a total of 520,000. Should we be looking forward to the day when computers consume the entire work force? Surely, even by the year 2020, we shall continue to need workers to grow food, build houses, and play Beethoven quartets. From every point of view, programmer productivity is a burning issue.

---

* Attributed to the Electronics Industry Association in a DoD briefing on the Strategy for a DoD Software Initiative (STARS).

Even as we have learned to look to Japan for workable approaches to improving the quality of our products, it is instructive to compare U.S. programming productivity with that of Japan. Although no two studies of productivity of either the United States or Japan arrive at the same numbers, all seem to find Japan far ahead of the United States. One citation suggests the average Japanese programmer produces 2,000 lines of code per month, while his or her American counterpart is generating fewer than 300.[2] I suspect that part of the reason for this discrepancy is that the average Japanese programmer is engaged in less complex projects than the average American programmer, but a more significant explanation for the difference probably lies with the greater use of software tools by the Japanese, and with the active participation of Japanese quality engineers.

Apart from the costs attending the development of new software, we are starting to lose sleep over the conceptual size of the projects now being considered. Where a large software system once numbered 100,000 lines of code, new systems are breaking the one million mark. With the power offered by modern chip technology, we can conceive of applications heretofore undreamed of. With the possible exception of science fiction writers, would anyone two decades ago have thought of the graphical computer-aided design systems that are used to generate complete VLSI (very large scale integration) chip designs? Would anyone have thought of connecting hundreds of such chips, once designed, into a distributed computing system capable of steering data and voice messages through various communications protocols across any path served by any combination of wire, fibre-optics, or satellite? Would anyone have conceived of real-time video picture enhancement capable of detecting and automatically pinpointing features of interest?

With these marvels—marvels even to those in the business of software—we encounter disquietingly complex conceptual structures wrought of our own cognitive processes. We have seen greater complexity before: the ecology of a farm pond, the structure and dynamics of a galaxy, our own bodies. But it is one thing to study that which exists, which has been designed or has evolved or has simply happened before we got there, and quite another thing to invent a structure of a complexity so great that it befuddles its own inventors. In a much-remarked paper,[3] David Parnas has questioned the very feasibility of the software that would be required to implement the Strategic Defense Initiative (Star Wars), and in the process has raised doubts among computer scientists and software engineers everywhere about how much we know about managing software projects that dare to extend the current bounds of complexity.

Awareness of the size of the software problem is reaching the highest levels of industry and government. In an attempt to improve the technology with which software complexity is managed, we now have in the United States three new enterprises directed squarely at the software technology problem:

- Microelectronics and Computer Technology Corporation, a consortium of 20 American suppliers of computer hardware and software. (MCC also addresses human interfaces and hardware.)

- Software Productivity Consortium, a cooperative effort of 15 defense electronics and aerospace contractors.

- Software Engineering Institute, an outgrowth of the DoD's ambitious project named Software Technology for Adaptable and Reliable Systems (STARS). The Institute is also affiliated with Carnegie-Mellon Institute.

The United States has no monopoly on software research and technology transfer. Abroad, three initiatives have attracted considerable note:

- Japan's Software Technology Center, with government, university, and industry participation.

- European Strategic Program for Research and Development in Information Technology (Esprit), formed by the European Economic Community, with tasks farmed out to companies in member countries.

- Alvey, an independent software initiative of the United Kingdom, which is also heavily involved in Esprit.

The funding of these ventures is continually undergoing revision, so it is not possible to state accurately the cost of these multinational and multicompany efforts. However, the total cost will certainly exceed two billion dollars by 1990—all this in the interests of attaining new levels of software complexity.

Most of the time, of course, we work within established limits of complexity. We do so, however, with programming teams smaller and perhaps less expert than those that will be required to implement the Strategic Defense Initiative, teams for whom the project at hand represents challenge enough. It seems that nearly every programming project taxes the imagination of its staff and provides new opportunities for error, error in understanding exactly what it is that is needed, error in translating the requirements into design, error in managing the entire process. As computers continue to proliferate and increase in power even as they decrease in space and cost, we find new applications for them that at once expand our capacities for performance and create new headaches for management.

Viewed from afar, software management is the management of complexity. Any number of approaches have been invented to ameliorate the task of managing complexity. Of these, perhaps the least difficult to implement is the concept of the *quality program.* Throughout the pages of this book we see how quality programs become part of the software solution. However, the notion of a quality program raises a problem of its own: If we are to use quality as a mechanism for reducing the pain of software management, we need to understand just what we mean by "quality" as it applies to software.

1.2 PERCEPTIONS OF SOFTWARE QUALITY

The connotation of "quality" seems to depend on the context in which it is used. One speaks of automobile quality in terms of the tolerance permitted in the fit of body panels, as measured in hundredths of inches. Using a different sense of quality, we also say that a car upholstered in real leather has greater quality than one furnished with vinyl seats (as measured in units of class). So too, with software. Analogous to automobile upholstery, a relational data base system has greater quality than a "flat" data base system. It gives the owner (or user) more utility, greater convenience, or, perhaps, just a sense of well-being. With regard to the fit of body panels, software may not develop squeaks with the passage of time, but as it ages it can become difficult to modify. Both notions of quality fall within J. M. Juran's concept of quality: fitness for use.

Restricted to software products, fitness for use is certainly inclusive. By why restrict quality to products? If, in our view of quality, we can also include the *process* that results in products that are fit for use, we can also address the problems of managing complexity. That is, to join in the attack on the fundamental software problems now facing us, software quality programs should also encompass the suitability of programming processes to the formidable tasks of producing complex software. In short, we can identify two sets of objectives for software quality programs:

- Software products.
- Software processes.

As we shall see, the distinction between the two sets is more apparent than real. Indeed, actions taken to satisfy one are required to fully satisfy the other.

Quality of the Software Product

Let us return to the business of defining quality, the issues of leather vs. vinyl on the one hand and manufacturing tolerances on the other. Just how do we perceive the fitness for use of the software product? Our perception of fitness depends on how we use it. Let us take a software-intensive central office telephone switch as an example.

The subscriber perceives the product's fitness in terms of reliability and availability. When the phone goes off hook, the subscriber expects to hear a dial tone, if not by the time the instrument is placed against his or her ear, then no more than a second or two later. Once having dialed, the subscriber expects to be connected to the called terminal. The only exceptions permitted are busy signals and announcements that the number is no longer a working number (or one of the many other discrete announcements with which telephone companies remind us of how fumble-fingered we are). If the subscriber forwards calls from office to club, he or she expects that no potential customers will be lost if the afternoon is given over to tennis. Call forwarding, like all subscriber features, must work unerringly as advertised. In brief, telephone subscribers define telephone switch quality as service dependability.

Quite different is the view of the people operating the central office. They, too, regard dependability as paramount, but they see it in different ways. To provide the subscriber with new service features, the operational staff must be able to install these features (update the software) without interrupting service. Thus, they want their dialogue with the switch to be clear and unambiguous. There must be no references to data files normally hidden from their view. If the installers forget which step of the installation process they are in, they expect to find out by querying the system. If they enter plainly inappropriate data (e.g., a trunk label where a file name was required), they expect to be admonished. Central office technicians want software that will limit the likelihood and magnitude of human error, whether the task at hand is extending service, troubleshooting a hardware problem, or going about such routine maintenance tasks as data backup operations.

The bookkeeping staff of the telephone company is also a user of the switch software. Although the staff anticipates its own fallibility from time to time in forgetting to redress a posting error, it will not accept software failures that charge calls to the wrong party. The bookkeeping staff perceives the quality of the switch in terms of the number of billing complaints received from subscribers.

Taking one more class of user, we have the maintenance programmers. Among the attributes of quality to which they are attuned, we find accurate and understandable software documentation, readable and well-annotated source code, and a software structure that does not violate the specifications of the software tools at hand. For example, if a patch is necessary, the patch installation tools must be capable of ensuring that the correct locations of memory and none others are overwritten.

We could go on with others who are touched by the quality of switch software, but the point is made: Many factors enter into the quality of large software products.

Quality of the Process

The most straightforward perception of a "quality" programming process has to do with the result of the process: The process is of high quality if the resulting product is perceived to be of high quality. Quality products are necessary to the definition of a quality process, but insufficient. Although good product quality can dependably result only from a good process, other views of quality need to be entertained, especially if quality programs are to be funded. Apart from the incontrovertible connection between process and product, the success of a software project is measured not only in terms of the product but of the events that attended its development. If the project manager had to give up every second weekend to replan the project as a result of a succession of mishaps that affected schedules, or if the project manager's boss had to dig deep into the firm's pockets to pay for cost overruns, or if the programmers had to spend most of their time drearily writing documentation (which will read drearily) instead of designing, we can hardly say that the process is of high quality.

To digress briefly, we may note that many firms have looked to the manager (or director) of quality assurance (or quality control or product assurance or what have you) to "take care of software quality matters." Where this has happened, we can suspect that senior management does not know much about software quality. Moreover, we can almost bet that, unless they have taken pains to school themselves in systems or software methodology, managers of quality assurance, with their background of viewing quality in terms of the product or service delivered to customers, will decide that the quality department should get involved in software testing. Although more thorough testing can be expected to benefit product quality, it is only part of a bigger solution to product problems, and it misses altogether the broader scope of software quality.

Good products are only one of management's objectives. The other objectives are meeting schedule, meeting cost, and manageability. A quality process addresses all of the objectives. General managers perceive process quality (although they may not know its name) by the extent of customer satisfaction or increased sales or some similar objective measure, and by increased profit—the result of lower costs. The knowledgeable software manager perceives quality in the smoothness of the development or maintenance process: infrequent replanning exercises, awareness of schedule slippages in time to take remedial action, no embarrassing interviews with senior management to obtain more funds, and confidence that critical parts of the system have been identified and are competently being dealt with.

Indirectly, management's ability to cohabitate with software is affected by the view of the process held by the people of the process. Designers who have to wait their turn to get to the word processor to document their work become noticeably (sometimes clamorously) impatient. Programmers who are unsure of exactly what it is they are supposed to program go about their work dispiritedly. Equally cheerless are testers who find that faults in the test support software cause system crashes several times a day.

What do these disgruntled workers do? They do what software people have been doing ever since computers were invented: They leave to take jobs elsewhere. Now, given the romantic allure of the life of the gypsy, migratory programmers will leave sooner or later in any case, but the problems of management are exacerbated when sooner, rather than later, is the rule. Worst of all, the more gifted software personnel, who are often the most stable, are the first to refuse to put up with unproductive process crotchets. In short, the programming staff's view of the quality of the software process is everyone's business.

The problem with processes is that they are seldom designed. They happen or, more euphemistically, they evolve. A banking house starts off with a small programming staff, possibly contract programmers working under the direction of a salaried supervisor, to build a modest management information system (MIS) for the timely reporting of the firm's equity and debt positions. A process appropriate to the small scale of the problem is more or less defined, as often as not by ad hoc procedures transmitted verbally. Other than language processors, tools are few. A decade later, when the firm is attempting to network an integrated set of MIS packages to its branch offices, the process by which the new software will be generated is the original process, repeatedly patched, with each modification a quick fix in reaction to the shortcomings observed in the course of the immediately preceding project.

To take another typical example, an instrument manufacturer uses a microprocessor in a new equipment design. The programmers are the engineers who thought to incorporate computing power as a way of providing unique features or of reducing hardware elsewhere. Working under engineering disciplines (not the worst thing they could do), they get the chip programmed, although with more effort than had been anticipated. Although the programming turned out to be a learning process, the product is successful. Some years later, the manufacturer is using a dozen microprocessors in its equipments (now graduated to "systems") and the programmers are dealing with concurrency, on-line downloading of reactive software into microprocessors, and other software matters standing at a considerable remove from engineering affairs. Indeed, in recent years the company has hired professional programmers with no engineering training, but the software development process has remained tied to what was appropriate to the design of electronic equipment.

The conscious design of software development and maintenance processes is one of the pillars supporting the fairly new discipline of software engineering. In fact, the term "software engineering" was originally coined by Prof. F. L. Bauer of the Munich Technical University in contradistinction to the prevalent practice of "software tinkering."* "Software engineering" seems to have a cachet about it that has induced any number of managers, either out of ignorance or wishful thinking, to call their programmers software engineers, quite independently of the approach to programming. In any case, the establishment of software processes based on thoughtful methodologies and supported by modern technology is the hallmark of successful programming shops. The six projects cited in Section 1.1, three in the United States and three abroad, start with the precepts of software engineering as a given.

To see how appalling software tinkering can be, consider two examples of mismanagement I have personally encountered. The first is from the engineering-cum-programming shop of an instrument manufacturer. The target computer was a ruggedized

---

* In 1967 at a meeting of a study group on computer science established by the NATO Science Committee.[4]

minicomputer destined for an airborne application. To the surprise of the programming manager, the machine came unbundled, and the cost of software—an assembler (yes, the program was to be written in assembly language), linker, and loader—had to be negotiated separately. The programming manager, outraged that the cost of the software would be $10,000, found a much cheaper cross-assembler and linker-loader that could be hosted by a machine located in a service bureau in a nearby city. However, in order to use the cross-assembler, some preprocessing of the source code was required. The preprocessing would be done on the firm's general purpose computer. This is the software testing scenario that finally developed: Source code was entered into the local computer, a tape was output, the tape was delivered to the service bureau, and a day later a load tape for the target machine was delivered so that a test could be run. Total turnaround time was three to four days, depending on the time of day the first tape was produced. Not including lost labor time, the total cost of developing test load tapes during the months before the project—hopelessly behind schedule—was abandoned was ten times that of the scorned $10,000.

The second example of an impossible process concerns a major financial institution that hired droves of programmers to develop an electronic funds transfer (EFT) system. Previously, it had contracted for custom software or for the modification of off-the-shelf systems. The EFT system represented the firm's initial venture into in-house software development. The programmers were immediately set to work designing and coding, and in short order the director of information systems (or whatever his title was) was able to report hundreds of new lines of code generated each week. Not long before testing was to start it become apparent that the programmers had never been given a clear idea of what the EFT system was supposed to accomplish. Subsystems were defined in general terms, and it was in those general terms that the new staff happily set itself to the task of programming. However, there were no testable specifications for the subsystems and of course there was no system specification. As it happened, some of the code was salvaged by the new director of information systems—it is likely that more was salvageable if one only knew what it did—and the system was finally completed at a cost overrun of about 300% of the initial estimate.

In both of these examples, the programmers were aware of the impending disasters long before senior management. However, business organizational hierarchies being what they are, there was no way to tip off the top brass that unpleasant surprises were in the offing. Moreover, as is so often the case, senior management had only the vaguest notion of what software development was all about, and were not inclined to ask questions likely to yield recondite answers. (Even today, when all else fails, programming managers turn to obfuscation.) In the absence of a standard process founded on proven principles— even if proven elsewhere—management had no way to interpret project status reports and no way to demand remedial action (which in both cases included firing the responsible manager) while such action could still prevent disaster.

In stark contrast to these two examples of processes of abysmal quality, we can also find established processes based on the tenets of software engineering, as documented in countless journal articles and reports, conferences, workshops, symposia, and books. In the better programming shops, the processes continue to evolve, not to correct last year's disaster, but (often with quantified knowledge of the effects of the current process) to take advantage of the latest technology. These quality processes exist not by chance but as the result of a deliberate quality program.

1.3 ELEMENTS OF QUALITY

No matter how it is perceived, it is hard to find anyone who has not a good word to say for quality. We're all for it. The only question is how do we get it? Simply paying more is not the answer. We have paid plenty and failed to get quality. Indeed, overpaying for software is a symptom of poor process quality. No, money is not the source of software quality, although we shall see where it helps. In fact, there are not one, but three sources of software quality:

- **People.**
- **Technology.**
- **Management.**

The canvas painted by people, technology, and management does not leave out much. Still, given the universal pursuit of simple solutions to difficult problems, the breadth of the foundation of software quality is worth noting, even at the risk of banality.

Certainly, to say that people are a prerequisite for quality is to drop a bromide square in the middle of the floor. Nevertheless, quality requires qualified personnel, and personnel qualifications for software development include smarts, aptitude, education, training, and attitude. Each of these can be addressed by a quality program, although within fairly narrow limits for the first two. Section 1.1 spoke of the burgeoning size of the software work force, which does nothing for one's confidence in being able to recruit at some selected level of intelligence or aptitude. Finding the right educational background is also compromised in a sellers' market, but through tuition reimbursement and adjusted working hours, companies can take aggressive remedial action. Certainly, training and encouragement of positive attitudes lend themselves to management actions.

Apart from influencing the quality of the cognitive processes that produce software, we have also to deal with the problem of maintaining staff stability. If firms employing programmers have no monopoly on losing people at the worst possible times or losing people in whom considerable education and training have been invested, a new chapter in the annals of professional migration has nevertheless been written by the programming population. In some companies, annual turnover rates of 25% are considered normal. Understandably, staff stability is a concern of quality programs, and, as it happens, improving stability is often a concomitant of improvements in management and technology.

Of course, the interest in technology transcends the influence it has on dissuading people from leaving for more automated pastures. Quality derives directly from tools, defect removal techniques, the ease with which previously qualified software can be reused, the choice of programming languages, and the very choice of development methodologies. None of these factors is independent of the others, which requires software managers to have a working knowledge of the entire software engineering spectrum. The difficulty is compounded by the rate at which the technology is improving, that is, the rate at which programming is becoming software engineering. Looking about the world of programming, we see levels of technology (and corresponding quality) dating from 1970, from 1980, and from the mid-1980s. The remarkable thing is that we can see all technology epochs in the same firm. Many programming shops lend new meaning to the term "living history." For example, we might have part of the MIS department working in BAL under DOS (actually, pre-1970) to extend the trusty old payroll system, some of that department developing PL1 code on virtual machines (1970) for a new set of modules to be added to the manufacturing control system, and yet another MIS group writing in one or another relational data base language for a new customer data base system. While this is going on, the product programming department is using Ada* for the new line of software-intensive products. In anticipation of the testing to start next month, two or three of the staff are running experiments with a recently purchased Ada source language debugger and coverage-based test system. And then there is the advanced concepts group using Smalltalk in their experiments with a software development methodology directed to module reusability. If they achieve any success, they hope to sell the idea to the product programming people; if not, maybe someone in MIS will offer his or her project as the subject of an experiment.

The technology pastiche of our hypothetical example is the result of several factors. Some of the outdated technology in use can be ascribed to ignorance of anything better; some to the simple fact that few software managers can be expert in all areas of a technology that is rapidly evolving. Also, newly minted technology must be experimented with before it becomes part of the standard process, and it is doubtful if any shop can run simultaneous experiments on all new methods and tools. Nevertheless, never have software managers had the option of so many ways to build software. The diversity of options is both solution and problem: There are better methods but novelty alone does not guarantee improvement. The product application, the corporate culture, and the speed with which staff can learn new ways and tools must all be considered.

Whatever the shape of the technology frontier within a specific firm, it is most certainly ragged across the entire industrial landscape, with some salients closely identified with specific companies, balanced by some anonymous redoubts. If the technology in use is uneven, so are programmer productivity levels and quality levels. A large part of any software quality program has to be directed to technology improvement, not simply the adoption of new technology but its proper use as well.

Updating technology usually costs. The people who provide the technology coin are called managers. Software managers put the costs of updates in their budgets—labor costs, training costs, software and hardware purchase or leasing costs. Senior management reviews the budgets and has been known to approve at least part of them. This is a common perception of the role of management, but an anthropocentric one; for management is not just people, it is also the framework of policies, procedures, and practices within which software is developed or maintained.

Apart from managers, software management consists of cost estimating procedures and tools, business planning and allocation of resources according to plans, and tracking mechanisms to determine variance from plans or (every now and again) adherence to plans. Management is also the climate in which the environmental needs of technical people are addressed, with attention given to technology, workspace, buffering from irrelevant nontechnical problems, and relief from administrivia (clerical work). Like people and technology, software management must be part of the solution to the software quality problem. Unlike people and technology, ill-considered software management can provide a climate in which improvement of people or technology is impossible.

From the foregoing, it would seem that enlightened senior management, technically astute middle management, and a high caliber staff would be sufficient to achieve software

* Ada is a registered trademark of the Ada Joint Program Office, U.S. Government.

quality. In theory, this is certainly the case. In practice, however, the attainment of software quality is best served by mounting a deliberate program to address the details attending the three main elements of quality. Moreover, the program should be managed. Companies involved in multi-million-dollar projects have cost management to monitor all project costs, program management to coordinate the work of diverse participating functions (design, manufacturing, and so forth), resource management to oversee the apportioning of capital assets over all projects, and so forth. Why not software quality management to manage software quality programs? Yes, why not?

1.4 SOFTWARE QUALITY ASSURANCE

The management of software quality programs is commonly called "software quality assurance" but the name is just about the only thing common to the management of software quality programs. This is understandable, since no two quality programs can be expected to address precisely the same purposes. Software quality assurance is actually somewhat of a misnomer, since

> *software quality assurance does not assure the quality of software, but the effectiveness of a software quality program.*

The distinction may seem overly fine, but it serves to rule out software quality assurance activities directed exclusively to testing, verification and validation activities, or the like. If we are to believe that software quality must be built into the product through the use of a process that itself has quality built in, then we must also accept that software quality assurance must be an aspect of all software development (and maintenance) activities.

To implement software quality assurance, the management of a software quality program, we need to have implementors. The day-to-day management of a software quality program is overseen by software quality engineers, often organized into a functional entity of their own, a software quality assurance group, department, or whatever. For brevity and generality, we refer to these as SQA functions. Such functions may report to software management, quality or product assurance management, or any other organizational entity that seems to make cultural sense. However, let us not lose sight of the dedication of the function to quality—it must avoid deep involvement in the problems facing other functions. Specifically, to manage the software quality program, SQA functions should be at as great an organizational remove from the technical staff as possible. Chapter 9 discusses the reasons for this detachment in some detail. For the present we simply recognize that in the face of adverse circumstances, when the SQA function is most needed, the interests of quality, cost, and schedule may be inimical, with the last two often the dominant influences on technical staff.

SQA functions operate in diverse ways, presumably in response to the most urgent needs. (Presumably, but not assuredly. Like software management, SQA is not always what it ought to be.) In some firms, software engineers keep track of reviews, test planning, and other tasks actually performed by the technical staff. In other firms, the software quality engineers actively participate in defect removal activities. Nearly always, the SQA function keeps tabs on needed corrections to the interim and final products of a software development or maintenance project. In some firms, software quality engineers take an active part in preparing or revising the documents that define the standard programming practices to be followed. In other firms, they only review these documents, sometimes with approval authority, sometimes without. Commonly, software quality engineers use audits of the technical process to determine the extent to which standard practices are complied with. Sometimes software quality engineers certify or qualify the technical staff's tools that have the capability to affect product or process quality. Some software quality engineers qualify the products of the technical staff; alternatively, some are content to evaluate the qualification plan prepared by the technical staff.

The most important role that software quality engineers can play is that of improving quality. By analyzing defect data, the SQA function can identify defect-prone elements of the development process or ineffective defect removal practices. The conclusions of these analyses are brought to the attention of technical management in the expectation that means of remedying the problem will be studied. Although it is rare for software quality engineers to have the authority to change tools and development or maintenance practices (other than product qualification), enlightened technical management will entertain any remedies that the SQA function cares to suggest. Plainly, the attention given SQA recommendations depends on the reputation earned by the SQA function.

Many software quality engineers are involved in attempts to predict the reliability of software systems. Trend analysis, reliability growth models, and fault mode analysis are among the techniques used for the purpose.

In nontechnical areas, software quality engineers may recommend or implement training programs for programmers, may analyze staff backgrounds relative to the programming tasks at hand, or may encourage the formation of quality circles to improve participatory management. Software quality engineers may analyze the accuracy of cost predictive models, as applied to past projects. They may correlate physical environmental factors with productivity or quality, as reported by various other companies, and compare the conclusions with local circumstances. They may keep track of the time spent by the technical staff in administrivia. In short, SQA functions can provide the bookkeeping necessary for technical and general management to productively participate in software quality programs.

From the description of all of these possible tasks that software quality engineers might perform, one is likely to conclude that some software quality engineers are more ambitious or efficient than others. Undoubtedly, this is true. However, the usual limitation to the scope of software quality assurance is not the predilections of the SQA staff, but the territorial imperative of technical management. Other influences are the funding available to the SQA function (a measure of general management's commitment to the quality program) and the abilities of the software quality engineers themselves. Software quality engineers who are software engineers are qualified to investigate, perhaps experiment with, new programming tools. Software quality engineers who are retread (let us hope they are at least retrained) welding inspectors are unlikely to get deeply involved in matters of technology.

Before leaving this overview of software quality assurance, let us look at the Japanese view of things. Ever since industry discovered that American consumers had discovered Japanese cars and home entertainment equipment, comparison of American quality practices with those of the Japanese has become common in the larger quality community. For the Japanese view, however, we shall not refer to a publication primarily read by the quality community, but to the IEEE's *Computer*. In the March 1983 number of *Computer*, Yukio Mizuno of Nippon Electric Company (NEC), writes about the scope of NEC's SWQC (software quality control) program.[5] While we see references to data collection and analysis and analysis of product problems, most of the SWQC program is directed to the people responsible for software development. Considerable emphasis is placed on quality circles (among other things, they are directly involved in defect removal tasks), excellent results are published, prizes are awarded programmers for more tangible recognition, and team goals are continually reinforced. This kind of attention to the first of the three elements of quality enumerated in Section 1.2, people, is prominent in the Japanese scheme of quality assurance.

This presentation of software quality assurance as a management tool is consistent with the management orientation of this chapter. In the next chapter we start to view software quality issues from a more microscopic aspect, and references to SQA functions are infrequent until we get to Chapter 9. However, it should be understood that it can be profitable to give software quality engineers a hand in the making of all policies having to do with software development and maintenance and in all matters involving the quantification of experience through measurement and data summaries.

1.5 FROM MICROSCOPY TO PLANS

The microscopic view of quality referred to in the preceding paragraph is the substance of Chapter 2, which concludes this first, or introductory part of the book. There are really two parts to the microscopic view: A qualitative summary of the specifics of software products that result in the perceptions of quality discussed in Section 1.2, and a discussion of the quantification of certain of the characteristics that influence quality or are regarded as earmarks of quality itself.

In Part 2 we explore in detail the three elements of quality—people, technology, and management—discussed in Section 1.3. Chapter 3 is devoted to the sine qua non of quality, the producers—in this case, the programmers—programmers being the inclusive category of producers comprised of analysts, software engineers, testers, designers, coders, and any other labor classification descriptive of professionals involved in the development or maintenance of software.

Chapter 4, the longest of the book, is given to the second element of quality, technology. Taking technology from the top, the generation of systems by data-driven, function-driven, axiom-founded, and other philosophies is surveyed, as is the reuse of software, in whole or in part. Programming and design languages, which in some ways are inseparable from development models, are also discussed. To many, the salient characteristic of technology is the aggregate capability of the tool set used for programming. To others, software tools are to the larger issue of technology as welding torches are to the issue of boiler design. In discussing software tools, Chapter 4 concentrates on the supporting role tools play in modern software technology. Quality cannot be discussed without including the methods used for finding and removing defects. In Chapter 4, defect removal methods are divided into two classes, passive and dynamic. The latter class, which involves the actual execution of code, is explored from two points of view, structural and functional.

The last part of the quality triplet, management, is the subject of Chapter 5. Here, we deal with the difficult problems of planning—including cost estimating (in contradistinction to soothsaying)—and the principles of software project control. Part 2 closes with discussions of the returns that can be expected from investing in a physical environment conducive to software development and maintenance, administrative relief from clerical tasks, and tools.

The third part of the book is given to the definition of software quality programs. Chapter 6 looks at the procedural schemes for software development. More to the point, the chapter examines the way these schemes lend themselves to built-in mechanisms for ensuring quality in the development process.

Chapter 7 deals with the use of these mechanisms as management "hooks." The chapter, concerned with other aspects of project control, also looks at organizational issues, the role of work breakdown structures in the quality program, and methods for determining adverse trends during the prosecution of a project.

Part 3 concludes with a chapter given to the special problems encountered after software is released. Although the quality program for major modifications of software is much like that for software development, minor maintenance actions need some separate treatment.

Taken together, Chapters 9 and 10 constitute Part 4, Quality Management. The first of these chapters addresses quality management, enlarging on the remark at the start of Section 1.4 that software quality assurance is the management of a software quality program. Here, the specifics of tracking corrective action, collecting defect data, and the like are individually described.

Chapter 10 is devoted to the measurements and methods used as part of a quality improvement program, the aspect of quality management likely to have the most lasting effect.

In the final part of the book, we come to the business of putting it all together, outlining the responsibilities of all functional groups and documenting each activity of a quality program. In short, Part 5 addresses *software quality plans.* Chapter 11 talks about the general content of quality plans, while the final three chapters each contain a sample quality plan. The plan of Chapter 12 is for a project of modest size, while the plans of Chapters 13 and 14 are typical of plans for development projects of hundreds of thousands of lines of code. The hypothetical projects to which the plans apply represent three different software application areas: Chapter 12 deals with management information systems, Chapter 13 with computer aided engineering, and Chapter 14 with military systems. The difference between the projects of Chapters 13 and 14 accounts for the essential difference between their quality plans: The quality plan of Chapter 13 is based on IEEE Std 730, and the plan of Chapter 14 is patterned after DoD-STD-2168.

1.6 SUMMARY

1. The sharply decreasing costs of computer hardware are causing an increase both in the amount of new software and in the complexity of software systems.

2. Software technology has not kept up with hardware technology, resulting in dramatically increasing costs and programmer shortages.

3. Software management has become the management of complexity. Software quality programs are one of the approaches to managing complexity.

4. There are two faces to software quality: quality of programs and quality of the processes that produce the programs. Both must satisfy the underlying tenet of "fitness for use."

5. The quality of the software product is difficult to fully quantify; worse, it is given to subjective evaluations by those who use the software. However, these can be anticipated.

6. Quality programs come from quality processes. Quality processes also address the objectives of cost, schedule, and risk containment.

7. Quality is rooted in the technology used to develop or maintain software, the caliber of the staff using the technology, and the managerial controls and support applied to the entire process.

8. Quality programs address the education and training of programming personnel and can also have a positive effect on the attitudes of programmers.

9. The level of technology is governed by programming methods and the software tools and detailed techniques that support the methods.

10. Apart from addressing such matters as planning, estimating, resource allocation, and monitoring deviations from plans, software management must also provide an environment conducive to programmer productivity.

11. Software quality assurance is a management tool. By managing quality programs designed to meet the objectives of product and process quality, software quality assurance ensures the effectiveness of these programs.

12. Software quality assurance can enter into the development or maintenance process in a number of ways, and considerable diversity is found within industry. The diversity results from differences among company cultures and the qualifications of software quality engineers.

1.7 REFERENCES

[1] J. Musa, "Software Engineering: The Future of a Profession," *IEEE Software* (January 1985) pp. 55–62.

[2] W. Myers, "An Assessment of the Competitiveness of the United States Software Industry," *Computer* (March 1985) pp. 81–92.

[3] D. Parnas, "Software Aspects of Strategic Defense Systems," *CACM*, Vol. 28, No. 12 (December 1983) pp. 1326–1335.

[4] *DACS Newsletter*, Vol. II, No. 2 (September 1979) RADC/ISISI, Griffiss AFB, New York.

[5] Y. Mizuno, "Software Quality Improvement," *Computer* (March 1983) pp. 66–72.

CHAPTER 2

The View from Below

Chapter 1 took a fairly lofty stab at defining software quality. Acting as the advocate of thousands of anonymous managers and software users, Section 1.1 reduced Juran's fitness for use to a matter of perceptions of the quality of programs and the process producing the programs. For consumers, fitness for use says it all, if in no great detail. For producers, fitness for use has a pleasant cachet to it; it represents a high-minded goal that should motivate managers and programmers to do the decent thing. As the least common denominator of quality, fitness for use entails one problem: Producers cannot design to it. It cannot be designed to because we do not know when we have achieved it. We need something more substantial to define good programs and to serve as objectives for programming processes. We start by dissecting the warm feeling evoked by the words "software quality."

2.1 FACETS OF QUALITY

Wearing our consumer's hat, the first things we see when we put software quality under a microscope are

- Reliability
- Usability
- Maintainability
- Adaptability

16

When we look inside these four "ilities" we find a host of others, the attributes the producer has to build in to achieve this top layer. Let's look at the four "ilities" in more detail.

The IEEE Glossary[1] offers two definitions of software reliability, one referring to an extrinsic effect, the other intrinsic, and both recalling the element of time found in probabilistic definitions of reliability for hardware:

> *"The probability that software will not cause the failure of a system for a specified time under specified conditions."*

> *"The ability of a program to perform a required function under stated conditions for a stated period of time."*

The new military standard on software quality, DoD-STD-2168, leaves ample room for waffling in its definition of software reliability:

> *"The degree to which the software consistently performs its intended functions."*[2]

In contrast to the DoD, NASA minces no words:

> *"The probability that software will function without failure."*[3]

All the definitions have merit. The first of the IEEE's seems most appropriate for systems in which a computer is embedded. We might wonder why the second IEEE definition restricts itself to the performance of a single function. The DoD's definition is rooted in our ordinary notion of dependability. The inclusively probabilistic NASA definition is no less intuitively satisfactory. If these definitions are insufficient in number, the glossary of the Data & Analysis Center for Software [sponsored by Rome Air Development Center (RADC)] has more.[4] Whether we rest our perception of reliability on the mathematical certitude of probability theory, reserve room for surprises by insisting on operation within stated conditions, or decide that consistency and not correctness is the crux of reliability, we have enough definitions available to choose from.

Usability is another matter, one I like to think of as related to the "perceptions" described in Section 1.1. However, other sources see it strictly in terms of what we used to call "user friendliness" (until we reduced the term to a cliché by invoking it every time we got angry with a program). Here are two examples:

> *"The relative effort for using software (training and operation)..."*[5]

> *"The effort required to learn the human interface with the software, to prepare input, and to interpret output of the software."*[2]

These definitions adequately encompass most of what we are concerned with in regard to the use of interactive software and go beyond that to address the human preparation of input data and the human interpretation of output. But usability means more. Consider performance. If a real-time program cannot process data sufficiently fast to prevent input queues from overflowing, it will be unusable for many operational conditions. We might contrive the definition of reliability to subsume performance adequacy, but only at the cost of muddying the meaning of reliability. A second, even more basic element of usability, connects the functionality of a program with user expectations.

If we are to consider usability as a prime facet of quality, we have to include in the definition its functionality and its performance when used in the intended operational environment. In other words,

> *Usability is the attribute of software that describes the extent to which it completely and, where applicable, conveniently performs the functions set forth for it, when operated in a specified environment.*

(This definition may not be the most succinct one possible, but contest entries for the most complete, accurate, and pithy—in short, usable—definition of software usability will be accepted until the close of business December 31, 2000.)

Although software maintenance is often referred to in terms of alterations of a program after it has been released to service, in our more circumspect moods of recent years we divide such alterations into two parts: modifications of functionality and all else. "All else" is what we mean here. (Modifications are discussed under the facet "Adaptability.") Once again, let us see what others say about maintainability:

> *"The effort required to locate and fix an error in the software."* [2]

> *"... ease of effort in locating and fixing software failures ... within a specified time period."* [5]

> *"The ease with which software can be maintained."* [1]

What the last (IEEE) definition lacks in profundity is made up by its refusal to brook any argument about the semantics of maintainability. Nor does the IEEE glossary run the risk of redundancy found in the second definition, which is from an RADC report. To the first two, more pointed definitions, we might consider adding something about the ease with which functionality is improved. For example, it is neither error nor failure that is being addressed when the speed of the search algorithm used by a link editor is improved by an order of magnitude to increase its salability to programmers.

The facet of adaptability can be reground to reveal three distinct faces of quality:

- Modifiability
- Expandability
- Portability

Modifiability refers to changing the way in which a function is performed. Let us take as an example a computer mounted in a sailboat. At one time it was specified that in the event of wind perpendicular to the starting line (a "fair start"), the computer aboard the sailboat would recommend that the start be made from the left side of the line on a port tack, since most boats could be expected to start from the right side on a starboard tack. After the hull had been holed four times by starboard tack boats (holding the right of way), the software supplier was asked to change the recommendation.

Expandability refers to adding new functions. Our onboard computer originally computed position from the outputs of an inertial guidance system. To reduce cumulative inertial errors, a Loran receiver was installed and the software was modified to accept the Loran inputs and periodically correct the computed position. There is negative expandability, as well. When the race committee ruled that boats that get sail selection advice from computers deserve an extra handicap, and the skipper decided that the advice isn't all that good anyway, the software supplier was asked to ship a new version with the sail selection module deleted.

As it happens, after two seasons in a salt atmosphere, the computer had taken on enough corrosion to impair the reliability of its operation. A new computer, designed specifically for sailboats and guaranteed for the life of the boat, was purchased as the replacement. The extent to which the software had to be modified to operate in its new environment is the substance of portability.

Without looking individually at modifiability, expandibility, and portability, others have concisely defined adaptability:

> *"The ease with which software allows differing system constraints and user needs to be satisfied."* [1]

> *"A measure of the ease with which a program can be altered to fit different user and system constraints."* [3]

The first definition is from the IEEE glossary and the second is from the NASA glossary. The two appear in concord, except for precedence. Like all the definitions presented thus far, these two provide a stage for targets we can design to. The specific targets are the layer of "ilities," hinted at in the beginning of this section, that lie beneath the four facets of quality. We start by identifying the attributes of reliability.

Reliability

The quality of software reliability is derived from the following attributes:

- Completeness.
- Consistency and precision.
- Robustness.
- Simplicity.
- Traceability.

We can see that "nesses," "sions," and "ities" are counted as "ilities." Later, we shall see a few other suffixes that also refuse to fit the mold.

"Completeness" describes the extent to which all of the parts required to implement a program's functionality are included in the operational program. Most of the time we might get away with omitting part of the code required to perform a given operation, but eventually the forgotten code makes its absence known. Returning to the example of our computer-assisted sailboat, leaving out the capability of switching from one Loran grid to another as the boat sails down the coast would result in erratic readings at some point. Erratic means unreliable. Software can be incomplete because something was not coded, because it was not designed, or because it was not specified as an explicit requirement. The last is the most frequent offense. One more common cause of lack of completeness—one that results from inadequate tooling (compounded by configuration control errors) for system integration—is failure to link a procedure or larger module into a system build, coupled with a forgiving link editor that only warns of unresolved externals.

In addition to the problem of partial functionality, we have also to contend with extraneous functionality. Call it negative completeness if you like. In the process of developing a system, segments of code are often compiled along with functional code to facilitate testing or to serve diagnostic purposes after a test has failed. Although only intended for temporary purposes, such code may inadvertently be left in at the time the system goes into the final qualification process. If the qualification tests do not invoke one of these testing relics (a not unlikely circumstance considering the enormous number of paths through a program) the presence of the superfluous code may not be detected until some operational circumstance uncovers it. The consequence is invariably a surprise. Changes made to released software can create negative completeness in a different way. Returning to our onboard computer example, if the deletion of the sail selection algorithm is effected not by the actual removal of the code and the path to it, but by the installation of a jump around the module, it is possible that during operation another program glitch (caused by weakness in another attribute, say, robustness) would cause the module to be unwittingly invoked. If the only consequence is that the skipper's face turns red from the realization that the computer is giving illegal advice, small harm has been done. A more serious example applies to accounting packages: leaving in the calculation of a tax deduction disallowed by new tax legislation.

Perhaps the most intuitively grasped attribute of reliability is consistency. Reliability is nearly synonymous with dependability. I used to own an airplane with an intermittent bug in the hard-wired digital logic of the transponder. The problem was manifested as inconsistent altitude readouts, which were generated by another instrument, but relayed to ground controllers by the transponder. Like many intermittent problems, it was difficult to find. After spending half the cost of a new transponder in an attempt to get dependable operation, I finally threw the thing away and bought a new one.

Inconsistent results from software are equally undependable. The behavior of a mailing list generator that seems arbitrarily to leave out a few names from time to time can only be described as unreliable. If our onboard computer, given what appear to be nearly the same inputs, suggests a course of 320° but abruptly changes it to 280° every few minutes, the entire function of course selection comes under suspicion.

The causes of software inconsistency are several. A common one is the improper handling of boundary conditions, not only in terms of the stated limits of operation of the system but also with regard to internal design targets. Another common cause of inconsistency is the improper treatment of numerical algorithms, for example, allowing a division to take place when the magnitude of the denominator approaches the magnitude of roundoff or truncation errors. Inconsistency of this kind is indistinguishable from *imprecision*. Informally, we often interchange the words *precision* and *accuracy*. To a scientist, however, the two are distinct. High accuracy results from a low level of systematic, or fixed, errors. High precision results from a low level of *experimental* (loosely, "random") error. The software equivalent of experimental error is the set of roundoff and truncation errors. Occasionally they are large enough to result in inconsistent behavior sufficiently noticeable to be considered unreliable.

Robustness refers to the capability of software to defend itself against anomalous input. In the early days of computers, the struggle to get a program to do what was expected under normal conditions was so arduous that the joy attending achievement of the norm eclipsed any concern that the program might bomb out under abnormal input. Not so today. Now we expect software to report the anomaly and keep on cranking away, doing the best it can at damage control. With regard to external stimuli, software needs to be designed to handle input beyond the stipulated ranges of data. Although the alphabet is specified to range from A to Z, there is no excuse for the program's bombing out when it sees a character code outside that range. At the very least, the program should report the problem in full particulars, and then abort. For most such input errors however, a less ruthless defense is possible; for example, the program can report the problem and go on to the next sales transaction.

Programmers are generally sensitive to the need for handling out-of-range data from external sources, whether the source is an 80 column transaction or the input from a Loran receiver. Frequently overlooked, however, are the data passed from one part of a program to another. A pointer to a data record may, for one reason or another, be incorrectly computed by one procedure and then passed to another. If the receiving procedure does not check the legality of the pointer before attempting to fetch the record from disk, the software operating system under which the program is executing may abort the program.

The attributes of reliability that have been discussed thus far—completeness, consistency, and robustness—interest the consumer as much as the producer. The last two attributes, simplicity and traceability, are invisible to users, but necessary goals for producers.

We hear much less of simplicity than of its opposite, complexity. If simplicity is a target for programmers to strive for, complexity (apart from that inherent to the problem) reports their failure. Complex software structures are to software bugs as laboratory nutrients are to microbic bugs. Not only do complex structures seduce programmers to wander away from the main thrust of problem solving into the jungles of involuted logic, where the climate encourages error; software complexity also makes it difficult to extract faults once they have been written into the program. The software community declared war on complexity around 1970, initially arming itself with structured programming, modular design, and the like, and later adding weapons directed toward data complexity: typing, private data, and delayed data binding. The battle continues, and complexity remains at the center of quality programs, exerting pronounced influence on technology.

Traceability between the requirements model for a program and the finished product is a means of assuring completeness. Also, the traceability of parts of the program structure to the program's requirement model promotes simplicity. As a prime attribute of reliability, traceability also refers to the sufficiency and accuracy of the test cases used to determine how well the program satisfies the requirements set forth for it. In this sense traceability is a quality technique. Generally, we can think of traceability in terms of a chain from the requirements model, through the development process, to the installation and final checkout of software.

Usability

To be usable, software must be reliable. That is, reliability not only is a primary facet of quality, but a prerequisite to another of the primary facets. Other attributes of usability are

- Accuracy.
- Clarity and accuracy of documentation.
- Conformity to operational environment.
- Completeness.
- Efficiency.
- Testability.

Accuracy is the easiest of the attributes to understand. If the program cannot come up with a sufficiently accurate result, it cannot be used. In this regard, accuracy may be compared with reliability. Even given the archetypical condition of unreliability, that is, a high rate of system crashes, failure to perform a computation correctly may represent a greater problem than failing to perform the computation at all. For example, under circumstances of corporate poverty so severe that no money is available for revising or replacing software, a batch payroll system running at night on the company computer can be permitted to bomb out from time to time. Although aborted runs are a nuisance, the payroll can be made up several days in advance, leaving plenty of time to recover from crashes. What cannot be tolerated is a payroll system that inaccurately computes paycheck amounts.

Anyone who has purchased software for personal computers knows of unclear and inaccurate user documentation. For those still using ledger sheets and typewriters, assembly instructions for toys manufactured in the Orient may serve as a reasonable analogy. Happily, there are also examples of good documentation for personal software to remind us of what quality programs can aspire to. Software for microcomputers is only a small part of the class of software requiring collateral documentation. For any systems that have to be installed by people other than the developers or that are intended to be used interactively, inaccurate or unclear documentation lessens the product's usability.

Every now and again it happens that software that works fine in the programming laboratory fizzles out in the real world. An airborne navigation system falls woefully behind real time because of the presence of irrelevant radio signals (noise). A data base management system consumes enormous quantities of disk space on a minicomputer when installed under an operating system designed to emulate features of an operating system popular on larger computers. Interactive process control software, which has been checked out for usability by members of the accounting department pretending to be machine operators, fails on the factory floor when used by people who have never before been confronted by keyboards and monitors. All of these examples represent failure of programs to conform to the operational environment they are destined for.

We have already discussed completeness, the fourth attribute of usability, so we can go on to efficiency.

Efficient software avoids waste of the resources available to it: memory, data channels, external storage, and time. The last is rarely thought of as a resource, but in the real world it most certainly is. With regard to usability, millisecond-pinching software is of immediate interest. Wasted milliseconds can easily add up to virtual system thrashing, overflowing input queues, and time for a coffee break between responses to the return key—any of which can be grounds for shipping the system back to the supplier.

In strict terms, testability refers to our ability to test software. Testability results from the accurate, complete, and unambiguous stipulation of individual software require-ments. In the requirements definition for a software system, the attribute of testability applies to each of the many facets of the system's behavior. As design progresses, testability applies to the requirements set forth for newly identified parts of the system. With regard to usability, however, testability also implies that the thought given to the requirements model—and the design that implements it—is sufficient to assure that the software can be used, at least insofar as its intended use is understood. Put differently, an untestable requirement will result when the person who specified the requirement did not fully understand its purpose. The result is that implementation of the requirement will be one step further from the operational behavior the users need.

Maintainability

Many programmers find it difficult to go back to code written six months earlier and make a small change. They look at statements like

$$\text{if } (kqky = 23) \text{ return}$$

and wonder where *23* came from and what the semantics of *kqky* are. If programmers have difficulty unraveling the riddles of their own code, how about the poor devils who earn their living maintaining the code others developed? This is the crux of the maintainability problem, one that we are painfully aware of since the costs of maintaining and adapting code represent perhaps 75% of all software costs. The attributes that make software maintainable are

- Accuracy and clarity (of documentation).
- Modularity.
- Readability.
- Simplicity.

In short, software needs to be understood before it can be efficiently and correctly altered.

Although documentation accuracy and clarity do not make the most significant contribution to maintainability, they make a significant contribution to the cost of making the software maintainable. Maintenance documentation, sometimes called logic documentation, is generally prepared during the course of development. It may be no more than a repackaging of design documentation, possibly augmented by some material to help the maintenance programmer get oriented. It may include installation information. It may be a complete new set of documentation prepared specifically for maintenance (and adaptation). It may be a combination of design documentation and new descriptions of the structure of the software. Whatever it is, a lot of labor goes into the process of producing it.

What a pity, then, to have piles of documentation that do not reflect the current status of the program, or perhaps never accurately described the actual program. What a loss to have tastefully bound material that can barely be understood because of vagueness, poor use of language, or diagrams that are difficult to read. Such documentation is of little use to the maintenance programmer who is attempting to understand the structure of the program and it may actually mislead him or her—eventually resulting in hours of lost labor due to rework.

Modularity helps make documentation more readable by lending some structure to the heap of paper. This is only one contribution modularity makes to maintainability but we defer discussing the others to continue addressing the topic of readability.

If documentation can be difficult to read, consider code. Trying to decipher unstructured code may require the use of all ten fingers as place-holders in the stack of listings. (Try turning pages with your nose or elbows.) Equally bad is inadequate annotation of the source code, which too often is accompanied by impoverished documentation and leaves the programmer nothing to resort to. Then we have "clever" programming, in which, for example, a coding scheme for efficiently storing data on disk is based on taking apart the bits of a key character or word of the data. Nor can we forget the magic numbers that suddenly appear in a program, reappear half a page later, and then once again, without giving a hint of their purposes as would declared constants. Every maintenance programmer has a favorite example of unreadable coding practices—perhaps one of these, perhaps one of dozens more.

Apart from its influence on the readability of code, structure is an essential part of simplicity. It may be recalled that simplicity, or more precisely, complexity, was discussed with regard to reliability.

Another strong influence on simplicity is modularity. In the sense of single-entry/single-exit program segments, we touch upon modularity when we speak of structured programming, but modularity—in a larger sense—also reduces the likelihood that a change made to one part of the program will unwittingly affect another. If all the code associated with generating reports is logically separated (in the least, in a separate compilation unit) from the code for adding to or modifying the data base, a change to a report generator is less likely to create surprises when data is updated. Going one step further, if the various report generators are all separated (notwithstanding their common use of certain procedures to perform universal operations, for example, opening files), inadvertent effects are further diminished.

Adaptability

Recall that adaptibility has three parts: modifiability, expandability, and portability. The attributes underlying modifiability are the same as those for maintainability. We may wonder if greater likelihood of error exists when correcting an existing error or when changing the way a function is performed. There seems to be no single answer to that, but stories are legion of buggy programs in which further attempts to clean up the program were abandoned because each fix created new bugs, and of programs for which additional improvements or customizing of functionality had to be curtailed by management, again because of the problems these essays encountered.

Adding functions to a system sounds more difficult than modifying existing functions, but in a highly modular system it may be easier. For example, if an MIS package comprises a single data base and a group of vertically oriented modules, each containing all the parts (such as input, reports, and so on) required to completely implement a function (inventory control, sales forecasts, or the like), it should be fairly painless to expand the package by adding a function completely independent of the others. This type of modularity, frequently seen in the MIS world, is emulated in systems software and real-time software by distributed processing architectures.

Other attributes of expandability include all those of maintainability and a new one, parsimony. Parsimony is like efficiency, only more so. By minimizing the use of time, memory, and other resources beyond the needs of the original release of the software, room is left for expansion. Resources are often traded off against each other in the interest of efficiency. In a frequently executed segment, memory may be bartered for time by using straight line code instead of iteration. In an assembly language implementation, use of more registers may be the way to buy time. Such tradeoffs may be inimical with expandability, and programmers should be apprised of any known potential for increasing the functionality of a program.

Portability, the third aspect of adaptability, describes the ease with which software can be moved from one operating environment to another, as from one computer to another or to a different operating system running on the same computer. Programmers who have wanted to move development tools from, say, VMS to UNIX, and have encountered conversion problems should be sensitive to the problem. Nevertheless, programmers often make their own programs difficult to transport. Portability is best achieved by first selecting high level languages for which standards have been established and then adhering to the standards. Language standards are often compromised by implementations of only subsets of the language—no two alike—or worse, supersets. With regard to the latter, the availability of nonstandard features can be an irresistible temptation to programmers.

Even when language standards are the same in two environments, the implementation may be different. Programmers who use Fortran do loop indexes outside the loop—a clear violation of standards—have discovered that some compilers increment the index at the top of the loop while others increment the index at the bottom, leaving a different value for the variable when the loop terminates. Some years ago my staff and I had an environment that allowed our computer to emulate a larger one. One emulation requirement was the substitution of three memory locations for three hardware registers. We soon discovered that we could write more efficient code in a compiler language by manipulating the three memory locations as though we were in assembly language. When we updated our computer to a more powerful one that also emulated the original model but had all of the model's hardware registers, we discovered we had several unplanned labor months of conversion work ahead of us.

With knowledge of the attributes of software quality, we should be able to build quality into the software product. Having done so, we should then like to measure the success we have achieved. Easier said than done. Few of these attributes lend themselves to the assignment of numbers. We will explore the issues of quality measurement, but only after placing quality within an even larger issue of programming measurements.

2.2 QUANTIFYING SOFTWARE CHARACTERISTICS

The value or essential characteristics of many of the things we buy or make can be summarized by a handful of numbers. A carton of milk costs 65 cents and contains 32 ounces. Use it by April 6. A page of material in camera-ready format for IEEE publications contains two columns of approximately 490 words each. A human baby takes nine months to make and is usually equipped with two eyes, two legs, and so forth. Assuming that people are not too fussy about the milk they drink, the first example is a fairly complete description. The next two, however, leave out those characteristics having to do with quality. Not all pages of all IEEE conference proceedings are of equal informational value, nor do all babies, however similar their gross characteristics, demonstrate similar behavior.

It is trivial to observe that any two arbitrarily selected software systems produced by the same company are not expected to do the same thing. It is also trivial to say that two software systems, each derived from 500,000 lines of code (LOC), are not necessarily expected to perform the same functions. The inverse of this is to say that just because two software systems do approximately the same thing, they ought to derive from approximately the same number of lines of source code—differences in programming languages, detailed design goals, and the like notwithstanding. This is plainly wrong, but we say it all the time. I am picking on lines of code—and its sibling, noncomment source statements (NCSS)—because they are the two universally accepted measures of software. There is nothing intrinsically wrong with them. They do measure something, but that something may impart far less information than the widespread use of the numbers warrants. More than anything else, the popularity of LOC and NCSS is a comment on how poorly software lends itself to quantification.

LOC and NCSS are used in all manner of ways. Most methods for estimating the cost of developing a new system are based on some given number of labor hours per thousand lines of code (KLOC). The estimate is then adjusted according to some gauge of difficulty, available tools, and so forth. We follow this practice despite the fact that we cannot know the number of KLOC until the job is done. (Admittedly, if the system is very similar to the project just completed, we should be able to estimate KLOC quite closely, but then why not just use the cost of the previous job?) The quality of software, at least with regard to reliability, is often stated in terms of known defects per KLOC. The productivity of a given programmer may be (covertly) recorded in hours per LOC.* As prominent as LOC may be among software engineers who want to quantify something—anything—about software, LOC strikes me as fairly remote from the bottom line of software: performance of useful functions. Has anyone ever seen a contract awarded to a software developer for the delivery of x KLOC? No, the contract talks of functions, features, performance, and the like.

The following example demonstrates the fallacy inherent in using LOC as a primary software descriptor. The example represents a source code segment used to compute a specified Fibonacci number. For those unfamiliar with the Fibonacci series, each number of the series is the sum of the previous two, given that the first two numbers are both equal to one. Put mathematically,

$$F_k = F_{k-1} + F_{k-2}, \qquad F_0 = F_1 = 1.$$

The computation of an arbitrary member of the series is shown coded in Lisp in Figure 2.1, in C in Figure 2.2, and in Basic in Figure 2.3. Each example is coded in an

```
(defun fib(k)
  (cond ((= k 0) 1)
        ((= k 1) 1)
        (t(+ (fib(- k 1)) (fib(- k 2))))))
```
Figure 2.1. Fibonacci Series in Lisp

---

*I once had a mathematician on my staff who was fine at mathematics, but had never quite got the hang of programming. Among other things, his programs were always twice as long as they need have been. Nevertheless, he programmed with great alacrity and even greater typing speed. Had I attempted to compare his productivity with that of his peers, using hours/LOC, he would have been the easy winner.

```
fib(k)
int k:
{
    if (k == 0 || k == 1)
        return (1);
    else return (fib(k-1) + fib(k-2));
}
```

Figure 2.2. Fibonacci Series in C (recursive)

```
20 IF K < 2 THEN FIB = 1 ELSE 30
25 RETURN
30 FIBOLD = 1
40 FIBLAST = 1
50 FOR I = 2 TO K
60 FIB = FIBOLD + FIBLAST
70 FIBOLD = FIBLAST
80 FIBLAST = FIB
90 NEXT I
100 RETURN
```

Figure 2.3. Fibonacci Series in Basic

acceptable style for the language. The first two figures are function subprograms, while the example in Basic, which does not support call-by-value functions, is coded in the form known in Basic as a subroutine. One does not need to know any of the languages[†] or, indeed, any programming language, to recognize that the three figures each contain a different number of lines of code. Figure 2.1 has four lines, Figure 2.2 has seven lines, and Figure 2.3 has 10 lines. All three do exactly the same thing.

One may argue that the Lisp and C versions are recursive, while the version in Basic (which does not support recursion) is necessarily more prolix since it is iterative, but the point remains: The language used can have marked effect on program size, without affecting functionality.

Programmer style can also exert a major influence. Suppose the C programmer had not recognized the intrinsic recurrence of the Fibonacci numbers, and had coded the function iteratively. We would then have the 14 lines of Figure 2.4, twice as many as the code of Figure 2.2.

None of these examples contains any annotation. Thus, anything said about LOC applies also to NCSS. NCSS, in contradistinction to noncomment LOC (which, oddly, is never seen but which is a more equitable basis for comparison), at least theoretically measures the number of discrete thoughts of the programmer without the influence of the (less significant) wordiness attached to those thoughts. To demonstrate this, consider Figure 2.5, another C language recursive version, but written in a style somewhat different from that of Figure 2.2. Here, although we see 8 lines of code, lines 5 and 6 constitute a single statement, divided into two parts simply for clarity. Figures 2.2 and 2.5 have exactly the same number of source statements.

None of this is to suggest that developing or maintaining a program of 100 KLOC is not a greater task than working on a 20 KLOC program, or that the 100-KLOC

[†] Although the choice of these three languages can be explained by stating that their marked differences are well-suited to illustrating the point, the real reason is that they are the only languages for which I have programming environments on my computer. Having once published an illustration with a bug in it, I now take care to test my examples.

```
fib(k)
int k;
{
    int i, f, fibold, fiblast;
    if (k == 0 || k == 1)
      return (1);
    fibold = fiblast = 1;
    for (i = 2; i <= k; i++) {
      f = fibold + fiblast;
      fibold = fiblast;
      fiblast = f;
    }
    return (f);
}
```

Figure 2.4. Fibonacci Series in C (iterative)

```
fib(k)
int k;
{
    int f;
    f = (k == 0 || k == 1) ? 1
             : (fib(k-1) + fib(k-2));
    return (f);
}
```

Figure 2.5. Fibonacci Series in C (recursive)

program presents significantly greater reliability problems, but we must be wary of the characteristics we ascribe to LOC or NCSS.

If it is so difficult even to speak of the size of a program, what of quality? At the very least, in LOC and NCSS we do have bulk measures of programming output. We can (and people actually do) speak of inches of thickness of documentation although the measure may at times be inverse to usefulness. Cost can be measured in dollars and schedule in months. But quality? As a bottom line measure, we could do worse than compute the ratio of pleased to displeased users three years after the release of software, but this anachronism is of scant help in determining whether the system should be released in the first place.

A popular exercise found in studies—some paid for by the government—is finding some kind of number to attach to each of the facets of quality, and then, by formula, combining the numbers into a single measure of quality. For example, reliability, usability, maintainability, and adaptability are each given a score based on some enumerable artifacts of the program or of the process that produced it. The scores are then weighted and added. Sometimes other, less visible, attributes—modularity, traceability, and the like—are included in the metric. In this misbegotten pursuit of quantification, some methods have seen fit to add cardinal numbers to ordinals. For the most part, the methods have not presumed to provide a dimension to the result. As my contribution to the science of software metrics, I submit

*The composite quality characteristic of software is measured in units of **qualitease**.*

One should not infer from this statement that summarizing certain of the quality-related aspects of software is impossible. For example, a recent study[6] published by the government rates efficiency as the ratio of actual utilization to the allocated utilization of resources, and portability as the ratio of the effort (I assume in labor hours) to transport to the effort to develop. Both of these measures have obvious intrinsic meaning. Others border on the arcane, but make sense on analysis if we can apply an appropriate multiplier. For example, verifiability is based on the ratio of the effort to verify to the effort to develop, and reusability is a function of the ratio of conversion effort to development effort. The ratio of faults per LOC is milked for four separate quality factors considered by the authors: integrity, reliability, survivabilty, and correctness.

The most straightforward software quality measurements are those that derive directly from testing experience, operational experience, and software structure. We turn to these now.

2.3 QUALITY MEASUREMENTS

We can measure

1. Failures per unit of time under operational circumstances.
2. Operational "incidents" per unit of operating time.
3. Calls for assistance per month.
4. Number of known defects (whether or not normalized to LOC).
5. Number of undiagnosed test failures (whether or not normalized to LOC).
6. Ratio of tests passed to tests run.
7. Number of seeded faults unrecovered during testing, or the ratio of recovered to unrecovered seeds.
8. Percentage of software actually exercised by testing.
9. Complexity.
10. Structural properties other than complexity.

Although items 1 through 3 apply only after software has been released, their validity as measurements is undisputable. Moreover, they are useful for maintenance purposes. Item 4 applies to both operational software and software during prerelease testing. Items 5 through 8 pertain to the testing period, while Items 9 and 10 can be measured independently of testing. Let us take these two first.

Complexity

A number of techniques have been developed to measure software complexity directly from source code. A 1982 survey[7] listed 13, and more have been developed since. Most of these techniques deal with either control flow or some measure of program size. Perhaps the best known of these are McCabe's Cyclomatic method,[8] *knot* calculations,[9] and measures derived from Halstead's "software science."[10]

McCabe's complexity measure derives directly from graph theory and is easily computed, either manually or with a static analysis tool, once the graph of the program has been generated. This measure lends itself quite readily to piecewise calculation, having a simple mechanism for combining the cyclomatic numbers computed for individual procedures. The method has considerable intuitive appeal, as the computed cyclomatic number relates to the number of processing paths that test designers need to consider.

Knot counts measure the number of excursions from sequential execution of processing nodes. If node y can be entered directly from node x, but only on the determination of an intervening predicate that would force control to a node beyond y, one knot is added to the total count. Like McCabe's work, this method has intuitive appeal, perhaps even more so than Cyclomatic number calculations. However, knot counts are not quite so easily determined as Cyclomatic numbers.

The use of Halstead's "software science" as a complexity metric is attended by some controversy. A disarmingly simple and easily automated computation combines the number of unique operators, unique operands (data), and the repetition in using these to compute a number called the program *volume*. The program volume relates directly to its actual size in a computer. Moreover, Halstead volume has been found to be related to natural language.[11] Although the distinction between operators and operands is not always as clear cut as in the programs Halstead examined, it remains true that volume is a more satisfactory description of program size than lines of code. Volume alone, however, does not seem to fit our usual notions of complexity. Nevertheless, it has been casually equated to complexity by many people. Other software science measures, all based on volume, more closely conform to our understanding of error proneness and poor maintainability. These employ measures of language level based on the ratio between volume and potentially minimum volume, an equation for difficulty, and an equation for computing the number of elementary mental discriminations made by programmers. Unfortunately, it is these and some ancillary calculations (some employing an arguable criterion for the rate at which humans can make elementary discriminations) that have given rise to most of the controversy that surrounds software science. Criticism has been directed to the rigor of the derivations of some of the equations, the assumptions inherent in the work, and the methods used to validate software science. The work by Shen and others[12] is a good example of the scrutiny to which software science has been subjected.

Much less work has been accomplished in finding measures of data complexity. Plainly, strong data typing (restrictions on the diversity of uses to which defined data may be put) reduces the opportunity for programmer error, but whether this is a matter of complexity is not so plain. More to the point, it is not clear how to quantify the extent to which languages support data typing nor the extent to which the data have been structured.

In a larger sense, data complexity might be viewed in terms of the interaction between data and architecture. Data independence, the dissociation of the values or structure of data from the rules governing their processing, is a measure of simplicity. Yet we often find data bound to code at compile time.

Consider a billing system for an electric utility, one that calculates customer charges using such factors as total electricity consumed, separate day and night rates, and customer commitments to minimum consumption. Effectively, a different billing formula applies to each customer. The most direct way to permit different billing formulas is to place the formulas directly in the customers' individual billing records. However, if the source code for the program requires fixed length billing records, flexibility in the expression of the formulas costs unused disk space and greater access time. Such "compile-time data binding" sometimes results from programming language constraints, sometimes from thoughtless design. Continuing with our example, we should not be surprised to see the designers provide a small auxiliary file of nothing but formulas, with each billing rate record containing not the applicable formula, usage information, and current rates, but a pointer to a record in the auxiliary file. Scarcely a straightforward approach to a straightforward problem. Unfortunately, studies of data binding do not yet suggest approaches to relating the binding of data to the quantification of complexity.

The complexity of data flow can also be considered. Ned Chapin has proposed a method[13] for calculating complexity based on the purposes served by individual data within program segments and the communication of data between segments that are iteratively called. The method requires that data usage types be weighted by subjective factors in the complexity formula, a feature that reduces the utility of the method unless the user has sufficient experimental data to adjust the factors to fit the history of reliability or maintainability.

Other Structural Measurements

Apart from violating structured programming precepts of control flow and data design, other ways exist for complicating software designs—to the detriment of reliability and maintainability. Some aspects of such design complexity are measurable, or at least lend themselves to measurement of their effects. Modularity is one of these.

Modularity describes the degree to which structural parts of a computer program are mutually independent of each other. Accordingly, a bottom line measure of modularity would be in terms of the number of other modules affected by a change made to one module of the system. This sounds simpler than it is, as each module—and, indeed, each possible change within each module—has a unique set of potential effects. The effect of changes within one module on other modules is sometimes called the *ripple effect*. Reflecting the concepts of information hiding,[14] we can begin to calculate the ripple effect for a given module by examining the number of assumptions of the subject module made by other modules with which it has some interaction, either in terms of direct interface or through shared data. Yau and Collofello[15] have quantified potential ripple effect in just this way, defining the result as the *design stability metric*. One interesting result of the experiment described by the researchers was the correlation of low module design stability with weak functional strength.

Functional strength (at its greatest when module performance is limited to a single function) is the highest of the seven categories of module strength (i.e., the contribution to modularity made by the internal view of individual modules) defined by structured design savant Glenford Myers.[16] In an experiment involving several hundred modules,[17] 50% of the high strength modules were found to be free of faults during testing, compared with only 18% of the weak modules. Evidence of this kind does not lead to modularity measurements, as module strength cannot be quantified except as an ordinal, but it points the way to the kind of analysis that provides insight into the reliability and maintainability of a design. The experiment provided some other pertinent conclusions: No significant relation was found between module size and fault rate, nor was one found between data coupling between modules and fault rate. Finally, looking at the calling structure, the researchers compared the fault history of modules of different fan-outs (i.e., different numbers of modules directly called). Of those modules calling only one other, 42% had no faults, while only 12% of the modules with seven or more descendents were free of faults. The suggestion is powerfully made that fan-outs should be counted.

Before moving on to the next topic of measurements, we can distill a verity or two from the discussion of the quantification of selected characteristics of program structures.

Although such analyses do not yield a qualitease metric, they can provide confidence in our estimation of whether the software has been constructed to certain accepted standards of good design. Moreover, the measurements that can be made—specifically, those having to do with complexity and modularity—relate directly to reliability, maintainability, and adaptability. Finally, if numbers of intrinsic meaning cannot be calculated, as in the assessment of modular strength, it may be possible to gauge positions within ordinal scales, as in "third best."

Measurements from Testing

The greatest source of quality data is that available from test activities. Later chapters deal more fully with the collection and use of test data, but an overview at this point demonstrates that there exists a meaningful counterpoise to the assignment of magic numbers of qualitease.

Let us start with the simple count of known defects remaining in a software system. As it happens, the count itself is much simpler than the explanation of why imperfect software is often released. Few people who have not suffered through the testing of large programs understand the influences dictating the release of software containing known problems. The reasons are several, and we start with the most common. For very complex software, attempting a fix to a minor problem may be imprudent, as more severe faults may be generated as byproducts. We might argue that software so complex should never have been allowed to progress as far as testing, but this hypothesizes a quixotic business world few of us have the luxury of working in. Also, software that was initially sound may in time have had its structure compromised by a series of maintenance or adaptation operations. Another reason to countenance known bugs is the cost (including the effects of a slipped schedule) of retesting after a fix is made. A minor anomaly will not stop the performance of scheduled tests. While someone attempts to find the source of the anomaly and formulate a fix, other planned tests continue. By the time the bug is identified and a fix proposed, test management may have to weigh the benefits of installing the fix against the circumspect course of repeating all—or a significant subset— of the previously passed tests. Regression testing, as it is called, may take days, weeks, or even months, depending on the application of the software and the testing tools available. Fixing a problem of minor significance may carry too high a price in retesting. Finally, some faults can be remedied only at the expense of some other operating characteristic. For example, reducing the time for writing into a common data base from one of many distributed terminals may require an increase in the probability of reaching a deadlock condition, wherein no terminal can gain access to the data base.

In any case, valid reasons do exist for leaving in known bugs or operational limitations (hence, some of the curious "features" described by software manuals), and it is a matter of history that large software systems have been successfully released with hundreds of problems of varying degree of severity.

The ability to judge severity is, of course, the key to bug permissiveness. A severity scale of three or four grades with "minor" and "major" holding down the poles is not sufficient. To determine the real significance of a defect, its severity must be related to the system's operational environment. For example, a three level severity scale for a computer operating system might be based on these criteria: (1) can cause frequent system crashes, (2) can cause infrequent system crashes or can cause user files to be clobbered, and (3) presents an inconvenience to the interactive user. In practice, each of the levels would have a number of examples attached to it, and, because no one can imagine every possible bug effect, the universal escape hatch "or equivalent" would be added to each level. For an airborne navigation system, examples of three levels of severity are (1) can cause aircraft to exceed airframe structural limits, (2) may require correction from pilot or cross-tracking system at half the specified time interval, and (3) may occasionally result in cross-controlled states of up to four seconds. Taking one more example of individual cases for a three level system, let us use a multiterminal accounting and record-keeping system: (1) can cause transactions to be posted to wrong account, (2) can cause system crashes during file maintenance procedures, and (3) with all terminals active, can reduce system response to 20% slower than specification allows.

Generalizing, a three-level severity scale should run from (1) prevents system from completing an operation, causes irrecoverable loss of data, or jeopardizes safety or equivalent (there, I've said it), (2) substantively impairs operation, and (3) presents operational inconvenience.

Severity assessment applies also to counting undiagnosed test failures, which in most ways is similar to counting known defects remaining in the system. The greatest difference is that we are a little less confident about releasing a system with a known failure mode but no information about the cause of it. One has to be faint of heart about these since, under circumstances different from those encountered during testing, the unknown bug may have an even more severe effect. The most common type of undiagnosed test failure is that resulting from intermittent operation of associated hardware, either within the computer system or within the associated instrumentation. Probes placed in the software may find the hardware anomaly and enable a software diagnosis (as well as a hardware diagnosis), but only if the right probe is inserted in the right place. Another reason some failures go undiagnosed derives from the use of uncontrolled test data input unsupported by an automatic input log. One criterion for determining how good a test has been planned is its repeatability. In this regard, it should be recognized that random data can be repeatable, provided the source is controlled. If not controlled, the test stimuli must be logged for the test to have proper value.

Another testing measurement is the ratio of tests passed to tests run (or tests passed to tests attempted). Once again, severity judgments must be applied for this criterion to have any meaning. As a quality criterion, tests passed/tests run has one advantage over defect counts and undiagnosed failure counts: Ratios are inherently normalized. A passed/run ratio of .9999 applies equally to strategic defense initiative software and a kitchen recipe data base. A count of 80 known defects (of arbitrary severity), intolerable for the kitchen (if we cannot get small, fixed-format data base programs right, what can we?), would be viewed by some software engineers as optimistic for the SDI.

The last two testing measurements we discuss are notably different from the others. Rather than a direct measure of expectations of the product's quality, these two measure how well the product was tested. The assumption that justifies their use as quality measures is the conventional wisdom that the better a product is tested, the less likely it is to be unfit for use. Chapters 4 and 9 deal with the technology behind these measurements and the management of their use. We touch upon them lightly here only with regard to their indirect use in gauging quality.

Let us assume that we know, prior to the start of any testing, the exact number of faults in the code. Assume also that we know the effect of each bug. We could then conclude that sufficient testing had been performed when we had witnessed the potential failures evoked by each of the faults. Of course, we have no such clairvoyance about bugs, but we can deliberately plant bugs, or *seeds*, in the code and observe our ability to find them through testing. We can then estimate the number of faults that existed at the start of testing from the equation

$$\hat{N} = \frac{A \times B}{C}$$

where

$A =$ the number of seeds planted prior to testing

$B =$ the total number of bugs that were found

$C =$ the number of seeds that were found, and

$\hat{N} =$ the estimated bugs, including seeds, that were in the code at the start of testing.

As it happens, seeding is not without its limitations, chiefly, our lack of prescience of the location of the unpremeditated faults. The accuracy of $\hat{N}$ depends on the seeds having the same distribution as the genuine articles. Nevertheless, the ratio of seeds recaptured to seeds planted indicates the extent of the testing that has taken place.

We can also measure the extent to which the structure of the software has been tested. Except for diagnostic tests run after a failure has occurred, test data are nearly always designed with regard to the functionality of the software rather than its structure. This statement holds even though functional tests of parts of the system—say, those of individual modules—are, in a sense, directed to the structure. As it happens, we can complete a seemingly comprehensive series of functional tests without having tested a very large part of the structure. To take a simple example, somewhere deep in the bowels of the software there may be a matrix inversion routine containing code to trap a singular or near-singular matrix (one that cannot be inverted because of dependent conditions between two rows or columns). During the course of testing, it is possible that only well-formed matrixes are operated on by the routine. It is also possible that the trap contains a bug, one that someday, during the operational life of the system, will emerge to sting an unwary user.

Code may also go untested because it is dead. Large software systems often have segments of code no longer used. A data base system may have started off with the capability of handling any ASCII character, but when the requirements model for the system was tardily released—months after design started – the only references to input were those for the tokens found on keyboards. Tests of the system exercised all of the algorithms for conversion from ASCII to storage format, but only for the expected input, not for the algorithms for other ASCII codes. Yet the other algorithms remain in the system, waiting for the peculiar operational circumstances to occur when some other defect in the system will inadvertently invoke them.

To determine the extent to which the structure has been exercised, special test instrumentation is required. Coverage analysis, as the measurement is called, is most valuable when the coverage is reported with respect to source code. At the source code level, coverage analyzers can be directed to statements, branches, segments between branches, combinations of branches and straight-line segments, and paths containing discrete numbers of embedded branches. Whatever the capabilities of the analyzer, reports of the coverage attained in testing are a meaningful and reportable quality measurement.

The final category of quality measurements comprises those made after software has been released. The most conspicuous of these are the failures reported by users. Formal reporting mechanisms are generally set up for these, and fault reports are normally given immediate attention on receipt. A count of these, perhaps weighted by severity as discussed earlier, is an obvious measure of reliability. Moreover, we would expect the frequency of failures to decrease in time, as latent defects are removed from the system. Accordingly, we want to count the number of failures per unit of time to confirm the improvement of the software.

Not all anomalous behavior can be classified as failure. Operational "glitches" are of interest, too, since they reflect the usability of the system. These are commonly reported using the same instruments as those for the reporting of outright failures. Examples of glitches (or, more euphemistically, "operational incidents") include unexplained delays in responding to keyboard input and superfluous characters that occasionally show up in sales reports. In the same vein we might also include deviations between user documentation and software behavior. Reports of the number of these per month are also a measure of quality.

Like the number of operational incidents, the number of calls for assistance represents a measure of usability, sometimes of the program, sometimes of the documentation provided users and installers. Sensitive to the need to provide prompt help, software suppliers provide not only telephone numbers to call, but some have technicians manning 800 numbers. Not all calls reflect software faults or usability as defined in Section 2.1. No matter how circumspect software designers and technical writers may be in anticipating user problems, or how clever the design of menus or the indexing of manuals may be, software users can always find a way to get into trouble. More than a few problems are caused by attempting to use software to do something it was not explicitly designed for. If the format of a spreadsheet suggests its use as a cataloguing tool, it is likely to be used that way. I know of no screwdriver designed for opening paint cans, but I have never opened a paint can by any other means. In any case, the count of operational incidents—whether or not the software supplier should assume responsibility— is an inverse measure of how pleased the users are, and pleasing users is what quality is all about.

In the first of the measurements applicable to operational software, reference was made to counting the number of failures per unit of time. Apart from the literal sense of the statement, this reference was also a timid introduction to the subject of software reliability modeling, which we take up next. The reasons for the timidity will become clear.

2.4 RELIABILITY MODELING

Few aspects of software engineering are as engrossing as reliability modeling. Perhaps seductive is a better word, for the practice of software reliability modeling has too often failed to fulfill its bright promise. Still, some study of modeling provides us with insight into the nature of software faults and their exposure through testing.

Viewing software as a functional entity with the potential for failure, we would like to be able to define that potential in some probabilistic manner. We do so for automobile transmissions, disk drives, microwave ovens, and light bulbs, why not for computer programs? Let us look more closely at the analogy.

For simple hardware devices (light bulbs, for example) we can rely on testing experience and calculate a mean time to failure (MTTF) based on the mean times before failure (MTBF) measured for many test bulbs. Moreover, we can calculate the MTTF for a new bulb, a bulb in use for 100 hours, and a bulb in use for 1,000 hours. Microwave ovens are more complex. With many components, each having its own probability of failure, the composite probability is calculated as a combination of those of the parts. Complex equipments or systems like microwave ovens are the paridigms on which software reliability models are based. A few definitions are appropriate:

$R(t) =$ the probability of no failure in the interval between 0 and t, is called the *reliability function.*

$F(t) =$ the *failure function,* is $1 - R(t)$.

$f(t) =$ the *probability density function* (pdf) of failure expresses the rate at which the failure function changes. Mathematically, it is defined by

$$f(t) = \frac{dF(t)}{dt}$$

$Z(t) =$ the *hazard rate,* is the pdf of the time to failure, given no prior failure. Mathematically, it is related to the reliability function by

$$Z(t) = -\frac{dR(t)}{dt}$$

The pdf describes the probability of failure during specific time intervals, whereas the hazard function is the instantaneous rate of failure. In reliability models, the hazard rate is updated at discrete intervals according to the precepts of the model. By selecting different hazard rate functions, we can generate diverse reliability models. During development and operation—at least up to the point at which modifications enter the picture—we expect to see reliability improve as defects are found and removed. Reliability models that reflect this expectation are called *reliability growth models,* and it is to these that most of the modeling attention has been directed. Figure 2.6 depicts a common expectation of reliability growth (or failure function decay).

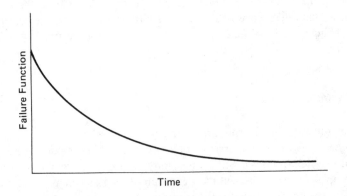

Figure 2.6 Exponential Distribution

The exponential failure decay of Figure 2.6 is not always approximated by real events. The transition period at the start of testing often results in a short-lived increase in failure rate. Intervals of increases in failure rate also occur, as programmers unwittingly replace obscure bugs with conspicuous ones. The parameters of the models are updated with each new failure or repair, or at specific intervals during which repairs are being made. For example, in models directed to the time between failures, plots of the nuclear hazard function might take the shape of those of Figures 2.7 and 2.8.

Both Figures 2.7 and 2.8 are taken from models that assume that the hazard function depends on the number of remaining bugs; the former expecting a uniform decrease in failure rate with each repair and the latter expecting that conditions will improve geometrically at each epoch. This is an example of the underlying assumptions that distinguish one model from another. We will take up the matter of assumptions again, but first let us look at the purposes to which we might put reliability models.

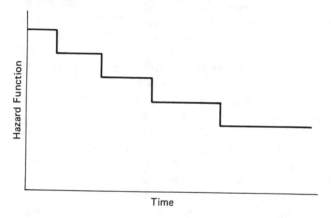

Figure 2.7 Uniform Improvement of Hazard Rate

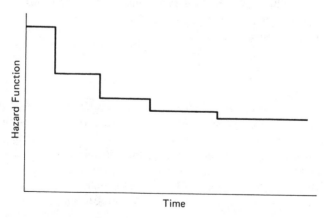

Figure 2.8 Geometric Improvement of Hazard Rate

Using Reliability Models

Assume it were decided that a program would not be released (or accepted from a software supplier) until it is demonstrated to be of adequate reliability. Using the acceptance paradigm, we can think in terms of the classic quality control reconciliation of consumer risk and producer risk. We hypothesize an acceptably low failure rate, lambda. We define alpha as the producer's risk that the hypothesis is correct, but is nonetheless rejected. We define beta as the consumer's risk that an incorrect hypothesis is accepted (that is, the failure rate exceeds the stipulated maximum). A distribution function of lambda, produced by the model from historical data, is compared to $(1 - \text{alpha})$; if greater or equal, the software is accepted. We can also define an unacceptably high failure rate, and compare the distribution function of lambda to beta; if not greater, the software is rejected. This is the end to which the Thompson and Chelson reliability model,[18] which can be used to generate distribution functions for any given lambda, was designed.

Alpha and beta are really confidence limits. Another use of confidence limits is proposed by Okumoto.[19] In his scheme, a confidence interval is applied to the prediction of future failure intensities made by a logarithmic Poisson model.[20] Specifically, given a failure intensity objective (presumably achievable with sufficient additional testing) and a current failure intensity, confidence limits are applied to the estimate that a specified additional amount of test time will achieve the reliability objective.

Apart from the added sophistication of confidence intervals, many of the software reliability models have lent themselves to the calculation of the additional test time required to reach some predetermined failure or hazard datum. Within the limitations of these models, this is a reasonably modest goal—assuming that the selected model seems to behave accurately over a period of, say, weeks or months.

Unreasonably immodest is the attempt to use software reliability models to extrapolate from a testing environment to an operational one. Nevertheless, this appears to have been a common goal of the early models. Perhaps the most widely used of all models, the Musa Execution Time model,[21] a predecessor of the logarithmic Poisson model, incorporated a "testing compression factor" to compensate for the greater stress that marks test activities.* A single parameter, no matter how artfully placed in a model, can scarcely account for all the differences between testing and operation that in the real world might affect failure rates, but this model gets an "E" for Effort. The success of the model actually derives from its being the first to incorporate both execution time and calendar time as independent variables.

Assumptions

Testing stress is only one of many influences on failure rate that can be modeled. No model takes everything into account. Some models take to an extreme the philosophy of Bayesian reliability model builders and give little thought to presuming specifics of a testing environment. In these models, all of the dependent parameters of the model are random variables having their own probability distributions that ripen with experience (time). Most models, however, are based on certain presumptions of the testing environment. Among the environmental factors that models have tried to account for are

- Testing stress, previously mentioned, of interest only if we attempt to predict operational reliability from test experience.

---

* Testing compression affects all models, whether or not it is explicitly accounted for. Readers interested in the subject are recommended a recent book by Musa and others.[22]

- Effect of defect removal as a function of discovery time (early fixes reduce hazard rate more than late fixes).

- Time spent in debugging failures relative to time spent in running test cases.

- Time available for testing as a function of calendar time.

- Availability of people for testing and debugging.

- Availability of computers and other hardware for testing and debugging.

- Probability that a failure will be correctly diagnosed and the defect removed.

- Probability of introducing a new bug incidental to the removal of another.

- Extent to which individual defects can differ in their vulnerability to exposure.

- Extent to which the removal of individual defects can differ in difficulty.

- Test management (e.g., no further testing until last failure diagnosed and a repair made vs. testing continues during preparation of new software release incorporating several fixes).

- Effect on failure of the number of bugs remaining in the software.

The last of these was the only assumption that the earliest software reliability models explicitly incorporated. The primordial group of models assumed that the failure rate was proportional to the number of bugs left in the program. This was another way of saying that all bugs are equally sensitive to the input domain of the system. Despite this simplistic approach, which is common to many of the models that have other explicit assumptions, even the early reliability models (for example, the Jelinski-Moranda)[23] have survived a surprising number of validation attempts—approximately as many as they have fallen to. In some validations, a model has worked for several weeks, departed from events for a while, and then returned to a usefully accurate approximation of failure experience. Users of reliability models should consider maintaining several models current with test history, selecting for predictive purposes the model hewing most closely to recent experience.

The assumptions dealing with the individuality of defects are a departure from hardware reliability theory—the root of software reliability modeling. The probability that a steel beam will fail under a given load is calculated without regard to microscopic variations in the crystalline structure of the alloy. The MTTF of a 256K RAM chip assumes that each memory cell is much like the others. Not so with software defects. Even when two bugs are identical (for example, two statements with inverted predicates) we cannot assume equal expectation of exposure by an arbitrarily chosen input data set. Ignoring the individuality of bugs is particularly noticeable during the latter stages of testing, when the estimation of model parameters should be maturing and when the model's vision of the future is most valuable.* Yet at this time the number of bugs has been so reduced that they cannot be considered members of a homogeneous class. Attempts at modeling bug personality are weak to nil. Still, some approaches have been made. The logarithmic Poisson model assumes that the hazard function of the next bug found is geometrically reduced from that of its predecessor. This assumption reflects the belief that the bugs found earliest are those most likely to be exercised by test data. A

---

* Early in testing, estimations of test completion dates or the number of additional tests required to reach a satisfactory level of reliability are moot. The governing parameter is the number of planned tests remaining. Also premature at this time is the decision to release (or accept) the system.

more ambitious attempt at modeling the relation between defects in frequently executed code segments and their probability of early discovery is the stochastic model of Bev Littlewood.[24] Here, expectations of failure are the composite of a model of individual bug occurrence rates. The model also takes advantage of its Bayesian nature by allowing failure rates to decrease between failure incidents, whereas most models counterintuitively assume that the hazard rate is constant between failures (as in Figures 2.7 and 2.8).

Further Observations

Anyone wanting to plunge into the waters of software reliability modeling would do well to start with the several surveys of models that have been published, three of which are listed in the reference for this chapter.[25,26,27] If the model used requires many parameters to be estimated—that is, involves many underlying assumptions—the validity of the assumptions relative to the testing environment should be considered. Otherwise, future failure rates could be predicted just as well by inspecting the smouldering entrails of a goat.

Bayesian models make fewer demands for ascertaining causality between the testing environment and failure. However, the Bayesian models require prior estimates of their parameters, estimates that can be accurately produced only if historical data have been collected and codified. Although improvement in the accuracy of parameters with the accumulation of new data is characteristic of Bayesian models (and more than characteristic, it is an article of faith for Bayesian reliability engineers), the "priors" as they are called do affect the final, "posterior" estimates.

Before using reliability models to estimate test progress, ordinary trend analyses—especially of test failure rates—should be performed. (These are discussed in Chapter 7.) Apart from the simplicity of trends and their promise of nearly instant intuitive comprehension, there is no point in attempting greater mathematical sophistication if trends are not present.

Reliability modeling may be regarded as an extension of certain of the quality measurements of Section 2.3 to provide statistical bounds on the inferences that can be made from the measurements. When applied to operational software, reliability models provide measures of goodness. Starting with the next chapter, we see how to build in goodness.

2.5 SUMMARY

1. To the user, the most prominent aspects of software quality are the reliability, usability, maintainability, and adaptability of programs.

2. The last of these, adaptability, can be divided into three parts: the ease of modification (apart from small maintenance operations), expansion, and transportation to another operational environment.

3. To produce software users perceive as having the characteristics of points 1 and 2, producers establish the following goals: completeness, consistency and precision, robustness, simplicity, traceability, accuracy, clarity and accuracy of documentation, conformity to the operational environment, efficiency, testability, modularity, readability, parsimony, and conformance to standards of programming languages.

4. For comparing the characteristics of one program to another or to external standards, lines of code (LOC) or noncomment source statements (NCSS) provide weak foundations. Nevertheless, they are commonly used.

5. Weaker yet are arbitrary quality metrics of no mathematical basis. Certain ratios have merit, such as reckoning efficiency by dividing utilized resources by allocated resources.

6. Although they do not translate directly into all of the characteristics of point 3, measurements derived directly from testing and operational experience and from the software structure itself provide incontrovertible evidence of quality and thorough testing.

7. Measurements of the important (to quality) attribute of control flow complexity are fairly easy to achieve. The equally important attribute of modularity, if not easily measured, can at least be ranked.

8. Testing measurements also are easily made. Those dealing with acceptance criteria, however, need to be normalized to severity levels, and in this case judgment cannot be avoided.

9. Measures of testing thoroughness and the usefulness of the tests performed can also be made.

10. Even after software is released, quality measurements can be made. Prominent among these is the count of problems reported per month or year.

11. Reliability models have been employed to place statistical confidence bounds on projected failure rates or defect counts. They offer great opportunity for misuse, however.

12. Reliability models differ from one another in their assumptions concerning the testing environment and failure causality, and in the extent to which the parameters of the model are single data to be estimated (with experience) or are random variables.

13. Simple trend analyses should always accompany the use of reliability modeling and may, in themselves, be sufficient for some of the purposes served by models.

2.6 REFERENCES

[1] *IEEE Standard Glossary of Software Engineering Terminology*, IEEE Std. 729-1983 (February 1983).

[2] *Draft Military Standard, Software Quality Evaluation* (DoD-STD-2168) Department of Defense (April 1985).

[3] *Glossary of Software Engineering Laboratory Terms* (SEL-82-005) National Aeronautics and Space Administration (December 1982).

[4] *Draft Glossary of Software Quality Terms,* prepared by IIT Research Institute for Rome Air Development Center, Data & Analysis Center for Software, Griffiss AFB (November 1985).

[5] T. P. Bowen et al., *Specification of Software Quality Attributes,* Vol. I, RADC-TR-85-37, Rome Air Development Center (February 1985) pp. 3–9.

[6] T. P. Bowen et al., *Specification of Software Quality Attributes,* Vol. II, RADC-TR-85-37, Rome Air Development Center (February 1985) pp. 3–6.

[7] W. Harrison et al., "Applying Software Complexity Metrics to Program Maintenance," *Computer* (September 1982) pp. 65–79.

[8] Thomas McCabe, "A Complexity Measure," *IEEE Trans. Software Eng.*, Vol. SE-2 (December 1976) pp. 308–320.

[9] M. Woodward et al., "A Measure of Control Flow Complexity in Program Text," *IEEE Trans. Software Eng.*, Vol. SE-5 (January 1979) pp. 45–50.

[10] M. Halstead, *Elements of Software Science* (New York: Elsevier–North Holland, 1977).

[11] A. Laemmel and M. Shooman, *Software Modeling Studies: Statistical (Natural) Language Theory and Computer Program Complexity,* Polytechnic Institute of New York, RADC-TR-784, Rome Air Development Center (April 1978).

[12] V. Shen, et al., "Software Science Revisited: A Critical Analysis of the Theory and Its Empirical Support," *IEEE Trans. Software Eng.*, Vol. SE-9 (March 1983) pp. 155–165.

[13] N. Chapin, "A Measure of Software Complexity," *Proceedings National Computer Conference* (1979) pp. 995–1002.

[14] D. L. Parnas, "A Technique for Software Module Specification with Examples," *CACM*, Vol. 15 (May 1972) pp. 330–336.

[15] S. Yau and J. Collofello, "Design Stability Measures for Software Maintenance," *IEEE Trans. Software Eng.*, Vol. SE-11 (September 1985) pp. 849–856.

[16] G. J. Myers, *Composite/Structured Design* (New York: Van Nostrand–Reinhold, 1978).

[17] D. Card et al., "An Empirical Study of Software Design Practices," *IEEE Trans. Software Eng.*, Vol. SE-12 (February 1986) pp. 264–271.

[18] W. E. Thompson and P. O. Chelson, "On the Specification and Testing of Software Reliability," *Proc. 1980 Annual Reliability and Maintainability Symp.*, IEEE Cat. No. 80CH1513-R, pp. 379–383.

[19] K. Okumoto, "A Statistical Method for Software Quality Control," *IEEE Trans. Software Eng.*, Vol. SE-11 (December 1985) pp. 1424–1430.

[20] J. D. Musa and K. Okumoto, "A logarithmic Poisson Execution Time Model for Software Reliability Measurement," *Proc. 7th International Conf. on Software Eng.*, Orlando (March 1984) pp. 230–238.

[21] J. Musa, "A Theory of Software Reliability and Its Applications," *IEEE Trans. Software Eng.*, Vol. SE-1 (September 1975) pp. 312–327.

[22] J. Musa, A. Iannino, and K. Okumoto, *Software Reliability: Measurement, Prediction, Application*, (New York: McGraw-Hill Book Co., 1987).

[23] Z. Jelinski and P. B. Moranda, "Application of a Probability-Based Model to a Code Reading Experiment," *1973 IEEE Symp. Computer Software Reliability*, IEEE Cat. No. 73CH0741-9CSR, pp. 78-80.

[24] B. Littlewood, "Stochastic Reliability Growth: A Model for Fault-Removal in Computer Programs and Hardware Designs," *IEEE Trans. Reliability*, Vol. R-30 (October 1981) pp. 313–320.

[25] R. Dunn and R. Ullman, *Quality Assurance for Computer Software* (New York: McGraw-Hill Book Co., 1982), pp. 305–328.

[26] C. J. Dale, *Software Reliability Evaluation Methods,* Report ST26750, British Aerospace Dynamics Group, Stevenage (September 1982).

[27] A. Goel, "Software Reliability Models: Assumptions, Limitations, and Applicability," *IEEE Trans. Software Eng.* Vol. SE-11 (December 1985) pp. 1141–1423.

CHAPTER 3

Craftsmen, Artists, and Engineers

A few years ago I was amused to read a guidebook on software quality published under the imprimatur of a military agency. In its nearly one hundred pages, the book told of reviews and audits, corrective actions, and the like—to the exclusion of a single word about the men and women on whose shoulders the whole business of software quality ultimately rests, the programmers. I have remarked this approach before and been told that the problem is that we know more about programming reviews than about programming programmers. As if that were the issue, or even an objective! No one really believes it is possible to legislate quality cognitive processes, but many of us do believe that sensitivity to the nature of programming work and the people who perform it is essential to quality.

Recall earlier references to software engineering, in which the production of reliable and efficient software is based on the application of sound engineering principles. In coining the term (in 1967), Dr. Frederich Bauer distinguished engineering from "tinkering." Tinkering was probably too strong a word to use, the better programmers having already established themselves as either craftsmen or artists. (By "artist" I do not mean to invoke a medieval class distinction, but to suggest that some programmers had learned to base their work on proven principles and methods.) In any case, quality programs can influence the migration of craftsmen and artists toward the status of software engineers. As we consider the effect of quality programs on programmers, let us recognize that however ungineered most programmers may be, many are as professional as the designers of refineries and RAMs.

3.1 THE PROGRAMMING PROFESSIONAL

Many people program computers. Students, scientists, engineers, and PC enthusiasts are only a few of the groups of people to whom the language of computers is as familiar as natural language. For many other people programming is not incidental to other work or a form of recreation, but is the means by which they earn their livelihood. Some of these programmers, the ones we are concerned with, are members of large teams working at a considerable remove from the people who will ultimately use the software. This is the essential difference between minor and major league programming. This section deals with how major league programmers, programmer turnover, teamwork, and programming aptitude affect quality.

In the beginning, a distinction between major and minor league programmers did not exist. Programming was performed for purposes known best to the programmers. We can gain some insight as to what the leading edge of the 1960s version of minor league programming looked like by reading Steven Levy's interesting book *Hackers: Heroes of the Computer Revolution*[1], in which he describes the computational activity of students and faculty at MIT. Even then, however, computer manufacturers and military contractors had extensive staffs for major league programming—although the major league of 1960 was not as large as it today.

My first contact with someone actually paid to program was in 1959. On my way to Florida to analyze some missile data, I stopped in Washington to pick up a new data reformatting program my hosts had contracted for. I arrived at the Washington office at the same time that the firm's computer finished punching the deck of cards containing the executable program. I was greeted by the programmer (bearded, but lacking the tennis shoes and blue jeans soon to become emblematic of the programming mystique) who thumbed through the deck as he approached me. "I'll be just another moment," he said as he studied the arcane perforation pattern on one of the pasteboards. Then he switched it with another card. "Did you change the program just now?" I asked. "Sort of," he answered. "How do you know it will work? Can we retest it?" He looked at me with a cool gaze: "Of course it will work." I thought of Miranda's lines: "O brave new world/That has such people in't!"

If the programmers of 1960 seemed to the rest of us to be members of an avant garde cabal— one that looked enticing enough to make us think about switching careers— they had more diversity than commonality. Their educational backgrounds included math, physical science, and just about anything else offered by academe. If I recall correctly, the most creative programmer I knew at the time, one who was soon to complete the first chess-playing program, had a master's degree in medieval literature. A few programmers had no degrees. Programmers working on development of operating systems may earlier have been electronic or computer systems engineers. The builders of general ledger programs included a few former accountants. Statistical packages included former (or part time) actuaries, and so it went. Some programmers were graduates of the new EDP training schools. Unlike today, there were few, if any, holders of computer science degrees, and few women were working as programmers thirty years ago, although women now account for a high percentage of the programming population.

Little else has changed since the time when programming was being established as a profession. Jeans and tennis shoes are in less favor these days, but diversity in all other respects remains. Oh yes, and programmer turnover is still a major concern.

Depending on whose survey we read, turnover rates during the 1960s era and in the present as well remain somewhere around 20%—considerably higher in the shops of some harried managers. Not surprisingly, these managers would like to know how to reduce the problem. One way, of course, is to reduce the effects of staff instability. Divide the work into small, discrete work packages, each of which should lend itself to completion within weeks or months (more on this in Chapter 7). But still, it remains that occasionally, to understand a subtle source of potential mischief, one needs to talk with the author of work previously performed. Perhaps even more importantly, teamwork is essential to large scale programming, and it is difficult to fashion a team from an itinerant work force.

We can rarely be certain of the reason a given programmer decides to change jobs. However, several factors have been cited to explain the aggregate motivation of programmers in motion. A fairly recent study[2] of 250 heterogeneous subjects examined four of the most frequently named causes: lack of job satisfaction (here as in all kinds of work), lack of identification with and involvement in the organization for which the programmer works, little belief that professional behavior will result in reward, and the programmer's own lack of a sense of professionalism. The first three of these turned out to be significantly related to turnover. I find particularly interesting the perception of little reward for professionalism. Perhaps because minor league programming comes readily to senior management, they find it easy to discount the fact that large-scale programming must bear the stamp of professionalism, and that programmers will be unhappy people unless they are treated accordingly.

Beyond the recognition that people get satisfaction from producing things that work, a direct connection between quality activities and job satisfaction is not apparent. Nevertheless, we expect that programmers would approach their work with a quicker step if they had up-to-date technology to work with. Updating technology, in any case, is a necessary element of a software quality program.

Quality circles, a form of participatory management so well known now that no explanation is required, can be a help in improving the programmer's sense of identification with and involvement in the organization. A gauge of the morale of employees is their feeling of importance to the organization. I once overheard a conversation among members of the plant guard force who apparently felt that the company revolved about them. I also recall getting the same sense from overheard conversations among secretaries, computer room personnel, and industrial engineers. In fact, to the extent that we can conceive of multiple spin axes, all these people were correct. The organization could not do without them. More important, they were aware of this, and acted the part. So too, with programmers: Programmers who sense their central part in the project or ongoing support effort are not only well motivated but are happier for it. I have seen programmer quality circles increase the participants' sense of their own importance to the organization and their involvement in it.

Making the Team

Earlier in this section I noted that one of the distinguishing characteristics of major league programming is the programming team. Teams of individuals are not always officially recognized as such. More often we speak of project staffs or the like, but when things are working well teamwork becomes apparent. Specific to software quality, peer reviews or walk-throughs are only as successful as the strength of the bond among members of the programming team. Looking at the Japanese model, we find the Senior Vice President and Director of Nippon Electric Company stating, with regard to software work,

"Here, teamwork will be the key. Team members working together are, in their collective wisdom, far more effective than individuals working alone."[3]

In the well publicized COCOMO* some 14 influences, in addition to program size, are used to estimate the cost of software production. By a wide margin, the most significant of these, as determined from analysis of actual projects, is the collective ability of the "personnel/team."[4] Evidently, the researchers find it impossible to separate the two. Team members, of course, easily make distinctions among the contributions made by the constituents of the team.

Teams Are Comprised of Individuals

Plainly, the contributions made by each person reflect the qualities the individual brings to the job. These include personality factors as well as intellectual ones. In his famous book on programmer psychology, Weinberg gives the following attributes as important: ability to tolerate stress, adaptability to rapid change, neatness, humility, and assertiveness.[5] The first of these may depend on the type of software. In a study of 580 information systems personnel (vice presidents, managers, supervisors, systems analysts, and programmers) the findings indicated "... that as a group information systems personnel have moderate to low levels of job-related stress."[6] Although this may be the case for information systems, it certainly is not for the environments of systems programming, large communications systems, and large military systems, which are ruled by desperately tight schedules and applications so removed from precedent that the requirements are a constantly moving target.

Stress is most apparent during periods of test, when system design defects that escaped the review process first become evident. Even as one tries to keep the test process going, new code, representing new design, constantly replaces existing code, providing exciting opportunities for mystifying library control blunders. A study of 63 computer users in the Dallas-Fort Worth area reported that none of 15 identified programming problem areas (e.g., preliminary system design and maintenance) was more troublesome than system testing and validation.[7] The sample size of 63 included sites representing commercial, scientific, systems, and data communications computing. Plainly, quality programs must address the tumult that can attend test and validation, both in terms of reducing the cause and ameliorating the effect.

In addition to personality factors and their correspondence to the programming milieu (from which we seem to have digressed with the issue of stress), we might look at intellectual qualities. The most controversial of these is mathematical aptitude. Scientific applications received the greatest publicity in the early days, and this gave rise to the notion that programmers had to be mathematicians of one kind or another. With the increasing prominence of emerging commercial applications it became apparent that most programmers were mathematicians of no kind. Inevitably, debunking set in, and in certain quarters the conventional wisdom became that mathematical aptitude was not a prerequisite for successful programmers. In fact, quite the opposite is true. In the next

* Constructive Cost Model.

chapter we touch lightly on the mathematical basis for producing correct programs, but even under ordinary informal programming regimens, it is obvious to anyone who has undertaken serious programming that logic or mathematical reasoning underlies much of programming, and that the programmer who was behind the door when logic was passed out will produce poor programs.

Another aptitude that seems significant is verbal ability. I have observed that programmers who speak and write well tend to produce quality software. I do not know why. Perhaps mastery of the syntax of one's native language is symptomatic of the ability to master the syntax of programming languages, but I suspect something more is involved. Even though I do not understand the connection here, I take comfort in the knowledge that the noted computer scientist, Edsgar Dijkstra, has made the same observation:

> *"I am engaged in teaching ... 'mathematical engineer[s].' The most powerful test that I know of for an applicant to be one of my students is that he have an absolute mastery of his native tongue: you just need to listen to him."* [8]

Quality programs cannot do much to improve the native abilities of the members of the programming staff. But quality programs can address the education and training of members currently on the staff.

3.2 EDUCATION AND TRAINING

Considering the diversity of formal education we find among programmers, we might wonder if the right education is always in the right place. That is, people who wandered into programming from some other field, or directly upon receiving some arbitrary undergraduate or graduate degree, may not have the best kind of educational background for the work they are now doing. Further, even when a square programming hole is filled by a square mortarboard, the programmer may be lacking essential skills for the job: fluency in the programming language, dexterity in the use of the operating system hosting the software development tools, and the like. If so, something should be done about it. We cannot expect quality software to be produced by people lacking the proper education and training for the job. We may (and often do) get quality results from programmers of unlikely classroom backgrounds, but this is a matter of luck, not expectations.

We tend to speak of education and training as a single concept, with little regard to the semantic content of each of the two words. Education is distinct from training, although there are times when the distinction is difficult to draw. Fundamentally, education provides people with the intellectual resources to learn, while training provides specific skills. Although some college curricula are tantamount to vocational training (an increasing and disquieting trend), we generally think of education as the product of colleges and universities, and training as the product of industry. We take up education first.

Education

Many employers currently provide tuition reimbursement of one kind or another for employees taking college or graduate courses, especially for those who are matriculated for a degree. Some also provide time during business hours to take courses not available at other times. Courses of particular relevance to programming professionals are those in computer science and software engineering. Computer science courses are fairly common today, and undergraduate and graduate degrees in computer science are only slightly less so. Software engineering is another matter. The paucity of schools offering courses of study leading to software engineering degrees may be symptomatic of the prevailing uncertainty concerning the academic background appropriate for software engineering. Nevertheless, an increasing number of schools are now finding their way toward offering software engineering degrees.

Programmers located near large schools have little difficulty finding courses of study to enrich their programming abilities. To make certain that the opportunity is not lost, companies may be able to engage faculty to teach some courses in-house, perhaps for academic credit. Unfortunately, a small percentage of the programming work force is not proximate to a college or university offering courses specific to the needs of software development or maintenance. However, few of these people cannot get to a school once or twice a week to take courses in mathematics, and a deeper understanding of mathematics—especially first order mathematics—can lead the motivated software professional to avenues of personal investigation equivalent to courses expressly directed to computer science. The sources for such investigation are mostly print: a vast library of book titles and the periodicals of the professional societies.

The three most prominent organizations are the Association for Computing Machinery (ACM), the IEEE Computer Society, and the Data Processing Management Association (DPMA). New developments in the science and engineering of programming are likely to find early publication in the periodicals of the societies, principally those of the ACM and the IEEE Computer Society. Of particular pertinence to education, these periodicals include several excellent tutorials: *Computing Surveys* (ACM), *Computer* (IEEE), and, although it is not billed as a tutorial, *IEEE Software*. To encourage programming personnel to extend their self-education, firms can purchase memberships for their employees in at least one of these organizations. Many programmers think nothing of using their own money to join one organization, but having done so, join no others. Cost reimbursement is a simple and inexpensive (generally $50 to $100 per year, depending on the number of periodicals taken) means of encouraging employees to extend their study.

Similarly, company libraries should include a number of titles dealing with computer science and software engineering. New books need to be purchased annually. From its inception, the science and technology of computer software has been in a restless state of evolution. Moreover, evolutionary software mutants appear every year, resulting in an ever-widening field of study.

Possibly the most popular source of software education is that offered by attendance at professional conferences and seminars. The professional societies hold several important conferences each year, distinguished from trade shows by the emphasis on prepared papers and panel discussions. Also of considerable value are the frequent software conferences sponsored by industrial organizations, such as the National Security Industrial Association (NSIA), the Aerospace Industries Association (AIA), and the Electronic Industries Association (EIA). Some of these are specific to software quality assurance. The total amount of new material introduced at these conferences is awesome. The "information explosion" we read about in the popular press may find its most prolix realization in the very field that is responsible for the handling of information. Moreover, many new ideas are initially published at conferences rather than in the journals, since the publishing queue of the societies' periodicals is rarely less than two years.

Many companies send their programming employees to at least one conference each year. The cost is that of travel, conference registration, and loss of three or four days of work—a small price.

Like all managers and professionals, software people are bombarded with mailings advertising professional seminars offered by private companies and a few colleges and universities. Certain seminars also carry the sponsorship of a professional society. Some seminars deal with fairly broad topics (e.g., new government policies concerning software acquisition), while others are more specific (e.g., relational data base design). Although individual attendance at a seminar is more costly than at a professional or industrial conference, seminars tend to provide a more focused structure. Also, it may be possible to arrange presentation to several staff members on company premises at a group rate (particularly if the seminar is given by only one or two people). One caveat: Seminars promising to deliver "the latest" have at times been known to provide hackneyed material last considered current five years earlier.

Summarizing this section, a number of diverse opportunities exist for enlarging the educational credentials of the programming staff. It's a good thing, too: The programmer who is technically au courant at a given time, will, without substantial further education of one form or another, be impossibly (but not irremediably) out of date three years later. To varying degrees, most companies offer support for employee education, but the educational program should be reviewed periodically to determine if it is as aggressive as it might be.

Training

Training is called for under a variety of circumstances:

- Introduction of a new programming language.
- Use of a new operating system.
- Use of a new software tool.
- A need for understanding the rest of the project (as background to the software requirements specifications).
- Introduction of new design or quality methods.

Most of the time, programmers are left to their own resources to learn programming languages and operating systems. They do learn that way, but the learning they get may not be in the best interests of quality. For example, a rich language like Ada provides many opportunities for misuse by all but the most adept programmers. Moreover, the language features most closely identified with realizing the attributes of quality (generic packages, for one) may be ignored by a programmer who decides that he or she has learned enough after mastering the basic set of instructions. To remedy this, a formal training program should be considered when a new language or metasystem is about to be used. The bad news is that this does not completely solve the problem. Given the usual staff turnover problem, there is always a new supply of people to be trained after the formal training has been concluded. The good news is that various organizations run training courses from time to time to which new hires can be sent. A two week diversion from the job for training may present scheduling problems, but in the long run, the commission of fewer errors will more than compensate for the two weeks.

If we were able to prepare perfect specifications for the behavior expected of software, it would be unnecessary for programmers to know any more about the projects they work on. As it happens, our specifications are usually models of imperfection (more on this in the next chapter), and programmers who know no more than the specifications perform work of low quality. We see this happening in the development of software that is barely usable in the operational environment for which it is destined, in real-time software burdened with problems of unresolved concurrency situations, and in commercial-application software incapable of working with other software systems across informational interfaces. Many years ago I joined a company engaged in a rapid staffing effort, to work on a project then about two years old. My first assignment was to join other new hires in a week long class to learn the architecture of the entire system. Many times during my subsequent assignments as an electronics engineer I found it necessary to draw on my classroom training to interpret properly the behavioral specifications presented to me. Training such as this is frequently overlooked, especially for replacements of personnel who left the company while the project was still under way. It is often called for, however, and should be considered in quality planning.

Progressive programming shops are forever acquiring or developing new software tools. Although tooling is an integral part of quality programs, training people in the use of tools is frequently neglected. New design processors, data checkers, or test systems are more often than not "thrown over the wall." The result is that programmers either are disinclined to use the fool thing or do not use it to its full advantage. Again, formal training programs are called for.

It is hard to imagine the programming boss saying to the staff, "Tomorrow I want you all to start using the Jackson Design Method," or, "Nancy, Pete, and Alma, whenever you can I want you to get together with Melvin to review his design," without having first seen to it that the people have been trained in JDM or in conducting design reviews. Yet this type of scenario happens all the time. Training is, of course, available from the same kind of people who conduct industrial seminars, as well as from many consultants. In many cases, at least one person among the staff is qualified to train his or her peers. In any case, to realize the expected benefits of new methods, they should be introduced by planned training programs. To digress a bit, I wonder why programmers think to include on their resumés languages, machines, and operating systems, but almost never say a word about methods. If I were using Warnier-Orr charts, I should be as interested in finding people with Warnier-Orr experience as I would people with experience in the programming language I was using.

Cross-Training

Despite the earlier brave words distinguishing education from training, gray areas do exist, none grayer than cross-training. Cross-training, at times unkindly called "retreading," attempts to provide sufficient classroom background to allow students to qualify for new careers. The typical impetus for this costly process is a scarcity of specialists of a given kind amidst a surplus of other kinds of personnel. Working our way around to programmers, let us hypothesize a company in one of the localities into which, for one reason or another, it is difficult to import a sufficient number of programmers who have backgrounds appropriate for the work at hand. Let our hypothesis also include a surfeit of electronic accounting machine operators.* Killing two birds with one educational shot, the EAM people are converted into programmers.

The shot had better be well aimed. Our scenario stacked the deck in favor of success: The training subjects had a related background. Cross-training EAM operators is much more likely to succeed than cross-training dental assistants. If the background of the subjects is the wind correction of a good shot, the depth and breadth of the training program is the bore of the gun barrel. A two-hour per week, after-hours program, lasting 20 weeks, is not going to do it. An example of a successful program is Lockheed's Data Systems Design and Development (DSDD) Training Program.[9] The goal is to increase the number of programmers available to work on military systems software. Applicants for the program are limited to employees with a technical degree or equivalent background. Once accepted, the applicants attend classes full time, Monday through Friday, for six months. Salaries are continued during the program, and no other assignments are made. In addition to courses specific to software development (programming, data base design, and the like), the students take courses in mathematics and engineering disciplines (communications, microprocessors, and so forth). To graduate 50 students each year, Lockheed provides the program with about 1.5 million dollars annually.

I was involved some years ago with a similar program, also in the military systems environment. The motivation was somewhat different, being colored by the company's belief that the programmers best qualified to work on our systems were among those relatively few people in the country expert in the highly classified application. Since most of the engineers in the company did some programming from time to time, we took the approach that programming knowledge was a reasonable prerequisite, and that the training program would restrict itself to large scale programming methods and to assembler language. (At the time, the use of assembler was defensible; it would not be now.) If I recall correctly, the program demanded about one day a week of the students' time, and lasted 6 months or so. Given the special circumstances of admission, this turned out to be sufficient, and the program was entirely successful.

Cross-training has also been considered as a method of staffing software quality assurance groups. The ideal software quality engineer is at once a programming expert and a quality expert. Given that a random selection of any million or so people will yield no one of that description (unless previously so trained), cross-training in either direction appears to be the obvious solution. As it happens, we have less a solution than a dilemma. Since quality engineers are also in short supply, the quality experts most likely to be available for cross-training are quality inspectors and the like. They are no more likely to have programming aptitude than bakers and Indian chiefs. Impaling oneself on the other horn of the dilemma, where does one find a surplus programmer?

It would seem that software quality engineers are not about to spring from any surpluses. Therefore, we must look to ways of making cross-training (in either direction) attractive to gainfully, happily employed people. Quality engineers must be given the opportunity to see that software quality is another phase in the ever-evolving history of the quality profession, one whose mastery is, if nothing else, another plank to shore up their job security. The seduction of progammers is more subtle. I suspect that the most likely candidates are those who, disaffected with the state of software engineering in their current situation, see in software quality engineering a direct way to do something about the state of software technology and management in their companies. At the risk

---

* We can assume they had been hiding all these years.

of getting several chapters ahead of ourselves, we might note that if software quality engineering staffs reach the 5% or so of development and maintenance staffing levels that many people foresee, we face a shortage much like the shortage of programmers noted in Chapter 1.

Concluding this discussion, we see that cross-training is a technique for filling staff shortfalls, often to the relief of staff surpluses. Cross-training requires the coordination of the managers for whom the trainees will eventually work, the managers who in some cases will have to give up valuable people, the trainers (possibly within the company, possibly without), and the personnel department.* Despite the fact that cross-training must be carefully approached, it may be the most reasonable approach to certain problems attending quality programs.

3.3 SUMMARY

1. Quality programs should encourage all programmers to assume the attitudes of software engineering.

2. Despite the diversity of the educational (and often vocational) backgrounds found among programmers, programming is a profession and it is to the employer's advantage to treat programmers as professionals.

3. Programmer turnover is a major problem, but one that can be attacked.

4. Large scale programming is not just a matter of employing many programmers, it requires conscious teamwork.

5. Notwithstanding the need for teamwork, the qualities of individuals remain a concern of quality programs. A variety of measures are available for employers to support individual efforts at self-improvement through education.

6. Education is not just a matter of upgrading. Without continuing education of one form or another, programmers rapidly become obsolete.

7. In the interests of quality, training should accompany the introduction of new programming languages, operating systems, methods, and tools.

8. It is important for programmers to have a comprehensive understanding of the project at hand. This, too, can be taught.

9. Cross-training can help fill staff shortages, frequently to the relief of other personnel surpluses. Cross-training is also a technique for filling software quality engineer openings.

3.4 REFERENCES

[1] S. Levy, *Hackers: Heroes of the Computer Revolution* (New York: Doubleday & Co., 1984).

[2] K. Bartol, "Turnover Among DP Personnel: A Causal Analysis," *CACM*, Vol. 26 (October 1983) pp. 807–11.

* Or, as it is often called in a curiously dehumanizing locution, "the human resources department."

[3] Y. Mizuno, "Software Quality Improvement," *Computer* (March 1983) pp. 66–72.

[4] B. Boehm et al., "A Software Development Environment for Improving Productivity," *Computer* (June 1984) pp. 30–44.

[5] G. Weinberg, *The Psychology of Computer Programming* (New York: Van Nostrand Reinhold, 1971), 149–150.

[6] J. Ivancevich et al., "Occupational Stress, Attitudes, and Health Problems in the Information Systems Professional," *CACM*, Vol. 26 (October 1983) pp. 800–06.

[7] L. Beck and T. Perkins, "A Survey of Software Engineering Practice: Tools, Methods, and Results," *IEEE Trans. Software Eng.*, Vol. SE-9 (September 1983) pp. 541–61.

[8] G. Weinberg, *The Psychology of Computer Programming* (New York: Van Nostrand Reinhold, 1971), 176.

[9] J. P. McGill, "The Software Engineering Shortage: A Third Choice," *IEEE Trans. Software Eng.*, Vol. SE-10 (January 1984) pp. 42–49.

CHAPTER 4

Technology

Chapter 3 made the point is that the quality of software depends on the qualities of the people producing it. In this chapter, the point is made that the quality of software depends also on the quality of technology that the producing people use. Technology is a matter of processes and tools. We cannot expect to get high-grade modern plate glass using the same technology colonial Americans used to make four inch window panes. Despite meticulous inspection procedures applied in the name of QC and despite the greatest imaginable diligence applied by well-instructed workers, the glass technology of 250 years ago will still result in unacceptable ripples and bubbles in the glass.

Software, too, is only as good as the technology that produces it. Defining what we mean by good technology is another matter. Since 1970 or so, software technology has exploded in diverse directions. We have various technological approaches for defining the behavioral characteristics of software, even more for designing its structure. Implementing the design in code involves a choice of radically different programming languages. Removing defects from final and interim software products raises not only procedural choices but an assortment of technological approaches. And even within the same general technical approach, a bewildering array of tools is available for use.

To paint so wide a canvas requires the use of a broad brush, especially if a technical level of detail inappropriate to this book is to be avoided. *Accordingly, the discussion of technology that follows deals with concepts, rather than the specifics with which the concepts are realized.* Although this chapter is *about* technology and its connections to quality, and not a text from which one may learn how to use technology, the generalist may find some of it overly technical and may choose to skip ahead to the summary in Section 4.5.

We start with the most fundamental of the technological concepts, that having to do with the translation of computing requirements into programming language.

4.1 PARADIGMS AND LANGUAGES

Apart from testing, the last stage of programming is the final encoding of the solution to the problem given to the programmers. Whether the problem is one of management information, communications switching, control of an industrial process, or the navigation of aircraft, the results of the design process must be conveyed to the computer through some instrument of translation. The most basic such instrument is assembler language (or assembly language), one step removed from the computer's native instruction set. Assembler language is tedious to write, difficult to read, and exposes the programmer to a level of hazard hidden by other languages. Assembler language is excusable only for time-critical parts of certain real-time programs, and seldom at that. From the point of view of technology, not much can be said about assembler language, since, for the best of reasons, no efforts at further advancing assembler language programming have been made for many years. In short, although assembler language programming can at rare times be justified, it is not part of quality technology. In the discussions that follow, we are concerned only with high-level languages. Before this section is out, we will see how high high can be.

Most of the software produced today is written in a language that deals with data on the one hand and, on the other, with procedures to use the data. The specification for the solution to be couched in a particular programming language is the result of a design process that is separable in technology from the language. The design itself attempts to satisfy some sort of behavioral requirements model, again separable in technology. Also separable in technology is the environment in which the solution will be tested and operated. Reflecting the mutual isolation of the technological elements, the term I use for this most common model of programming technology is "disjoint programming." No derision attaches to the word "disjoint," which, when used by mathematicians as an adjective, simply means having no parts in common. Total continuity is absent also in the more technologically advanced approaches to programming that follow. However, none of these is as fragmented as the programming with which we have become most familiar.

Disjoint Programming

Disjoint programming starts with a definition of the requirements of the system to be programmed. The requirements may be set forth in the form of a detailed specification, or they may result from an exercise in rapid prototyping. We leave the methods of producing a behavioral requirements model in the disjoint paradigm until Chapter 6. For the present, we move on to the design phase, wherein, by one means or another, detailed specifications of each part of the program are produced.

Most design processes are attempts at decomposing the software problem into a discrete set of software elements. All the processes share the same goal: Replace the complexity of the programming problem with a set of inherently less complex constituents of a programming solution. Some of these processes are directed to the structure of the data and some to the logical structure of the procedures that will process the data. In the end, both kinds of approaches result in discrete, but related, definitions of data and procedures. Modularity is the attribute that describes the mutual independence of the elements of the solution. Greater independence ensures greater likelihood that individual design efforts will result in a working and maintainable system.

One way to look at problem decomposition in the disjoint paradigm is to consider the level of abstraction of the solution at various points in the decomposition process.

> *At the start, when we know much about the problem and nothing about the solution, the solution is very abstract. At the end, when we have compiled source code and bound data, the solution is concrete.*

Despite the diversity of the several modern methods for reducing the problem to a solution, we frequently encounter among them the concept of *information hiding*, initially formalized by David Parnas some years ago.[1] The idea here is that the specification of any piece of the solution should contain nothing beyond the minimum amount of information required to implement the specification—whether by further decomposition or by code. The Parnas method results in modules having code "hidden" from other modules, thus making it impossible for one module to depend on the implementation of the specification (formally, the description of the data used by the module) peculiar to another module. The result is intermodule independence.

I suspect that more programming shops than not use ad hoc decomposition processes, as distinguished from formal processes such as Parnas'. However, the better of the home-grown methodologies I have seen are based—not always consciously—on the precepts of information hiding. Typically, programmers tentatively partition the program into components that will satisfy the external requirements, and then refine the component definitions to hide as much data as possible within the components.

A few formal methods are worth noting in order to illustrate the diversity of design methods.

> *The fact that the software mustard can be cut in many ways underlies the fallacy of prescribing an arbitrarily selected method in the name of quality.*

Perhaps the most widely used of the formal methods is *structured design*, derived from strategies devised by L. L. Constantine. Structured design is concerned with the coupling among modules that makes them interdependent, the self-sufficiency of modules (called cohesion) that promotes their independence, and the architectural relations among the modules. The central decomposition method,[2] based on an analysis of data flow, regards modules as information transformers. It is augmented by other strategies, as well, including the Parnas approach. G. J. Myers has extended structured design to the express achievement of *functional decomposition*,[3] a divide-and-conquer strategy that iteratively divides and subdivides the functional requirements into constituent subfunctions tentatively identified as modules. The modules are then regrouped to take advantage of commonality.

Two design methods emphasizing the structure of data are the Jackson Design Method[4] and the Warnier-Orr approach.[5] Both methods are finding increasingly wide use. Both—especially Warnier-Orr—are noteworthy for another reason: their use of graphics in addition to text. Graphics add new dimensions (well, two of them, anyway) to the programmer's ability to conceptualize the evolving design of a system, particularly with respect to data flow and system states.

As an example of the power of graphics, the Petri net of Figure 4.1 depicts the relation between system states or "events" (circles) and the transitions (squares) between them. States marked by circular black tokens enable transitions at the end of the corresponding arrowheads. When a transition occurs, one token is deleted from each enabling state and one token is added to each consequent state. For Figure 4.1, try describing in words the conditions that govern the possible sequences of states.

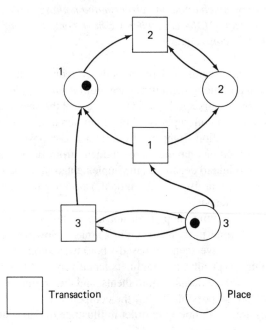

Figure 4.1 Petri Net

The more advanced design methods utilize formal graphic semantics; that is, each symbol has specific meaning, and the interconnection of the symbols follows syntactic rules. A well-known example of a graphically supported design method is SADT,* [6] which is also compatible with the Jackson, Parnas, and structured design methodologies. SADT is applicable not only to design but also to the analysis of requirements, which makes it somewhat disjoint from the other methods of the disjoint paradigm.

The most popular mechanism for documenting design decisions is a software design language, although HIPO (hierarchy plus input-process-output) has a number of adherents and there remain those who have yet to break their knotted ties to flow charts. Increasingly, data dictionaries are being used in large systems to define the relations among data. Taking one documentation scheme as an example, we find an enormous number of species belonging to the genus "software design language." Home- grown design languages are often used strictly for documentation, while others, available from software suppliers, are equipped with analyzers capable of finding some classes of error.

---

* SADT is a trademark of SofTech, Inc.

Appropriately for the disjoint paradigm, design languages are usually restricted in capability to but one phase (most commonly, detailed design) of the problem decomposition process.

Working backwards from design to requirements definitions (which is art imitating what is all too often life), we find requirements defined at several levels of abstraction. For example, a marketing specification of some performance features can be construed as a requirements definition. If the marketing specification leads to a composite systems specification, one in which computing devices compete with other electronic equipments for the attention of systems engineers, we have yet another level of requirements modeling. The software requirements model that emerges from the analysis of the systems specification, like as not, is disjoint from that specification, save for some backwards references.* Most requirements are specified in pure prose, alleviated every now and again by a diagram or two. Apart from the difficulty of interpreting specificationese, over-reliance on words tends to obscure the relations between functional specifications that are removed from each other by 100 pages. Worse, prose specifications do not easily serve as vehicles for analysis. Structured requirements languages, similar to design languages, help, but even greater help is found in hierarchical schemes, wherein one peels off layers, as of an onion, to iteratively gain an understanding of what the system must do. Documentation methods that lend themselves to the onion model are state diagrams (of which the Petri net of Figure 4.1 is a special case), data dictionaries, and data flow diagrams. See DeMarco's book[7] for techniques to layer structured data flow analysis.

In the disjoint paradigm, structured requirements models do not necessarily lead to quality system designs, as continuity between the two is lost. However, structured design documentation is likely to produce structured code, unless deliberately sabotaged by "clever" programming. Structured code, characterized by logical processes having but one entry and exit and by restrictions on the use of data, was one of the earliest inventions directed toward software quality. Structured code is encouraged not only by structured detailed design, but by programming languages. Indeed, it is impossible to structure code in certain languages (e.g., COBOL and RPG). Other languages (e.g., Fortran 77 and PL/1) give programmers the opportunity to structure or not. On the surface this sounds satisfactory, since nonstructured code can be caught in reviews and reworked. However, structure is not something that one easily (or efficiently) adds on when translating a cognitive process to code. When developing code, the programmer should think in terms of structured control constructs and data privileges. Initially, many programmers thought this impossible, but nonetheless rapidly developed fluency in the structured culture. Languages such as Pascal (and its variants) and C offer some capability to violate the tenets of structured control flow, but—perhaps because the offending goto constructs are thought outre when used in these languages—the opportunity is not generally abused. Pascal also permits programmers to define classes of data in terms of the operations that may be permitted on them. Such *user-defined data types* represent a significant expedient in the battle against programmer error. (User-defined data types represent a form of data abstraction. More formal treatment of abstract data types underlies object-oriented programming, which we come to shortly.)

Of the several dozen languages in current industrial and academic use, none has equaled Ada in attracting the attention of software professionals dedicated to quality. In addition to the structured capabilities of Pascal, Ada also supports concurrent pro-

---

*Five will get you ten that at least one substantive contradiction can be found between the two.

cesses (sometimes an inescapable consequence of the physical world, but sometimes an attractive alternative to forcing unnatural control linkages between inherently independent processes), generic program elements (change the parameters and the code is reusable), and—more than any other common language—information hiding. Recall that the discussion of problem decomposition in the disjoint paradigm began with the concept of information hiding. In Ada, information hiding extends directly to the code, where the specifications and the processing body of a procedure can be compiled separately. Indeed, if we were to view the specifications as the data of a procedure and the body as the methods used to operate on the data, we would have an opportune introduction to the topic of object-oriented programming. However, the object-oriented paradigm will have to wait until the programming paradigm is finally defined.

Abstractions and Paradigms

Programming paradigms have their origins in the ways that people abstract the sense of programming problems. The word "abstraction" was used earlier intuitively, but to make certain we know what we are about, let us try for a better definition. The second definition of abstraction offered by my favorite dictionary is "The act or process of separating the inherent qualities or properties of something from the actual physical object or concept to which they belong."[8] In software, we identify a few of an object's qualities or properties, and use them for the purpose at hand while temporarily ignoring all other properties. Principally, we are concerned with properties that capture the quintessence of the object, to the exclusion of properties that describe the way it does its thing. We can look on computer programs themselves as abstractions of processes. This is true at the most general level: The Turing machine of computer science is an abstraction of all automata; that is, of all programmed machines. The Petri net of Figure 4.1 is an abstraction of a set of asynchronous processes. Data flow diagrams are abstractions of the sequences of transformations on interrelated data.

The disjoint paradigm, the term we used to describe the most common of all programming milieux, is a paradigm in the sense that it is a model of how to go about approaching a programming process. However, it is a weak paradigm, for the disjoint paradigm is quite nearly a boundless set of models, each member of the set representing one technique of defining programming behavioral specifications, one design decomposition method (and its tools), and one programming language. Nevertheless, commonalities do exist: The programming languages are all procedural, the means for expressing one set of decisions are not necessarily the same as those for any other set, and the run-time environment is independent of the programming process.

Although, as we saw, the disjoint paradigm can be supported by quality-oriented technology and although it represents the way most programming is currently accomplished, let us take a look at another class of paradigms, the models that increasingly are pointing the way to the future of programming, and for which we needed to coin the term "programming paradigm." These models are based on abstractions of classes of programming languages. In these models, languages and paradigms are inextricably intertwined, the division between designing and coding is blurred to the point of vanishing, and at least some data binding generally awaits execution time.

Several of the paradigms that conform to this definition are discussed briefly, starting with the object-oriented paradigm remarked in the discussion of Ada.

The programming of our disjoint paradigm is based on functional abstractions. Given a set of functions—loosely, procedures—we apply inputs and obtain outputs related to the inputs by the encoded functions. The data are our variables. Alternatively, we can think of the input as a specific data structure and consider our variable to be the set of functions that can be applied to the data. The alternative is the essence of the object abstractions. Wegner[9] formalizes this concept by speaking of the class of all expressions of the form $f(x)$, where f is a function and x is an argument of f. In the function abstraction he varies x over all the arguments of a particular f. In the object abstraction he fixes x and allows f to vary over all the functions applicable to x.

If we think not of data structures and algorithms but of the system concepts they implement, and if we loosely (for now) define these concepts as *objects*, we see that at any given time during problem analysis the objects of a system define our knowledge of its state and behavior. If the objective is an air traffic radar system, we start off by knowing that we have a radar, as in Figure 4.2. It is an object. Other objects we know about are the individual members of the class "aircraft" that the radar points to. On further analysis, the radar transmitter becomes a time reference, and the aircraft become the transmission returns. In the next stage of modeling the problem, the returns are seen to be transponder codes, encoded altitudes, and time related to the transmission (by now, interrogation transmissions)—more objects. Eventually, many of the recognized objects are quite small in scope (for example, display graphics). In functional decomposition, we would arrive at a hierarchically structured set of programs that would have direct relevance to the functions of the system. In the object-oriented paradigm, data abstraction leads us to a set of objects about which a software system is configured, as in Figure 4.3. Functions are distributed among the objects. (The illustration, of course, is a gross oversimplification.)

Apart from its effect on the design process, a way to contrast object-oriented programming to conventional programming is to consider the latter as founded on separate data and procedures, while the concepts of the former are objects and messages. Objects are inseparable collections of data and the methods (operations) performed on them. For example, our range object has the data for the time of interrogation and the time of the response, and one method for reconciling the two to form aircraft range. Objects communicate with each other by exchanging messages. Specifically, an object asks another object to do its thing with its data (hidden from the first object) by sending it an appropriate message specifying the operation that the receiving object is to perform. In Figure 4.3, the position object would ask the range object to perform the range calculation for a given aircraft identification (another datum).

There are other differences between conventional programming and object-oriented programming. In the former, the state of a procedure or subroutine is lost after the procedure completes its operation. Objects, however, have states, and can retain the value of their states when the methods are completed. Conventional programming entities generally are mutually disjoint. However, objects may share certain characteristics with other objects, may be members of the same *class*. Viewed so, a given object is considered an *instance* of the class, populated with values for the internal state variables *(instance variables)* of the class. New procedures cannot be created from existing ones, but new objects or classes can be derived from existing classes. In so doing, characteristics of the antecedent are *inherited* by the descendent. For example, at the control consoles, the

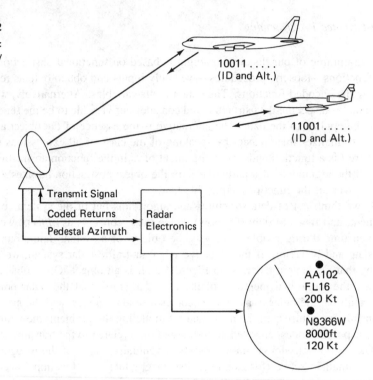

10011 . . . . .
(ID and Alt.)

11001 . . . . .
(ID and Alt.)

Transmit Signal

Coded Returns

Pedestal Azimuth

Radar
Electronics

AA102
FL16
200 Kt

N9366W
8000ft
120 Kt

Figure 4.2 Air Traffic Control Radar

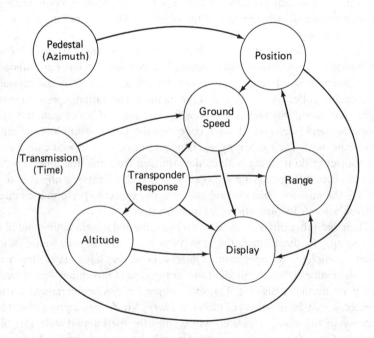

Pedestal
(Azimuth)

Position

Ground
Speed

Transmission
(Time)

Transponder
Response

Range

Altitude

Display

Figure 4.3 Radar System Objects

block of information for each airplane and the block's location on the display inherit a format template and a set of placement rules common to all aircraft display objects.

One of the problems in decomposition processes is to make certain that the design decisions reached at each stage of development are traceable to the predecessor stage. Through inheritance, however, defined classes are unmistakably members of the class from which they are derived. (This remains true even for those languages that allow inherited methods to be modified or replaced.)

The foundations of object-oriented programming are abstract data types, data hiding, and inheritance. Several languages supporting these exist, each implementing the basics of object-oriented programming to a somewhat different degree. SIMULA was the prototype, followed by Smalltalk. More recently, we have C++, Lisp-based Flavors, C-based Objective-C,* and the last language named in the discussion of the disjoint paradigm, Ada. C++, Objective-C, and Flavors permit the programmer to depart from object-oriented concepts to write code in the conventional data structures and procedure bodies of the base language. C++ and Flavors have another advantage over Smalltalk: In creating a new class (called, in Flavors, a "flavor"), the programmer may select characteristics to be inherited from more than one predecessor class.†

Ada differs from the other languages in that it is not designed for specific conformance to the object-oriented paradigm. Ada's intrinsic separation of data structures and procedure bodies is reconciled to object-oriented concepts by encapsulating data and programs in packages. The specification part of the package declares the public data and the procedures manipulating the data, which we can interpret as the instance variables of an object and the functions used by the object for operating on the variables. The messages of object-oriented programming become the instantiation of generic parameters. Nevertheless, it remains that Ada is an incomplete realization of the object-oriented paradigm. Ada has no built-in capability for inheritance, although a limited form of inheritance can be achieved by deriving data types from exported types. Even this is not without cost: As pointed out by Booch,[10] in doing so the safety of encapsulated data types is lost. Ada is also incomplete as an object-oriented language with respect to invoking methods. Ada does not lend itself to run-time binding of method names in messages, which the paradigm calls for. Further comment on the capabilities and limitations of Ada as an object-oriented programming language can be found in reference.[11]

Even as the programmers of twenty years ago decried the inefficiency of compiler languages as compared to assembler languages, the efficiency of languages addressing object-oriented programming has been questioned. Cox has measured the cost of message communication compared to procedure calls, and has shown that execution time ratios of approximately two can be realized in Objective-C at some cost of storage space.[12] Aside from toy problems, solving a software problem two ways for the purpose of comparison is rare, so the efficiency question remains alive.

Anticipating Section 4.2, it would be inappropriate to conclude this brief discussion of the object-oriented paradigm without some mention of the purpose most prominently proposed for it. Earlier in the discussion of the paradigm a comparison with functional decomposition was drawn. Implicit in the comparison was the opposing alternative: system composition, that is, building a system from existing software components. In the functional decomposition approach, we proceed by functional abstraction, ending

---

* Objective-C is a trademark of Productivity Products, International.

† Put perhaps too preciously, in Flavors one "mixes flavors."

with a set of functions to be programmed. In the object-oriented paradigm, once the problem has been analyzed, we can proceed by identifying the objects of the system, determining the interfaces among them, and then implementing the objects. Unless we are new to the business, the likelihood is great that most of the objects or their classes have previously been implemented and can be reused. Quoting Wegner, "Function abstraction emphasizes reusability of functions for varying data, while data abstraction emphasizes the reusability of data objects for various operations ..."[13] Since a large system will have a large number of elements, to be of practical use as a reusability approach, the object-oriented paradigm requires the establishment of some kind of library of implemented classes and a mechanism for matching library entries with the objects defined at the start of the system composition process.

The Fourth Generation

We hear much about fourth generation languages. Of course, one person's fourth is another's third and yet another's fifth. The nth generation of languages, computers, chips, and so forth, is simply a dramatic way of saying that a technological revolution is at hand, and whoever says it first establishes an instant reputation as a foresighted leader.

> *If the many languages that have been touted as belonging to the fourth generation have anything in common, it is that they are nonprocedural, in contrast to the assembler, compiler, and interpreter languages in which most of the software we now use has been written.*

If we can equate the fourth generation with nonprocedural languages, object-oriented languages would seem to be of Generation 3.5, since the object-oriented part of their programming use is nonprocedural.

It is not difficult to understand why people want to dub the class of nonprocedural languages a new generation of programming languages. In the more familiar languages, a method of solving a problem is coded. In nonprocedural languages, the problem is more or less stated. For example, relational data base environments permit the use of declarative statements to reconstruct data in new relations to represent the information sought. To further illustrate the difference between procedural and nonprocedural languages, Figure 4.4, in conventional programming style, finds the largest of ten values, while Figure 4.5 depicts the way a nonprocedural language might be used for the same problem.

```
real s(10);
int i, big;
big := s(1);
for i = 2 to i = 10
      if (s(i) > big) then big := s(i);
print big;
```
                                        Figure 4.4.

```
set S contains:
          10 numeric values
          Big;
Big => S(i) over S;
print Big;
```
                              Figure 4.5.

The program of Figure 4.5 merely defines the existence of the ten values and of a variable *big*, provides a definition of *big*, and commands the computer to print *big*. Forming *big* is left to the language processor, which needs no more than the rigorous definition of *big* provided by the program.

Information Systems. Of the languages the fourth generation is purported to comprise, the most familiar, now numbering in the dozens, are those directed to information systems. An early one (so early it usually escapes the designation of fourth generation) is RPG, short for report generator language. Later well-known examples include Focus, Ramis, and Nomad. These are not just languages; collectively they form a paradigm, complete with development and run-time environments. The earmarks of the environment of fourth generation information systems languages generally are a data base management system (DBMS), a query language or report generator, and a data dictionary to ensure the correctness of the DBMS entries. Given the inclusiveness of the term fourth generation, some languages also provide constructs for procedural programming.

The fourth generation languages used for information systems can be thought of as application generators. An application—anything from a data collection system to an accounting system—can be built much faster using these languages than using purely procedural languages. Indeed, we have to be careful in measuring programmer productivity: Lines of code per month are markedly fewer when using an application generator, but only because the languages permit the generation of far more succinct programs. Of course, recalling the arguments of Section 2.2, productivity measured with regard to functionality is higher by an order of magnitude. The gain in productivity is not without cost: The fourth generation is a prodigious user of machine resources. Also, an expert in software maintenance fears that application generators may increase the cost of software maintenance.[14]

Beyond MIS. Beyond the intrusion of the fourth generation in the lives of application programmers, we see a variety of nonprocedural languages dedicated to other types of problems. For several years, programmers have used compiler-compilers, or translator writing systems, as they are sometimes called.* Given the semantics and syntax of a language as input, compiler-compilers produce output suitable for direct translation by a code generator into the machine language of the target processor. Thus, programmers, unfettered by the greatest part of the cost of compiler design and implementation, can freely invent new languages for solving specific classes of problems. For example, a graphical language (itself a nonprocedural language) for expressing concurrency conditions in software-intensive systems uses a compiler-compiler for producing the code corresponding to graphical symbols.[15]

The greater the level of abstraction each encoded operation implies, the fewer the number of operations required to encode a solution. Accordingly, languages capable of high levels of abstraction, frequently called *very high level languages* (VHLL) have found application in rapid prototyping (more about this in Chapter 6). An example of a VHLL is New York University's set-theoretic language, SETL. The application of SETL to rapid prototyping was demonstrated in the prototype compiler for Ada, the first such compiler—prototype or production—certified by the government. While the

---

*Compiler-compilers are favorite projects for computer scientists, and a great number have been produced. One such is YACC—Yet Another Compiler-Compiler.

compiler may be too inefficient for production purposes, it is interesting to note that despite several updates to track the evolving Ada specification, the entire Ada effort took only 100 labor-months to complete.[16]

Another important example of nonprocedural languages is Prolog, developed to express rule-based programming, the formalization of human methods used to arrive at solutions to problems. Thus, it joins Lisp as a language embraced by researchers in artificial intelligence. Prolog is a logic programming language. Such languages, also referred to as relational languages, allow unknown values to be found from known values where the relation between unknowns and knowns can be defined. In Prolog, relations are defined by a set of definitions, the clauses of which specify the constraints for which the relationships are valid. I have not learned Prolog, but I have been told by Prolog enthusiasts that the language is not difficult to learn, and that once learned it is very satisfactory to use. A recent tutorial[17] on Prolog by Ruth Davis succinctly describes how the language is used.

Other Paradigms

We can list some other programming paradigms that, despite attracting considerable attention, have not yet achieved sufficient "industrial strength" to find their way into ordinary use. I have included only those paradigms that software and quality managers, alert to any technological developments having to do with fault-freeness, have queried me about.

Functional (or *applicative*) languages are highly expressive nonprocedural languages that hold the promise of executable specifications to replace other methods of specifying the requirements for components of software systems. Exactness in specification technology has obvious application to software quality.

The quintessence of software exactness is found in *mathematical programming*. The idea here is that programs can be regarded as mathematical objects when their behavior is analyzed within a formal system of mathematics. Using formal systems (e.g., the predicate calculus) as an accompaniment to program development, the programmer produces not only code but a proof of the code's correctness with respect to its specifications. Even with the help of powerful theorem-proving tools, realization of mathematical programming is both tedious and itself error-prone. Quality engineers who have heard that programs can be proved correct, have (in my experience) heard references to mathematical programming, but it simply is not practicable for any but the smallest programming components.

Provable specifications have received as much attention as provable production code, as in AFFIRM,[18] the Vienna Development Method (VDM),[19] and Anna,[20] all of which formalize abstract data typing. VDM applies not only to specifications, but also to implementation. Unlike the other paradigms of this section, VDM has been used with some success in industry, particularly in the U.K. Anna, a superset of Ada for formally specifying the behavior of an Ada program, takes the physical form of annotation statements inserted in the text of the subject Ada program. If the Anna statements are viewed as the program design language for the underlying code, apart from proving the correctness of the specification in Anna, a link is also established between the proved specification and its implementation.

If industry remains cool to programming paradigms born in academe, the same can scarcely be said for the topic of the next section, one of the hottest items going in the quest for software quality.

4.2 REUSABILITY

A shipwright steaming and shaping an oak plank to be placed in a sailing vessel carefully works his piece to fit exactly in the space where it is to be fastened. He gives no thought to some later reuse of the plank in another boat, nor do we expect him to. On the other hand, we do expect that the auxiliary engine he installs is one of several, perhaps many, made from the same set of design drawings and manufacturing fixtures. Without the ability to reuse the design, the engine would be prohibitively expensive.

Historically, the design of new software systems has usually been undertaken as though the components of the system were oak planks. The result is that the cost of much software, if not prohibitive, is grimly discouraging. Curiously, cost (or programmer productivity) may not be the most important advantage that accrues to reusable components. Quality may be. As we shall see, the cost associated with finding existing components that can fit into a software scheme cannot be ignored. However, components that have stood the test of time, perhaps been improved over time by the gradual elimination of latent defects, have obvious merit with regard to quality. As an illustration, consider a study[21] of 887 modules—some new, some reused from earlier projects, and some that were modifications of existing modules—developed for flight dynamics software projects. Of the new modules, only 44% were fault-free, in contrast to 98% of the reused modules. Fifty-two percent of the extensively modified modules were fault-free, while 69% of the slightly modified ones had zero defects. The more somber count of modules with high fault rates varied from 27% for completely new modules to 2% for reused ones. The same study also showed cost advantages for reusability but, as we would expect, not to the same extent as quality.

Scale and Scope

Reusability can apply at any level of component hierarchy. At the highest level, discrete, separately compiled and linked modules are logically associated by common data files. This is not uncommon in information systems applications, where stand-alone sort programs or file update programs see service in a variety of applications. Operational linkage is effected by job control language statements. A modern example might have a standard query module for a relational data base system, followed by a custom analysis module, in turn followed by a standard report generator. But what of the components in each of these stand-alone programs? They represent another concept of reusability, one invisible to the designer of the JCL file.

It is plain that the higher the structural level of the reusable component, the more effectively the concept of reusability has been executed. If a system comprising three subsystems requires the development of only one new subsystem, two-thirds of the potential for new code has been eliminated at one stroke at the cost of only three new interfaces—perhaps only two if the two reused subsystems have previously played together. Ada packages may be considered to be at this level. It is at the other extreme, however, where we have witnessed the greatest utilization of reusability. Countless programs have been written drawing on one or more libraries of subroutines or procedures. Of course, the choice of programming language has something to do with this. A programming cliché gives the number of existing, powerful subroutine packages as the reason Fortran can never become extinct. Programmers grinding out a solution to a missile trajectory problem are unlikely to think of themselves as soldiers in the reusability campaign when they write a call to a matrix inversion routine, yet in a very small way they are. Nevertheless, reusability at the level of utility routines is old hat. What captures our interest today is reusability at higher structural levels.

We have been addressing code reusability. Just as there are structural levels, so there are conceptual levels. Designs may be reusable even when the code they lead to is not. For example, the design of the PL/1 code for separating message packets may be reusable for a later generation system executed in Chill. Libraries of subroutines are common; not so libraries of design language files organized by component. Nor are we likely to find libraries of abstract data types, although the shop programming in a paradigm supporting abstract data types is likely to have use of the same ones again and again.

The fault data presented earlier alluded to modified code. Often called "re-engineered" code, this is the most common form of reusability at higher structural levels. A programming shop working the same set of problems from year to year is likely to find that the solution to a problem previously programmed almost fits the problem at hand. The subsystem that enhanced the signals from satellite BIGBOUNCE is an almost perfect fit for the signals from METALASTIC. Just change a few things here and there, and the code can be reused.

Almost. Modified components should not be construed as equivalent to unaltered reused components. Of particular interest to people concerned with reliability is the potential of harmful side effects resulting from modification. Testing after modification must be no less circumspect than testing of virginal code. Even then, we cannot have the same confidence that the component is free of latent defects as we do with unchanged code. Also, before such code can be modified, we have to take the time to thoroughly understand it, which is quite different from having only to understand the specifications of a candidate for reusability. Nevertheless, apart from the use of subroutine libraries, it remains that most code currently reused is really re-engineered. Although smaller components within a major component may be reused without alteration, the whole undergoes some kind of transformation before being installed in a new environment.

Successes and Problems

Notwithstanding the support given to the goal of reusability by object-oriented programming and abstract data types, most of the lore of software reusability necessarily derives from the disjoint paradigm. As noted earlier, reuse of utility routines stored in libraries is the most conspicuous kind of reusability. However, if only because we seldom recognize it as such, another historical form of reusability should be pointed out. As it happens, principles underlying this kind of reusability presage much of the future.

The ancien regime of programming might have had several programmers employed for a month generating a program to determine, for each hour of the working day, the average number of cables that might be queued up for transmission to Europe, given certain office activity parameters. In another shop, programmers would be working on the problem of computing the statistical distribution of idle hours for milling machines on the factory floor. Eventually, someone noted that the programs to solve both problems—indeed, a whole family of problems—were remarkably similar. The approaches to problems of this sort took the form of simulations; specifically, simulations of discrete activities. Such simulations had the same basic elements: random function generation, activity cells, time as an independent variable, and so on. Why not provide a set of universal software resources, building blocks of discrete simulation, that could be configured for solving the problem at hand? Thus were born discrete simulation packages, general ledger programs, production control systems, and all the other familiar general applications programs.

Within our present context, these applications programs are reusable programs; have been reused thousands of times. Conceptually, we may regard fourth generation languages as the second generation of reusable applications packages. Whatever the authors of a fourth generation language had in mind at the time of its development, the result is a touchdown that can be cheered by the fans of reusability.

Still, even within the software for a fourth generation language, or within the structure of a custom system that does not lend itself to general solution, we have to deal with the problem of reusable components. Successes here have been harder to find. Nevertheless, including re-engineered code, reusability at the component level increasingly attracts attention. For example, it is reported that in a study of 16 NASA programs, ranging from 57,000 to 239,000 lines of executable code, some 68% of the code was found to have been lifted from existing software.[22]

Most examples of successful reuse arise from staff members' recognition that the problem currently being solved has elements in common with one or more systems developed earlier. We wonder how such a thought could not occur. Doesn't the programmer addressing the problem of synchronization between the satellite and the ground receiver recognize that this is almost identical to a problem solved two years earlier? Frequently, the programmer does. However, if the programmer working on the problem is the same one who solved it two years earlier, he or she may want to redo the component to perfect it to his or her satisfaction. One thinks of the old adage that engineers never know when they are finished. More likely, though, the programmer of two years ago has been promoted and another programmer is working on the current synchronization routine. The new programmers would probably prefer to start afresh than to take the (nonsatisfying) time to understand the existing code sufficiently well to modify it. Also, programmers seldom have a way to determine if any existing code, other than their own, is a direct or near fit to the current problem.

Finding previous work analogous to the current problem implies either mechanization or memory. We take up mechanization in a bit, but let us now look at the memory solution, which accounts for most of today's reuse of code. Remembering that a component of a few years ago will serve today's purposes implies continuity of staff. Such recall is really part of one's "corporate memory," to use the popular term.

Unfortunately, corporate memory has finite recall. Although one may remember that something like the current need was done two years ago, one is not likely to remember enough about the behavioral specifications of the existing component to determine whether it is an exact fit for the component now required. The fundamental problem, one that *must* be solved if mechanization is to be essayed, is the informality of most component specifications. Ordinary natural language is inadequate for specifying to form, fit, and function requirements. Assume that a top-down design regimen has defined the need for a component in terms of a data interface and a functional description in natural language from which we excerpt, "Given the outflow and inflow vectors, calculate the internal rate of return by an iterative present value method solution and return the computed value as a percentage." Even in this simple specification unknowns abound: Are the values in the outflow and inflow vectors both referenced to the start or to the end of each unit of time? Is the computed percentage placed on the stack or is this a call-by-address procedure? To what accuracy is convergence tested? What error-handling takes place if the iteration does not converge?

Informal specifications hinder reusability, which requires formal specifications. Moreover, to implement mechanized searches for reusable components, the term formal specification must imply more than completeness, testability, and so on. A formal specification must possess mathematical exactness, as in the definition of abstract data types. A formal specification must reflect the concept of information hiding, in that it tells us everything we need to know about functionality and nothing about implementation. For example, to specify solution by an iterative method is to confuse a design specification with a requirements specification.

> *The less we need to know about implementation and the more we know about external specifications, the more reusable the component will be.*

Still, it is naive to assume that we never need to know anything about implementation. I recall helping a colleague some years ago to debug a program. I was convinced nothing was logically amiss. After a while I asked why she had selected the particular quadrature (numerical integration) routine her program called. The subroutine library had several such routines, each using a different method. She answered that she had chosen the first one listed. On examination, we discovered that the method selected is notoriously unstable for integrands containing a singularity, as hers did. So here, specification of the method was an important adjunct to the specification of outward behavior.

Mostly, however, we can say in a formal external specification all we need to about a component. The time for writing the specification is not when the component might be a candidate for reuse, but at the time it is designed. Generally, design in the disjoint paradigm does not depend on formal specifications. Accordingly,

> *if reusability is to be taken seriously, we have to prepare a formal specification at extra cost. Perhaps this has been a restraint on more reuse of code.*

An even greater restraint on the reusability of components above the structural level of utility subroutines is the matter of generality. The higher the level of a component, the more likely it is to be specific to its initial purpose and no other. Designing generality into a product is costly, and the environment for most programming sacrifices future efficiency for present exigency. Ada's generic package may be a significant help in this regard.

Decomposition or Composition?

In the ideal environment for reusability, programmers have access to the formal specifications of a library of existing components. They also have a formal specification for the problem to be solved. In some manner the programmers select those components that satisfy the requirements of the problem. Perhaps a few new components have to be programmed, used first on the current problem and later added to the library. This is the composition paradigm. Plainly, the chances of successful use of existing components increase with their generality, which places an onus on the people who define the external specifications of components destined for reuse.

Composing a program from a collection of existing components requires methods quite different from those most programmers are accustomed to. Wegner suggests that artificial intelligence holds the secret to composition.[23] He proposes a knowledge-based development model that uses a data base of multiple versions of existing application programs. Recall the discussion of object-oriented programming in Section 4.1. At several locations current research on composition methods is pursuing the line of a library of existing objects supported by a search/compare mechanism that attempts to match the library entries with formally defined objects in the problem space.

Object-oriented programming also provides reusability solutions in decomposition methodologies. Decomposition proceeds as new instances of classes, with salient class characteristics transmitted through inheritance. Initially, the system is partitioned into a small number of objects, each at a high level of abstraction. Following the principles of stepwise design refinement, the initially defined classes increasingly become more representative of the problem space as new objects are defined at ever decreasing levels of abstraction. Eventually, the defined objects reach the level of concreteness of the objects stored in a library, and a search for identical or close matches can begin. Although decomposition is used to arrive at a set of objects, if most of the necessary objects are found in the data base of existing objects, it is still correct to say that the system is produced mostly through composition. That is, the production part of the development process (rather like bottom-up integration) is a matter of assembling pieces to form a working whole.

Whether or not one uses the formalism of the object-oriented paradigm, reusability is encouraged by standard interfaces for components so that their relation to other components can be analyzed for conformity. Standards—a subject always of interest to quality professionals—go beyond interfaces. The reusability of components implies some degree of sameness in the way solutions are arrived at. Capitalizing on this, we can define templates of general solutions (components) at various structural levels. A template found in a library can be modified to be specific to the problem at hand. In the object-oriented paradigm, templates are classes, and their uses are their instances, or objects. In Ada, generic packages, deliberately designed to apply to a number of systems including some yet unknown, are instantiated for the current need.

Languages and Reusabilty

Once more the ubiquitous Ada has crept into the discussion, as it has into every technological area of discourse. Let us summarize the salient aspects of Ada with regard to reusability.

Ada's generic mechanism permits parameterization of subprograms and packages with types, functions, values, and objects. Generics directly support component generality by acting as templates for families of components, capable of being instantiated for specific purposes. Ada packages provide a means for encapsulating, making external interfaces explicit and—helped by Ada's strong typing—exact, while hiding implementation details.

Before leaving the subject of reusability, we might note that Ada is not the only member of the small group of languages directed, wholly or partly, to reusability. Very briefly, two other examples follow to illustrate the scope of the concept of reusability.

OBJ,[24] a language with facilities for algebraic objects (objects here are collections of sets and functions), also supports the instantiation of components of great generality. OBJ is more a specification language than a production language, and we may view OBJ as an example of a language that addresses the reusability of design, rather than production code.

The second example is really a group of languages, namely those operated on by the experimental system Draco.[25] The languages of interest are referred to by Draco's developers as domain languages, which we may loosely consider languages for modeling, at high levels of abstraction, objects and operations peculiar to specific classes of problems. Programs in such *domain languages* are interactively transformed by Draco into executable programs. In the Draco approach, the objects and operations from one domain language can be implemented by their being modeled in those of other domain languages. Such modeling can be the vehicle for translating elements of solutions from one problem to another—yet another form of reusability.

At the most elementary level, software reusability implies knowledge of what one has. At more advanced levels (e.g. Draco), reusability concepts depend on mechanization. Mechanization, from esoteric reusability aids and theorem provers down to the more pedestrian systems for keeping track of design information and code, takes us into the realm of software development environments, a fancy name for integrated tool kits.

4.3 SOFTWARE DEVELOPMENT ENVIRONMENTS

Since the earliest days of computers, programmers have had software tools to work with. Assemblers, compilers, link editors, and the like, are all software tools. Today's programmers take these for granted, and a well-equipped tool kit for a given programming language might include

- Screen editor
- Word processor
- Context-directed editor for requirements language
- Requirements analyzer
- Context-directed editor for design language
- Design analyzer
- Data base manager
- File comparator
- Source code librarian
- Static analyzer
- Compiler
- Private library manager
- Link editor
- Data dictionary

- Test case librarian

- Pretty printer

- Source level debugger

- Dynamic test analyzer

With luck, some of the tools may be graphical. Programmers working in modern paradigms may have tools specific to the paradigm, say, a theorem prover or something for run-time data binding. In any given environment, certain of the intertool boundaries that are implied by the foregoing list will be different. For example, aided by an appropriate user interface, the data base manager may subsume the functions of the private library manager. Nevertheless, the list is functionally representative of a modern set of tools for programming productivity and quality. Properly used, the composite set of tools can find inconsistencies and other defects in requirements and design documents, can find a variety of bugs in code even before active testing, can organize stub and test driver harnesses, can implement traceability techniques, can provide structural insights for debugging, can speed up debugging and discourage patching, can ensure that the only components submitted for an integration test are the authorized ones, and can support other quality-oriented functions.

As independent tools, the list represents a good tool kit, but today's technology demands more. We want the tools, or at least a minimum number of subsets of them, to be integrated. That is, the tools should have common programmer interfaces and data bases, perhaps the capability, as provided by Interlisp, of allowing one tool to be invoked from within the context of another. Tool kits that meet these criteria are the ones referred to as *software development environments*, or sometimes computer-aided software engineering (CASE) environments. Even more than the quality of air in the office, the amount of acid in the drinking water, or the prevailing state of anxiety, the environment that most affects productivity and quality is the one viewed from a virtual machine terminal or microprocessor-based workstation. Figure 4.6 is a schematic representation of a software environment spanning all development activities.

Given appropriate representatives of the general categories of tools listed above, environments can be organized toward different ends. Apart from the support of specific paradigms, environments can be fashioned to implement rapid prototyping (by including a very high level langugage (VHLL) or an executable design language) to support data-oriented design approaches, or to support process-oriented design methods. When environments are that specific, excepting the environments appropriate to modern programming paradigms, we usually find several separate environments, perhaps one for requirements and design, one for code and debugging, and one for testing.*

We can fashion our own environments from purchased, contracted, or home-grown tools, or we can buy an environment directed to one or more given phases of programming. Taking the latter route implies accepting another's vision of how to go about the programming business. There is nothing wrong in so doing, and quite a lot that can be right. However, care must be taken that the purchased environment and its concomitant methodology are compatible with other phases of programming work. The following examples represent available systems.

---

* As will become apparent later, testing, that is, the attempt to expose the presence of bugs, is distinguished from debugging, the attempt to locate and remove a bug.

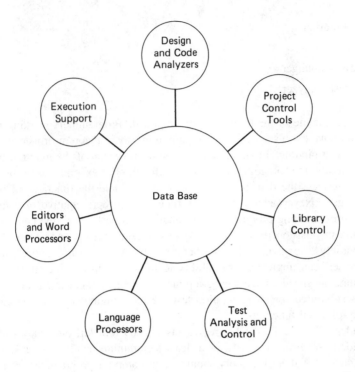

Figure 4.6 Software Development Environment

Available Software for Environments

The SREM system of TRW is directed to software requirements and preliminary analysis. After system interfaces and their mutual messages are identified, a network of stimulus-response relations is developed to model these. Details of the functional requirements are entered in a structured language and can be analyzed for consistency and completeness. The resultant functional specification can be validated through simulation. With the addition of more design information (e.g., timing), the data base contains a complete software specification. An interactive graphics package is available for analysis of the stimulus-response networks. SREM is an outgrowth of work done for the U.S. Army, and I understand that there is no charge for the software package. TRW does charge for training and support services.

The Teledyne Brown people have a system called TAGS that is used with a high resolution graphics work station. The TAGS input/output requirements language (IORL) is a compilable language consisting of graphical engineering symbols and mathematical expressions. Prior to compilation, IORL schematic diagrams are statically analyzed for conformance to syntactical rules and for the presence of various fault types related to logical construction, data flow, and data definition. The static analysis is followed by compilation and dynamic simulation. Although a password system provides a measure of library control for the IORL documents in the data base system, more formal configuration management is supported by a separate TAGS module that assists in ensuring tracking of trouble reports and distribution of change information.

The comprehensive SOLID system developed by Grumman Aerospace Corporation includes tools applicable to every part of the software life cycle. The system's support of the top-down development model starts with SRIMP, its program for modeling re-quirements. Although SRIMP performs no simulation, it does provide structure reports, hierarchy charts, attribute reports, and functional flow diagrams. Most of the SOLID tools are directed to planning and management: incrementally detailed test planning, configuration control, cost estimating, and so on.

The foregoing software development environments require a mainframe or max-imini computer as a host. Recently, a number of tool sets for software development have been released for operation in desktop computers. KnowledgeWare's Informa-tion Engineering Workbench/Workstation provides graphic tools to assist in top-down decomposition, data planning and modeling, business data flows, and hierarchical struc-tures. NASTEC's CASE 2000 system emphasizes management of the development of requirement definitions, designs, and the structural relations among the parts of a de-sign. Context-directed editors accept both graphical and text input, as for example in the preparation and maintenance of data flow diagrams. CADWARE,* which also sells a comprehensive software development environment, offers a product of special inter-est. Their "SYLVA Foundry" is actually a set of tools for developing CASE tools and providing an open architecture interface with existing tools. Such a system can be used to shorten the implementation time for customized environments, the topic of the next section.

Tools should not be thought of simply as adjuncts to software development and maintenance processes. For example, the difficulty of maintaining diagrams had discour-aged a client of mine—one who spends most of the time maintaining software—from basing problem analysis on structured flow diagrams because of the difficulty in chang-ing paper diagrams. Upon the acquisition of a tool (CASE 2000) for creating, storing, and modifying such diagrams in a computer, the client revamped his analysis process to conform with DeMarco's structured analysis.[7]

Thus far we have considered environments focused on requirements and design activities and on management. A growing number of test environments also are becoming available. We encounter some of these in Section 4.4, but let us note an early one here as a representative of the class. For programs written in Fortran and two of its variants, the RXVP80[TM] system of General Research Corporation supports source code control, static analysis, and execution coverage analysis.

Customized Environments

Home grown software development environments have the advantage of being able to provide technical support for all the technologies involved in software development and maintenance. This is not to say that the advantage is often fully taken, nor does it say that a home grown environment cannot include purchased or leased systems where it is feasible to plug them in. However, the do-it-yourself approach carries no penalty with regard to compatibility with external influences (call them environments of broader scope), such as those framed by management procedures and disciplines. The design of one's own environment is driven by a number of technical, managerial, and cost factors.[†] At the highest level, the principal technological considerations are

---

*The proximity of New Haven (CADWARE's location) to my home has led a few people to confuse me with CADWARE's president, also named Robert Dunn. We are not related.

† But not, one would hope, by a not-invented-here attitude.

- Level of abstraction of requirements.
- Design orientation: process or data.
- Reusability goals.
- Use of prototyping or simulation.
- Test philosophy.
- Coupling (through data base) to management tools.
- Host.

The first three items have received considerable discussion in this chapter, prototyping and simulation are met in Chapter 6, and testing issues are the substance of much of Section 4.4. The last two items are elaborated on in this section.

Management Tools. The list of generic tools printed near the start of this section ignored those that often are thought of as lying in the province of software management rather than technology: configuration management tools, cost estimating tools, and the like. Whether or not such tools are central to the technology of developing or maintaining software, their purpose is integral to the business of developing or maintaining it. In the long view of things, such tools support the technical work performed by programmers. Accordingly, to ensure that management information is traceable to the actual evolving or changing product, we want these tools to operate on the data base built by technical decisions. For example, a cost estimating program that needs to know the number of defined modules and the state of their completion ought to get such information from the catalog of software components initially built as part of the problem decomposition process and updated by subsequent work (e.g., completion of code and unit test). Similarly, configuration management documents should be based on the constituents of a system catalog. There is little point to reporting the current edition of a deleted module, and much point to making certain that a change notice identifies a module as it is known to the programmers.

Other management systems should draw their input from the data base of a software development environment: critical path or other project control programs, status reporting systems, work breakdown structure packages, cost accumulation systems, traceability systems (used for test case design), and defect data collection and analysis software. Tight coupling from the design data base to management tools helps to ensure the quality of management.

Another concern is the direct input of programmers to management systems, for example, status reporting. Why not have the programmers report through the same interface they use for technical purposes? Beyond the issue of consistency, we should recognize that nothing is gained by divorcing programmers from the concerns of management. Consider programmers assigned to components on the critical schedule path. If, out of curiosity, they inspect the project control system and discover the number of tasks gated by their current assignment, they may be more easily motivated to speed and diligence than by all the exhortations the supervisor can summon up.

Hosting the Environment. Software development environments have been hosted on a diversity of hardware and operating systems. For large scale programming, typical hardware configurations are mainframe or maximini (most popularly, VAX) computers, in a multi-user, multi-tasking environment supporting a number of simple terminals, smart terminals, or computer-aided design workstations, all of which are worked into Figure 4.7. The distinction between smart terminals and computer-aided design workstations is not always easy to draw, since both are really microcomputers. Salient features of the workstations are high resolution graphics, disk storage, and a design-oriented operating system. However, these features are not exclusive to workstations.

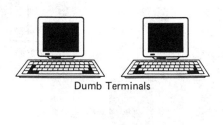

Dumb Terminals

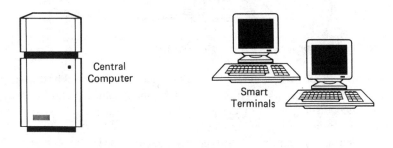

Central
Computer

Smart
Terminals

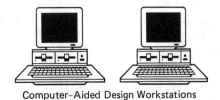

Computer–Aided Design Workstations

Figure 4.7 Terminal Alternatives

With the advent of CASE tools for desktop computers, a popular alternative environment comprises a network of microcomputers, one of which serves as the common data base, as in Figure 4.8. One can also conceive of a network of microcomputers with a distributed data base.

However it is organized, common data bases are fundamental to software development environments. Programmers must have access to a common library, to common system data, and to common tools.

Returning to the star configuration of Figure 4.7, a singular advantage to the use of computer aided workstations is their capability to off-load processing tasks from the central computer. Program design tools, like those for VLSI design, have an insatiable

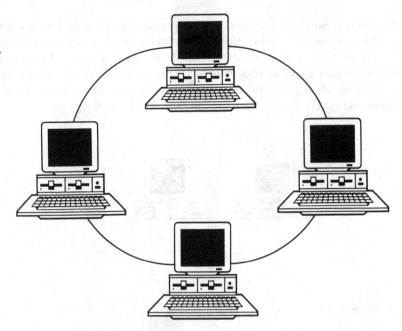

Figure 4.8 Microprocessor Ring Configuration

appetite for computer resources. A Petri-net analyzer can quickly devour all of a programmer's workspace, while graphics can consume machine cycles like they were going out of style. Placing much of the processing burden in the workstation is one way to avoid thrashing at the central computer.

Operating systems must also be considered. Operating systems with powerful command languages and in which a rich stock of tools are already embedded have an obvious selling point. The archetypical operating system for hosting a programming environment is UNIX.* Indeed, it is generally regarded as an environment in its own right, certainly for programs written in C. Programmers can augment UNIX's basic repertoire of utility functions with their own, incorporating the commands in the language of the command interpreter (the shell).

An important attribute of a software development environment is the capability to assemble small tools into larger ones. This generally amounts to being able to direct the output of one program to the input of another (as provided by the UNIX pipe). We can get the same functionality by storing output in temporary files, but this can get cumbersome, even with the use of catalogued procedures to combine command language statements. Operating systems that offer this capability are to be favored as hosts. Other features that lend themselves to the construction of a custom environment are forms management (as in DEC's VMS All-in-One), a built-in data base manager, and windowing.

We cannot overstate the importance of an effective development environment to a quality program. When talk turns to the ways in which capital investment can be used to improve software quality, the requirements, design, and code aspects of development (or maintenance) environments should get equal billing with test support. *After all, defects that can be prevented never have to be removed.*

---

* UNIX is a trademark of Bell Laboratories.

4.4 DEFECT REMOVAL

Next to defect prevention, no topic is as pertinent to quality issues as defect removal. As it happens, defect removal is a major concern with regard to programmer productivity. Some 35% to 50% of programming labor is spent on removing defects from software. For a number of years, we have known that one way to reduce the cost of defect removal is to detect and remove bugs early in their lives. Consider that a defect implanted in the requirements definition for a software system may be excised through a review conducted some time before the specification is implemented (meaning, before the start of the next design activity). If not caught by the review, the defect may later fall as a side effect of a design review, possibly even a code review. Bugs hardy enough to survive all reviews may still be exposed by any of a number of testing processes.

> *If it takes exercise of the full system to catch a bug in the definition of software requirements, the cost of removing it is likely to be 25 or so times the cost that would have been incurred had the defect been uncovered by the review of the requirements specification.*

The inflation associated with not removing a defect at the first opportunity has several roots, not the least of which is rework. A requirements defect that is allowed to propagate to final system testing will have been implemented in design and code and the affected portions will have to be redone. The testing that was directed to the discarded code is likely to be repeated when replacement code is prepared. Worse, many if not all of the system level tests will have to be repeated to ensure that the changes did not produce unwanted side effects.

Let us go on. No amount of testing can guarantee that latent defects will not find their way to the users of the delivered system. Thus, for released software, the cost of defect removal is further increased by the cost of distributing code updates, possibly compounded by attendant costs in documentation updates and configuration control.

It seems reasonable, then, that we should be as concerned with the technology of defect removal as we are with the technology of defect prevention, which is what the first three sections of this chapter are mostly about. This statement is scarcely profound. From the historical perspective, defect removal (specifically, testing) and software quality assurance were once synonymous.

Technology: No and Now

In the distant past, software defect removal meant no more than testing the product before inflicting it on users, and fixing anything that was found to be wrong. The philosophy underlying the design of test cases was the demonstration that nothing was wrong; perhaps less a philosophy than a self-fulfilling prophesy. In some cases, few tests were actually designed: The product, once it was made capable of "cycling through," was handed over to selected users with the request that they report any problems they found. (We still believe in beta testing, but as the successor to some kind of alpha.)

One could scarcely hand over an essentially untested software package to the designers of a satellite launch system and say "Try it when you have a chance and let us know what you think." The time came when all recognized that more thorough testing could not be avoided, a truism that—if it does not quite capture the level of today's technology—announced the beginnings of an organized attack on defects.

Today we understand that the war with defects can be waged on two different fronts, passive defect removal and active defect removal, as in Table 4.1.

Table 4.1

Passive Methods	Active Methods
Requirements reviews	Functional testing*
Design reviews	Structural testing*
Pseudolanguage analysis	
Code reviews*	
Static analysis*	
Formal verification*	
Symbolic execution*	

*Applicable to code.

Passive methods, when applied to code, are often referred to as "static testing." By the term *active defect removal*, or if you will, *dynamic defect removal*, we mean actual execution of the program, in whole or in part, as it is intended to be delivered to users. Active testing is synonymous with the usual sense of the word *testing*; it is, in fact, the only defect removal method of twenty years ago.

Beyond an exercise in taxonomy, the distinction between passive and active defect removal bears directly on both programmer productivity and software quality. Active methods do not directly expose defects, they only provide evidence that a defect exists. To actually find the bug, the cause of a test failure or an anomalous test result must be diagnosed. Alternatively, defects found by passive methods can be removed with no further investigation of cause. We know what caused the problem. The fix is another matter, but at least we know what to fix.

The significance of all this is that diagnosis is no small matter. A bug that caused a test to fail in two seconds may take two hours, days, even months to be located. Many bugs are so carefully concealed in the warp and woof of the program that they elude all effort to bare them, inviting the decision that the search be abandoned. (Defects of grave consequence are, of course, never allowed to be left in the system, even if the system must be delivered a year late.) Among the most evasive bugs are intermittent ones, particularly those associated with software written for computers embedded in instrumentation systems, wherein the physical conditions that induced test failure may not be repeatable at will. Over a complete test cycle, the time spent in debugging may exceed that spent in running planned tests by hundredsfold.

To the extent possible, passive methods should be used prior to the start of active testing so that the code submitted for testing is less likely to require extensive debugging. Plainly, in the interest of timely defect removal, the first three passive methods of Table 4.1 beg to be employed before active testing. Reinforcing the temporal primacy of passive defect removal, we discuss the passive methods first.

Passive Defect Removal

In the usual course of software development, the first defects available to be removed are those found in the requirements definition that serves as the basis for ensuing design activities.* Reviews of requirements definitions have the greatest payoff in terms of cost avoidance. However, such reviews also are the most expensive to conduct. In addition to evaluating the testability of individual stipulations, it is necessary to establish conformance of the requirements specification to the operational environment of the system ("environment" used here in the larger sense), its completeness, and its feasibility. These criteria are not easily established. For example, what can we do with a requirement that, summarized, might read, "Inquiry screens shall be intelligible to operators with at least one week of training," when the training program has yet to be established. This matter goes beyond testability: Until the operators have been trained, no one knows exactly what their performance levels will be. Not surprisingly, reviews of requirements models rarely find more than 50% of the defects contained in specifications.

Requirements reviews are often regarded as an element of "modern programming practices"—whatever that means. Nevertheless, their inherent labor intensiveness requires that we place them in the category of low-technology practices. Low technology or not, they are an indispensable part of the disjoint paradigm. Even as low a defect yield as 50% is important when we consider the cost of tardy removal of a requirements defect.

One way to get the greatest benefit of a requirements review is to use a checklist. Checklists, such as the one given by reference,[26] serve not only to assist memory, but as a focal point for defect removal.

Equally labor intensive are design reviews. These are normally held at the end of discrete design stages; say, preliminary design, intermediate design, and detailed design. The substance of each is a function of the defined development process (as a prerequisite of quality, we assume one exists). Again, checklists such as those given by reference[27] are used. Design reviews often follow the format of walk-throughs, a programming adaptation of show-and-tell. In the walk-through format, the author of the work reviewed explains, point-by-point, how the design under review satisfies the functional specification addressed in the design. In addition to looking for confirmation that the specification has been met, the reviewers, who frequently interrupt the exposition with questions, also evaluate the design for compliance with local design standards, general standards of good design, and the presence of any assumptions, limitations, or constraints introduced by the design.

Reviewers are generally taken from several groups. A rule of thumb is that the team should include one or more representatives each of

- The group responsible for the work antecedent to that reviewed.

- The groups that will implement the work reviewed.

- Software quality assurance, or an equivalent group involved in the entire development process.

- Librarians, technical editors, or others who will officially receive the work.

---

* System prototypes modeled in VHLLs reduce the importance of documented requirements specifications and the concomitant importance of requirements reviews. If they achieve industrial strength, the use of executable specifications will obviate the need for any kind of requirements review, except for those specifications that augment the executed model. An analogous situation with regard to design reviews will obtain with the use of paradigms based on executable design languages.

With the exception of the last category, which in any case is more or less optional, most review teams have no structure other than a designated chairman. An example of a more formal structure is that described by Fagan[28] for IBM's design and code inspections, in which roles are designated for the author, a reader (or interpreter), a tester, and a moderator. In sharp contrast to IBM's formality are peer walk-throughs,* wherein the participants are likely to be of the same functional group as the author. Peer walk-throughs, in general, are distinguished from reviews by an avoidance of formal review requisites such as preparation and the use of traceability mechanisms.

The cost of design reviews can be reduced significantly by the use of design language pseudocode analyzers. These systems can detect many of the defects to which reviewers would otherwise have to be attentive, and can also generate structural summaries that help to reduce the reviewers' preparation time. Apart from their attractiveness in cost avoidance, analyzers offer the advantage of machine infallibility. Defect types that are vulnerable to detection by pseudolanguage processors include data inconsistencies, improper sequences of processing steps, and interface anomalies. Design languages are widely praised for their encouragement of structure in design, but another salient advantage of design languages over non-machine readable forms of design documentation is that they lend themselves to automated defect detection.

Most of the discussion of design reviews applies also to code reviews. Many programmers have felt that code reviews are unnecessary, since compilers (some say static analyzers as well) and testing can find any bugs introduced in the process of writing code. Admittedly, it would be foolish to review code prior to compilation and, if available, static analysis (more about this shortly), but only reviews of one format or another can determine conformance of code to design. Moreover, certain kinds of defects such as inverted or incomplete predicates, missing data validity checks, incorrect access of array components, and others are not likely to be found by compilers or static analyzers and may not be detected by a finitely bound set of dynamic tests. Many years ago, to persuade a programming department to start reviewing code, I prodded them into reviewing a group of modules that had completed unit testing. The inducement was that if fewer bugs were found than the number of modules, I would forever be quiet on the issue of code reviews. The reviews found as many bugs as had earlier been exposed by testing.

Like requirements and design reviews, the effectiveness of code reviews is greatly enhanced by checklists, as in reference.[29] Checklists, preparation, and an accurate log of required corrections are the earmarks of code reviews sufficiently productive to find up to 85% of defects.

When programmers say that static analysis should be substituted for code reviews, they are not entirely wrong. Even more than design language analyzers, static analyzers for source code are effective at finding bugs, and they should be given the opportunity to do so before code reviews are held. Again like design language analyzers, static analysis systems can generate structural reports (of which program graphs are the most important) and cross-references of data usage, all of which not only speed up code reviews but help in debugging test failures.

Since static analyzers operate on source code, one is needed for each programming language being used. What should be a powerful argument for language standardization is all too often turned into a weak argument for eschewing the value of static analysis.

---

* So informal are peer walk-throughs that they are usually spelled "walk-thrus."

Nevertheless, any programming shop with a staff knowledgeable about compiler design can prepare a static analysis system for each of its languages of choice. If carefully done only the front end of the system needs to be language-specific, although—depending on the diversity of languages to be handled—this may restrict certain capabilities of static analysis. Static analyzers can be purchased or leased, and some of these are noted when we get to the topic of dynamic analysis (for which static analysis is an operational front end).

Table 4.1 noted two other types of passive defect removal: formal verification and symbolic execution. The former refers to proofs of correctness, related to the mathematical programming briefly noted toward the end of Section 4.1. Not in widespread use, proofs are tedious and error-prone, even given the availability of powerful theorem provers. Moreover, ad hoc methods are generally required to prove program termination (halting). Current thinking tends to follow the argument that the role of program proofs—if any—is more appropriate to program construction, as in mathematical programming paradigms. Nevertheless, formal verification, which offers the potential of 100% effectiveness, can be considered as a candidate for program elements for which reliable operation is especially critical; say, the internal self-checks for nuclear power plant control software or the file protection code of a multi-user operating system.

For production programming, symbolic execution remains mostly a high-technology goal, notwithstanding successes attained by academe. Also called symbolic evaluation and symbolic testing, the technique permits symbolic, or algebraic input to a program. Assuming we have an algebraic input specification, the algebraic output can be compared to the input to determine if the program performed as expected. The program is not actually executed, of course. (If it were, we could not call the technique passive defect removal.) Rather, the source code and algebraic input are processed by the symbolic execution system, which interprets the behavior of the source statements in response to algebraically valued variables. Algebraic simplification is performed at each step of the symbolic execution.

Symbolic execution sounds too good to be true, which is a fair appraisal of its current status. A thorny problem for which totally satisfactory solutions have yet to be worked out is that of algebraic expressions for subscripts, wherein ambiguity can exist in determining which element of an array is referenced in, say, a symbolic assignment. Worse, within loops we cannot know within which iteration the subscript expression was formed. Another set of problems (inherited from correctness proofs) arises in regard to calls to external procedures and functions, although this can be mitigated by methods akin to the use of stubs in top-down testing. Those interested in pursuing the matter should consult the work of King[30] and Howden.[31] To step from symbolic execution to literal execution is to move from the technology of passive methods of defect removal to active ones. And so we do.

Active Defect Removal

As indicated in Table 4.1, we can divide the technology of active testing into two categories: functional and structural. Functional testing is the kind all programmers are familiar with; structural testing on a large scale is known to few.

> *Functional testing is testing with regard to the expected functional behavior, while structural testing is directed to the way the functions have been programmed.*

Now this sounds like a nice clean division, but nothing in software is ever that neat. As it happens, when we test a module to the behavioral specifications set forth for the module during the design phase, we are at once functionally testing the module and structurally testing the system. The significance of this is that not all behavioral specifications used as yardsticks for functional testing derive from the requirements specification for the entire system: The greater number actually derive from the design process. With this understanding, we go on to discuss the technology of functional testing to *any* external specification and structural testing at the *code*, not the design, level.

Functional Testing. At any structural level, the fundamental issues of functional testing boil down to designing that set of test cases that provides confidence that the program conforms to its specification. Use of the word "confidence" is not intended to imply that a statistical measure of test adequacy can be estimated. That we can do so is speculative. See Sections 2.3 and 2.4. Rather, we are faced with the problem of covering each of the testable provisions of the specification, determining the input and output domains applicable to each function, judiciously selecting combinations of specified requirements to be tested, determining the performance and volume responses that need measurement, and finally designing the test cases that will meet these objectives.

Perhaps the most commonly used approach to test case design addresses the input domain of the system. For each individual specification, a representative set of input values is selected, and the stipulated behavioral response to the input is calculated. The input and the response ("expected results") are documented as a single test case. Where applicable, subordinate test cases may be designed to check behavior at the extremes of the input domain specific to the specification. Such "range checks" for numerical calculations easily come to mind, as do those for real-time data handling operations, where we might check performance at minimum and maximum data rates. In the second example, operation at maximum data rates may overlap with *stress testing*, or pushing time-related system stimuli to the point of saturating machine resources. Another kind of test of saturation of machine resources is called *volume testing*, where we attempt to determine the sheer volume of data that can be handled.

Critical to quality are tests of the program's capability to defend against input that is outside the range that the program can handle. To exercise input data checks, circumspect test designers always stipulate test cases of invalid data.

Often overlooked in the design of functional tests is the output domain of the program. Even with test data directed to the nominal input and boundary conditions related to a stipulated function, the correct results may fall only within a confined portion of the output domain of the function. To take a simple example, a procedure to evaluate the oscillating function $\sin(x)/x$ may, even with diverse input, be tested so that all test output is in the region of zero. Such input will not reveal the presence of a bug that affects only output values close to 1.

Testing individual provisions of the external specifications is one thing. Testing combinations of them is another. Consider a requirements model with 1,000 testable specifications. Taking just two of these at a time requires a minimum of 499,500 test cases. Taking three at a time requires another 166 million test cases. Taking four at a time.... Fortunately, nothing is gained by testing most of the combinations. Also working in our favor is the nesting effect that arises from individually testable aspects of the required system behavior. For example, a requirements model for a word processor may have one testable specification citing the keys to be used for cursor control and a second stipulating that attempts to move the cursor off screen should have no effect. Any test of the second (four are required, one for each direction) automatically subsumes testing of the two specifications in concert.

Nevertheless, it remains that many functions need to be explicitly tested together. In a multi-tasking system, the function of on-line noninterfering manual updating of the data base must be tested with each function with which interference is a potential threat. In the usual approach to designing tests of combined functionality, test designers attempt to identify each meaningful combination and design a test for it. To reduce total test time, combinations are often tested in lieu of tests of individual functions. This practice may shade subtle bugs. The approach is largely ineffectual in reducing test time anyway, since combination tests usually fail the first time, and the first step in diagnosing the failure is to design ad hoc tests of individual functions.

When conscientiously carried out, all the functional testing performed on a large system can add up to a formidable number of test cases, but rarely as many as writers on software testing recommend. Extrapolating from published examples, one researcher discovered that

"1.8 million lines of source code or 19,000 pages of external specifications require more than 250,000 test cases to satisfy the coverage criteria." [32]

Plainly, this much testing is impractical even for huge development projects, especially when we consider that many tests will be repeated (*regression testing*) after corrections. At the system level, the quoted researcher found 40,000 test cases adequate to cover his 19,000 pages of external specifications. From my own experience an average number of test cases per 100 pages of external specifications or 1,000 NCSS is meaningless. The variance is too high for statistical purposes. At the one extreme I have seen a ratio of 0.23 test cases per thousand NCSS suffice, and at the other extreme I have seen situations where no fewer than 60 test cases per 1,000 NCSS were required to provide satisfactory coverage. The disparity is not only a matter of application diversity, although that is a major factor. We have also to consider the number of discrete inputs that can interact, the need for sensitivity analysis (smoothly varying input while looking for roughness in the output), and behavioral variants for different system states.

The earlier references to individual, testable specifications were somewhat glib. They can be identified easily enough (para. 4.3.9.1.2 of document ASY349.16, and so forth), but many of the testable requirements carry with them explicit dependencies on other requirements. For example, the requirements model for a system states the effects that should result from a given operation, but may also state exceptions based on prior sequences of other operations. At a more general level, we are really back to the problem of finding appropriate combinations of testable specifications. Various *traceability* mechanisms have been devised to capture the interaction of specifications. Simple two-dimensional tables, diagrams employing simple semantic rules (e.g., CSC's system verification diagrams,[33] particularly useful during integration), and more complex diagrammatic methods (e.g., IBM's cause-effect graphs)[34] have all been used to determine the minimum number of test cases to cover the functionality of large software systems.

We have considered test design based on the input domain and the output domain of programs. Now let us look at the program domain itself.

Structural Testing. Despite the profusion of functional test cases that attend each stage of testing, much of the system's structure will remain untested. At the macro level, perhaps as little as 10% of code written in conventional programming languages is functionally related to testable requirements. The rest is housekeeping: calculating and rearranging pointers or indexes, opening and closing files, saving intermediate results, and so forth. While the housekeeping tasks are directly supportive of the system's functionality, it is unlikely that all the code associated with them will be tested to the same degree of sufficiency as coverage of explicit functional stipulations.

At the micro level, experience tells us that certain sequences of processing steps, interleaved with decision points, will remain untested by pure functional testing. Many individual branch-to-branch paths will be untrod. At multiple-predicate decision points, some of the conditions directing control will be evaluated, others ignored. Even at the level of unit testing, where the programmer of the code gets a chance to test it to his or her satisfaction—testing that usually includes at least some structural testing to confirm that the design works—parts of the code remain innocent of exercise.

Beyond the unit test level, testing to the structure of software can mean little other than testing to some level of structural coverage.* The alternative, attempts to analyze on a large scale the effect of data on arbitrary combinations of code segments, is equivalent to diagnosing failures that have yet to occur. We can define several levels of structural coverage testing:

- Statement coverage.
- Branch-to-branch segment coverage.
- Coverage of paths containing a given number of branch points.
- Coverage of individual predicates.
- Data coverage.

Each of these is used as a criterion to be satisfied. For example, one might determine that 95% of all statements must be executed before testing can be considered complete. The first three criteria are listed in ascending order of significance. The fourth criterion, which recognizes that decision points often contain multiple predicates, is one that is best used in conjunction with the second or third. Data coverage is discussed later.

Theoretically, it is possible to design test cases that, in the aggregate, would test every statement in the program, but the manual labor required to do so would be Herculean. Also, aside from the problem of keeping track of what has been tested and what has not,[†] to reach previously untested segments it is often necessary to work out the input values that will satisfy multiple path predicates of the same set of variables. If structural testing beyond that normally performed by programmers at the unit test level is to be accomplished, mechanization is required.

Structural testing's own Deus Ex Machina is sometimes called a dynamic analysis system. The term "dynamic analysis" has been used both as a synonym for any dynamic

---

* One of the "others" is dynamic detection of data flow anomalies. These are improper sequences of operations in which data are defined, undefined, and referenced. For more on this, see reference.[35]

† Worse yet is keeping track of branch-to-branch segments that have been tested. For anyone who wants to try it, I recommend using variously colored pens on copies of module program graphs.

testing and as a descriptor of mechanized evaluation of the effects of testing. It is in this latter sense that dynamic analysis is used here. In addition to coverage analysis, dynamic analysis can refer to data flow analysis, the evaluation of embedded assertions, and performance analysis. Dynamic analyzers need to know the structural properties of the software under analysis. Accordingly, each dynamic analyzer is accompanied by a static analyzer. In addition to providing structural analysis (e.g., generating program graphs used to relate segments to branch points), the static analyzer also instruments the source code with probes for detecting execution of specific points. Schematically, the composite system, with the static analyzer acting as a preprocessor, is used as in Figure 4.9.

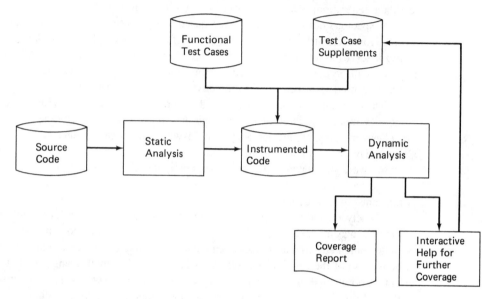

Figure 4.9 Coverage-Based Testing

A number of dynamic analysis systems are available. Their capabilities, as well as the source language they support, vary over a spectrum that includes the several coverage criteria previously listed, cumulative coverage over a series of test runs, and assistance—through coupling to automatic test generators—in formulating input data to improve the percentage of coverage. Table 4.2 lists representative systems for popular languages.

Automatic test data generation has its problems, of which perhaps the most bothersome is one inherited from static analysis preprocessors: the generation of infeasible test paths. These are apparent paths that, owing to mutually exclusive conditions, cannot actually be executed. Consider the following program segment that reads sequential records until it has found two that begin with dollar signs, at which point it returns the count of the number of records read:

```
twice := count := 0;
while NOT EOF
begin
    read next record;
        if twice = 2
```

```
        then return;
    if next record(1) = '$'
        then twice := twice + 1;
    count := count + 1;
end;
```

From the program graph, a path exists directly from the top of the loop to the return statement. In fact, it cannot be executed, since a minimum of two iterations is required before the condition on twice will permit the path to the return to be taken. Interactive assistance to the user, as provided by the SADAT[36] system, rather than fully automatic test data generation, is a way to cope with the infeasible path problem.

A specious objection to coverage-based testing is that it takes more time than it is worth. However, little extra time is required if, as suggested by Figure 4.9, the dynamic analyzer serves as a test bed for running functional test cases. The only additional testing required will be the tests that augment the functional test cases for the express purpose of meeting predetermined quality objectives of coverage criteria.

Thus far, automation has neglected coverage to data criteria. However, data coverage may be of more significance to data-driven programs than coverage of statements, branches, or paths. Consider a system in which a relational data base is embedded. Can we have confidence that the system has been adequately tested if only 50% of the domains were populated, referenced, or manipulated during testing? In general, data coverage criteria can be based on percentages of entries, domains, relations, or whatever is relevant to the structure of the data.

Closely related to coverage-based testing is *mutation testing*. Although viewed by some as a way to find simple bugs (e.g., a variable incremented when it should have been decremented), mutation testing can also be considered as a technique to measure the effectiveness of the set of test cases. Consider this: If a small change made to the code produces no change in the results of any of the tests, we have evidence of insufficiency in the full set. Therefore, let us make a small change (say, invert a relational predicate)

Table 4.2

Analyzer	Language	Source
RXVP80™	Fortran	General Research Corp.
JAVS	Jovial/J3	General Research Corp.
LDRA Test Bed	COBOL	Liverpool Data Research
	C	Associates, Ltd.
	Coral 66	
	Fortran	
	Pascal	
	PL/1	
Softool 80	Fortran	Softool Corp.
	COBOL	
TCAT	COBOL	Software Research Assoc.
Logiscope	Ada	Verilog USA
	Fortran	
	Modula 2	
	C	
	Pascal	
	Cobol	

and rerun the full set of tests. If at least one result changes, we can feel good about the whole thing and make another small change and again rerun the full set, and then we can make another small change and ...

If this Sisyphean variant of fault seeding seems impractical, try mechanization. As implemented by the inventors of the technique, the mutation test bed, after forming each mutant program, reruns the test set only as far as the first different result.[37] One problem of mutation testing is that of equivalent mutants. Mutant programs can produce the same results but, in the process, consume different computer resources. Progress, however, continues to be made in developing algorithms to detect equivalent mutants.

Still a young technique, and one held back by the cost of analyzing test results, mutation testing has not made much of an impression on the providers of software tools. However, work continues at the Software Engineering Research Center (SERC) of Purdue University, where mutation testing lies at the heart of the center's MOTHRA test system. MOTHRA has automated much of the manual activity surrounding mutation testing and several of SERC's industrial sponsors are now experimenting with the system.

Test Environments. In addition to the mechanization of structural testing, there are other ways in which tools lighten the load of beleaguered test teams. Anyone who has attempted to assemble a knocked-down child's toy or yard machine has wrestled with the problem of organizing a swarm of pesty nuts, washers, odd-looking thingamajigs, and what have you. Programmers building a system have to cope with the equivalent in stubs, drivers, link files, and dummy data sets. Organized into a library of some sort (often called a "scaffold" or a "test harness," depending on whether the emphasis is on top-down or bottom-up integration), the support code used for testing can be managed, available when needed, and distinguished from incorrect look-alikes.

The benefits of test support libraries to software development are obvious. Less apparent is the profit that accrues to maintenance. During the operational life of software the system may be torn down (that is, parts may be deleted or revised) and rebuilt any number of times. Saved in a library—rather than being dispersed among dozens of dusty tapes somewhere in an archive that would gladden the heart of an archaeologist,*—the support code of development, is reusable for rebuilding the system. This, of course, assumes that the support code is maintained as the system metamorphoses. In this case, quality benefits as much as productivity. Tests are only as valid as their support software. Just as reused operational code should be more fault-free than new code, so should reused test support code.

Test managers move the automation of testing a notch higher. Not only the harnesses or scaffolds are under interactive control, the procedures to generate test input and record test output are interactively controlled as well. Data input files may be catalogued and the more ambitious systems may even have the capability of comparing any two results files. Extrapolating a bit, we have has an automatic regression test system, one that can rerun a battery of tests to see if a modification to the target program caused any unwanted side effects.

Test managers capable of handling large programs are fairly rare. At the unit test level, they are quite common, except perhaps for the features of comparing results and automatically sequencing tests. In particular, many programming shops have developed

---

* It's not called "throwaway code" for nothing.

systems, tailored to the production methodology in place, to interactively translate unit test procedures or code structure into test data.

No technological barriers exist to the design of complete test environments capable of handling large systems. All we have to do is define "complete." Here is a wish list:

- Test harness/scaffold catalogs.
- Semiautomatic or automatic test data generation.
- Dynamic analyzer.
- Command file for setting up test from catalogued components, stubs, and so forth.
- Catalogued sets of test data and expected results.
- Automatic sequencing of tests.
- Automatic recording and cataloguing of actual results, including monitoring of performance or temporal relations among independent processes.
- Automatic comparison of results with selected benchmarks. Benchmarks selected from expectations or any previous set of results.

Whether or not technology stands in the way of fulfilling this wish list, money does. But solving money problems is one of the things we pay management for, isn't it? Perhaps a good case for funding wish lists can be made in the next chapter.

4.5 SUMMARY

1. Most programs are written in procedural languages, which attempt to map computer execution steps into programming statements.

2. In current programming practices, analysis of requirements, design, and coding are usually disjoint activities. The results from each may not be consistent.

3. Design methods for large programs are motivated by the desire to decompose the complexity of a large problem into many less complex, more manageable, problems; thence into solutions.

4. In the more orderly of these methods, we see the system evolve into solutions at ever-decreasing levels of abstraction.

5. A common precept underlying many modern design methods is that of information hiding; loosely, the belief that the specification of any piece of the solution should contain nothing beyond the minimum amount of information required to implement the specification.

6. Fourth generation languages and languages based on abstract data types take a more holistic view of the software process than do procedural languages. Rather than forcing solutions into maps of computer processing steps, these languages permit solutions couched in terms more closely identified with the problem.

7. Advanced programming paradigms provide more unity to the design, coding, and run-time environment of the product.

8. The object-oriented paradigm, which derives from the concepts of information hiding and abstract data types, is particularly well adapted to the generation of systems that reuse program elements previously developed for other applications.

9. The languages most commonly referred to as fourth generation languages are those that are used to provide quick solutions for management information applications.

10. Other languages that may be thought of as belonging to the fourth generation are those pertinent to the support of computation itself. Among these are languages directed to artificial intelligence.

11. Paradigms based on formal mathematical concepts hold the promise of freedom from faults, but currently are impractical for wide application in industry and business.

12. The reuse of designs and code reduces cost and increases quality.

13. The application generators of the fourth generation are an example of reusability at a high conceptual level. For program components, reusability is best served by functional generality and specifications of mathematical formalism.

14. A goal of reusability technology is to be able to build large systems by composing them of reusable components.

15. Software development environments (i.e., highly integrated tool kits) can be fashioned to support specific programming regimens from combinations of purchased and custom-developed tools.

16. Beyond purely technical support, such as that provided by compilers and the like, the constituents of development environments help to ensure that management of the development process accurately tracks the evolving technical solution.

17. Development environments can be hosted by diverse combinations of hardware and software. Operating systems having powerful command languages and built-in utilities are favorite foundations for development environments.

18. The cost of removing defects, whether in documentation or code, dramatically increases with the time the defect is allowed to remain in the system.

19. Defect removal techniques that do not require actual execution of code—that is, passive methods—are much more efficient than those that do. Actual execution only reveals the presence of defects and must be followed by diagnostic effort. Passive methods find faults directly.

20. Among these passive methods are reviews of requirements models and design data, reviews of code, machine analysis of design data, and static analysis of source code.

21. Active testing, or the execution of production code, is generally directed (at least after unit test) to the program's functionality.

22. Functional test cases usually address the input, and occasionally the output, domains of the program. Test sufficiency, particularly with regard to combinations of functions, is improved when the design of test cases is driven by traceability mechanisms.

23. Active testing directed to the domain of the program, or structural testing, further improves test sufficiency.

24. Except for testing to design interfaces, structural testing beyond the level of unit tests generally amounts to mechanized evaluation of the percentage of statements, branches, linear segments, paths, or predicates that have been exercised. Much of the desired percentage of coverage can be achieved during the execution of functional tests.

25. Analogous to development environments, test environments abet the efficiency and manageability of testing. They also encourage more thorough regression testing and the reuse of "throwaway" test support code.

4.6 REFERENCES

[1] D. L. Parnas, "A Technique for Software Module Specification with Examples," *CACM*, Vol. 15 (May 1972) pp. 330–336.

[2] E. Yourdon and L. L. Constantine, *Structured Design* (Englewood Cliffs, N.J.: Prentice-Hall, 1979).

[3] G. J. Myers, *Composite/Structured Design* (New York: Van Nostrand Reinhold, 1978).

[4] M. Jackson, "Constructive Methods of Program Design," reprinted from *ECI Conference 1976* in *Tutorial: Software Design Strategies*, IEEE Cat. No. EH0149-5 (1979) pp. 24–42.

[5] K. Orr, "Introducing Structured Systems Design," *Tutorial: Software Design Strategies*, IEEE Cat. No. EH0149-5 (1979) pp. 72–82.

[6] D. T. Ross and K. E. Schoman, Jr., "Structured Analysis for Requirements Definition," *IEEE Trans. Software Eng.*, Vol. SE-3 (January 1977) pp. 6–15.

[7] T. DeMarco, *Structured Analysis and System Specifications* (New York: Yourdon Press, 1978).

[8] *The American Heritage Dictionary of the English Language* (Houghton Mifflin Co.: Boston, 1982), p.6.

[9] P. Wegner, "Varieties of Reusability," *Proceedings Workshop on Reusability in Programming*, Newport, RI (September 1983) pp. 30–45.

[10] G. Booch, "Object-Oriented Development," *IEEE Trans. Software Eng.*, Vol. SE-12 (February 1986) pp. 211–21.

[11] G. D. Buzzard and T. N. Mudge, "Object-Based Computing and the Ada Programming Language," *Computer* (March 1985) pp. 11–19.

[12] B. Cox, "Message/Object Programming: An Evolutionary Change in Programming Technology," *IEEE Software*, Vol. 1 (January 1984) pp. 50–61.

[13] P. Wegner, "Capital Intensive Software Technology; Part 1: Software Components," *IEEE Software*, Vol. 1 (July 1984) pp. 12–22.

[14] N. Chapin, "Software Maintenance with Fourth-Generation Languages," *ACM SIGSOFT*, Vol. 9 (January 1984) pp. 41–42.

[15] F. Vidondo et al., "GALILEO System Design Method," *Electrical Communication*, ITT, Vol. 55, No. 4 (1980) pp. 364–71.

[16] P. Kruchten et al., "Software Prototyping Using the SETL Programming Language," *IEEE Software*, Vol. 1 (October 1984) pp. 66–75.

[17] R. Davis, "Logic Programming and Prolog: A Tutorial," *IEEE Software*, Vol. 2 (September 1985) pp. 53–62.

[18] D. Musser, "Abstract Data Type Specification in the AFFIRM System," *IEEE Trans. Software Eng.*, Vol. SE-6 (January 1980) pp. 24–32.

[19] C. B. Jones, *Software Development: A Rigorous Approach* (Englewood Cliffs, NJ,: Prentice-Hall, 1979).

[20] D. Luckham et al., *Anna Preliminary Reference Manual*, Stanford, CA: Stanford University (1984).

[21] D. Card et al., "An Empirical Study of Software Design Practices," *IEEE Trans. Software Eng.*, Vol. SE-12 (February 1986) pp. 264–71.

[22] B. Silverman, "Software Cost and Productivity Improvements: An Analogical View," *Computer* (May 1985) pp. 86–96.

[23] P. Wegner, "Capital Intensive Software Technology; Part 2: Programming in the Large," *IEEE Software*, Vol. 1 (July 1984) pp. 24–32.

[24] J. A. Goguen, "Parameterized Programming," *IEEE Trans. Software Eng.*, Vol. SE-10 (September 1984) pp. 528–43.

[25] J. Neighbors, "The Draco Approach to Constructing Software from Reusable Components," *IEEE Trans. Software Eng.*, Vol. SE-10 (September 1984) pp. 564–74.

[26] R. Dunn, *Software Defect Removal* (New York: McGraw-Hill Book Co., 1984) pp. 95–96.

[27] R. Dunn, *Software Defect Removal* (New York: McGraw-Hill Book Co., 1984) pp. 96–98.

[28] M. Fagan, "Advances in Software Inspections," *IEEE Trans. Software Eng.*, Vol. SE-12 (July 1986) pp. 744–51.

[29] R. Dunn, *Software Defect Removal* (New York: McGraw-Hill Book Co., 1984) pp. 121–23.

[30] J. King, "Symbolic Execution and Program Testing," *CACM*, Vol. 19 (July 1976) pp. 385–94.

[31] W. Howden, "Symbolic Testing and the DISSECT Symbolic Evaluation System," *IEEE Trans. Software Eng.*, Vol. SE-3 (July 1977) pp. 266–78.

[32] N. Petschenik, "Practical Priorities in System Testing," *IEEE Software*, Vol. 2 (September 1985) pp. 18–23.

[33] M. Deutsch, *Software Verification and Validation: Realistic Project Approaches* (Englewood Cliffs, N.J.: Prentice-Hall, 1982) pp. 51–89.

[34] G. Myers, *The Art of Software Testing* (New York: John Wiley & Sons, 1979) pp. 56–73.

[35] J. C. Huang, "Experience with Use of Instrumentation Techniques in Software Testing," *Proc. NSIA Natl. Conf. Software Tech. and Measurement*, National Security Industrial Association, Washington (October 1981) D1-D10.

[36] U. Voges et al., "SADAT—An Automated Testing Tool," *IEEE Trans. Software Eng.*, Vol. SE-6 (May 1980) pp. 286–90.

[37] T. A. Budd et al., *Theoretical and Empirical Studies on Using Program Mutation to Test the Functional Correctness of Programs*, Georgia Institute of Technology (February 1980). This report is also found in the *Conference Record* of the *Seventh Annual ACM Symposium on Principles of Programming Languages* (January 1980) pp. 220–33.

CHAPTER 5

Management

Within the context of software quality, the word "management" takes on a diversity of meanings. When referring to people, we may use the word to mean general managers, quality managers, software managers, logistics managers, and anyone else who sets policies that can affect the quality of software. To these managers it is management itself that is responsible for notable successes in software quality (and cost reduction). To technical staff, management is the nebulous entity responsible for software failures. Often overlooked by both managers and managees is the fact that management is more than managers. As pointed out in Section 1.3, management is also the framework of policies, procedures, and practices within which software is developed or maintained. We start with that framework.

5.1 DEFINED PROCESSES

Quality does not exist in the absence of established processes for software development, maintenance, customer service, or other functions relevant to software applications. Taking development as an obvious example, the selections of technology, when used and how used, provide the basis for the development process. But for that process to be executed as it was intended to be, and for it to form the foundation that allows many individuals to work in concert, it must be defined. The definition takes the form of

94   *standards.*

There are three distinct levels of standards: The practices "everyone knows," documented standards, and the standards implied by the tools in use. The first of these have no place in a process directed to quality. The last represent the highest level, since they are integral to the process. In a sense, we can say that software tools provide self-defining elements of the software process. In most programming shops, the process is defined by a combination of both documented standards and tools. Untooled elements of the process certainly require documented definition, such as the specifics attending reviews. The subject of the next chapter, the overall development process (a specific waterfall or operational model or whatever) needs to be defined in sufficient detail for each member of the team to know the expectations for each element of work. Moreover, not only technical activities require definition. Standards are also needed that define an acceptable work breakdown structure; that is, the division of activities into discrete tasks at several hierarchical levels, each task sufficiently well defined to be manageable at its given level.

The definition of the process serves several purposes; the obvious one of providing guidelines for members of the programming team, and less obvious ones intrinsic to software quality. With a defined process, we have the basis for project control (more about this in Section 5.4). We have also a known environment for measurements of influences on quality (and productivity). For example, measurements of design faults found during test have little application to quality improvement if the design methods in use are a constantly moving target. In short,

> *one of the quality responsibilities of managers is to make certain that the framework within which software processes take place has built-in structural strength.*

The establishment of a defined process is the most obvious evidence of a management commitment to quality. We shall look at some others.

5.2 COMMITMENT TO QUALITY

Beyond making certain that software processes are deliberate rather than haphazard, software managers have ample opportunity to demonstrate their commitment to quality. Not the least is providing the coin to acquire the tools of a quality-oriented programming environment. Librarians, dynamic analyzers, data base systems, and other software tools require money, whether developed in-house or purchased. Workstations are not cheap either. Although the costs may be considerable, depending on the languages used, the number of programmers, documentation standards, and the like, managers should be aware that tools not only improve quality, they also improve programmer productivity. Even a librarian, installed for the primary purpose of ensuring the correct edition of each program unit during integration or delivery of customized software packages, saves money. Library control tools reduce labor intensive library policing and (given the opportunity for human error) the cost of retesting after one discovers that an obsolete edition of one program unit had been incorporated in the tested program load.

Thus, capital intensive tools provide a return on investment by reducing labor intensive activity. A study by Barry Boehm and others of productivity influences estimates that, "All other factors being equal, a project with a very low level of tool support will require 1.49 times the effort required for a project with a very high level of tool support."[1] This is the software equivalent of Crosby's dictum that quality is free.[2] Intensive tooling is essential to those programming shops that employ advanced software technology (e.g., object-oriented programming or mathematical programming). However, the cost effectiveness of tools is most evident in the disjoint paradigm. Consider a documentation-driven approach to software develoment, as imposed by the DoD on its contractors for mission-critical projects. In these projects, programmers may spend half their time producing project documentation. Without exact cost reckoning, we can easily imagine the difference in programmer productivity between two environments, one in which each programmer has a computer terminal and one in which four programmers are expected to share a terminal. Worse, I am familiar with programming shops that do not offer programmers word processors, but expect documentation to be produced either by the screen editors used for coding or in longhand. From the quality point of view, we know that the easier it is for programmers to keep their documentation current, the more likely it is that the delivered documentation will be usable.

Tools are not the only part of the programming environment that can demonstrate management's commitment to quality, and like tools, the other parts also are conducive to improving productivity. No Catch 22 here: These other parts are the physical environment, education, and relief from administrivia. Each requires an investment of capital, expense funds, or both.

The most important attribute of the physical environment is space. Air quality, proximity of offices to test laboratories, noise level, and views of the surrounding woods all influence the quality and quantity of work, but space is the prime influence. Programmers need handy access to documentation, code listings, test results, and even the standards that define the work they do. Some of this, of course, appears on the screens of their terminals, but only one page at a time (even with windows). In addition to paper storage, programmers need to have their terminals within a swivel or less of their primary work space, most often the cleared area in the middle of the desk. The frequently encountered table or desk, surmounted by teetering open shelves to hold books explaining the programming language or operating system, a monitor jammed in one corner, a telephone under some papers in the other corner, is not an adequate environment for programming. Proper storage units and work surfaces are.

Expense, not capital, is required to implement an education program, as discussed in Section 3.2, and both are required to lessen the waste of programmer hours in dealing with administrivia. Why programmers are expected to personally prepare priority mailings, distribute notices of review meetings, book conference rooms for reviews and other team activities (has one ever seen an office suite with a sufficiency of conference rooms?), fill out forms for cost-to-completion exercises that could mostly be automated, and the like is beyond me. Clerical help comes at half to a quarter the price of programming talent. Spreadsheet programs are only a few hundred dollars the copy. To assume that programmers can fit in administrivia time at no cost to programming time is plainly wrong. But worse, administrivia often has the highest priority of all task classes: The marked-up acceptance test specification has to reach the subcontractor by the end of business tomorrow, the revised cost estimate must reach the customer by Friday. These priorities can be satisfied only by interrupting the tasks that senior management believes the programmers (and first level supervision) are being paid for, and the most significant cost of having design work placed on a LIFO stack is poor design quality.

We have still other measures that can be taken of management's commitment to quality: the willingness to fund the additional cost of developing software components that can be reused, the top-level support for a software quality function to manage the quality program, and the initiative to replan an underestimated or redirected project, no matter how unpleasant the immediate consequences may be. In brief,

> *the commitment of all levels of management to quality is not a matter of platitudes, but one of tangible consequences.*

5.3 PROJECT PLANNING

Thus far, we have been looking at management in the large; that is, the effect of management on the overall programming environment. Now we turn to the effect of management on the quality of individual projects, and we start at the beginning—with planning.

The quintessential issue of project planning is identifying the activities required to complete the project and then ensuring that resources will be available when they are needed. For development, this means having people, hardware tools, software tools, and physical space in time for each planned activity. Failure to anticipate the need for, say, high speed data links between a remote prototype installation site and the programming shop will preclude use of the in-house software development environment to support on-site problem solving.

Work Breakdown Structures

To many managers, project planning begins with the development of a work breakdown structure (WBS). This is a collection of hierarchically related tasks or activities that in the aggregate are believed sufficient to perform all the work of the project. Figure 5.1 illustrates the first two tiers of a typical WBS. In a complete WBS, we would see the implementation task, for example, further broken down to the level of identifying individual module design, code, test, and review activities. Not all activities need be identified at the start of a project, indeed, not all can be. The individual software elements of our example remain undefined until sometime after the project has been started. Also, although we can anticipate ab initio that analysis of defect data will be performed, not until enough of the data have been collected can we know all of the individual analyses that are warranted. Thus, like software systems themselves, the details of the WBS evolve during the course of the project. Nevertheless, the ontogeny of the most detailed WBS item starts with the identification of its first hierarchical predecessor.

Regardless of its position within the hierarchy, the identification of each WBS item entails the definition of the inputs, the outputs, and the organizations that will perform the work. The outputs may be viewed as the expectations for a successfully (and completely) performed task. To take a high-level example, the output of the qualification task for a spreadsheet program might be defined as the successful completion of tests designed to demonstrate compliance with project goals, followed by the successful training of a heterogeneous group of management and accounting personnel who are given only the user's manual and built-in tutorial as training aids.* In a low-level example, one of the qualification tasks might be the design of test cases.

---

* The definition of "successful" would be found in process standards, as would a description of test case sufficiency.

Development
Requirements Analysis
Preliminary Design
Implementation
Integration and System Tests

Quality Assurance
Audits
Data Collection and Analysis
Qualification

Logistics
Beta Test
Hot Line Support
Distribution

User Documentation
Preparation
Publishing

Figure 5.1. Work Breakdown Structure, Technical, and Support Tasks

Given the expectations for each WBS item, project control partially rests on tracking the status of the individual tasks. An important service performed by software quality assurance organizations is the determination that tasks have not only been nominally completed, but that they have been completed in accordance with established standards.

Although rough schedules may be prepared prior to the development of the WBS (often as not by backing into a demand completion date), schedules can be made much more useful by recasting them in terms of the WBS. This lends tangibility to milestones, making their tracking easier and their reporting more secure. Accordingly, the popular aid for progress forecasting and tracking, the Gantt chart, is often depicted in terms of linear sequences of WBS items.

The WBS also provides tangible micro-milestones for input to critical path systems such as PERT. The better of these project-control tools report not only the milestones on the critical path (those milestones that directly control the completion date) but those on subcritical paths (the ones having "slack"). The value of seeing the subcritical paths is in knowing exactly which activities are the real constraints to starting any given task. In a complex network of interrelated tasks, the real constraints often are not apparent. Given the true gating conditions for starting a task not on the critical path but nevertheless considered crucial with regard to performance, managers can request that the quality assurance activity related to the gating tasks be intensified to minimize the possibility of slippage. For example, experiments calibrating the performance of an interrupt handler for an instrumentation system are assumed to be constrained by the availability of code for the module. In fact, subcritical path analysis shows the gating constraint really is the availability of hardware interfaces and data generators.

Once the WBS is defined, detailed consideration can be given to staffing details. How many people will it take to perform each task? Laying out the tasks on a Gantt chart or other calendar-oriented planning aid provides an estimate of the number of people required on a monthly basis. However, the manager cannot wait for the development of the WBS to begin the staffing effort. Coordination with other projects from which staff may be drawn begins even before the decision to proceed with the project is made. With regard to development personnel, one of two conditions will probably exist: Either the new project will be started just in time to avoid the need to reduce staff once current commitments are completed, or the number of present employees who can be made available will be woefully inadequate to staff the new project. Except where backlogs measured in years are tolerated, the quiescent or steady-state model of technical staffs seems not to apply to programming.

In any case, the size of the project staff and the rate at which it is built up must be estimated early to leave maximum time in which to take appropriate actions. Although we know that salaries are not the only costs involved, estimating staff requirements is generally equated with cost estimating, one of the blacker sciences of software management.

Cost Estimating

The dominant cost estimation fault modality is underestimation and for this reason, cost estimation is a quality consideration. The understaffed project falls behind schedule bit by bit, raising the risk that heroic rescues will be undertaken. Usually the forms taken by heroic measures are either reducing the scope of the more vulnerable labor-intensive tasks, such as some testing, or adding hordes of new people at a rate that cannot be absorbed. The fallacy of the latter solution was put neatly by F. P. Brooks, Jr. some years ago in the oft-quoted Brooks's Law: "Adding manpower to a late software project makes it later."[3] So inevitably, the first method of rescue eventually prevails, and quality invariably is the loser. In addition to testing, other tasks likely to be shrunk if not deleted altogether are reviews, maintaining the currency of the requirements model, documentation of test cases, preparation of user manuals in time for qualification, preparation of maintenance documentation in time for the first alterations of the program by people other than the developers, and defect data collection and analysis.

Plainly, managers need to do more than estimate just the total number of labor-hours that will be used. Estimating labor as a function of time is required to align staff availability with work demands. In this regard, many software managers have observed that the shape of the composite staff over time is that of a Rayleigh curve, as in Figure 5.2. Nevertheless, to ease the number of variables to be juggled, software managers generally assume a linear build up. (Which gives rise to the popular locution "ramp-up.")

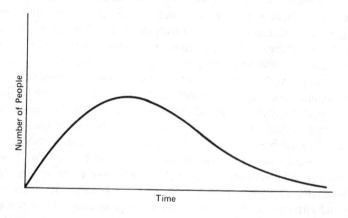

Figure 5.2

The shape of the rise is the least of the problems attending cost estimation prior to the start of the job. The major problem is that the manager does not really know what the job consists of. The software requirements are still only faintly defined, one has only a vague notion of the software structure that will emerge and less than that of the number of program units that will be coded, reviewed, and tested, and on it goes. It has been asserted that the error during the feasibility study phase in estimating cost-to-completion is more than quadruple the error of estimates made at the time detailed design specifications are prepared.[4]

Software activities are not the only kind of work that is difficult to estimate. Parallels can be found in estimating engineering design costs and pricing a season's worth of snow plowing. For both of these, the experienced estimator relies on historical information, whether remembered or documented, tempered by risk considerations. So too, with software. Typically, software managers start with a guess of the size of the software system that will be delivered to users. In particular, the estimator thinks in terms of the number of lines of code (LOC) that will be written. A close alternative is the number of noncomment source statements (NCSS). Recall the discussion in Section 2.2 of the use of these as independent variables for programming measurements. The variance in the number of statements written to solve a given problem is as high for cost estimating as it is for measurement. Worse, the number of statements has direct cost causality only with respect to the coding tasks; the relation to analysis, design, testing, and documentation tasks is indirect.

Still, where a new project can be related to one or more predecessors, LOC has some bearing on the cost. The arguments of Section 2.2 on language differences do not affect the programming shop that uses the same programming language from one job to the next. Assuming a fairly stable programming staff (probably the shakiest of the assumptions that must be made), style does not change markedly between jobs. If successive projects are related closely enough, there may even be a reasonable ratio between the writing of a given number of LOC and other tasks. If some guesses can be relied on for the shape the structure of the program will take—not too difficult to do for a job with predecessors—managers can establish difficulty factors for the various parts to adjust the estimated labor hours for these. In short, LOC are used as the prime quantifier, adjusted for presumed difficulty, and applied with multipliers for tasks other than code-writing.

Not a very scientific way to go about things; the method is a singularly unreliable way in the absence of both a stable process and precedence. Indeed, given precedence and process stability, LOC can be dispensed with altogether. Yet like countless software managers found everywhere, I, too, have reported software estimates in the cast of LOC. The reason for doing so was to comply with the tacit demand of senior management that there be a quantitative basis for all cost estimates. LOC are quantities, they can be added, multiplied, and added again. The truth is that my estimates were really based on extrapolating from earlier work, or in the absence of precedence, hunches, tempered by more hunches about the stability of the behavioral specifications for the software.

Some help is available to managers in the form of estimating models. Two that are widely known are the model of Walston and Felix[5] and the CoCoMo model.[6] Both include a number of influences on cost as well as LOC. For example, the classic Walston and Felix model accounts for complexity of the application (at the one extreme, batch storage and retrieval; at the other, sensor-based processing), the development environment, programming methods, the customer and user interfaces, previous relevant experience, the ratio of staff size to project duration, documentation, and various constraints on software design (e.g., timing requirements), for a total of some 29 distinct influences on productivity per thousand LOC.

Considerations such as these are incorporated in today's estimating tools, such as RCA's Price-S, Larry Putnam's SLIM, and the tool sold by Software Productivity Research in Acton, Massachusetts. The discrete influences used by each model and the way in which the influence is quantified differ, of course, from model to model. None, however, is capable of quite getting away from LOC or NCSS. Either of these itself can be only an estimate at a time when cost estimates are most important.

Although we can only guess at LOC at the time initial cost estimates are needed, we have a fairly good idea of what the software is supposed to do once the project has ended. What we really need is a way of quantifying the overall behavior in a way that will yield a requirements based parameter for cost estimating. Allan Albrecht has devised such a parameter, *function points*, applicable to the class of software variously called management information systems, electronic data processing, or commercial software. That is, Albrecht's parameter is applicable to the greatest single area of computation. The parameter, determined from weighted counts of external user inputs, outputs, inquiries, and relevant files, has been shown to correlate closely with delivered source LOC.[7]

Unfortunately, not all software lends itself to function point calculations. But all software applications have some countable external characteristics. Here are some admittedly simplistic examples: Telephone switches have numerable "features" to be supported, numerable subscriber lines, and numberable trunk lines. Electronic countermeasures sets have numerable radar types or classes of types to identify. Word processors have a given number of editing options and a specified number of operating system interactions. All programs have a finite number of external data sets.

Of course, we must go beyond simply identifying the external characteristics that can be counted before we use them as cost modeling criteria. We must also apply weights to each. For the constituents of function points, Albrecht used heuristic methods to determine the weights. Managers who have kept records of past projects can do the same with the characteristics important to their own software.

No matter how methodically costs are estimated, it remains that the estimates will be inaccurate if the premises behind the estimates are subsequently violated. Hence, the next topic on the influence of management on quality.

5.4 ADHERENCE TO PLANS

Quality management also means project control. Given defined standards and policies, and given thorough project planning, the game can still be lost in the playing. Software development lends itself all too easily to lapses in compliance with local standards and project plans. Often, software managers lay the blame on changes in the external specifications, but the programming shop itself can account for most of the grief.

Tools are available to ensure project control. The work breakdown structure is such a tool, and so are quality assurance and configuration management functions. Reporting requirements, rather than just a periodic bother, can be viewed by managers as an opportunity to review their own performance. Finally, quantified variance from plans can be used to sound an alarm that remedial action is required. We shall return to these and other mechanisms for project control in Chapter 7.

5.5 SUMMARY

1. Standard processes must be defined and documented to establish the methods by which software is developed, maintained, and supported.

2. The strongest standards are those built around the tools in use.

3. Among other purposes, a defined process serves as the basis for project control.

4. Management can demonstrate its commitment to quality in several tangible ways: funding for tools, a proper physical environment, education, extra cost to make software components reusable, and all manner of ways to relieve programmers from routine administrative matters. In the long run, these pay for themselves.

5. Project planning resolves to identifying the activities required to complete the project and ensuring that necessary resources will be available to support these.

6. A work breakdown structure is the basis for detailed project planning.

7. Milestones for critical path analysis should correspond to items in the work breakdown structure.

8. Although its accuracy is vital to quality, cost estimating is generally based on estimates of the size of the eventual program that are of questionable accuracy.

9. Managers should explore analysis of outward characteristics of software requirements as a basis for cost estimating.

10. Control of ongoing projects is required to ensure the satisfaction of process standards and project plans.

5.6 REFERENCES

[1] B. Boehm et al., "A Software Development Environment for Improving Productivity," *Computer* (June 1984) pp. 30–44.

[2] P. Crosby, *Quality Is Free* (New York: McGraw-Hill, 1979).

[3] F. P. Brooks, Jr., *The Mythical Man Month* (Reading, Mass.: Addison-Wesley, 1975), p. 25.

[4] B. Boehm, *Software Engineering Economics* (Englewood Cliffs, N.J.: Prentice-Hall, 1981), p. 502.

[5] C. E. Walston and C. P. Felix, "A Method of Programming Measurement and Estimation," IBM Systems Journal, Vol. 16, (1977) pp. 54–73.

[6] B. Boehm, *Software Engineering Economics* (Englewood Cliffs, N.J.: Prentice-Hall, 1981).

[7] A. Albrecht and J. Gaffney, Jr., "Software Function, Source Lines of Code, and Development Effort Prediction: A Software Science Validation," *IEEE Trans. Software Eng.*, Vol. SE-9 (November 1983) pp. 639–48.

CHAPTER 6

Process Models

In Chapter 4 we looked at some of the technology used to develop and maintain software. Little attention was paid to the armature upon which technology hangs—that is, the overall scheme within which software gets developed and supported forever more. A few paradigms that span all activity from requirements analysis to implementation were explored, but these are largely outside the mainstream of today's software development practices.

When sufficiently inclusive to account for such miscellaneous activities as installation and user support, software models are usually referred to as *life cycle models*. The locution is a curious one, since over the full life of software, the only thing cyclic is the use of development practices for behavioral modifications. Presumably, biological analogs suggested the term, but the analogy is a slim one. We might suppose that the software life cycle is the epitome of reusability, with the bytes of obsolete programs revived in new software systems. However, the "software life cycle" entered the vocabulary of software engineering long before anyone took reusability seriously.

The most elementary life cycle model has two elements:

- Development.
- Operational life.

Used in this grand a sense, development entails all activities between software conception and the successful installation of the first (or only) system. The operational life includes technical support to users, removal of latent bugs, adaptation to new operating environments (especially operating systems), performance or function enhancements, and modifications that add (or delete) features or alter the behavior of existing features. We are interested in the quality of all these activities, but we are particularly interested in quality during development, since this is the time when quality is built into the product for both performance and the ease of future change.

The overwhelming majority of software is developed using technology from the disjoint paradigm, as it was called in Chapter 4. The disjoint paradigm lends itself to a series of equally disjoint development states. In nearly all programming shops, the differences of kind that characterize these states are somewhat muted by concatenating the several states into a composite process popularly known as a *waterfall model*. The name waterfall comes from the popular graphic depiction that shows the states overlapping, as in Figure 6.1. The overlap is intended to imply that during the overlapped state the overlapping state is completed or at least refined. That is, the activities of the overlapping state are subject to iteration after the state is initially exited.

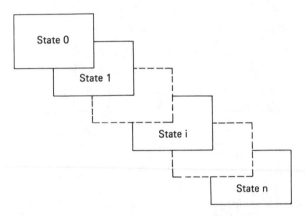

Figure 6.1 A Waterfall of Development States

6.1 THE WATERFALL MODEL

The states of the waterfall model are generally referred to as phases, or sometimes as stages, suggesting a sequential set of tasks, each having plainly defined inputs and outputs. In the most common implementation of the waterfall, the *document-driven* model, outputs are in the form of documents (including code listings and test reports). Apart from any technical purposes it supports, the waterfall has been used primarily as a management device to divide the job of developing software so that incremental progress is made visible. Collaterally, the end of each phase is taken as a control point for deciding whether to continue, replan, or abandon the project. Since each phase is further divided into smaller work breakdown elements, as discussed in Section 5.3, the waterfall can be regarded—at least for programming tasks—as the top tier of the work breakdown structure.

Forms of the Waterfall

Just as the waterfalls that transport real water take many forms, from a series of small cascades off rock ledges to sheer drops of several hundred feet, so do programming waterfalls. Here are some published examples, including a few that venture into operational life:

The First is a notably concise waterfall, sufficient to show the bare bones of arriving at a software solution.[1]

- Requirements analysis and definition.
- Design.
- Implementation.

The next example extends the waterfall beyond development.[2] (Note that the author distinguishes programming from other software development activities.)

- Definition.
- Design.
- Programming.
- System test.
- Acceptance.
- Installation and operation.

In this example requirements and the operational life are given considerable prominence.[3]

- Understanding requirement.
- Specification of requirement.
- Design.
- Implementation.
- Testing.
- Maintenance.
- Evolution.

At this point it is becoming clear that all software engineers and managers do not see the waterfall the same way. In fact, some seem unwilling to see it the same way twice. The next example represents a waterfall restricted to development tasks, as published by one author on page 54.[4]

- Requirements analysis and specification.
- Design.
- Code and unit test.
- Integration.
- System test.

In the same book on page 188 we find this waterfall, evidently for software-driven instrumentation systems.[5]

- System specification.
- System design.
- Software requirements.
- Top-level design.
- Detailed design and code
- Unit test.
- Software integration.
- Software test.
- Hardware/software integration.
- System qualification.

In the last example, it is obvious that the author was much concerned with testing. This example also illustrates the imprecise, but common, practice of using artifacts of the software life cycle (e.g., system specification) as equivalents of the activities that produce the artifacts.

The point of these five illustrations is the diversity that can exist in the definition of the states of the software life cycle. Yet each exists for the purpose of placing the opportunity for management evaluation and discretion at points considered to be of immediate importance.

Viewing waterfall definitions for development, it would appear that the end of one phase signals the end of that activity for all elements of the system. Taking design as an example, waterfalls make it appear that all design is completed before any coding is begun. Indeed, process models have been defined just this way, but none I think in modern times. Although it simplifies management reporting and decision making to assume that development phases hold for all system parts, across the dam, the assumption is not realistic. Consider a system divided, during some preliminary design phase, into two parts. The first and larger part is straightforward and considered insensitive to changes in the behavioral specifications of the system. Not only is the second part likely to be affected by external decisions, but many behavioral specifics will be defined only after scheduled meetings with potential users, say, two months hence. There would seem to be little purpose in delaying design of the larger portion of the system until all the behavioral details have been worked out. And having designed the larger part, why not go ahead and code it, indeed, test it—at least to the extent possible while the second part of the system plays catch-up. Going one step further, certain software elements within the first part may lend themselves to more rapid development than others, or may proceed faster simply because they are in the hands of more capable programmers. It makes little sense to hold up the rapidly developing elements on behalf of their slower siblings.

Asymmetric development is one of the precepts of top-down programming, wherein the only restraining stipulation is that a given unit may not be implemented (i.e., designed in detail, coded, and tested) before its superordinate. Top-down programming, which in many interpretations implies top-down testing as well, represents the most liberal departure from lock-step, across-the-dam waterfall thinking. The problem, of course, is that the disarmingly few phase completion milestones of the waterfall are multiplied, and by factors that become ever larger as development progresses, into a number large enough to dissuade managers from invoking the very options the waterfall is designed to produce.

To solve the problem, let us steal another page from hydrography and place a few large rocks in the lower rapids to create a waterfall of many branches. Ignoring any attempt to portray iteration, as was done in Figure 6.1 with overlaps, Figure 6.2 illustrates a portion of such a waterfall. Figure 6.2, plainly a tree structure, seems familiar. It is nothing less than the top tiers of a work breakdown structure for development, as the first paragraph of Section 6.1 presaged.

Requirements Analysis

Preliminary Design

Design of Subsystem

    Design of Module 1.1
    Coding of Module 1.1
    Test of Module 1.1

    Design of Module 1.2
    Coding of Module 1.2
    Test of Module 1.2

    Design of Module 1.3
    Coding of Module 1.3
    Test of Module 1.3

    Design of Module 1.4
    Coding of Module 1.4
    Test of Module 1.4

Design of Subsystem 2

    Design of Module 2.1
    Coding of Module 2.1
    Test of Module 2.1

    Design of Module 2.2
    Coding of Module 2.2
    Test of Module 2.2

    Design of Module 2.3
    Coding of Module 2.3
    Test of module 2.3

    Design of Module 2.4
    Coding of Module 2.4
    Test of Module 2.4

Design of Subsystem 3

    Design of Module 3.1
    Coding of Module 3.1
    Test of Module 3.1

       ⋮

Subsystem Integration

System Test

Qualification Test

Figure 6.2. A Waterfall with Divergence and Convergence

Although boxes like "Requirements Analysis" have subordinate WBS elements, and each of the implementation phases (given in Figure 6.2 as module design, coding, and test) has WBS elements not only for the obvious technical work but also for reviews and test preparation, the congruence of WBSs with waterfall trees is the key to preserving the principles of management discretion without compromising top-down or other asymmetric principles of development methods.

Process Drivers: Logic vs. Data.

Figure 6.2 suggests a waterfall model based on program logic. That is, the system is divided along the lines of logical operations, using one or another decomposition strategy, perhaps one of those noted in Chapter 4. If the most common approach is taken, the program structure develops as the result of a hierarchical decomposition of the requirements model. In the process, various algorithms are decided upon, some at so high a level that they are tantamount to computing strategies, and some at the low level of, say, search techniques. A process model that stresses functional decomposition may be thought of as *logic driven*. As data are needed to complete a given level of logic design, the data are designed. Alternatively, one may start out stressing data design, with the design of data structures and the rules governing their use refined at each step of the development process. In a *data-driven* (or data decomposition) process model, as the final forms of the data become clearer, the algorithms that operate on the data are designed when needed. Recalling the discussions of Chapter 4, logic-driven construction results from approaches that emphasize abstraction of logical processes (in the other sense of the word "process"), while data driven construction results from abstracting the data aspects of the problem. As it happens, one would not expect to find construction processes defined such that either the logic orientation or the data orientation completely overwhelms the other. Nevertheless, most of the design processes I have seen are strongly influenced by functional decomposition.

Since logic-driven process models are so prevalent, an example of a data driven process is worth looking at. The scope of this book limits the depth to which any design topic can be illustrated, and the example is necessarily simple. Let us assume we have undertaken the job of developing a system to perform the following functions for a library:

- Retrieve an abstract of the contents of any given book.
- Form a list of those books having, in their abstracts, any given key word.

We further assume that we are and choose to continue ignorant of existing data management systems or theory.

A likely place to start our preliminary design is with the abstracts. We look through the existing card catalog and find abstracts ranging from a dozen words to over a hundred. To accommodate this range, we decide to place the abstracts in a file of their own, with each abstract occupying a contiguous storage block of variable size. We also decide to include with the identification of the book the address of its abstract. We do have a modern operating system to run our software under, so we recognize that we need only a logical address—the operating system will provide the physical address when we assign a physical device to the file, thus binding the addresses at run time.

Now we look at the phrase "any given book" in the first of the defined requirements. After consulting with library officials, we learn that one might identify a book by author and title, by title alone, by author alone, or by Library of Congress number. In the case of title only, if the library has more than one book by that title, the abstracts of all are to be retrieved. In the case of author only, the abstracts of all the books by that author are to be retrieved. We decide that the Library of Congress number will be the key identifier, and that the data block containing the key will also contain the address of the abstract. With this, we now decide that author names and titles will each exist in separate files but will point to the file containing the key block. However, the name of an author may point to a number of key blocks. Moreover, the possibility of duplicated names for books requires also that a given title be allowed to point to a number of key blocks. Finally, we have to deal with a query containing both author and title.

At this point we would give anything for a relational data base system, but we have never heard of them. In any case, we are now ready for what I shall call intermediate design, the structural definition of each file.

Because the number of books for a given author or title are both variable, we decide to store the pointers to key blocks for author and title in threaded lists, or data chains, wherein the end of each entry contains the address of the next. Among other advantages, this allows us arbitrarily to add new books under an author's name or under a title without large movements of data.

Thus far, we have ignored logic. However, we now look at the data so far defined and discover that we require

a) Data entry algorithms for all four files so far defined.

b) An interactive query screen.

c) A pointer look-up algorithm with indirect indexing. modes and with the capability of conjunctive indexing (to handle queries containing both author and title).

d) A retrieval screen with bidirectional scrolling.

We currently have item d in our library of programs. Input is a logical address, and the program does the rest. We nearly have items a and b, and we make a note to modify them as needed. For item c we need more definition, but we are not yet finished with data design. We now attack the most detailed level of data design, logical representation of data.

Since we want to reuse the programs that perform functions a, b, and d, the formats for alphanumeric data and screen control are already established. For item c, we must construct the exact representation of the data blocks containing authors and titles along with their pointers. With this accomplished, the behavioral specifications for item c can be completed while we continue with further detailed data design.

Happily, the only remaining details are those required to implement the key word in context (KWIC) requirement, but this affects only the file of abstracts. As it happens, we have on hand a KWIC system that wants only that the data be stored in ASCII code, so that completes the last of the data design tasks.

The simple-minded example just concluded is obviously more appropriate to small scale programming than it is to large scale programming, but it does illustrate a decomposition process that lends itself to staging, with the design of logical operations subordinate to those of data.

We speak of "hooks" as control devices embedded in a process to provide management with visibility of progress and opportunity for decision. Diverse management actions can be hung from hooks: remedial actions for redressing schedule slippages, changes to project goals ("Marketing says to include the zeta feature, now that it is obvious we've got time and money for it."), and even abandonment of the project. Hooks are also the means to ensure that the quality program is being complied with. In the waterfall model, we find hooks in the rites of passage that mark the transition from one phase of work to the next.

The most common hooks rely on documents produced at the end of each phase. Although a bit removed from the cognitive processes that actually produce programs, documentation (mostly in natural language) explains to management the work that has been accomplished. That such documents are extrinsic to actual development and as such may be viewed as cost drivers is another matter. In any case

> *The strength of the document-driven process is the ease with which it accommodates hooks.*

Assuming that they have been evaluated with respect to process standards, the artifacts of each waterfall phase—requirements specifications, design documents, review records, and the like—provide the evidence to gauge project status. Beyond status, once these artifacts have been found to meet specifications for *phase exit criteria*, they define the current state of the software system itself. That is, during development they are the tangible representation of the system that will eventually be produced. These harbingers of product performance and chroniclers of technical decisions can be placed under library control to define the system at the end of each waterfall phase. When this is done, the material that is placed under control becomes a development *baseline*, the foundation on which the next phase will rest. Baselines are the formal hooks of product control throughout the life cycle.

Waterfall Problems

Despite its popularity, the waterfall model is not without notable problems. Perhaps the most remarked of these is that the whole concept falls apart in the presence of unstable requirements.

Even when given reasonably stable requirements, we still have to cope with the iteration built into the model. It is one thing to graphically depict iteration with over-lapping boxes, and quite another to actually manage iteration. A requirements document is baselined. During early design work we may discover that the document contains an unfeasible requirement or a contradiction. The model calls for iteration, a revision of the requirements document. Because we have a requirements baseline, updating the document cannot escape control, at least in theory. In fact, the designers cannot wait for official release of a new document (or revised pages). They have their own schedules to meet. So they proceed in the full and certain knowledge that the document will be revised—someday. Plainly, we have a problem of library control. However, we have a second problem: Resource control. How is management to know that additional work in requirements analysis is necessary? Where are the staff to perform this? (By now they surely have been assigned to other tasks.) How much will it cost? What computer resources for simulation or text processing or whatever are going to be required? Reasonable questions all, and questions that can be addressed by management. Only a formal mechanism can guarantee that management will learn of the necessary rework, but a formal mechanism for timely changes of earlier work can be an impediment to progress. Bad news in either case.

The tacitly accepted—but otherwise ignored—iteration of requirements analysis during development is nothing compared to the iteration of design phases during design itself, coding, and testing. Here, we must contend with changes that can occur daily. Programmers can report the time spent on task iteration, but it is impractical to iterate design reviews daily or to maintain the currency of baselines.

We see in Chapter 7 that makeshift solutions can be contrived, but it remains that the waterfall, invented to place hooks into the development process, can be pretty slippery at times.

6.2 DEMONSTRATION-DRIVEN VARIANTS

The problem of unstable requirements can be ameliorated if the users of software can be involved during the interval when requirements are being defined. One way to do this is to have the programming staff work directly with users during the preparation of requirements documents. However, this requires that the users understand the implications of the programming jargon that—despite the best intentions to produce a "what" document—somehow insinuates itself into the team effort. An alternative and increasingly popular approach has programmers translate their comprehension of the problem into a model that demonstrates their interpretation to the potential users. In the process, it may become evident that the programming staff has not been told of all of the required software behavior.

Rapid Prototyping

Implementation of the demonstration driven variant of the waterfall implies the construction of a prototype software product. We use the word prototype to refer to a computational model having behavioral characteristics similar to the final, or "production," product. It is not a prototype in the sense that, with refinement, it will evolve into the production product. Rather, it is a model of the behavior of the production product. (Prototyping need not be restricted to requirements modeling. In Section 6.3, we examine prototyping at other times during development. However, this capability so changes the ground rules of the waterfall that we can no longer continue thinking in terms of a demonstration driven variant of the waterfall.)

To build a prototype, programmers commonly use an application generator or a very high level language (*VHLL*) selected for the speed with which the prototype can be constructed. Speed is essential, and the realization of demonstration driven waterfall variants is most often referred to as "rapid prototyping." Recall the description in Section 4.1 of application generator languages as nonprocedural (popularly called fourth generation) languages processed by application generator systems to produce executable programs. As final products, these programs are suitable only for applications in which computation resource utilization is immaterial. However, even where efficiency is important, as it usually is, the result is usable as a prototype. The point is that programmers can write a program much faster in a nonprocedural language than they can in a compiler language, and the issue in the demonstration driven variant is not efficiency but confirmation of the model of the computational problem.

Application generators have narrow problem domains; each operates on a limited set of problems. VHLLs are of more general application, but require that more thought be given to the solution domain. The speed with which one can program in VHLLs, still more expressive than conventional languages, recommends their application in rapid prototyping. Actually, expressiveness is the only thing these languages have in common. Examples of VHLLs that are used for rapid prototyping are APL, Lisp, and SETL. The last of these was noted in Section 4.1. APL and Lisp are not generally thought of as VHLLs, yet the one advantage universally claimed by APL devotees is programming speed, and Lisp's expressiveness in manipulating symbols allows the programmer to deal with information at a comfortable remove from tedious logical processing operations.

When used to refine, or even propose, behavioral specifications for software, prototype systems need demonstrate only the features considered important to the users. The concerns of a prototype for an aircraft flight director have to do with maintaining heading in crosswinds, tracking navigational signals, staying within allowable angles of roll, pitch, and yaw, and the like. The prototype is used to check out the adequacy and correctness of the algorithms that will be used. The manner in which the user inputs navigational data is mostly fixed by hardware limitations, so it has little relevance. On the other hand, the prototype for a manufacturing inventory control system is concerned with the ease with which the user can manipulate the variables of expected production schedules, goods on hand, cost of borrowing, and also with the suitability of the error-defeating guidance it provides for updating inventory information and other largely static data. Determining the operations that ought to be demonstrated if the prototype is to serve as a requirements model should be part of the quality program. Of course, one can prototype everything, but the time spent constructing the prototype would be that much longer. Any external specification that will be passed on to more than one designer must, of course, be stipulated in an adjunct document if it is not prototyped.

How does the prototype become the de facto requirements model? Users observe its execution (or examine hard copy of the results), tell the designers what they want improved or what was left out, and the prototype is revised. The revised model is again evaluated and the process repeated until all operations are satisfactory. The prototype should then be put under configuration control so that the designers of the production software have an unambiguous reference, and the observer should be asked to sign the control document or an artifact of the demonstration, as appropriate.

In comparing prototype models of behavioral specifications with voluminous documented specifications, we see three major advantages to the prototype:

- Little if any interpretation (with consequent opportunity for error) is required.

- The user is directly involved in the development process.

- The test cases used for evaluation of the model can be saved for evaluation of the final product, thus ensuring traceability in the validation process.

Compared to completely document-driven waterfalls, the demonstration driven variant does not as easily lend itself to hooking. Documents are inspectable, tangible artifacts of programming. However, when placed under configuration control, the approved model is baselined no less than a written specification. The main problem that arises is finding hooks during the process of prototype iteration. Baselining each model would defeat the purpose of *rapid* prototyping. Still, a solution exists. For the observer's evaluation of demonstrations to be maximally useful, the evaluations should be documented. Just as a baseline becomes the reference for the further work, so the evaluations of prototype behavior are the references for further development of the prototype. Given documented evaluations, hooking becomes a matter of noting the number of problems evinced in the evaluation reports and the interval between the reported demonstrations.

6.3 ALTERNATIVE MODELS

For those whose enthusiasm for software engineering is dampened by the waterfall, perhaps an alternative model for the development portion of the software life cycle should be entertained. We start with models based on paradigms introduced in Section 4.1.

Models Based on Object-Oriented Programming

We can employ object-oriented programming within the waterfall model. However, object-oriented programming also lends itself to the formulation of demonstratable models of the computational problem that, with further programming in the paradigm, will evolve into implementation of a solution. Although the problem cannot be programmed in terms of process abstractions independent of the solution domains, models can quickly be produced to demonstrate behavior in any critical area. Recall that objects derive from previously defined objects or classes and lead finally to a run-time system in which commands are bound to implementation specifics at execution. Unlike models with discrete phases for various stages of design, coding, and preliminary testing, object-oriented program evolution can be viewed as a continuum: The structure of the system gains specificity with time, but at all times is described in the same kind of language.

In the discussion of rapid prototyping we saw that the test cases used to evaluate the requirements model can serve double duty in the subsequent evaluation of the final product. To the extent that the product's behavior was modeled, the quality of validation is thereby ensured. With the continuum of object-oriented programming, we have the added insurance of verification: Each development activity necessarily derives from its predecessor.

The Operational Model

Depending on functional programming (see *Other Paradigms* in Section 4.1) and on program transformation mechanisms still more studied than available, the operational model has limited industrial utility. However, the concept provides food for thought when designing a process model, particularly with regard to means of verification. In the operational model, we verify direct products of development rather than documents prepared at some remove from actual development.

As in the object-oriented programming model, early demonstration of behavior in the operational model leads to final system implementation. However, here it is required that systems under development metamorphose during their evolution. Nevertheless, verification to predecesser work is at all times assured. The model is distinguished by the construction of a functionally programmed operational requirements specification, not directly executed but demonstrated by an interpreter. Containing no implementation specifics, the model is independent of the execution environment of the eventual production model.

After the model has been accepted, the specification is converted stepwise into a practical software system; that is, the specification's problem-centered structures are transformed into structures that can execute in the stipulated run-time environment. Because the formality of the operational specification is ensured by the constraints of the interpreter that demonstrates it, the required transformations lend themselves, at least in theory, to mechanization. From a practical point of view, complete mechanization, required for large software systems, is still in the future. Even when done manually, however, the state of the system after each transformation can be verified. An example of the transformations required to go from the process-oriented abstraction of the operational specification to the implementation structure can be found in the discussion by Pamela Zave.[1] Examples of languages that have been applied to the operational model are PAISLey[6] and Gist.[7,8]

TRW's Spiral Model

The discrete phases of this development model give it a superficial likeness to the waterfall. However, each of the phases, or spiral "rounds" as Barry Boehm puts it,[9] to a great extent replicates in method the round immediately preceding it. The rounds most nearly conform to the following progression of phases found in waterfalls:

• Operation concept.
• Software requirements.
• Software product design.
• Implementation (starting with detailed design).

The resemblance to the waterfall fades as we look at the series of activities within each of these. Early in each round, alternative means of completing the round are identified (anything from design approaches to make/buy tradeoffs) as are the constraints applicable to each. Risk analysis is featured in each round and may lead to prototyping to resolve key issues. Unlike the demonstration driven variant of the waterfall discussed in Section 6.2, prototyping may take place at any time in the spiral model.

The spiral model is wed to no particular technology. Any of the paradigms of Section 4.1 may be employed, individually and in combination. One would expect that the economic feasibility of prototyping during any round would necessarily be influenced by the technical approaches of that round or of its immediate predecessor. However, the character of the risks at issue may permit prototypes to be easily constructed using technology independent of that used for product development. For example, in the development of a programming environment (TRW-SPS) the user interface options were modeled by Unix shell scripts, unrelated to the specific methods for defining system behavior or pursuing design decomposition.

Boehm states that, although in its current state of development the spiral model works well on internal developments, further work is required before the model can be used for the development of contract software. The problem here is that the flexibility and freedom to revise plans, an intrinsic part of the model's strength, do not conform with contract "accountability and control."

6.4 CONCLUDING OBSERVATIONS

Development process models may derive directly from technology, as does the operational model, or may form a metastructure supporting a mix of technological approaches, as does the spiral model. At either extreme and points in between, the model should provide technical discipline and opportunities for management discretion. The construction of a process model must take into account not only technology but also known constraints on implementation, and even more so, known liberties that may be taken with the implemented product. For example, process models for projects having no predetermined implementation language can provide greater freedom during the formulation of external specifications than can projects destined to end up in one source language or another.

To minimize the effects of bad marriages, process models should be constructed to the purpose of employing methodology isomorphic to technology. This is easiest when the technology has means for verification built into it. Suppose that a process model combined rapid prototyping to refine the requirements model with a composition process for design (see Section 4.2). A management review at the end of the requirements modeling phase would not only include the results of prototype demonstration, but the extent to which the prototype incorporated models of existing components. Software components reused from previous projects would be subject to certification based on the known (measured or otherwise assessed) quality of the components. A management review, held when the structure of the system has been arrived at and the plan for developing new components has been prepared, would review evidence of such certification. Eventually, before beta testing, the test cases used to demonstrate the requirements model would be reused to evaluate the final product, thus ensuring the product's fidelity with respect to the requirements model.

We do not see a need for formal process models in software projects undertaken by a single person or a handful of people who (1) are the end users of the software and (2) work in constant communication with each other. At the risk of some iconoclasm, we can draw the conclusion that

> *Well formed process models should have as their goal the reduction of the complexity of large-scale programming to the efficiency and manageability of programming by computer hackers.*

6.5 SUMMARY

1. The management of technology throughout the software life cycle is defined by process models.

2. Most software development has been governed by waterfall models, in which technical activities are divided into discrete sequential phases, each marked by output in the form of documents or code.

3. In the most common, or document-driven, implementation of the waterfall model, each phase is marked by output in the form of documents.

4. Despite the diversity of waterfalls in use, all provide management checkpoints (hooks) at the end of each phase.

5. From all but the earliest design work until testing of the completed system, the waterfall may turn into a set of parallel sequences to account for different rates of development.

6. Design generally follows along functional decomposition or data decomposition lines. The choice affects the process model.

7. The success of the waterfall model depends on the success with which requirements can be defined initially.

8. Although iteration of each phase is inherent in the waterfall concept, full use of phase exit hooks during iterations becomes an impediment to progress.

9. To improve the accuracy and completeness of requirements definitions, we can use rapid prototyping during the analysis of requirements to provide demonstration of the programmers' understanding of the required behavior.

10. System prototypes can be fashioned rapidly using application generators or very high level languages.

11. Models centered on the technology in use avoid mismatches with methods.

12. Suitable process models must also reflect the constraints imposed by implementation technology (e.g., a given programming language), but should not restrict decisions unaffected by implementation technology.

13. The "spiral" model provides risk analysis, with prototyping to further assess risk, throughout software development.

6.6 REFERENCES

[1] P. Zave, "The Operational Versus the Conventional Approach to Software Development," *CACM*, Vol. 27 (February 1984) pp. 104–18.

[2] P. Metzger, *Managing A Programming Project*, 2nd ed. (Englewood Cliffs, N.J.: Prentice-Hall, 1981), inside cover.

[3] C. V. Ramamoorthy et al., "Software Engineering: Problems and Perspectives," *Computer* (October 1984) pp. 191–209.

[4] R. Dunn, *Software Defect Removal* (New York: McGraw-Hill Book Co., 1984) p. 54.

[5] R. Dunn, *Software Defect Removal* (New York: McGraw-Hill Book Co., 1984) p. 188.

[6] P. Zave, "An Operational Approach to Requirements Specification for Embedded Systems," *IEEE Trans. Software Eng.*, Vol. SE-8 (May 1982) pp. 250–69.

[7] R. Balzer et al., "Operational Specification as the Basis for Rapid Prototyping," *ACM SIGSOFT*, Vol. 7 (December 1982) pp. 3–16.

[8] M. Feather, "Mappings for Rapid Prototyping," *ACM SIGSOFT*, Vol. 7 (December 1982) pp. 17–24.

[9] B. Boehm, "A Spiral Model of Software Development and Enhancement," *ACM SIGSOFT*, Vol. 11 (August 1986) pp. 14–24.

CHAPTER 7

Project Control

The consequences of projects that have become unmanageable demand our interest in project control. Cost overruns and the souring of user relations gain most of the attention drawn by poorly controlled projects, but quality is another casualty. The project that is losing money or running out of time is the project most likely to have its planned tests curtailed and most likely to deliver unusable documentation.

Software loss leaders are losers for everyone.

Examination of projects that have run amuck reveals that chaos rarely springs from a single event. Management may not have learned of impending disaster until all was lost but, as with termite damage, things had been eroding bit by bit. Had management been aware that problems were brewing, it may have been possible to take remedial actions. However, when we learn the week before the scheduled start of integration that a six month postponement is required, it is too late to install the source level debugger that would have speeded unit testing. Although appropriate remedial management alternatives are outside the scope of this book, the information part of project control is not. In this chapter we look at means for determining current project status and forecasting future status. We also look at how the manner of organizing project teams influences project control.

7.1 FROM HERE TO THERE

The consuming interest of project managers is delivering a software system on time, within budget, and in usable condition. Periodically during the course of development, managers formally assess the status of the project. Informally, they do so every time another hitch develops. In the popular expression, the problem of project management is "Getting from here to there," and knowing the real whereabouts of "here" occupies a major part of managers' energies. Sure, direct reports provide weekly summaries of progress made and milestones achieved, but the previously scarred manager is always suspicious of the pertinence of reported progress and of the straightness of the road marked by milestones. Managers need a technique of certifying reported progress and they have it. It is called task control and it relies on our old friend, the work breakdown structure.

Using the Work Breakdown Structure

Work breakdown structures (WBS) were introduced in Section 5.3 in regard to project planning. Building a useful WBS takes care; using it for project control requires only diligence. Useful WBSs reflect a natural set of discrete activities and their relationships, rather than a parcel of diffuse responsibilities or a group of milestone aliases. An example of a weak work breakdown element is "Development of system test criteria." This can engage some of the designers' thoughts almost from the inception of a project. A much stronger WBS element is "Design of system test cases," since this work will result in tangible, measurable output. Another weak WBS element is "Preliminary design review with customer." Except for the people charged with administrative planning to support the review (e.g., arranging for lunch), the preliminary design review is a milestone and does not reflect the completion of the many design tasks that give the milestone meaning.

A WBS useful for project control comprises tasks of specified input and output. The task cannot be started until all the input is present. The task cannot be considered complete until the expected output is produced. Let us take as an example the task defined as the coding and unit test of module SMD. Defined inputs are the following:

1) Detailed design specification for SMD.

2) Minutes of the review of the detailed design specification for SMD. (Note: if the minutes identify any required specification changes, the revisions must exist in one form or another for the specification to be a valid input.)

3) Test data for populating file JDD, used by the module.

Let us assume that inputs 1 and 2 exist, but that input 3 is not yet ready. The manager must decide whether to allow coding to begin, with a hold placed on testing until item 3 is ready, or to delay the entire task. The decision probably will rest on whether the programmer assigned to the task can be reassigned to another. In any case, we see a poorly defined task, one that could easily have been divided into two tasks—coding and unit testing—each with a set of necessary and sufficient inputs. Rule: To avoid the WBS from becoming a housekeeping nuisance (tracking waivers, and so forth), tasks should be defined such that required inputs apply to the entire task.

Let us look at the outputs of the task as originally defined (coding and unit testing).

1) Code listing as output by compiler, with no errors.

2) Minutes of code walk-through.

3) Error-free output of static analyzer.

4) Test report showing successful completion of planned tests.

If all four items are completed, the task is completed. This raises the question of how the keeper of project status knows that all four have been completed. The answer is that the programmer's supervisor—a quality engineer or whoever is designated by the governing (and documented) procedures—certifies ("signs off") that each of the four outputs has been *completed to standards*. In short, a direct link connects task control and the set of standards discussed in Section 5.1. Moreover, real project status is measurable in terms of the tasks that have been certified as completed.

Well, almost. No one can be certain, at least until late in the development process, that task completions add up to project completion. One may learn during integration that the behavior of Module SMD was improperly specified. One may even learn that it was never necessary. Worse, the manager may tardily learn of a new set of functions that have to be designed, coded, and tested before the software system can be usefully employed. All of this means that no matter how carefully the WBS is constructed, it may have to be modified any number of times. The WBS is a management device that reflects, but does not form part of, the software solution.

Thus, not only does the WBS have to be amplified from time to time to reflect new levels of delineation as the specifics of the software solution become more plainly defined, but tasks previously defined may have to be reopened (that is, changed in status from complete to incomplete). Nowhere is the regression of task status more obvious than as a byproduct of the iteration inherent in software development. A common example is the revision of preliminary design tasks required during any of the activities needed to implement the design: detailed design, coding, system testing, or whatever. Indeed, this is where project control is most likely to falter.

> *In the haste to get design errors or shortcomings fixed so that progress can continue with minimum interruption, certification of the revisited design tasks is likely to be ignored.*

Since task status regression is to be expected, does this mean that the WBS is not very useful after all? Not at all. What it means is that we need yet another tool for project control.

Baselines

Baselines are definitions of the software system at all stages of its life, including the prenatal states. A requirements model for a software system defines the behavior of the future system, and as such is the definitive descriptor of the system prior to the emergence of its structure. The requirements model is a baseline from which design can proceed. In time, artifacts of the design process will supersede the requirements model as the definition of the future software, and a new baseline will have been created. And so it goes, until, some time after the intial release of the software to users, we have the baseline for Version 4, Revision 2, consisting of protected master code files, code listings, installation instructions, and the like.

However, baselines are more than definitions of software systems. Baselines can also be regarded as collections of the output of the WBS tasks that result in system definitions, and regression in the status of any task contributing to a baseline is tantamount to regression in the status of the baseline itself. Since each baseline represents a known state of the software, baselines are maintained under library control. Thus, regression of the status of a baseline should require that the instruments of library control come into play to guard against the chaos of undefined software states. If checks are made to certify the completion of tasks required to implement the revisions, then the same formality that attaches to the initial certification of task control can apply to the completion of task rework. The common term for a system of baseline control is configuration management. Apart from helping to maintain task control during task iterations, configuration management has other utility for project control, and we turn to that now.

Configuration Management

Configuration management is not peculiar to software. Long before computers entered our lives configuration management had been used to assure that automobile spare parts manufactured years after introduction of a new model would be identical to the original parts. Configuration management applied to manufacturing drawings, installation diagrams, and anything else needed to establish a hardware process. Bersoff defines it as

> "... the discipline of identifying the configuration of a system at discrete points in time for the purpose of systematically controlling changes to the configuration and maintaining the integrity and traceability of the configuration throughout the system life cycle."[1]

If baselines were never to change, we would have little need for configuration management. A baseline would be a declared collection of documents and files and that would be that. However, the character of software is change, and change needs to be controlled.

The primary instruments of configuration management are library control tools and procedures and change boards. Library control, which we touched on several times in the preceding chapters, is the protection provided to documents and files to make certain they are not inadvertently destroyed, altered without authorization, or misused. The first two require no explanation. Protection from misuse means that obsolete program units must not be erroneously linked with other parts of the software system to form a new program load, that fixes to a subsystem be dispatched only to those customers that bought the features supported by the subsystem, and so forth. Library control tools cover a wide range. We have code control systems such as DEC's CMS system for VAX users, module control systems such as DEC's MMS, document control systems found in some of the off-the-shelf environments discussed in Section 4.3, and simple mechanisms such as those built into obdurate link editors to reject module files having edition information different from that found in the link file. Library control procedures include the prescribed steps for delivering source code to an integration test team, conducting audits of controlled material, and publishing information related to changes. Software standards should describe all library control procedures.

The other configuration management instrument is the change board. Aliases include configuration management board, software change board, and—forthrightly— change control board. The board can take as many forms as its appellations. It may consist of one person (less a board than a splinter) attached to a mature product for which no further enhancement is planned or several people representing diverse interests: marketing, technical staff, customer service, and so forth. The board may judge the worthiness (and cost) of changes requested by users or marketing, or may simply pass these along to people charged with keeping track of product and project status. The board may decide whether to proceed with rectifying latent faults or, again, may only make certain that the decision made by others is duly recorded and procedures set in motion. Change boards may be project-peculiar, or may cover all projects and products. Both types of boards may exist in the same company: boards dedicated to a single project to expedite required changes, and boards dedicated to operational, hence less protean, products. Whatever the form, no changes that fall under the province of a change board may be made without the board's imprimatur. In addition to the ranges of responsibility and authority, boards also differ in their methods. Some meet weekly or twice a week, some monthly, some only when called to meet. Some periodically conduct audits to assure consistency between documents or between documents and code, some await the audit reports of others charged with the responsibility (e.g., Quality Assurance), and still others accept all on faith. I suspect that the following enter into the way change boards are established: corporate culture, past problems, size of projects and products, number of installations of products, and tool capability. The last is no small matter: A code control tool that reveals the edition and date of last compilation of each item in a program load markedly reduces the bookkeeping of even the most actively involved change board.

Although the emphasis of configuration management is change control, we should not ignore control of newly released software. Configuration management procedures handle the release of all software, newly minted as well as revised. Such procedures call for confirmation that test plans have been successfully executed, that user manuals and the like have been found to be consistent with the code, and that the software is properly labeled (as by updated edition number). Generally, the chairperson of the change board is required to sign a release instrument. In theory then, the board provides the final quality check. In practice, the board looks for approval signatures from the technical and quality departments (certainly the former, increasingly the latter) before affixing its own. That is, the board provides management restraint, rather than actual quality assurance.

With this discussion of the release mechanism, it may appear that we have finally gotten from here to there. In fact, the software may have gotten there, but we have not. Project control requires one more input associated with the WBS, insight to potential schedule threats.

Will the Real Critical Path Please Stand Up?

Getting from here to there is a matter of hurdling one crossbar at a time. The track for industrial projects, far from straight or oval, not only is convoluted, but hides its convolutions in a fog of misconceptions. Consider the set of tasks and interdependencies, depicted in Figure 7.1, that comprise the development of an interactive software system. The numbers above each task represent the number of calendar weeks to perform the task.

123

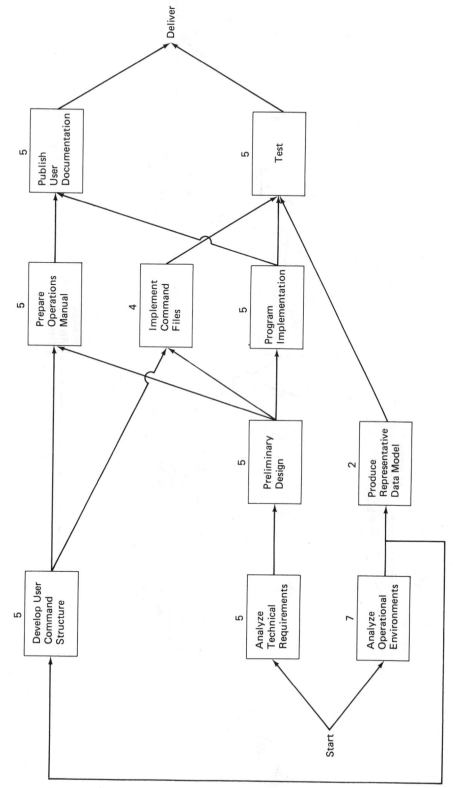

Figure 7.1 Task Dependencies Drawn to Show Technical Tasks as Critical Path

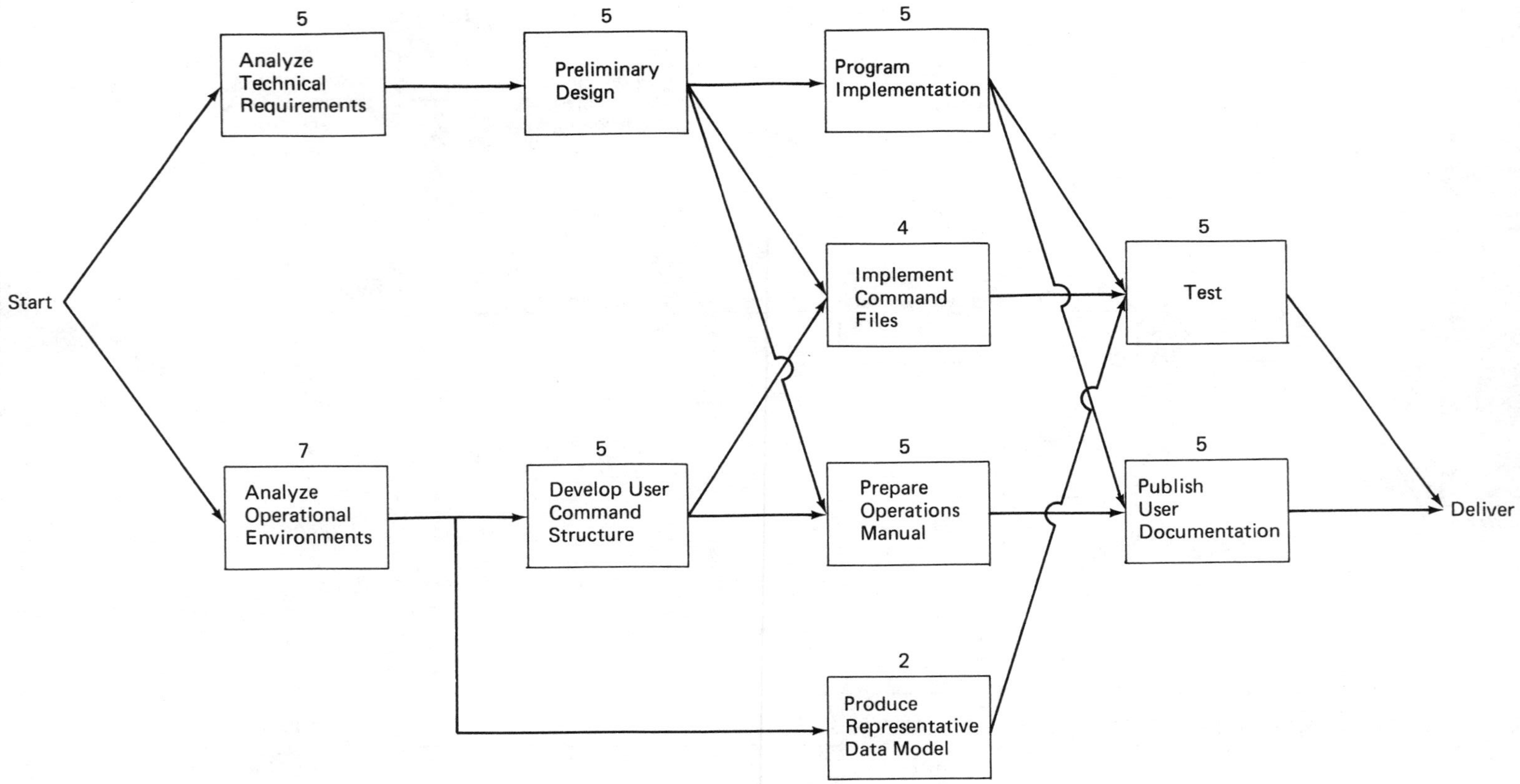

Figure 7.2 Task Dependencies Drawn to Emphasize Critical Path

Through oversimplification of task delineation and omission of iteration, the diagram trivializes the problem, but it will serve our purposes.

Drawn by a technical manager, the network places the technical tasks of requirements analysis through test in a straight line in the center of the diagram. However, the time to perform these can slip a total of one week without affecting delivery. Earliest delivery, as constrained by the time to execute each task, is actually determined by the analysis of operational environments, the development of a user command structure, the preparation of an operations manual, and the publication of user documentation. Figure 7.2 illustrates the network redrawn to depict more clearly the cumulative effect of task duration and dependencies.

Determining the critical path is no problem with modern analysis programs, as noted in Section 5.3. Every manager performs the analysis during the planning stage of a project. Often as not, the manager learns that project completion will be too late to meet marketing or contractual obligations. However, remedies are available: Increase staff for those critical path tasks that can profit from more workers, add new tool capabilities to improve worker productivity, and plan the use of overtime. Remedial action is not limited to modifying the project plan. As the project unfolds, the critical path tasks are given extra managerial attention.

Unfortunately, the network is not static. The task definitions and dependencies may be invariant,* and even the estimates to perform tasks not yet undertaken may remain constant, but with the passage of time actuals replace estimates. Whether the actuals are less than or greater than the estimates, mapping current status onto the network may result in new topological consequences. For example, in the network of Figures 7.1 and 7.2, the path from technical requirements analysis through test may become the critical path if the technical analysis takes a week longer than estimated and the analysis of the operational environment takes two weeks less than the estimated duration. Wise managers know they must periodically update their critical path analyses with actuals to determine the tasks that most deserve close scrutiny.

7.2 SYMPTOMATIC ANALYSIS

Section 7.1 dealt with the certification of progress and with recognizing the significant schedule drivers inherent in the project plan. However, no project can be considered completely under control unless the manager can fathom the phenomona underlying reported progress. Even when critical path analysis indicates that the delivery date is unthreatened, progress reports can be analyzed for symptoms of disturbances too early to show up on schedules tied to task definitions and milestones. These analyses have in common the use of trend studies. What has happened and what is happening point to future events. Put more eloquently by T.S. Eliot (in *Burnt Norton*),

> *"Time Present and time past*
> *Are both perhaps present in time future,*
> *And time future contained in time past."*

---

* In practice, they are frequently redefined over the course of a project.

Those who find poetry incompatible with software project management* may find more relevant eloquence by analogy to the headline that appears from time to time in nearly all newspapers:

> *"Investors wary while awaiting Commerce Department's monthly report of leading indicators."*

Indeed, analyses such as those we will look at in this section were called "software leading indicators" by the group that developed them at ITT Programming, under the direction of Ray Wolverton.

Staffing

The first of the symptoms we look at is also the first that needs to be considered in the chronology of many projects. Projects for which staff on hand are fewer than needed have to be concerned with the timely addition of people. Failure to do so will obviously jeopardize other project plans. Now, if the schedule calls for a staff of 100 on February 1 and 150 on March 1, and so forth, a current staff of 120 on the first of March provides factual evidence that the staffing schedule is in trouble. Predictably, the project manager will lean harder on the boss to accelerate reassignments or on the personnel department to recruit more aggressively . However, the project manager needs to do more—specifically, to work up a contingency plan to deal with the projected shortfall. But how short will the shortfall be, and when will staffing catch up?

Let us chart the planned and actual staffing as in Figure 7.3. A linear 10-week buildup is expected, followed by a planned plateau. We see also the beginning of a planned stepped decrease of staff, the whole plan roughly approximating a Rayleigh curve. Actual staff buildup also is linear, but at a rate lower than that hoped for. In fact, by the fifth week the total staff is only 86% of that expected. Extrapolating, the staff will not reach the peak until after the twelfth week. This projection would seem tolerable. After all, in a project of this duration there should be more than two weeks of slack built in. However, let us look at the curve in Figure 7.3, which represents the cumulative effect of insufficient staff during the buildup phase. Although both planned and actual (including extrapolated) increases are linear, the cumulative shortfall is parabolic, at least until after the start of the planned plateau. This translates into a parabolically increasing schedule slip. One way to handle this, as shown in the illustration, is to continue to increase staff size until the cumulative shortfall is reduced to zero. In this case, the staff should peak at 36% more people than initially planned. Brooks' Law[†] notwithstanding, adding staff this early in the project will probably help to maintain control later on, certainly more so than if the project manager were to wait until severe slippages became visible to the senior management.

As noted earlier, other remedial actions are also possible. Probably the most common approach to this common problem is to use a combination of remedies. But this is beyond the point: By analyzing what has happened and continues to happen, management can take effective control actions. In the example case, we do not know

---

* Would anyone find science fiction incompatible?

[†] Brooks' Law: "Adding manpower to a late software project makes it later."[2]

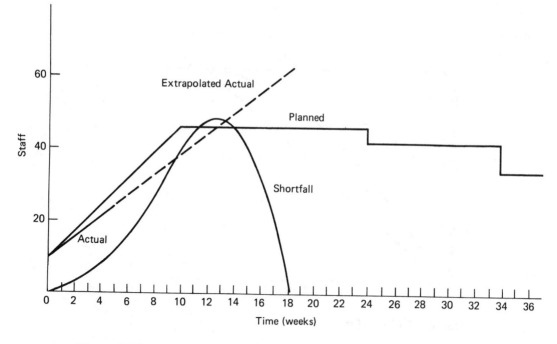

Figure 7.3 Building Staff for a New Project

why staffing is going badly, but the simplest analysis displays the symptom, and little additional analysis is required to estimate the effect.

Design of Discrete Functions

Let us turn our attention to the long interval in the decomposition of a large software subsystem during which individual testable functions are being resolved in the detailed design of separate code units. We want to know what is going on, but task control provides little help. The natural set of WBS tasks, corresponding to hierarchical design activities and discrete structural units, does not quite tell the story of progress in a way that might reveal underlying technical problems.

In the simplest illustration, we have N functions to be translated into detailed design someplace or another. Figure 7.4 shows two idealized trends that might be encountered. The straight line tells us that each individual function is much like the others. Either we have every programmer's dream of a straightforward problem domain, or an incredibly brilliant job was done at codifying the requirements model. The arcing curve is perhaps more typical. As more and more functions are translated into coding specifications, interactions among them become more evident and design proceeds more cautiously. Also, some rework of earlier design may be required. Comparison of design rate data with a curve to which the data of earlier projects have been fitted provides some insight into the complexity of the current job relative to its predecessors. Since the planning of other project activities was most likely influenced by an estimate of the overall complexity, the insight gained by this symptomatic analysis may lead the manager to revise several parts of the project plan.

127

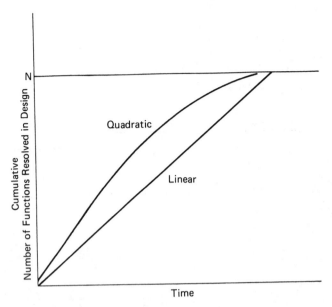

Figure 7.4 Design Progress

In the years before management learned that software project progress can be forecast during the course of development, the 95% syndrome was the source of both anguish and humor: Shortly before the software system is due to be released, and every week thereafter for an interminable interval, the system is reported as 95% complete. Actually, there is no need to wait until the release date approaches to see the 95% syndrome at work. It can strike during any phase of development. In Figure 7.5 we see the limiting case (this side of design regression) of the arc of Figure 7.4. That is, the rate at which discrete functional requirements are resolved in design asymptotically approaches the number of functions. This is a clear signal to management to examine in detail the problems that are occurring. If the signal is ignored, the eventual announcement of a disastrous slip in the schedule may lead to the decision to abandon the project as infeasible. However, the symptom may be acted upon now and, although the remedy may be harsh (such as revisiting the overall design concept), at least the project will be saved.

Testing

Testing tasks, too, can take months to be completed. This is especially true of integration testing, wherein problems in the design of the structure of the system may first be detected. Consider Figure 7.6. In this illustration, as in others on testing, the curves represent cumulative numbers of tests.

Anticipating greater complexity in tests as the system grows, the planned rate of test execution is slower in the later stages of integration than in the earlier. Nevertheless, we see that the rate of execution is still slower than that planned. Several reasons could account for this: Modules are being added to the build at a slower rate than expected because of coding delays, the test environment is more inefficient than had been believed during testing, the test team has been hit with a succession of viral outbreaks, the test

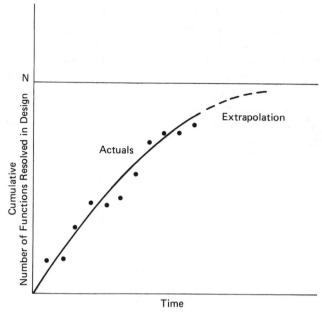

Figure 7.5 The 95% Syndrome during Design

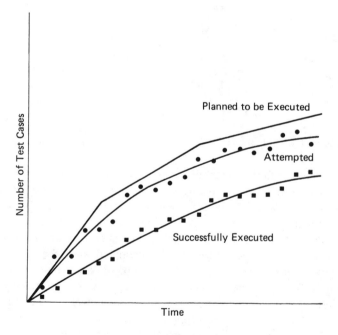

Figure 7.6 Testing: Plan and Reality

plan was deliberately optimistic, or the code is too buggy. The fact that the success-rate curve follows the attempt rate suggests that buggy code is not the problem. (more on this shortly). In any case, the situation invites examination. More than one project has been lost in integration. The symptomatic analysis suggested by Figure 7.6 applies not only to integration, but also to other test series involved in the process model in use. Of course, the possible causes of symptoms differ in each. For example, a sluggish test attempt rate during acceptance testing may result from the short hours kept by the customer personnel witnessing the tests. Whatever the cause, something can be done about it once the problem is known.

A more sensitive indicator of code quality is the comparison of successful and unsuccessful test case execution history. This can be plotted either as a ratio of the two, or as the separate, smoothed, scatter diagrams of Figure 7.7.

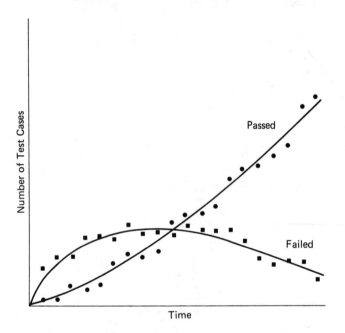

Figure 7.7 Typical Test History

The illustration is fairly typical of a smoothly running test program. At the start, we see a high failure rate, mostly because testing bugs compete with product bugs in causing tests to fail. There is another reason for seeing more failures than successes, one that holds for the entire test program: Excluding those test cases repeated during regression testing, test cases may fail several times for each success. Also in the early period, the execution of new test cases may be attempted while the debugging backlog continues to grow. This is especially true for tests of fully assembled systems. Toward the end of testing, however, the number of successes may increase rapidly if there has been a cumulative bunching of fixes. This is the case shown. Although few managers will relax until the daily fail/pass ratio approaches zero, at no time during the test series does Figure 7.7 suggest that trouble lies beneath the observations.

Not so the diagram of Figure 7.8. Here we see the failure rate, after easing up once the initial trauma of a new test program has worn off, start again to increase. Since test successes continue to increase, we are not likely to panic. Nevertheless, we may have a debugging process that is going badly, a possible symptom that the bugs found in later tests are more intractable than those found earlier.

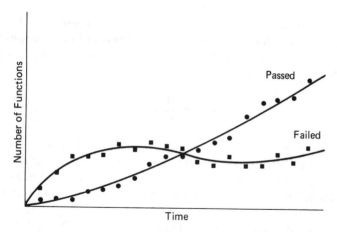

Figure 7.8 Test History Inviting Further Analysis

There is another difference between Figures 7.8 and 7.7. Figure 7.8 plots, not test cases, but functions tested. Assuming that more than one test case is required to provide evidence that a given function has been correctly satisfied, the two figures are not exactly equivalent. The significance of the distinction lies in the philosophy behind the test series: From the aspect of validation, functions may be of more interest than test cases.

Not all symptomatic analyses are illustrated with time as the independent variable. For example, the rate of recompilations, frequently employed as a leading indicator, illustrates little. If recompilation is a routine Friday night affair, absolutely nothing is learned from the rate. On the other hand, if recompilation of a system is performed whenever the number of lines of patch code exceeds some stipulated maximum, what is really being analyzed is the rate at which the size of fixes changes. Not much insight from that. Alternatively, recompilation could be performed when the number of patches, as distinguished from lines of patch code, exceeds a threshold. In this case, what is analyzed is the rate at which fixes are being performed. However, this practice is no different from analyzing the rate of test successes. Without also looking at the rate of test failures, we have no way of knowing the effect of bug discoveries on the rate at which fixes are made.

The last example of symptomatic analysis during testing not only takes no profit from observations as a function of time, but requires a different independent variable, the number of bugs that have been found. In Section 2.3 we encountered fault seeding as a technique for measuring the quality of testing. Recall that one can form an estimate of N, the number of faults (including seeds) in the code at the start of testing, from

$$\hat{N} = \frac{A \times B}{C}$$

where

$A =$ the number of seeds planted prior to testing

$B =$ the total number of bugs that were found, and

$C =$ the number of seeds that were found.

The estimate of the number of starting bugs is only as reliable as the randomness of the seeding process with respect to both the program domain and the capability of the test data to explore the domain. Before using $\hat{N}$, the premise of randomness should be tested. As it happens, the ratio

$$E = \frac{B - A}{\hat{N} - A}$$

is a way of measuring the seeding effectiveness. Ratios evaluated after a considerable number of bugs have been found—at a time when the total number of detected faults is likely to be greater than the number of seeds—will approach 1 as B increases. If seeds are being recaptured more or less in proportion to the total number of detected bugs, a line can be passed through the scatter diagram of the pairs (E_1, B_1), (E_i, B_i) ... (E_n, B_n) with a high correlation coefficient;* say, a coefficient of .95. This is depicted in Figure 7.9. If, however, each batch of bugs contains a different proportion of seeds, the low correlation coefficient that is calculated signals that estimates of N are not to be trusted.

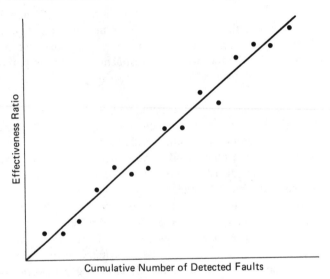

Figure 7.9 Fault Detection with Reliable Seed Recapture

Analysis of Resource Consumption

At various times during development the designers estimate the system resources that will be used by the program. Such resources include execution time, memory, input/output ports, and the like. Typical times to generate estimates are

- During the project feasibility study.
- At several points during preliminary design.
- After each subsystem or major component has been designed to the point where detailed design can begin.

* Any book on statistics has at least one formula for calculating the correlation coefficient.

- After the detailed design of each subsystem.
- After the testing of each program build.

For projects that were initially underestimated in either scope or complexity, it is typical that the estimates of resource consumption grow monotonically with refinement. For example, Figure 7.10 illustrates the growth in program storage as it may have been estimated at various times prior to testing. Here we not only see the anticipated memory requirements increasing at each estimate, we see them growing at ever increasing amounts as each new design activity adds another increment of memory to the original estimates.

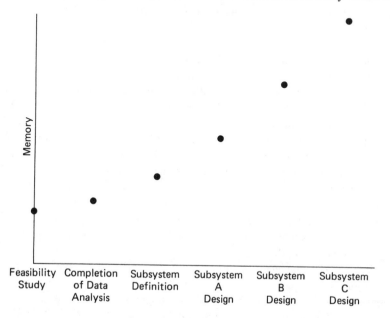

Figure 7.10 Growth in Estimated Memory Requirements

It is axiomatic that the later one discovers that luck and computer power are running out at the same time, the greater the amount of mischief that occurs. The worst time to discover that the computing equipment has insufficient memory is when a program load cannot be done. By definition, this situation marks a project out of control. If we may skirt a contradiction in terms, the best time to discover that resources have been exceeded is when remedial action can be taken in the form of providing more memory, changing the design approach, or reducing the scope of the software.

Five will get you ten that an underestimated memory requirement is accompanied by an overestimated design rate, as seen in Figure 7.5. Equally likely is the combination of an overestimated throughput capability and one or another symptomatic testing progress problem. We can conceive of various links between the leading indicators of resource consumption and the others discussed earlier. Sometimes a strain on computational resources is the cause and difficulties in design or testing the result. For many years we have known that programming productivity suffers when programmers are up against the need to optimize design. Sometimes resource leading indicators and others signal difficulties arising from a common source—most often underestimation of the computational problem. Whatever the case, even the least hint of problems raised by symptomatic analysis of resource utilization should lead to a closer examination of other leading indicators. Something is probably amiss, even if no single analysis is sufficiently conclusive to raise fears that a project is ripe for loss of control.

7.3 HELP FROM THE ORGANIZATION

The title of this section should not be construed as a suggestion that a hit man be contracted to keep a project under control. Rather, the title means that the way one organizes a project bears on its controllability. The connection between organization and control is scarcely unique to programming, but it is worthwhile to cast certain aspects of the connection in software terms.

People are segregated in different organizational entities primarily in the interests of specialization. Someone who does the same sort of work day in and day out, eventually gets pretty good at it—recall Adam Smith's division of labor. Thus, we find personnel from the contracts department who in minutes can write terms and conditions by entering memorized merge tags in their word processors. The systems operator has had to rebuild user directories so often that the whole drill is now a rote procedure. Programmers working in the C language for the last two years are now so fluent in the language that they are assigned only to projects using that language. And so it goes. But nothing intrinsically distinguishes the people performing software testing from those who designed and coded the programs under test. Nor is the configuration control clerk kept separate from administrative assistants simply because the configuration control work has been learned so well.

What impels management to distribute authority and responsibility among several organizations is not just a matter of productivity. We are taught in grade school that bicameral legislative bodies such as the U.S. Congress provide a natural system of checks and balances. So too, the charters of internal organizations. We look briefly at some of these, and we discuss, also, the use of external people to help keep projects in control.

Putting Teeth in Hand-Over Operations

Requirements models are turned over to system design teams. On very large projects, system designers hand their abstract concepts of the final product to design teams for translatation into structural specifications. Perhaps coding is performed by yet another group of programmers. Each time work gets handed over from one organization to another, the receivers, by quietly proceeding in their use of the material, tacitly accept that material. Phase transition criteria are implicitly satisfied—well mostly, anyhow. Perhaps not all of the local standards have been completely observed, but the substance of the work must be reasonable or the receivers would refuse to accept it. That is, the receivers will refuse the work if they report to a boss different from the one the givers report to. In short,

The essence of task control can largely be accomplished simply by having the outputs of tasks implemented by people who had made no contribution to producing the output.

We still have to make certain that process standards are maintained, of course. For example, a coder's agreement that a piece of detailed design contains sufficient information to code from says nothing about whether the design was reviewed or computer resource allocations were made—or any other ancillary business having to do with detailed design.

From the aspect of top-down development, we have been discussing a *horizontal* division of labor. A penalty of inefficiency attaches to any horizontal segregation of personnel. Part of the inefficiency derives from the very need to complete tasks sufficiently well to hand the results over to others. The vernacular (c. 1987) contains an expression for this: no gain without pain. The other cause of inefficiency is the learning process the receivers have to go through before they know as much about the problem as the givers. We cannot simply pick up a stack of documents outlining the master scheme for handling data, resolving problems of asynchronism, dividing functions into a set of computational tasks, and so on and instantly start designing. On very large projects, the cost of all this is small relative to the risk. On more typical projects, the cost can be sufficiently high to reduce the practicality of horizontal organizational divisions to the barest minimum number. However, on even the smallest jobs, the people responsible for the requirements model should be different from those who build the software to satisfy the model. This is more from the point of quality than control: Requirements analysts are specialists in understanding the needs of users—human users, instrumentation systems, or whatever the company's business entails—while designers and coders are specialists in the effective use of computational resources.

Independent Test Teams

Test teams composed of personnel other than those who generated the code under test may be viewed as another horizontal level of organization. However, the transition from code generation (possibly via local unit test) to integration testing involves the start of system composition, with a concomitantly different point of view. Hence, we view a separate test group as a *vertically* distinct organization. This despite the fact that in small programming groups independent test organizations are no more common than uncommon. For small projects—say, those involving fewer than 20 programmers—a compromise plan has integration performed by the programming group, but tests of the completed system performed by a separate organization. "System testing," as it is often called, emphasizes evaluation of system behavior under simulated operational conditions, with no regard to exercising internal interfaces or other structural specifics of the system.

The use of organizationally independent testers is often thought, correctly, to be a technique for reducing the risk of delivering software of poor quality. However, it has further merit for project control. More than the programming group, test groups represent the attitude of the potential users of the software. Handing the system—or in the case of integration testing, its parts—to another organization is tantamount to bridging the gap from chiefly technical concerns to those of the marketplace or the user community. We sometimes see this in project plans in which all testing from integration on is considered in the light of validation. As anyone who has jumped across a brook knows, before bridging a gap we want to be certain that the departure point is well established. Independent test organizations can be counted on to protest if the material given them is not ready for test or is in a condition likely to compromise the test schedules.

We discussed configuration management earlier in this chapter. The importance to project control of maintaining the integrity of baselines needs no further emphasis, but let us consider how we can be certain that configuration management is given the attention appropriate to it. The answer is the same as that to similar management concerns: Appoint someone to give the matter full-time attention. That is, rather than have a configuration management board of all equals (with regard to interest in the subject), let the board be organized by a *configuration manager*. A large project may require its own full-time configuration manager. Several small or medium sized projects may share a configuration manager. To ensure independence, the configuration manager may report to the project management directorate, to a product assurance directorate, or to some office other than that of software development. As long as we have an independent configuration manager, we might as well provide staff: library control personnel and any clerks involved in the distribution of releases. If there is a strong feeling that library control people outside the technical directorate may be a bureaucratic impediment, then provide the configuration manager with people to perform library control audits. If at least this much is not done, then let the configuration manager make certain that quality engineers perform such audits—which, of course, brings us to an independent quality assurance organization.

Quality Assurance

In Chapter 9 we explore the merits of quality assurance as a discipline, much like configuration management. Here, we note that if the discipline is vested in a vertically segregated organization, the members of that organization will have the opportunity to raise to ever higher levels of management any problems that cannot be solved at the working level. Given a workforce that cares about getting the job done and getting it done correctly, most problems will be solved on the spot without the need to involve higher authority. Still, the members of the separate quality assurance department function like the cop on the beat, maintaining order as it were. Conventional wisdom among quality control people is that independent management of a quality program makes certain that "the foxes aren't let in with the chickens." This maxim may overstate the case for software quality (or for that matter for any design assurance program), but it has some relevance. Perhaps it is more fitting to say that an independent software quality assurance organization keeps the cocks away from the hens.

7.4 HELP FROM OUTSIDE

The ultimate in a vertical division of labor occurs when outside organizations are used in the interest of project control. Now no program manager will admit to needing help from without, and the role of outsiders in project control is considered a byproduct of other services they perform. Nevertheless, the most telling result of the involvement of outsiders has to do with project control. We look at two such groups, independent verification and validation teams (IV&V) and the users or customers.

As we know it in the software world, IV&V exists nowhere else. Something like it is involved in the design of nuclear power stations, but IV&V is ours alone. Also, for the most part, IV&V is an invention of the U.S. military, conceived at a time when it was beseiged by programming disasters. Moving away from the point a bit, we may wonder why the government has singled out software for so much attention. When government project managers are asked why, to the exclusion of other nonnuclear development, IV&V was invented for software (along with standards and specifications to direct the way contractors should go about software development), they remark about the much lengthier time over which other design disciplines evolved. Software, their reasoning continues, never had a chance to slowly develop doctrinal engineering methods. Once computers began to find their way into weapons systems, the size of software projects exploded to keep apace of the rapid growth in computer hardware technology. The reach of software, however, exceeded the grasp of its inchoate management methods. A series of financial, schedule, and performance calamities drove the military to impose external project control mechanisms.

So far I haven't defined IV&V. Let us start with V&V. The *V* that stands for verification can long-windedly be defined:

"Verification: Procedures that attempt to determine that the product of each phase of the development process is an implementation of a previous phase; that is, that it satisfies it."[3]

Now to define the other *V*:

"Validation: Procedures that attempt to determine that the product of each phase of the development process will lead to satisfaction of the most abstract requirements set ..."[3]

Frequently, the meaning of validation is restricted to comparison of the software system that results from development with the requirements model for the system. Boehm puts the definition of V&V more succinctly:

"Verification is doing the job right and validation is doing the right job."[4]

Connections between verification and task control, and between validation and testing are obvious.

Now for IV&V. On a number of large projects the government has hired contractors, unrelated to the contractors responsible for developing "mission-critical" software, to perform certain of the phase exit evaluations. For example, poring over design documents, the IV&V contractors attempt to establish definite connections to predecessor documents (in this case perhaps a requirements specification). Looking at the process in reverse, the IV&V contractors try to trace all provisions of the requirements document to the design. To find substantive discrepancies, the IV&V contractors need to become intimately familiar with both sets of documents; no small matter, achieved only at a costly level of competence. Assuming that the IV&V contractor has been able to engage staff with the ability to do all this, the development contractor can use the IV&V's findings as a check on the effectiveness of its own phase exit control evaluations. Never mind that the cost of IV&V is enormous—the government is footing the bill.

Note that I did not suggest that the IV&V findings *replace* the task control procedures of the development contractor. Given the arm's-length learning process inherent in IV&V, the results of the independent evaluations are rarely timely enough for effective task control. Nevertheless, an IV&V operation that finds a host of substantive problems that escaped the developer's own defect removal process rings a tocsin signalling that the process is not all it is cracked up to be.

A final word on IV&V: The same kind of arm's-length V&V activities performed by an independent contractor, when performed by a vertically separate organization within the development contractor's company, is also considered by many to be IV&V. But to equal the defect-removal effectiveness of well-organized reviews and internally designed tests, such IV&V, no less than when performed by an independent contractor, will be far costlier than a defect removal program developed along the lines proposed in this book. Repeating a recurring theme of the book, to profit from the task control afforded by independence, a software quality assurance organization can be formed to manage the software quality assurance program.

User Participation

Who is as interested as the project manager in getting a usable product on time? The user, of course. Project managers can capitalize on this interest: Letting the user become engaged in the definitive specification of the requirements model is one way. Letting the user participate in testing the product is another. In the former case, the sharp user will be certain to let management know if the specified behavior is incomplete or incorrect. In the latter case the user, never forgetting the end purpose of the software, will warn of technical goals that have been misunderstood or unfulfilled before the finality of acceptance testing (or its equivalent). Project control profits in either case.

The "user" has many faces: a member of a firm's own accounting department, a customer contracting for a software product or a system embedding software, one of many customers of proprietary software, and more. Engaging the user in the development process entails few logistical problems, except in the case of multiple users, such as those who buy off-the-shelf software. In the case of multiple users, we can select a representative set of users with whom a mutually respectful working relationship has previously been established. Precedence for this practice is well established. For years, publicly offered software has been "beta tested" by selected customers before becoming generally available.

Chapter 6 dealt at some length with rapid prototyping, the most direct way to get users involved in the requirements process. If project plans do not call for rapid prototyping, an oral presentation of the requirements model—one that points out each behavioral aspect in detail—can be substituted, although to less effect. In fact, this type of presentation is required by military customers as a Systems Requirements Review (SRR). The point is that user involvement should not be viewed solely as a hurdle to be jumped before payment is made. The user can be used.

7.5 SUMMARY

1. A consequence of losing management control of projects is poor product quality.

2. A key to project control is task control, which depends on the certification of reported status and progress.

3. Tasks of the work breakdown structure are not certified as complete until they have satisfied local process standards.

4. Certification of iterated task completions is as important as the first time the tasks are undertaken.

5. To maintain project control, baselines, the collection of task outputs that define software at all stages of its life, may be changed only with proper authorization.

6. The control of baselines is vested in the discipline of configuration management.

7. Tasks on the critical schedule path normally get the most managerial attention, but the composition of the critical path changes with time.

8. Certain status and progress reports lend themselves to analysis for possible symptoms of potential trouble.

9. The cumulative effect of a slow staff increase rate is insidious, but can be diagnosed early enough for remedial action.

10. General technical problems may underlie a slow rate of resolving specified functions in design.

11. Several leading indicators can be applied to testing for the early determination of the adequacy of test planning and code quality.

12. Analysis of the updates of estimates of computer resource (e.g., memory) consumption can reveal overoptimistic technical assessments of feasibility.

13. The way a project team is organized bears on control methods. There are two kinds of organizational segregation of functions: horizontal and vertical.

14. Horizontally segregated organization uses the hand-off of task results between work phases for built-in task control.

15. Vertical segregation separates test teams from other development functions, as well as from configuration management and quality assurance.

16. Although costly, independent verification and validation teams can be used to measure the effectiveness of task control mechanisms.

17. Although their primary role in development is unrelated to task control, potential users of software products can play a silent role in task control.

7.6 REFERENCES

[1] E. Bersoff, "Elements of Software Configuration Management," *IEEE Trans. Software Eng.*, Vol. SE-10 (January 1984) pp.79–87.

[2] F. Brooks, Jr., *The Mythical Man-Month* (Reading, Mass.: Addison-Wesley, 1978) p. 25.

[3] R. Dunn, *Software Defect Removal* (New York: McGraw-Hill, 1984) p. 59.

[4] B. Boehm, *Software Engineering Economics* (Englewood Cliffs, N.J.:, Prentice-Hall, 1982) p. 728.

CHAPTER 8

Software Is Forever

Actually, it only seems that computer programs last forever. A usually reliable source advises that the software written by Lady Lovelace for Charles Babbage's differential engine was retired some time ago. The mortality of Ada's code notwithstanding, we are surrounded by software antiquities still performing useful work. Some of the oldest software still extant is found only when we probe into the structure of large systems, finding the kernel of the system much as it was when first placed into operation, but now engulfed by layers of applications added as the requirements of the system grew.

In other software archaeological digs, we find systems still being used much as they had been in earlier, gentler, times. A payroll system written in 1401 Autocoder is painlessly installed on a S/360 run in the 1401 emulator mode. A few years later, it runs under software emulation on a larger machine in a DOS environment. Later it is adapted to OS/MVT, thence to a virtual operating system, and on to new hardware and new operating systems ad nauseum. In a variant of long-lived systems, individual modules are one-by-one rewritten in more modern languages to make changes easier or files are restructured to live more amicably with modern file management systems. Nevertheless, at the level of programming-in-the-large, the system remains much as it was when first installed. At the level of programming-in-the-small, we see modules in which most of the code has been replaced in groups of a few lines at a time.

In the petrified forests of software, the analogy to the cell-by-cell mineral replacement of organic material is the statement-by-statement replacement of code. The form remains the same, but the functionality evolves into something quite different.

8.1 EVOLUTION

Keeping software useful is big business, $30 billion annually by one reckoning.[1] The longevity of software is also a serious quality matter. First, we want to make certain that software now in development is capable of the long life that a proper return on investment demands. Second, we are concerned that in altering existing programs we do not lessen the ability to make further alterations at a future time. By recognizing that software systems undergo change even before their initial release, we can combine the two quality issues into one by thinking of software as a continually evolving product. In this chapter we are concerned with the quality view of evolution once software has been made operational. As noted in Section 2.1, much of the capability of keeping software operational is established by its beginnings; in particular by the qualities of simplicity, modularity, and readability of code. Nevertheless, with the greater part of all programming activity expended on operational software, any capability for change that is built in during the formative period can eventually be destroyed.

The programming expended on operational software is commonly referred to as *software maintenance*. Occasionally, we see reference to "maintenance and modification," in which "maintenance" is used to describe changes that have no effect on the external behavior of the software, and "modification" used to describe changes that do. Section 2.1 spoke of the "maintainability" and "adaptability" of software. However, these terms were used in the context of describing the quality attributes of software, a somewhat different matter from describing programming activities. In any case, most programmers use the one word, maintenance, to refer to any change.

Although "maintenance" is used to cover several distinct kinds of change, we should not infer that the processes attending all change activities should be the same. To this end, we turn to the taxonomy of software maintenance devised in 1976 by E. B. Swanson, who divided maintenance into three classes:

- Corrective.
- Adaptive.
- Perfective.[2]

Corrective maintenance refers to any remedial programming initiated by operational failure to perform as expected. The most conspicuous corrective maintenance is, of course, the removal of latent bugs, but improving a user interface that too frequently results in operator error is also corrective. Adaptive maintenance covers programming actions required to permit the software system's operation in an environment different from the original one. Adaptive maintenance arises when operational environments themselves are altered, or when the use of the system is to be extended to operational environments beyond the ones initially planned. Typical environmental adaptations have to do with accommodating new or modified operating systems, hardware, or data bases. The third category, perfective maintenance, responds to changes in the behavioral specifications of the software. As the word "perfective" suggests, these include improvements suggested by users, but we extend the sense of perfective maintenance to include the addition of entirely new functions, the modification of others, and even the deletion of designated functions.

As prominent in quality quarters as corrective maintenance may be, it is not the principal consumer of the billions of dollars spent annually on maintenance—perfective maintenance is. Fairly recent research[3] estimates that perfective maintenance consumes 55% of all maintenance resources, most of it going to enhancements. (Corrective maintenance, at 20%, is not even second. Adaptation is the place horse at 25%.) As noted in the opening paragraphs of this chapter, useful software is hard to kill—one keeps extending its uses bit by bit.

We usually think of adaptative and perfective maintenance as activities applied to mature software; that is, software that routinely performs its tasks with little in the way of operational glitches. We certainly would like to restrict modifications to software that is not, at the same time, the subject of extensive debugging effort. Responding to changes in the external specifications while the internal specifications are undergoing change is a risky business. On the other hand, once software is operational, little time passes before users find new features they would like added or existing ones they need changed. Given that new software is likely to have bugs that escaped preoperational testing, how do we determine when it is safe to entertain adaptive and perfective maintenance? One way is to look at the rate at which bugs are found and removed. If problems are being reported at a greater rate than they are being solved, the software is in no state to be extended. Figures 8.1 and 8.2 illustrate, respectively, favorable and unfavorable conditions for undertaking maintenance actions other than corrective maintenance.

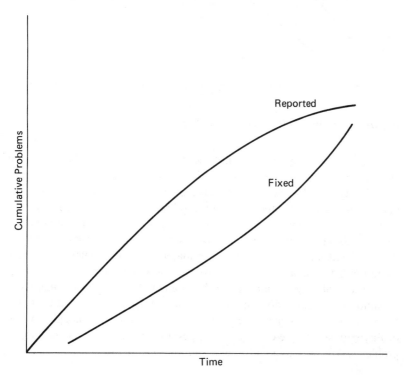

Figure 8.1 Stabilizing Software Release

Software stability applies not only to software when it is first made operational, but to each subsequent release incorporating changes to the operational specifications. Over the course of several releases, we might expect to see a problem reporting history like that of Figure 8.3. Plainly, after each release prudence demands the deferring of all

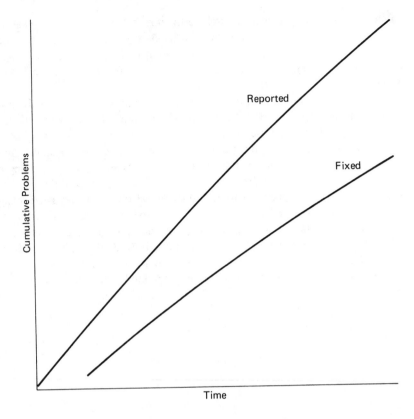

Figure 8.2 Software Release Remaining Unstable

maintenance but bug removal until the problem rate starts decreasing, but the stability criterion of Figure 8.1 should be considered also as an input to management planning.

In Figure 8.3 we see releases leaving successively fewer residual problems to greet a new release. This is symptomatic of a good process for software maintenance. The result of a poor maintenance process is seen in Figure 8.4, evidence that either configuration control is going awry, or the software structure is crumbling under the onslaught of ill-considered maintenance work. The majority of the problems may be minor, but the overall effect on quality gives the product a low reputation.

The goal of management is to build a maintenance process that yields not only the evolution of functionality, but also that of quality, as evidenced by Figure 8.3. Figure 8.4 is evidence of management failure. As it happens, enough notable instances of quality regression have occurred to suggest that maintenance can be subject to significant problems. We shall look at these and at their solutions.

8.2 MAINTENANCE PROBLEMS

Because many of the maintenance activities are congruent with those of development, it should come as no surprise that development problems are visited anew on maintenance. As discussed in Chapter 4, many of these problems are attacked with new technology.

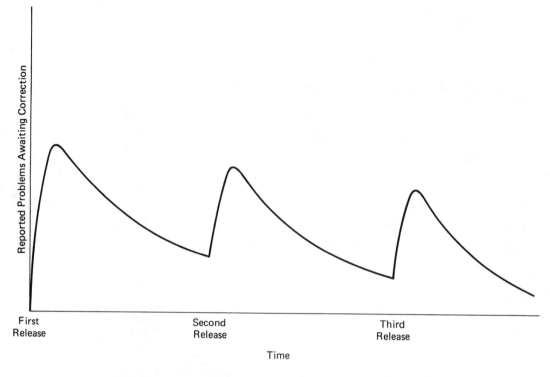

Figure 8.3 Software Gradually Improving with Time

Perhaps the most striking problem unique to current maintenance is that much of the software now in "the maintenance phase" bears the scars of outdated technology.

Back to the Roots

The greater part of software maintenance is expended on programs written at a time before structured programming became the rule, using older programming languages of little or no data typing capability, and using data manipulation techniques designed more for efficiency than understandability. (This statement, should not be construed as an indictment of the maintainability of the most common language of all, COBOL.) Enough has been written on the poor readability of unstructured programs that we shall not go into it here. Also, we have heard more than enough about the potential for damage wrought by the intricacies of "clever programming," a frequent concomitant of unstructured programming.

We hear less frequently about the problems created by data handling techniques devised at a time when memory and speed figured more prominently in programming constraints than they do now. A file handling routine written for data stored on magnetic tape may have unnecessarily complex search routines appropriate to sequential access but irrelevant to random disk access. The files may long ago have been converted to disk, but to the error-inducing perplexity of maintenance programmers, the complicated methods for retrieving data remain unchanged. Similarly, to save precious microseconds in inner loops, older programs may have used structures of several tiers of data pointers. These, too, have an inherent complexity that all too easily leads to programmer error. Most

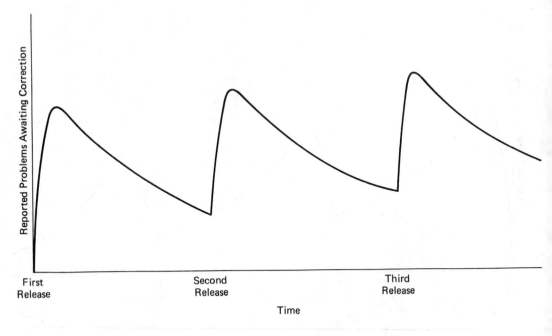

Figure 8.4 Software Deteriorating over Time

likely, faults accompanied the use of the pointers when the software was in development, and faults will accompany their use when the software is modified.

Truly old programs, those dating back before 1975 or so, present yet another impediment to change: documentation—more precisely, lack of documentation or documentation awkward to use. Few archaic software systems had documentation embedded within source files. Flow charts, the most common means of documenting control flow, were often drawn at a level of detail meaningful only to the programmer who drew the diagrams. (This is also true of programming aids that generate flow charts from source code.) Similarly, file layouts often referred to cryptic designations provided by the programmers, rather than using data labels found in the external specifications. If today's programmer is given the job of extending the salesperson's field by four characters, the programmer must first find out what the original programmers called salesperson and where the salesperson symbols were put.

Perhaps the most vexing problem encountered in aged software is that of patches. Patches are to maintenance programmers as jury-rigged electrical systems are to those who rehabilitate old buildings. What do the patches do? How do they relate to data labels in the source code? Is this a patch of a patch or of compiled code? Worse, when adding a new function, the maintenance programmer is bedeviled by fear that a patch somewhere will cause the changes in source code to generate failures in processes seemingly unrelated to the new function. Of course, recent code can also be patched. However, younger code can be expected to be less patchy than old code. Moreover, we have gotten smarter in recent years: If circumstances require us to coexist with the evils

146

of patching, we now know about such things as patch documentation and linking with controlled patch files.

More on Complexity

The concern for the complexity often found in old programs should not lead us to believe that new programs are immune to the problem. Section 2.1 touched on the effect of complexity on maintainability—one reason why complexity is the Darth Vader of quality programs directed to development. If complexity can attach to new programs, so can it attach to maintenance. Plainly, the addition of a single function increases the overall complexity, no matter how well the addition is made. Not so plain is the effect on complexity of corrective maintenance or modifications of existing functionality. Looking within individual models, we would expect the increase in complexity resulting from a change made to a given module to be contained in that module. The total increase in complexity should be no greater than the sum of any increases to complexity of the code within the altered modules. However, changes often affect complexity at the level of programming-in-the-large. From a study by Kafura and Reddy[4] using both code and structure complexity metrics, it appears that the complexity of both tends to increase with corrective maintenance, the very form of maintenance that we would least expect to affect complexity beyond the bounds of individual maintenance.

One of the structural complexity metrics used in the Kafura and Reddy study was that of Yau and Collofello,[5] a metric that defines the design stability of a module in terms of the potential ripple to other modules of a change in the subject module. The potential ripple effect, in turn, is a function of the number of assumptions of the module made by other modules. The concept of information hiding, wherein a module knows nothing of another module save its interface specification, reduces the extent to which complexity increases as a result of maintenance. Modern programming methods notwithstanding, experience dictates that we can expect to see software complexity increase from revision to revision. One measure of a maintenance quality program is the extent to which increases of complexity are contained.

From Simple Origins...

Complexity of a different kind further compounds maintenance. With time, many software systems give rise to a number of variants. The software for a telephone switch contains different modules for different customers, reflecting the features bought by each customer. Even different installations for the same operating company may have differing configurations. The same condition holds for accounting packages. The software driving an electronic countermeasures system is somewhat different for each aircraft type in which the system is installed. And, by definition, we have the variants of any software that result from adaptive maintenance to accommodate different operating systems.

In most of these cases, diversity evolves as the original program is adapted to new applications. The variants, created in response to marketing opportunities, may have been hoped for in the original product plan, but were unlikely to have influenced the original software design. In some cases, telephone switches for example, the capability to produce variants is demanded at project inception and is reflected in the software architecture. Regardless of how variants come to be, we need to know precisely what software is in a given installation in order to interpret problem reports or to issue new releases. The problem here is one of configuration control. We have not one product baseline, but a family of them. Software producers need to be able to account for the exact software configuration at each installation. Where configuration management fails to maintain the information, we have inefficient problem diagnosis and overly complex installation instructions for new releases. We may also see new editions of software going to the wrong users. Configuration management, always a quality concern, takes on a new face during the operational life of software.

If software development is encumbered by quality problems begging to be solved, software maintenance has more. But like the problems of development, solutions have been found.

8.3 MAINTENANCE SOLUTIONS

Chapter 1 introduced the theme that quality derives from people, technology, and management. So too, maintenance quality. In this section we deal only with those matters peculiar to maintenance. Nevertheless, to the extent that the age of software permits the use of new technology, the quality solution for development applies throughout the software life cycle.

People

For maintenance, little can be added to the substance of Chapter 3 other than one point, and the point cannot be made too emphatically. The policy of many firms is to leave maintenance to the same programmers responsible for development. For one reason or another, other companies prefer to separate maintenance activities from those of development.* Too often the people engaged full time in maintenance are less able than the development staff, evidence that management regards maintenance as inferior work. Although maintenance may not require specialists in conceiving software architectural strategies, evaluating languages, or translating design paradigms into a defined process, maintenance requires all the other skills of development programming. Perhaps more so, since modification is often more taxing than development. (Ask most programmers, and they will tell you that solving a problem from scratch takes less work than adapting an existing solution.) Creativity aside, good people are required for good maintenance. Since most programmers themselves prefer development to maintenance, management needs to sweeten the maintenance pot, perhaps by financial reward.

Management

Except for conceptual work in developing a system architecture, programming maintenance encompasses the same kind of technical tasks required for development. Programmers design, code, test, debug, and document (or revise documentation). Accordingly, the same process that governed these steps during development can be applied to maintenance. To prevent loss of management control of maintenance projects, tasks need

---

* Sometimes, freeing development programmers from maintenance tasks is the only way management can find staff able to undertake new development projects.

definition, and checks need to be established to ensure that tasks are completed to standards.

The same kind of reviews and test preparation required for development are required also for maintenance.

Another Turn of the Wheel. What is different about maintenance is the need to recognize just which development steps need to be replicated for each maintenance project. If, on examination, an exercise in corrective maintenance requires that a segment of code be revised to conform to a (correct) design, then only those development tasks from coding through testing need be repeated. On the other hand, if the correction requires rethinking some of the large scale design decisions, it may be necessary to replicate preliminary design and all the steps subsequent to it. Adding or modifying external behavior always requires that a maintenance project be started with the tasks associated with requirements analysis.

Maintenance tasks differ in one respect from their development archetypes: In revisiting development methods during maintenance, it is not sufficient to limit the scope of activity exclusively to the problem (or enhancement) at hand. Maintenance programmers are always conscious of side effects; of producing unexpected changes elsewhere in the output domain. For example, a change confined to the design of a single procedure may unwittingly alter the results produced by other modules. Older programs using global data areas are notoriously vulnerable to side effects. The programmer, unaware of all the uses of common data, discovers that changing one common variable will correct the behavior of the faulty module, only to create problems in other modules.

Actually, concern for side effects exists also with respect to changes made during development. However, we hear less about the problem during the initial set of development stages, because at that time no operational software yet exists to be affected by the failure to detect an inadvertent side effect.

Configuration Management. With no help from technology other than the use of straightforward tools, management can directly solve the problems introduced by variant releases. During the operational life of software, configuration management procedures are most conspicuous in controlling the initiation of changes and in maintaining the integrity of configuration records. Requests for changes to the external specifications of the software system are reviewed by a change board before any controlled documentation or code files are permitted to be altered. Programmers may contemplate the effects of the requested change, but until the change is authorized, the hands of the programmers are figuratively tied behind their backs to keep them away from keyboards. If the change board authorizes a change, the board should also make certain that the proper place in the development process is reentered, as discussed above. In some firms the board itself is capable of making the decision, reducing the lead time before a modification can be undertaken.

If management takes the doctrinaire position that no change, even an emergency fix, may be undertaken without the authorization of a change board, configuration management will be as much a bureaucratic problem as a solution. When a valued customer reports that the freshly updated system repeatedly bombs out, common sense demands that a short cut be found to regain the customer's confidence. Investigation of the report presents no problem (there is no harm in looking), but this begs the issue of a management policy on implementing emergency fixes. One valid approach is to insist that configuration management procedures accompany the distribution of fixes, thus ensuring the capture of change information for updating configuration records. Perhaps more common is the requirement that all problems be reported on special forms (often called *Problem Reports* or *Program Trouble Reports*) copied, or even directed, to the configuration change board. The board can then follow every step of the process of resolving a problem.

Such reports—we shall abbreviate them as *PTRs*—contain administrative information (location reporting the problem, name of reporter, and so forth), the exact identification of the affected software release, a description of the operational circumstances under which the problem arises (e.g., whenever the master and transaction files are merged directly after the transaction file is queried), and, of course, a description of the symptom. Other information may be also be appropriate. Examples are the version of the operating system under which the faulty program is run, or the exact identification of peripheral hardware associated with the problem.

The configuration management system is generally charged with maintaining records of installed software configurations during the operational life of software. This requires nothing beyond bookkeeping so routine we should be able to ignore it, which is the very problem: Sometimes the bookkeeping *is* ignored. No matter how fruitfully variants have proliferated, record keeping is simple enough, given the appropriate data base tools. We simply have to do it.

Technology

The earlier example of inadvertent side effects is one attacked by the concept of information hiding. Other contemporary technical practices are directed as much to improving the maintainability of software as to its initial development. We saw much of this in Chapter 4. During the operational period of software—except for restructuring, which we will come to shortly—we have no special technology except for the care that should be taken to confine change to cleanly defined program domains. Such care not only addresses the problem of side effects, it also adds assurance that changes are fully implemented.

Most of what has been written on the maintenance of operational code has been concerned with processing logic. Faulty control logic is, perhaps, the most common instigator of corrective maintenance. Recall however, that corrective maintenance accounts for much less change than adaptive or perfective maintenance. As it happens, we rarely add an enhancement without altering any data specifications. A study of the differences—all of which were enhancements—between two versions of Unix found that data declarations were more frequently changed than any other type of statement. 18.4% of the data declarations were modified, compared with 11.4% for the closest competitor (if statements).[6] We care about this because altered data are prolific producers of side effects. Design taken primarily from the view of data abstraction is likely to produce fewer interlocking data structures than design that emphasizes logic abstraction. In any case, during maintenance, when so often the easiest route to enhancing behavior is to modify an existing data structure, technology favors adding, rather than modifying, data structures whenever possible. In practical terms, this boils down to altering as little data as possible at the expense of adding new data structures.

Let us take an example. Consider a Fortran subroutine using a COMMON two-dimensional array, whose columns represent attributes (color, specific gravity, and so forth) of chemical compounds, a different compound for each row. To add a new feature to the program, we require a new attribute, taste. We could extend the array in the subject subroutine, but we would then have to modify the COMMON statement throughout the program, raising the potential of side effects elsewhere. It would be much better to declare a local vector just to handle the taste attribute, and add logic as necessary to deal with the now fragmented set of attributes. Annotation of the new logic should make certain that readability is not overly degraded.

The principle of minimum tampering with data structures extends to external data, such as system files. These, too, are part of the software structure we want to preserve. Going one step further, and recalling inadvertent side effects as a recurring maintenance problem, we need to consider another aspect of software structure: unit interfaces. To the extent practical, these should be altered as little as possible. Ideally, we want to confine a change completely to a single module, with no change to its global data declarations or dummy parameters.

Reviews of maintenance actions should raise the issues of change containment, except for the rare cases where proposed changes are already encapsulated. Another quality action that can be taken is a study of the effect on the rest of the system of each alteration of public data or interface declarations. Wherever the change is found to have rippled to another part of the structure, the effect on that part should then be analyzed.

Restructuring. It is all very well to talk about containing changes and analyzing ripples, but what does that do for software so ill-structured that a change to any statement selected at random threatens to bring down the entire software edifice? This is the condition, perhaps overstated, of much of the older software that accounts for the greater part of maintenance programming. Without regard to the extent such programs were structured in their natal state, the venerability of some of these systems implies that they have weathered countless earlier maintenance actions, most of which eroded their structure.

What one can do about these programs is restructure them. To suggest restructuring at the level of programming-in-the-large is tantamount to suggesting the programs be redesigned, which, of course, implies subsequent recoding—in short, surrendering. Within each module, however, restructuring is not entirely impossible. For COBOL, the most common of all languages spoken by elderly programs, at least one tool has come to my attention for automatically refashioning code to conform to the precepts of structured logic flow. The Recoder[7] system parses COBOL programs and iteratively transforms the result into a program graph. In successive passes (as many as 32,000), the initially complex graph is recursively transformed into a program graph representative of structured code, from which new COBOL code is generated. The system runs slowly on IBM mainframes, but when the job is complete the program has a new start on life. In fact, considering the nonstructuredness with which old COBOL code had likely started its first life, we can say that the result of the restructuring is a software product made better than new.

Maintaining The Support Environment. The same screen editors, static analyzers, compilers, and other elements of the software environment (see Section 4.3) used for development are required for maintenance programming. We are especially concerned with two project-peculiar elements of the environment that may not themselves be maintained: the system configuration data base and test support tools and data. The former may easily be "locked up" at the conclusion of the initial development work, to serve as a permanent record of the product. This is particularly likely if master configuration records are maintained by personnel primarily occupied with hardware records. While there is nothing wrong, and quite a bit right, in having such records secured, we should recognize that a copy of the data base should be available to the maintenance programmers for modifications that span a number of modules.

With regard to testing, after a set of changes has been made we want to perform regression testing to detect latent side effects. Most of the test cases used for the last release still apply and can be used for regression testing. The ones that do not apply will be replaced by the tests designed to address the modified feature, or (in the case of corrective maintenance) the tests redesigned as a result of discovering that a bug had reached the users. The updated set of test cases is then saved for use in regression testing the next time around. Similarly, data reduction software to help interpret the results of testing should not be discarded after development, but should be updated as necessary and saved. If anything is reusable in old software, test cases are.

Keep the Measurements Coming. Although not quite a solution to maintenance problems, measurements of software during its operational life provide some means of determining its future maintainability. Whatever structural measurements were made when the software was intially placed in operation should continue to be made after each subsequent release. See Section 2.3 on structural measurements. In particular, despite the precautions taken to avoid adding undue complexity to the software, we want to make certain the structure has not reached the point of decrepitude where further attempts to maintain it are ill advised. In Figure 8.4 we saw one effect of increased complexity, a slow but steady increase in the number of problems found in new releases. This, too, is a measure of a system ripe for restructuring or, if that is not possible, complete redevelopment. Yet another measure of the same effect is the cost of maintenance. If the cost continues to climb for equivalent feature additions, maintenance may be abandoned on financial grounds.

Measurements of the system resources used by the software should also be continued. Taking memory as an example, if we learn that precious little of it remains for further expansion, we have also learned that the time has come to start planning for hardware modifications (more appropriate to software installed in dedicated machines than to MIS software) or for a study to determine the efficiencies that might result from a complete redevelopment. A primary goal of maintenance quality programs is the extension of the useful life of the product, but if code death is inevitable, the earlier we can make funeral arrangements the better off we shall be.

8.4 REQUALIFICATION

No one interested in software quality would think of releasing a new software system without qualifying it. Whatever methods are used to qualify new software should be applicable to subsequent releases. Let us look at the possible substance of a new release:

1. A set of fixes to minor problems deferred until enough fixes have been collected to warrant the expense of a new release.

2. One or more new or modified features.

3. An adaptation to a new operational environment.

4.   Any combination of the above three possibilities.

5.   An emergency fix distributed to all users, often released as a patch.

Except for the last, requalification implies all the formality associated with qualification: controlled test material, independent evaluators, and beta testing where appropriate. We do not encounter a proper discussion of qualification until the next chapter, but
we can make the point here that if qualification is designed to keep erratic or unusable
software out of the innocent hands of users, requalification is equally required. For the
first of the five categories of new releases, requalification has sometimes been ignored in
the belief that software qualification addresses software suitability, not latent bugs. Not
so, and to do our best at uncovering problems we need to evaluate performance in as
close a verisimilitude of the operational environment as possible.

With regard to emergency fixes, the very word *emergency* suggests that a lengthy
requalification exercise is inappropriate. However, for fixes distributed to multiple users,
the software producer committed to quality will want to follow up closely the experiences
of a few users after the fix is installed, perhaps even have his or her own programmers
install one or two fixes and stick around to see the results. Of course, except for software
embedded in instrumentation systems, I have never actually seen this happen, but we
can always hope.

8.5 SUMMARY

1.   Software systems commonly continue to evolve from their original form to handle
      new or modified features, minor improvements of operation, and new operational
      environments. Software systems also change as latent defects are removed.

2.   Improvements other than bug removal and changes to the behavioral specifications
      of software account for over half of all software maintenance. Such maintenance
      should not be attempted until stability, with respect to defect removal, is attained.

3.   Software maintenance should be directed to the evolution of quality as well as utility.

4.   Alterations of programs developed under older technological regimens confronts
      software maintenance with a major problem. These programs are more difficult
      to maintain and do not easily allow an infusion of new technology to the change
      process.

5.   Poor documentation is a frequent concomitant of old software.

6.   Maintenance programmers struggle to avoid adding untoward complexity to software.
      In time, a system may grow too complex to make further change practical.

7.   In time, many software systems develop tree structures of variants, representing
      either adaptations to diverse environments or offerings of selectable features. This
      presents problems in configuration management.

8.   Although firms often give maintenance work to their less experienced or less capable
      programmers, maintenance programming is no less demanding than development.

9.   For modifications structurally equivalent in scope to defined steps of the development
      process, changes should be made by retracing those steps.

10. Avoidance of unintended side effects is a key precept when altering operational software. Solutions to the generation of side effects include minimum alteration of system data and an attempt to encapsulate individual changes within single modules.

11. A configuration management system must be capable of controlling all new releases of software. To prevent "backdoor" releases, a change board can ensure cognizance of all change actions by screening all problem reports.

12. Although not easily accomplished, complete restructuring of software simplifies the maintenance of overly complex systems.

13. Maintenance requires the availability of the same software development environment used prior to the first release.

14. Maintaining a current set of regression test cases enhances the quality of software maintenance. The first such set is the one used for the initial release.

15. With each release software structural characteristics and the consumption of system resources should be remeasured.

16. Except for emergency fixes, software should be requalified prior to being rereleased.

8.6 REFERENCES

[1] G. Parikh, "Exploring the World of Software Maintenance," *ACM Sigsoft*, Vol. 11 (April 1986) pp. 49–52.

[2] E. B. Swanson, "The Dimensions of Maintenance," *Proc. Second Int'l. Conference on Software Eng.*, IEEE (1976) pp. 492–97.

[3] C. B. Ramamoorthy et al., "Software Engineering: Problems and Perspectives," *Computer* (October 1984) pp. 191–209.

[4] D. Kafura and G. Reddy, "The Use of Software Complexity Metrics in Software Engineering," *IEEE Trans. Software Eng.*, Vol. SE-13 (March 1987) pp. 335–343.

[5] S. Yau and J. Collofello, "Design Stability Measures for Software Maintenance," *IEEE Trans. Software Eng.*, Vol. SE-11 (September 1985) pp. 849–856.

[6] D. Gustafson et al., "An Analysis of Software Changes During Maintenance and Enhancement," *Proc. Conference on Software Maintenance—1985*, IEEE (1985) pp. 92–95.

[7] E. Bush, "The Automatic Restructuring of COBOL," *Proc. Conference on Software Maintenance—1985*, IEEE (1985) pp. 35–41.

CHAPTER 9

Software Quality Assurance

Section 1.4 defined software quality assurance (SQA) as the management of software quality programs. The section noted that despite the sound of things, SQA assures not the quality of software, but the effectiveness of the quality program. From a management prospect, the essence of a software quality program is found in the conscious consideration given to the effect on quality of technology, management practices, and project staffing. Without a framework within which such considerations are given substance, a quality program is illusory.

With tongue in cheek, we are tempted to say that in the real world we need a conscience to keep conscious the consideration of quality—but the framework for a software quality program has more to do with bookkeeping, accounting, and technical analysis than with the inspection associated with traditional quality control. In theory we know that these quality activities do not have to be performed by people other than technical staff, as Sections 1.4 and 7.3 pointed out. Still, it makes good sense to entrust the management of a software quality program to a software quality organization. Doing so has become so common today that this chapter discusses software quality assurance activities in the context of independent software quality assurance organizations. Although we start by looking at the SQA organization itself, we should not lose sight of what SQA really is: the set of activities that give substance to a software quality program.

9.1 SOFTWARE QUALITY ASSURANCE ORGANIZATIONS

As we saw in Section 7.3, an important purpose for having SQA organizations is the independence they lend to the monitoring of technical activities and the assessment of

155

software products. Independence provides the basis for both objective evaluation and management constraint. But we have independence and then we have independence. An SQA organization reporting to the software project leader is less independent of the project leader's internal imperatives than an organization reporting to the project leader's boss—say, the technical director. Of course, the SQA organization reporting to the technical director has less independence from the director's immediate objectives than an organization reporting to the president.*

> *With regard to acting as the "cop on the beat," the effectiveness of software quality assurance increases with the management distance of the SQA organization from the pertinent development or maintenance personnel. With regard to all other SQA tasks, management separation is of minor importance.*

I have heard heated arguments about whether SQA organizations within the technical directorate can be effective. The arguments seldom seem to take cognizance of the existence of other management tools for providing independent constraints on deviations from project plans or standard methods. If other methods have proved effective to prevent circumvention of the prescribed development or maintenance process, it makes little difference where one places SQA in the management hierarchy.

In whatever harbor an SQA organization is berthed, we need also to look inside it. We turn first to its members.

Software Quality Engineers

Few professionals staffing an SQA organization have received any formal training in software quality assurance, although courses are now being offered at two colleges that have come to my attention. Most of the professional staff have backgrounds in either programming or quality assurance. However they arrived on the SQA scene, the effective software quality engineers have a knowledge of current software engineering practices. A prerequisite for formal cross-training of quality professionals is the ability to program computers, which in some cases means that cross-training has to start with training in programming. This is followed by training in software engineering. Training in software quality assurance comes last, most of it on the job.

The SQA novitiate entering from the secular software world requires considerably less training. Primarily, training should consist of memorizing the mantra, "Quality management is risk management," learning some statistical techniques, and reading the local software quality assurance standards. The rest is on-the-job training.

The National Security Industrial Association (NSIA) conducted a survey in 1983 to determine the constituency of SQA organizations. As reported by Ken Mendis, then Chairman of the Software Subcommittee of NSIA's Quality and Reliability Assurance Committee, the typical software quality engineer has one to five years of software engineering experience, and the typical head of an SQA organization has over five years of software experience.[1]

Since few SQA organizations were more than a decade old at the time the survey was taken, we can see that industry has found it more practical to cross-train software

---

*If software is but a constituent of the company's goods or services, an example more likely than president is the director of quality assurance or an equivalent position.

157
Section 9.1:
Software
Quality
Assurance
Organizations

professionals than people from the quality community. Plainly, it is less costly to train software professionals than quality professionals for the performance of software quality engineering tasks. However, few software professionals grind out their daily programming lives in anticipation of the tap on the door that means they have been nominated to join the SQA organization.

Section 3.2 addressed strategies for inducing members of the software community to try their hands at SQA. However, let us recognize the dim likelihood that the SQA manager will attempt the seduction. Software quality assurance will fail if the SQA manager and the programming manager do not have a good relationship. Such a relationship is unlikely if the latter perceives the SQA manager as skulking about the programming offices, trying to steal away promising programmers. Programmers are going to be invited by their current supervisors to explore transfer to the SQA organization. The way it works is this: The SQA manager tells his colleague in the technical directorate that he is shorthanded and would like to cross-train someone from the technical department. Does the programming manager have anyone who could be transferred?

Unfortunately, programming managers nearly always have someone who can be transferred—the person who has done nothing useful for the last six months, the malcontent, or the programmer who produces the most troublesome software. The proper question is "Can anyone be spared to whom you would feel comfortable entrusting the management of the quality program?" The point is that the programming manager has as much to gain from constructive software quality engineers as the SQA manager, and both their interests are served by getting the right people on the job.

Another approach to engaging staff is that of rotating people between the technical and SQA departments. Programmers serve a tour of duty of six months to a year as quality engineers, and then return to their technical tasks. The advantages to the SQA manager are several: minimum training of new people, a larger labor pool to absorb staff fluctuations, and the eventual ability to deal with a technical staff comprised of quality proselytes. Technical management also gains by reduced risk of having to cope with quality engineers of inadequate technical competence or insensitivity to the nuances of development. Once again, the practice of rotation must not be used by technical management to "dump" its least valuable people. Transferees must be given to understand that their temporary assignment is a genuine opportunity to expand their software engineering horizons, not a career derailment to limbo.

Rotation is not without problems. Technical staff on temporary assignment are likely to remain mindful that their technical management will have the most to say about their future earnings and promotions. In the event of contention between technical and quality people, the transferee may be less inclined to stand ground than would a permanent member of the quality staff. Effective rotation requires that transferees be convinced of the corporate citizenship of their managers before the temporary transfers take place; moreover, that the ratings provided by quality managers for the periods of rotation govern merit increases for those periods.

SQA Documentation

Even as we have called for documented standards to establish the software development and maintenance processes, so must we have documentation of the role played by the SQA organization. Whether we call such documentation SQA Standards, SQA Operating Instructions, SQA Procedures, or some other name, the responsibilities of the SQA organization need to be made explicit. Beyond the usefulness to the software quality engineers—especially new members of the staff—exact descriptions of SQA activities need to be available for reference by the technical staff. Programmers asked to supply defect data records, for example, should know the use to which the data will be put.

The constituents of the set of SQA standards will, of course, depend on the specific tasks assigned the SQA organization. A typical set of standards might cover

- Pro forma software quality plans.
- Each type of audit performed by the SQA staff.
- SQA responsibilities in activities controlled by other organizations. Examples are the SQA role in design reviews and change board tasks.
- The criteria for SQA approval of test plans, procedures, and reports.
- The criteria for SQA approval of software purchases, software releases, and other noncasual interfaces with the outside world.
- The tasks performed by software quality engineers in vendor surveys and surveillance, and in acceptance of purchased software.
- Defect data collection.
- Analyses of defect data.
- Failure prediction methods.
- Criteria for determining which software elements require closest SQA attention.
- "Feedback" reports to technical management.
- Reports made to senior management.
- Qualification or other testing for which SQA is responsible.
- SQA solicitation of user feedback and SQA tasks on receipt of user complaints.
- Retention and control of quality records.

As applicable, each standard should note how and when tasks are performed. "When" may be a matter of frequency, but in most cases it relates to specific events. For example, vendor surveys should be completed x weeks prior to award of contract.

In addition to the standards prepared by the SQA organization for its own purposes, a more senior standard—call it a policy document if you like—needs to be published by that level of management common to both technical staff and software quality engineers. Depending on where the SQA organization is placed, such management most often means the technical director or the vice president of operations or the president. The policy document is needed to spell out the authorities of the SQA organization. It at once restrains the SQA Organization from excessive zeal and sanctions specific involvement of software quality engineers in the software development and maintenance processes.

From Precincts to Empires

A favorite topic of conversation among SQA managers is the "ratio," meaning the ratio of software quality engineers to technical staff. Ratios generally run from 1:20 to 1:10. The range results from the diversity of roles assigned SQA organizations. An SQA organization responsible for configuration management and complete authority for all system level testing, including test design and operation, requires far more people than an organizations charged only with analyzing defect data. SQA organizations that have to contend with overseers from government agencies have a further overhead burden not necessarily directly related to the quality of products.

The true cost of software quality is not the cost of the SQA staff, but the cost of performing quality-related work, whether performed by quality engineers, programmers, or members of other groups.* The size of the SQA organization depends not only on the size of the technical organization, but on the quality responsibilities apportioned SQA. Determination of the SQA role should be made in the light of such intangibles as corporate culture and the maturity of the programming process, as well as more obvious influences: government contract requirements, testing philosophy, and the record of customer satisfaction.

In the sections that follow, we see the SQA organization assigned those tasks specific to the software quality program (as distinct from the technical aspects of defect removal). Repeating an earlier statement, a separate SQA organization is not necessary for these jobs to be done, it just makes things easier.

9.2 THE PEACEKEEPER

In the role of ensuring that process standards and project plans are properly followed, the software quality engineer has earned the sobriquet of "the cop on the beat." Because this might raise the image of nightsticks and parking summonses, I prefer the more constructive sounding "keeper of the peace." In any case, both conscious and unwitting opportunities abound for project personnel to take destructive liberties with the well-laid plans for developing and maintaining software. The SQA peacekeeper maintains order in the presence of potential chaos.

Chapter 7 dealt at some length with techniques for project control, with considerable emphasis on certifying that tasks are completed in accordance with prevailing standards. Although such certification is often performed by first level supervision, the job is sufficiently time-consuming to intrude on other responsibilities of technical management: planning, coordinating with technical management of other elements of a large system, and technical direction. Thus, if left entirely to technical supervision, evidence of noncompliance with the prescribed project course is likely to be given short shrift. The natural emphasis of technical management is on getting on with things, making the decisions that will affect tomorrow's work. Yet certification of yesterday's work is an essential element of quality management. Enter the software quality engineer to audit selected reviews or walk-throughs, project documents, library control records, and tests. Typical of the discrepencies that are found are

- Requirements specification contains several nontestable functional requirements that actually lent themselves to quantification.
- Review never held, not completed, or not minuted.
- Test plan omits estimate of time required on mainframe computer for test execution or data analysis.
- Test case specification for system level tests completed too late for review prior to start of tests.

---

*To be complete, cost of quality must account also for certain training and tool acquisition.

- Module not entered into library control following unit test, as required by local process standards.

- Integration tests conducted with program loads inconsistent with test plan.

- Library control records show data base document not updated with other design documents.

- Test set up not consistent with test specification.

- Customer-requested change implemented without approval of change board.

- Vendor given verbal permission to make changes to external specifications without paper follow-up.

After discussion to confirm that the finding is a true discrepancy and not a misunderstanding, software quality engineers document their findings in memos or, more formally, discrepancy reports. These are directed to the people responsible for the discrepancy. If the problem is one that is frequently encountered, indicating a disquieting trend to deviate from the prescribed standards, the report is copied to appropriate management with the trend noted. Inevitably, from time to time, technical and quality people disagree on whether a discrepancy has been found. The programmer says that the warning reported by the compiler or the static analyzer is no problem, while the quality engineer says that it flags a violation of local coding standards. The programmer argues, "I am allowed to nest loops more than seven deep as long as they are not all of the same kind." The quality engineer says, "No, the standard is clear on that point: 'No more than seven iteration constructs may be nested.' " Adjudication of the point may have to be made by cognizant technical management, to whom the initial discrepancy report must then be directed.

More profound disagreements may also have to be adjudicated. The quality engineer may find that design documentation is not being baselined, but is kept in an informal and unauthorized local library by the project manager, who, citing expediency as the reason, is not disposed to follow the standard practice. This may require that the software quality manager get involved; may lead to a discussion between the quality manager and the project manager's boss. If the SQA organization is part of a larger quality directorate, the issue may ultimately reach the level of the technical and quality directors. We hope not. The objective, always, is to solve the problem on the spot. Nevertheless, the potential of escalation to ever-increasing levels of management helps to solve the problem at the working level.

The discrepancy report not only describes the problem, but states the (negotiated) date by which it should be rectified. More than the problem itself, the date for closing the problem is likely to stir up some controversy, especially if little latitude can be granted because of the problem's effect on other scheduled work. In any case, the problem and scheduled closing date get added to a composite log of "correction items," as they are often called. With the log maintained on a computer, it is a simple matter to generate a "tickler" report to check on items as their due date nears.

Following up on discrepancy reports is a small, if sometimes disputable, matter compared to follow up of technical problems uncovered by reviews, walk-throughs, static analyzers, and tests. The minutes of a review or walk-through document problems, assign someone to solve them, and assign a date for the solution. Daily test reports do the same. Follow up to make certain that corrective action was actually taken is less direct. The bookkeeping associated with this can be cumbersome, especially when purported solutions turn out to be faulty, or when the subtlety of a problem requires preliminary investigation before final assignment for the solution can be made. In assuming the responsibility for logging and tracking all such problems, SQA organizations make a strong contribution to the quality program.

No stretch of the imagination can make the role of peacekeeper an attractive one. However, in the next role described for the SQA organization, we find more rewards.

9.3 THE SURROGATE

Concerned above all else with the reliability, usability, maintainability, and adaptability of software, the software quality engineer has much in common with the ultimate users of the product. Unlike the users, the quality engineer is never more than minutes away from the developing product and has the opportunity to make certain that every effort is made to design and test the product to achieve the users' goals. Participating in review meetings or independently reviewing the artifacts of design, quality engineers can judge whether the attributes (see Section 2.1) of the four "ilities" are being built in. Direct participation in the defect removal process also affords the quality engineer the opportunity to make certain that the process is thorough.

The most conspicuous defect removal role played by software quality engineers is in testing. From the inception of a project, quality engineers discuss with their technical counterparts the test techniques and tools that are appropriate to the project. Although the test plan and the design of test cases for informal (or development) testing are generally produced by the programmers, these are reviewed in detail by the quality staff.* For test plans, special importance is attached to the availability of test resources in time to support the tests, and to the level of detail specified for test case descriptions and test reports. Using techniques to trace all functional requirements to the demonstration of their realization, quality engineers make certain that all such requirements are covered by the set of test cases. Although particular importance is given tests at the full system level, since it is at this level that user requirements are formally addressed, quality engineers also look for traceability in the functional testing of major system components. The more astute quality engineers also analyze the test cases to make certain they are feasible. They fear that some functions may evade testing when the tests directed to them must be abandoned with no time left to design new ones. I once saw a test designed for a real-time signal acquisition system that required the use of enormous amounts of random data. Correct operation was to be indicated by the cross-correlation (a mathematical averaging operation performed on two random processes) of the output with the input. The test would have been as conclusive as the design was clever. Unfortunately, the post-test data processing required to form the cross-correlation function would have taken several months on the most powerful computer available to the testers. As it happens, sufficient time remained to design a new test, less conclusive but doable.

If we view the quality department as the organization having the greatest proprietary detachment, we find it the obvious choice to prepare and conduct qualification testing of the product. Tests are designed not only to demonstrate narrow conformance of the

---

* Some companies give to a separate department the responsibility to plan and perform all tests, at least at the full system level, and—in a much narrower view of SQA than that given in this book—name that department "Software Quality Assurance." Essentially, such departments are the independent test groups noted in Section 7.3.

software to the formal requirements model, but, indirectly, to evaluate the model itself. Large volumes of data, data at extreme rates, invalid data of every imaginable violation of the specifications, are all used to supplement the nominal operational conditions. Determining the success of qualification tests frequently involves more than just checking off successes and failures. Judgment often needs to be exercised. For example, the new compiler compiles every source code file it is supposed to, and aborts compilation of every source code file in deliberate violation of the language specifications, but certain of the object code files are woefully inefficient compared to performance by the competition. Should something be done about optimization for the next release, or is the current product so bad it cannot be released without immediate improvement? Similarly, how many minor problems should be tolerated before deciding that the product is not yet qualified to be unleashed on innocent users? Judgment calls, all. It helps to have criteria for qualification established beforehand. Along the lines discussed in Section 2.3, a detailed guide to severity ratings, couched in terms specific to the product's use, is established before testing starts. Armed with a predetermined maximum acceptable number of problems for each severity class (or a weighted sum), the qualifiers are at least spared the final judgments.

Apart from qualification, SQA organizations are also the logical groups to perform, or at least manage, testing specifically directed to evaluating product usability. Sometimes called alpha testing, these test operations rely less on prepared test cases than on simulated user experience. A software house may have its own managers use the new spreadsheet for a month or two before releasing it. However, the management of a software house, more computer literate than the general marketplace, is less likely to be inconvenienced by minor documentation errors or cryptic menus than would the typical user. The SQA organization contracts with several management consultants to use the system over a period of time on real problems, periodically interviewing the tester/users to see if something needs to be fixed up before release. The SQA organization of a supplier of machine tool software might try out new releases by using them, along with in-house machine tools, to fabricate actual parts from drawings provided by cooperative software customers. In all such testing, the goal is the same: answering the question, "Is the product fit for use, and, if not, what must be done to make it fit?" As the surrogate of all the unwary users out there in Computersville, the SQA organization wants to be the first to know.

9.4 THE COLLECTOR

We have come across programming measurements in Chapters 2, 7, and 8, and we encounter them again in the next section of this chapter and in Chapter 10. We have not, however, discussed obtaining the data used for measurements. As it happens, gathering software data is often harder than reducing the data to measurements. The reasons for this are historical. The development of programming methods did not depend on measurements as did engineering and scientific disciplines. We needed hard data on the performance of various lubricants and bearing designs before we could design today's disk drives, but like the software process itself, we were able to use nothing beyond our cognitive powers to arrive at software decomposition strategies. Thus, the programming culture has no equivalent of engineering's omnipresent laboratory notebooks. With no clear motivation provided, programmers, asked to start recording data (other than test results), tend to do the minimum recording they can get away with. Moreover, without an interested party to act as custodian of the data, that which is collected is usually discarded (or stuffed in a box and sent to the warehouse archives) at the conclusion of a project.

Measurement, however, is a historical imperative of the quality community, and SQA organizations are keenly aware of the uses awaiting hard data. In particular, software quality engineers find great value in the data of least interest—or so it would seem—to programmers: data related to defects or failures. As noted at the beginning of this section, uses of data are discussed elsewhere. Our immediate interest is in collecting data. Defect and failure data come from three sources:

- Passive defect removal.
- Active defect removal and qualification testing.
- Alpha testing and failures or other anomalies experienced by users.

While the circumstances for collecting the data from each source are different, none defy the aggressive SQA organization.

Passive Defect Removal

Defect data from passive defect removal operations are found in

- Minutes of walk-throughs and reviews.
- Independent documentation reviews.
- Output from pseudolanguage processors.
- Output from source code static analyzers.

Even the SQA organization that has heretofore ignored data analysis likely maintains a log of defects from walk-throughs and reviews so that correction items can be tracked (see Section 9.1). For the purpose of further analysis (discussed in Section 9.5), it remains simply to categorize these in whatever fashion the analysis requires. For example, we may want to label each defect as either a substantive fault or one of form (such as inadequate code annotation). On the other hand, more ambitious analyses of code faults may require division into the classes of logic faults, data handling faults, interface faults, and so forth. Software quality engineers who are copied on the minutes of these reviews have only to negotiate with technical staff the details of how minutes are to be taken to have the data they need.

Similarly, we would categorize defects found in independent reviews of documentation and other artifacts of development. Since the independent reviewers are most likely the same software quality engineers who analyze the faults found, data collection is no more than recording their findings in the proper data base.

Static analysis systems for design representations and source code produce hard copy of all faults and potential faults. Improvising a scheme to collect copies of these reports and translating the output into the defect data base should present no problem. What does require some thought is the timing involved. Static analyzers are most useful when used by the authors of the work analyzed. Translating analyzer output to a defect data base the first time a programmer has used the analyzer on new code is analogous to recording, as evidence of poor spelling ability, a novelist's typographical errors before the author has had a chance to use the word processor's spelling checker. The defects worth recording are those found in design and source code statements that have reached the program library. These defects may have been inserted after the initial (possibly informal) release of the design or code file, or they may have escaped the notice of both the programmer and the people reviewing the work.

Active Defect Removal and Qualification Testing

Records of defects found in active test are the most elusive. Programmers are not wont to record bugs, especially during test periods in which bugs are found with any frequency. During formal tests—say, qualification testing—formal problem reports or trouble reports (see Section 8.3) contain all the information needed for analysis (or will if the reporting form also contains the information developed during diagnosis). Further, any test series for which test reports are prescribed as part of the standard test process at least alerts software quality engineers to look for the results of diagnoses for inclusion in a defect data base.

Informal testing, such as that conducted by programmers during unit test and the early, building, phase of integration, is another matter. We do not wish to burden testers with detailed reporting requirements. The job of the programmers is to get on with the business of fixing bugs and continuing test, and any involved reporting is bound to interfere with that work. However, we can reasonably require that programmers record the bare essentials of bugs, especially if the programmers are provided with simple tabulation forms—data base interfaces or paper—for these. If the date of bug capture is important, as for trend analysis, then we need to have the daily number of failures reported. If we care about knowing the number of defects created by each task, we can ask the programmers to include in their daily reports the number of diagnosed bugs that seem to be traceable to requirements analysis, preliminary design, detailed design, coding, data entry, support systems (test fixtures, library control), or whatever. If failure-prone modules (see Section 9.5) are of interest, we can ask that the daily report include the identification of each module in which bugs were found, or, more precisely, the number found in each.

Let us assume we want *all* of the above, and further want the programmers to make a judgment of bug severity; say, (1) abnormal termination or production of gibberish, (2) inaccurate but recognizable output, or (3) cosmetic. We then have four dimensions of reporting. These can be handled by two forms, each having a two-dimensional table to be filled in with a number. Let us assign Form A to the dimensions of severity and problem source (requirements analysis and so forth), and Form B to the dimensions of module identification and generic fault type (logic and so forth). The two forms can be correlated by common fields, say, date and project identification. Thus, we might learn that on April 27, among other defects, program unit XQ12Z40 turned up with a catastrophic logic bug traceable to its detailed design.

The last statement is not necessarily correct. Most of what we learned was not available until after the catastrophic failure was diagnosed. Since diagnosis cannot be guaranteed to be complete the day of a failure, the dates on the forms really represent the dates of diagnosis, not the dates of failure. This discrepancy should have little effect except for those attempting to fit failure data to a reliability growth model.

Whether in-house surrogates for the user community (alpha testers), selected users given restricted software releases (beta testers), or the general user community, a formal reporting mechanism is a necessity. This was noted in Section 8.3 and in the discussion of problems that develop during qualification testing. With regard to qualification testing, we saw that we require only the inclusion of diagnostic information on problem reports to capture defect data. The difference between qualification testing and the data sources now under consideration—alpha testing and user feedback—is only that reports from the latter two must include operational circumstances. Alpha testers and users cannot merely refer to a feature, but, if only to permit the problem to be diagnosed, have to describe the conditions under which the failure or anomaly was observed. The software quality engineer adding the problem to the defect data base should have enough information from the description to make a severity judgment. Since these problems are bottom line ones—defects in released or quasi-released products—it is important that the SQA organization make such judgments.

With the basis for a continuing supply of defect data, software quality engineers will devote a considerable part of their time to analyzing the data and evaluating the results of their analyses, generating measurements such as those of Chapters 2, 7, and this one. Apart from the processing of defect data, however, other analyses need also be performed for a complete system of software quality assurance.

9.5 THE ANALYST

At the most general level, software quality assurance covers all analyses except those directly related to system functionality or programmer productivity. Even productivity analyses tend to rely heavily on the work of software quality engineers, since quality and productivity are so intertwined. Of immediate interest, however, are the analyses that bear directly on the quality of delivered software systems.

The Analyst as Plotter

Section 7.2 discussed various trend analyses that could provide early clues to control problems. Staffing trends, functional design rates, test progress trends, and increases in the consumption of system resources were all seen to be symptoms of project health. With the possible exception of staffing analysis, we find that trend analysis is seldom attempted outside of SQA organizations. Making the point for the nth time, software quality assurance is the management of software quality programs, and quality management requires that obstacles to quality be noticed if they are not to be tripped on.

Once again relying on data base software, the quality engineer keeps inputting fresh data on staff currently engaged, discrete functions now resolved in design, tests attempted and tests passed, and estimates of required memory, computer operations per second, and so forth. With the data base now updated, the quality engineer calls for plots of cumulative data against time. Although we can apply statistical tests to these plots, the shape of the plots is usually sufficient to determine the presence of adverse trends. Armed with these plots, the quality engineer prepares periodic reports, perhaps weekly, fortnightly, or monthly, directing the readers' attention to any disquieting trends that need to be attended to.

Consider the tasks of keeping track of project events, gathering data, plugging data into a data base, drawing reports, distributing reports, and (if necessary) discreetly reminding those in charge that reaction to a report is overdue. In sum, these activities are similar to the job of the peacekeeper (Section 9.1). These tasks seem so easy we may wonder why software quality assurance had to be invented to perform them. There is no obvious answer, but perhaps the reason that trend (and other) analyses fall to SQA organizations is found in the detachment of software quality engineers from the daily technical decisions that occupy the rest of the project staff.

Failure Mode and Effects Analysis

Not a task commonly undertaken by software quality engineers, failure mode and effects analysis (FMEA) is standard practice among quality engineers concerned with the reliability of hardware. Nevertheless, the need occasionally arises to determine the effect of software failures on system behavior.

In an operating system serving many users, we want to be able to predict the possible ways in which the security kernel might fail and, given failure, its effect on users who are logged on, on on-line files, and on users attempting to log on. Taking a hardware analogy, in what ways can the decoupling components of a computer system's power supply fail, and what will be the effect on the system? Will error-detection circuitry catch the failure and gracefully shut down the system before damage occurs, or will files by the dozens be clobbered before the intervention by the console operator or by software? Such analyses, although time-consuming, are relatively straightforward for hardware. Consider a decoupling capacitor in the power supply. It can fail in one of two ways: It opens up or it shorts out. The decoupling circuit can be analyzed for both conditions, and the effect can be predicted. If the effect is intolerable, we can pay more for a vastly more reliable capacitor, or we can provide redundant capacitors.* By contrast, although they may be incorrect, individual software statements do not of themselves fail. For example, x := pi will always replace the value of x with pi. If a failure occurs it is because the value of pi has been clobbered by some other fault in the program, or because the statement should have been encoded x := twopi. (If we know that the latter is true, we would change pi to twopi, which would make FMEA moot.) In neither case will it help to pay more for the statement or encode it twice. Let us look at a statement that, with the omniscience reserved for those who hypothesize, we know to be faulty:

$$\text{if } (x > y) \text{ return}$$

The bug is the sense of the predicate. The procedure should be exited if y is greater than x. Now, knowing all we can know about the bug, we can predict what will happen if the statement is executed. It may even be practicable to relate the conditions under which the statement should be executed to the input domain of the program as seen in functional terms. The problem is that in the nonhypothetical world we do not know that the statement is faulty.

---

* Say, by putting two of double the capacitance in series, if the catastrophic failure mode is a short.

The components examined for software FMEA must be of a larger scale than individual statements. It may be impractical to analyze individual statements, but certain kinds of components can be analyzed *if we can succinctly abstract the behavior of the component.* As an example, let us take a queue. A bug in a queue (or, if you prefer, a queue manager) can cause it to fail in the following ways:

1. New input not added to queue.
2. Entries not delivered on request.
3. New input added, but not at end.
4. Delivered entry not the oldest.
5. Infinite looping or program halt.

The last is not considered further because the failure is not unique to the component under study. Let us place the queue in a communications multiplexer that combines several asynchronous queues to form a serial data stream of several sources. For each of the first four failure modes we can predict the behavior of the multiplexer. For the first, we lose data. For the second, we fail to deliver output data, or output data is delivered intermittently. In either case, recognition of a failure may be possible if the output rate of the multiplexer can be compared to the sum of the input rates. For the third and fourth failure modes, garbled data will be output with no easy method for recognizing in real time that a failure has occurred.

The benefit of the queue FMEA—assuming the effects of its potential failure are considered sufficiently serious—is that it tells us to add software to compare input data rates to output data rates and to add sequence coding to identify garbled data. Is this likely to happen? Not generally. Laboring under the assumption that software is not going to fail, we are loathe to further complicate it with possibly purposeless check logic. Examples do occur, however, as in the logic for password protection or for spacecraft control. Indeed, if majority logic computation, using different algorithms, can be considered for fault tolerant software, as it was for the space shuttle, we can also consider performing software FMEA and making use of the results. In any case, we are more likely to decide to undertake the FMEA of a component if we believe it to be prone to failure.

Failure-Prone Modules

Analysis can indeed reveal modules likely to fail. For the purpose of finding candidates for FMEA, such analysis is conducted late in the development period. However, failure-prone analysis starts much earlier, and for a different reason.

Early Forecasting. If, while a software system were still being designed, we were sufficiently prescient to predict which program components were most likely to fail, we would take pains to assign our best programmers to them, we would take extra care to review the designs, and we would make sure the source code got extra attention during code reviews and testing. Although we cannot have foreknowledge of their identity, we do have methods for predicting which modules are likely to be troublesome. Modules that have been reengineered a number of times, palimpsests of the history of a long-lived product line, are more likely than others to be buggy. Quality engineers who keep good records know which modules these are. New modules for which the external specifications have been revised an untoward number of times during development are also among those likely to have more than their share of bugs. Again, the quality books show which ones these are.

Once coded, we can apply further criteria to identify failure prone modules,* all to the purpose of giving them an extra measure of defect removal attention. If the system contains modules of mixed language types, the lower the language level the greater the likelihood of faults. Admittedly, the effect of different compiler languages may be argued, but few carry the argument to compiler vs. assembler languages. (See, for example, Lipow's comparison.)[2,3] A number of experiments have demonstrated that the modules of greatest complexity are those that most bear watching, although the relation of fault density (faults normalized to module size) to complexity (as measured, for example, by cyclomatic number) is not as striking as often thought. Many people also believe that the number of faults increases with the size of modules. This is more arguable. I suspect that the belief is generally correct, but that only for very large modules (several hundred source statements) can we expect anything like proportionality. Indeed, for smaller modules, experiments suggest that fault density may vary inversely with size.[4,5] One study suggests that it is not so much size as the number of unique operands (Halstead's n_2) that can be used to predict fault content.[5]

As with so much in software engineering, the most reliable predictors are those that derive from personal experience. The structural attributes of software are not physical measures of intrinsic meaning. Software measures have to be related to the specifics of the development or maintenance process and the software product. On examination we might discover that large modules have lower average fault densities than smaller modules, simply because the larger modules contain a high density of text messages. Alternatively, examination may reveal that the larger modules are disproportionately buggy; further, that the larger modules contain a high percentage of register operations. In short, local historical information is required to determine reliable indicators of failure-prone modules.

> *To profit from early identification of failure-prone modules, a data base should be developed containing not only defect data but various measurements of both the internal and external specifications of the modules in which defects are found.*

At the risk of repetition, measurement is at the core of software quality programs, and software quality engineers should spend a major part of their time collecting and storing data.

Some of the internal specifications both promising as predictors and capable of being measured by tools are itemized in the following list. Quality engineers and programmers may know of others peculiar to their software environment.

- The four basic Halstead measures (n_1, n_2, N_1, N_2).

- The number of each of several types of statements (branches, loop control, assignment, and the like).

---

*If a bit of semantic pedantry may be forgiven, modules are fault-prone until they are coded, and failure-prone thereafter.

- Total number of statements or non-comment statements.

- Complexity (cyclomatic number, knot counts, and the like).

- Number of variables shared with other modules.

- Number of other modules invoking or being invoked by the subject module.

A Digression on Pareto Analysis. The procedure of singling out modules having internal characteristics markedly different from most of the modules in the system is a form of Pareto analysis, named after the early twentieth-century economist who discovered that 80% of the wealth was controlled by 20% of the population. Reliability engineers have been using Pareto analysis for some years now, applying the technique to various problems in which it is necessary to separate the "vital few" from the "trivial many," to use the terms coined by J. M. Juran. Simply put, Pareto analysis is a statistical method to identify the minority of agents that exert the greatest effect. The translation of Pareto methods from hardware oriented quality analyses to those of software quality is another sign of the origin of software quality assurance in the traditions of quality management.

Much of the next chapter is based on Pareto analysis, as is the detection of failure-prone modules from testing experience.

Test Experience. Because modules that were found, from analysis of their designs or code, to be fault-prone or failure-prone will get extra care and handling, testing should not reveal the existence of noticeably failure-prone modules. Does anyone care to believe that? No matter how much experience lies behind it, early identification of fault-prone modules inherently is prophesy. Test experience is reality.* Since using test experience to predict failure during operation is adding new prophesy to reality, we still cannot completely avoid the saying of sooths, but such is the nature of all predictor methods.

Before getting into the mechanism of predicting failure-prone modules, let us look at the purposes to which we can put the predictions derived from test experience. First, if we know that a given module is among the more failure prone, we still have time to identify it—assuming other criteria are met—as a candidate for FMEA. We can also place it high in the list of modules to be rewritten at the earliest opportunity. Alternatively, if examination of a failure-prone module finds it handling an inherently difficult problem, we may consider revisiting some higher-level design decisions. Finally, we can earmark it to be used only with the greatest caution in other software systems.

Identification of failure-prone modules requires even more modest effort than identification of fault-prone modules. Given the large number of modules we can expect to find in any large system, statistical data abounds to separate the vital few from the trivial many. The experience of Albert Endres, who first published on the phenomenon of failure-prone modules, has been duplicated many times. Let us use Endres data[6] as an example. The system studied by Endres' contained 422 distinct modules. Endres tabulated the number of modules containing one fault, the number in which two were found, and so on, to form a table, excerpted as follows:

---

*If testing reveals errors in the system architecture, a succession of changes during testing may, in any case, introduce new faults into previously sound modules, thereby undoing earlier Pareto analysis.

Number of Modules	Number of Faults
220	0
112	1
36	2
.	.
.	.
.	.
.	.
.	.
1	15
1	19
1	28
422	512

Applying Pareto's 20/80 criteria as close as the data allows, we find that 21% of the modules (those having two or more faults) contain 78% of all the faults in the system.

Although Endres' data fits Pareto's demographic data as though it were planned, we might look at other ratios as well. One percent of all the modules were responsible for 15% of the faults. 5 percent of the modules were responsible for 23% of the faults. 10 percent of the modules contained 24% of the faults. And so forth. Computing these other ratios helps us arrive at the number of modules we can examine in detail, while remaining consistent with the resources available to support investigation. Perhaps our quality plan has allocated only 20 labor-days for the study. In this case, assuming we can investigate an average of one module per day, we need to pare the number of modules to 5% of the total. However, since these account for 23% of all faults, we know we shall be putting our resources where they are most needed.

In investigating failure-prone modules, quality engineers reapply the same criteria that were used for early detection of fault-prone modules, except that complexity, size, and similar calculations should be updated. The number of changes to the external specifications of each module also should be updated. Further, quality engineers look at the code itself—at least the code of the worst offenders—to see if the code substantively violates code standards (weak use of data typing, excessive loop nesting, and so forth). The possibility exists that none of the indicators will prove anything. Perhaps the bugs were isolated problems with no perceptible pattern of poor code. Alternatively, grounds may be found for abandoning one or more modules or for requesting the programming staff to rewrite the code or even revise design.

We do not need to wait for the conclusion of testing to search for failure-prone modules. Fault counts can be tabulated at regular intervals once a sufficient number of modules (for statistical purposes, say, 50) have entered testing. Until testing of the entire system is undertaken, however, the criteria for failure-proneness should be based on any sore thumbs that stick out of the tabulation, for example, the four modules that accounted for 15% of the faults in Endres' data. The earlier these modules can be reworked—assuming the earmarks of poor code are present—the smoother the rest of testing will be.

Test Sufficiency

In the narrowest sense of quality assurance, testing, quality engineers analyze the testing that has been performed to determine when the product has been sufficiently tested.

Generally, such analysis is restricted to testing at the full system level, that is, with all the parts in place. Before we get further into the subject, let us accept the most prevalent test of test sufficiency: By definition, testing is complete when all the planned test cases are run. However, with analysis, aggressive SQA organizations backed by a management commitment may learn that enough is not enough.

Summarizing material from Section 4.2 and earlier in this chapter, two measures of test sufficiency are satisfaction of predetermined functional coverage and structural coverage. The criterion for the former is nearly always 100% for individual testable functions. Criteria for the latter are usually between 90% and 95% of one type of coverage or another: branches, statements, paths of given length, or combinations of segments and branches. (We should note here that decision-to-decision path coverage and statement coverage are equivalent if either attains 100%.) By itself, structural coverage is insufficient for determining when enough testing has been performed. Used to augment functional testing, as suggested earlier, coverage-based testing calls for the execution of additional test cases if, after completion of the planned test cases, the predetermined structural coverage criterion has not been attained.

Seeding (Section 2.3) provides another basis for determining test sufficiency. The simplistic view in some quarters is that testing may not be considered complete until all seeds have been recaptured. This is doubly fallacious. First, and most obviously, the seeds are not the bugs that have the potential of remaining in the delivered product, and the possibility exists that all the real bugs will be removed before all of the seeds are found. Second, recalling that our interest is test sufficiency and not specious guarantees of bug-free programs, retrieval of an arbitrary number of seeds does not provide quantitative evidence of sufficiency without further analysis. Accordingly, it is necessary to start with quantitative criteria for sufficiency.

Since the basic purpose of seeding is to provide confidence in the full set of test cases—augmented if necessary— quantitative criteria based on seeding ought to be based on confidence limits much like those used by quality control engineers in accepting or rejecting, on the basis of samples taken, the hypothesis of product acceptability. In the following metric of Duran and Wiorkowski,[7] which expands on Harlan Mills' original (unpublished) work in seeding, the symbols used in Section 2.3 are both altered and augmented for clarity.

Given that that the number of real bugs detected is a subset of an initial total of some maximum size, we want to place confidence limits on that maximum size. The joint probability of finding exactly a of A planted seeds and n of N real faults is found from

$$q(a, n, A, N) = \frac{\binom{A}{a}\binom{N}{n}}{\binom{A+N}{a+n}}$$

Taking α as the risk of rejecting a true hypothesis ($1 - \alpha$ establishes the confidence limits we are concerned with), we compute the largest N such that

$$\sum_{k=0}^{n} q(a, k, A, N) > \alpha$$

Giving the name N_{max} to this value of N, the procedure yields $100(1 - \alpha)$ percent confidence that the true value of N lies between the inclusive limits of n and N_{max}.

Duran and Wirokowski also develop the case where no real bugs are found.

Assuming the procedure has been programmed, application means plugging in updated values of a and n, holding A and α constant, until $N_{max} - n$ is within some predetermined criterion. Of course, none of this works unless it can be established that the seeds are representative of the real faults. We speak mostly of randomness, but we should realize also that we are unlikely to sow seeds other than the simplest of bugs, while many statements may be involved in some real bugs. To ensure that test sufficiency may be inferred from evidence provided by seeding, we should examine ratios between real bug detection and seed recovery, as in Figure 7.9.

An entirely different concept of test sufficiency—different in that it is directed elsewhere than the sufficiency of deliberately designed test cases—is provided by the trend of failure history. Much like the testing trend plots of Figures 7.6 through 7.8, we plot the decreasing rate of failure once the system is running with all components present. That is, in the absence of a pathological distribution of bugs with respect to input data, we expect the rate to decrease. Moreover, the failure rate decrease should be reasonably smooth if testing progresses at a fairly constant pace, each week accounting for similar numbers of actual test hours. In the classic case, the failure rate decreases, perhaps exponentially, until it is asymptotic to zero. Then we claim that testing is complete. (If seeding is employed, failures caused by seeds must, of course, be purged from the failure history.) To be more certain about the decision, we can, by applying reliability models as in Section 2.4, attempt to bound the assumption of near-zero failure incidence with confidence limits.

Actually, this technique should be used not so much as a measure of test sufficiency as a measure of test insufficiency. That is, if the failure rate is not steadily decreasing at the time all other measures of sufficiency have been met, and, further, has not reached an acceptably low rate, the system is not yet ready for release.

Testing has three major objectives:

1. **Defect detection.**

2. **Demonstration that requirements have been met.**

3. **Evaluation of reliability.**

Test sufficiency means, not only that the first two objectives have been met, but the third as well. If the time between failures, given intensive test loading, has not increased to the point that reliability objectives have been attained, the system is not ready to be released. It is unlikely that much analysis of testing will occur beyond tallying test passes—unless, of course, software quality engineers do it.

Although the analysis tasks of software quality engineers seem more than sufficient to keep them busy, we have yet to discuss analysis leading to quality improvement. I have saved that for a separate chapter—the next—mostly as a way of emphasizing that quality improvement is, in the long run, the most important work of software quality management.

9.6 THE PLANNER

This chapter started with the remark that software quality assurance provides a framework for software quality programs. The framework needs to be put on paper. Just as a project development plan—to the end of implementing management decisions on how the project will be conducted—delineates the steps taken to produce a software product, so we require a quality plan to ensure that deliberate provisions are made for tasks specific to quality. The plan has to go beyond the activities of the software quality organization, to which this chapter has been devoted. Software quality plans should address all tasks specific to quality.

A software quality plan does not have to be a separate document. It can easily be incorporated in a development (or maintenance) plan, either as a separate section or, better yet, woven into the fabric of the development plan. For example, a section of the development plan given to testing can call for the analyses to be made, the uses to which they will be put, and the identification of the people performing the analyses.

Whether separate or part of the development plan, the planned software quality activities still have to be written. If software quality assurance is the management of software quality programs, and if a software quality organization exists to make certain that software quality assurance happens, it is obvious that the people to write software quality planning documentation are the people of that organization.

Apart from their preparation, software quality plans are the substance of Part 5 of this book. When we get there we shall see that software quality engineers require yet another tool: a word processor. Of necessity, quality plans are documents of many words.

9.7 SUMMARY

1. The management of software quality programs is made concrete by the establishment of a software quality assurance (SQA) organization.

2. The effectiveness of SQA increases with its organizational independence.

3. SQA organizations are staffed by software quality engineers, few of whom have received any formal training in SQA.

4. The cost of training programming personnel for SQA is less than the cost of training people from the quality community.

5. Even with cross-training, staffing SQA organizations is difficult. A promising solution is to rotate selected personnel between the technical and quality organizations.

6. Analogously to the standards for defining technical processes, software quality standards define the way software quality programs are managed.

7. Depending on the tasks assigned SQA organizations within the software quality program, the size of the organizations generally ranges between 5% and 10% of that of the technical organizations.

8. Through audits of the technical process and tangible products of development and maintenance, software quality engineers provide objective visibility for task control.

9. Essential project bookkeeping is performed by software quality engineers to track the correction of both procedural deviations from plans and technical problems discovered in defect removal activities.

10. While the interests of the technical staff during testing concentrate on removing bugs, the diverse tasks of software quality engineers reflect their assumption of all the concerns of users of the product.

11. SQA organizations are often given the responsibility for qualifying products, which, in addition to formal qualification testing, may included extended testing in a verisimilitude of the operational environment.

12. Collecting defect data and tabulating the data in various ways is a prerequisite for the diverse analyses performed within software quality programs.

13. Despite some difficulty in their acquisition, defect data from development testing are necessary constituents of a defect data base.

14. Data base software can be used to reveal adverse trends.

15. Failure mode and effects analysis (FMEA) is practical at the software component level provided the behavior of the component can succinctly be abstracted.

16. FMEA is most likely to be performed on modules believed to be prone to failure. Even before they are tested, modules can be tentatively identified as failure-prone by an unstable history of external specifications and by analysis of their internal specifications.

17. Modules thought to be fault-prone are earmarked for special care in defect removal procedures.

18. Pareto analysis is used to identify failure-prone modules from their internal specifications.

19. Pareto analysis of testing experience is used also to identify modules likely to continue to fail.

20. In the sense of defect removal and demonstration that behavioral specifications have been met, test sufficiency may be determined by the satisfaction of coverage criteria or criteria based on fault seeding.

21. Statistical confidence bounds can be established for test sufficiency decisions based on seeding.

22. With respect to evaluation of reliability, test sufficiency is based on failure trends. The confidence placed in favorable trends may be statistically bounded by reliability modeling, assuming good fits are found.

23. Software quality organizations take an active role in quality improvement, and assume the responsibility for planning (and documenting) software quality programs.

9.8 REFERENCES

[1] K. Mendis, "Personnel Requirements to Make Software Quality Assurance Work," in *Handbook of Software Quality Assurance*, ed. G. G. Schulmeyer and J. I. McManus (New York, NY: Van Nostrand Reinhold, 1987) pp. 104–118.

[2] M. Lipow, "Number of Faults per Line of Code," *IEEE Trans. Software Eng.*, Vol. SE-8 (July 1982) pp. 437–39.

[3] M. Lipow, "Comments on 'Estimating the Number of Faults in Code' and Two Corrections to Published Data," *IEEE Trans. Software Eng.*, Vol. SE-12 (April 1986) pp. 584–85.

[4] V. Basili and B. Perricone, "Software Errors and Complexity: An Empirical Investigation," *CACM*, Vol. 27 (January 1984) pp. 42–52.

[5] V. Shen, "Identifying Error-Prone Software—An Empirical Study," *IEEE Trans. Software Eng.*, Vol. SE-11 (April 1985) pp. 317–324.

[6] A. Endres, "An Analysis of Errors and Their Causes in System Programs," *Proceedings 1975 Int'l. Conf. on Reliable Software*, IEEE Cat. No. 75CH0840-7CSR (April 1975) pp. 327–36.

[7] J. Duran and J. Wiorkowski, "Capture-Recapture Sampling for Estimating Software Error Content," *IEEE Trans. Software Eng.*, Vol. SE-7 (January 1981) pp. 147–48.

CHAPTER 10

Quality Improvement

When we speak about improving quality, we speak of two domains: the quality of a given product and the quality of the process that produced the product. Both are covered in this chapter. Of the two, the latter is the more important, since improvement of the quality of the process affects not one but many products. Moreover, improvement of the process also implies reducing project cost and schedule risk.

Frequently, the best way to improve the process is to upgrade the staff. Software managers do not need a defined quality program to know this, nor do they wait for one. Let us assume a metric exists (one does not) for evaluating the quality index of individual programmers. To properly represent the thinking of management, we postulate a metric that accounts for both quality and productivity, one that includes annual counts of functions designed, lines of code produced, (inversely) numbers of produced problems that reached system level testing, and any other numerable attributes of programmer output that catch our fancy. We now rank the staff and find "measurements" ranging from 452 up to 1,296. The management alogrithm for improving quality is simple: Replace people between, say 452 to 600, with new staff expected to measure 1,000 or greater. Shedding members at the bottom of the stack in favor of those measuring up to the top performers is standard management practice. Unfortunately, with no metric to properly rank people, we have a most unscientific basis for our decisions. With considerable confidence, we can usually name the poor performers who have been on the staff for at least a year or two, but judgments of new hires are likely to be premature, especially with regard to quality. Moreover, although we want to hire new people at the level of our best present staff, we have only a resumé, a couple of interviews, and notoriously unreliable

176

reference calls to guide us.* At best, the "inchworm on the fencepost algorithm," as I call it, is generally a slow way to upgrade staff. It is even slower for those companies loath to hire and fire, relying instead on attrition to peel off the people at the bottom of the stack. Since the programmers higher up are the ones more likely to feel that a faster track exists for them elsewhere, this policy may get no results at all.

As discussed in Section 3.2, we can improve the quality of programming personnel through education and training. We cannot, however, improve the innate abilities of the people. Accordingly, the emphasis of quality improvement has been on the other two basic elements of software quality: technology and management.

Fortunately, technology and management lend themselves to deliberate programs of improvement. The effects of these two elements of quality are measurable, although not always as measurable as we should like. Measurement is, in any case, the basis for the archetype of quality improvement, the industrial model of process control.

10.1 THE INDUSTRIAL MODEL

In the industrial model for controlling processes, illustrated by Figure 10.1, the results of each step of a process are monitored and compared with standards. The standards may be established theoretically or may be heuristic, the experience of previous

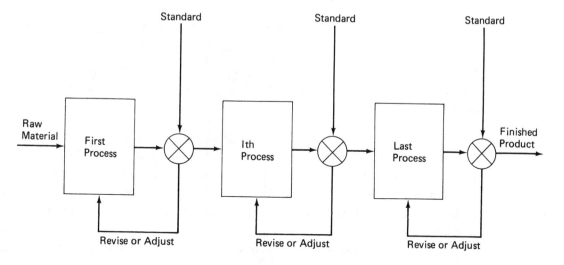

 Represents Comparison Point

Figure 10.1 Industrial Process Control Model

---

*If we knew with certainty more about programming aptitude, we could also use aptitude tests to screen candidates. Indeed, companies have tried testing, as with the Programmer's Aptitude Test, developed by people at IBM. See Weinberg for reasons the test is not an accurate predictor of programming talent.[1]

achievement. If the measurement falls below standards, the process is revised. If the process is an ongoing production operation, the machines involved are retuned or parts are replaced. If a prototype process—stretching the process control model to serve the immediate purpose of quality improvement—the machines or their use are redesigned. To take a simple case, let us assume that the process of Figure 10.1 manufactures tennis balls. The nap of every thousandth ball is measured using a fuzzmeter. If the measured nap is too long or too short, the production line is stopped and an operator tweaks an adjustment in the fuzzmaking machinery.

For the new production line, the model works a bit differently. We are concerned not only with the nap of the felt when new, but how much play the ball will take before it fuzzes up beyond some new standard. Perhaps two standards are necessary: so many hours of play before a mean of x millimeters of attached fuzz are produced and so many hours of play before the fuzz can be hit off the ball by an intermediate B player. Plainly, the measurements are getting tougher, even if the balls are not. In the case that the tested balls do not stand up to measurement (bounce up?), tuning may not be enough. The machinery itself may have to be redesigned.

Before using the industrial process control model as the prototype model for a quality improvement program, we need to stand back and admit that of the many hits taken by software development and maintenance processes, none has been over a tennis net. The obvious objection is that sampling, which works with a homogeneous population of tennis balls, is hard to apply to software, wherein the elements of the population have much less in common structurally or functionally. Less obvious but of equal importance, no software quality measurement is as exact as the nap height of felt, nor can we predict the response to a change in the software process as exactly as we can the response to a change in the production of tennis balls.

Still, the industrial model of process control has the potential of serving as a model for software quality improvement—really the only model that can be implemented—if certain constraints are present:

- Products are divided into a great enough number of pieces, say 50 or more, to provide a statistical basis for evaluating experimental changes at the module level.
- The process is fairly stable from project to project, so that historical measurements have currency.
- The process is established with sufficient definition to formulate the exact change to be tried.
- Copious amounts of data are collected and converted into programming measurements.

More than the problem of nonhomogeneity or the exact correlation between process elements and measurements, the last of these constraints is the stumbling block that often prevents software quality improvement programs from getting off the ground. But unlike the other problems, the collection of data and their analysis have clear solutions.

10.2 ANALYSIS

Section 9.4 spoke of the methods for collecting data. At the risk of vivid writing, for the purpose of quality improvement the section should have been printed in boldface.

To one extent or another, software processes are always undergoing change. Sometimes the change is a necessary consequence of an external influence, for example, customer insistence that customer personnel must be capable of maintaining the product. Changes also come about in direct response to complaints about the product, for example, user proclamations that documentation cannot be understood. Another common reason for revising processes is to suit the style of the newly hired software director. Self-motivation to produce a better product is another instigator of change. Despite the diversity of reasons for change, without data—really, without measurements— intuition and hallway conversations usually govern the revision to the standard operating procedures or the software tool kit.

For example, conventional wisdom has it that systems composed of small modules are more reliable than those made up of large modules. Contracts for software have been written that actually restricted maximum (and minimum, as well) average module sizes. Nevertheless, few software engineers have actually observed any direct correlation between module size and reliability.* In 1987, an interesting set of measurements on the effect of module size on reliability was made public. Applying rigorous statistical methods to data gathered from 325 Fortran V programs comprising 5,692 subprograms totalling over a million lines of executable source code, a number of software hypotheses were tested. Two are relevant to module size: The number of faults detected during formal testing decreases markedly as the average subprogram size *increases*, and also decreases as the variability of module size increases.[3] The researchers hypothesize that the first phenomenon may result partly from the decreased coupling required to implement a given design with larger modules and they suggest that the second finding may result from the fragmenting of functions to meet arbitrary size standards, the very thesis of my 1979 paper.

In short, cherished beliefs are scarcely the equal of measurements when it comes to deciding how to change process standards. Not all beliefs are wrong, of course. For example the cited study[3] found that faults increase with use of COMMON and the number of IF statements, which should surprise few.

What would be most valuable for determining where and how we can improve quality would be a single number that could be applied to each of the facets of quality identified in Section 2.1, or, failing that, to each of the attributes behind the facets. For example, based on our experience, we would like to assign numbers to the extent of software completeness, testability, maintainability, and so forth that we have actually achieved. Section 2.2 touched upon the fallacy of applying metrics to all aspects of software quality but, because attempts to do just that—especially with regard to quality improvement—continue to be published under respected imprimaturs, we digress briefly to consider the central problem encountered in producing single number metrics: the intransigence of arithmetic.

Two Plus Two and Other Problems

In our earliest formal encounters with mathematics, at the age of five or six, we learned that all numbers could be divided into two kinds: cardinals and ordinals. Of the two, cardinals were the more useful, since we could use them to determine the amount of

---

* In 1979 I coauthored a paper, "Modularity Is Not a Matter of Size,"[2] in a futile attempt to dissuade publication of proposed government guidelines calling for average and never-exceed module maxima.

change a quarter should return when used to buy bubble gum. Cardinals were also used for adding the number of bushels of corn Farmer Brown harvested from each of his two fields. Ordinals, we were taught, were much less useful. Yes, the boys' room is the first door on the left, Mrs. Wendell's classroom is the second door, and so forth, but that was about it—well, not quite. Ordinals are the numbers used for ranking. In those green years we could use ordinals to say that the Red Sox were in first place, the Yankees in second, the Indians in third, and so on.

As it happens, although we cannot truly measure testability, maintainability, and many other attributes, we can make judgments on a scale of, say, one to ten. A document might score 5 on testability, 8 on readability, and 2 on conformance to a standard format. Since the three numbers are no more than subjective estimates of rank, they really are ordinals, and as we learned so long ago, ordinals have no place in calculation. Nevertheless, in misguided essays at establishing numbers for comparison, often to determine whether quality improvement programs pay off, such ordinal numbers have been averaged, root-mean-squared, or whatever, to come up with composite quality numbers. But we cannot treat ordinals this way! With apologies to electrical engineers, Plantagenets, and Tudors, I take the liberty of vividly putting the matter to rest:

> *When connected in series, an inductor of two henries and one of eight henries form an equivalent circuit of ten henries, but there is no way one can add Henry II to Henry VIII and get Henry X.*

By combining the rankings of disparate attributes, metrics of serious intention have gone beyond the assessment of single documents or quality attributes to "calculate" overall quality indicators. Testabilty, maintainability, document completeness, and so on are added or averaged to produce the Henry X of software quality. Published metrics have even called for the addition of Boolean variables to ordinals or cardinals.

> *A metric is a standard for measurement, and among engineers (software engineers as well as others) the word measurement implies precise quantification. Precision and contempt for the rules of arithmetic cannot coexist.*

Arithmetic modesty is called for even when working with real cardinal numbers.

As part of a product improvement program we can subtract the calculated complexity of a module from the complexity calculated before the module was simplified. But we cannot add module complexity to module failure rate to attempt to get a more comprehensive number for comparison. Nor does it help to use weighting factors. When operating on the means or variances of statistical samples of different sizes, we weight the mean or variance of each by its sample size. The mathematical justification for this is intuitive. Not so an attempt to come up with a measure of test sufficiency that, by arbitrary factors, individually multiplies the structural coverage percentage, functional coverage percentage, and number of test cases before adding the three. Weights do not in the least reconcile dimensionless ratios and actual counts to their addition.

In short, we must be careful to base quality improvement on actual measurements or explicitly proclaimed assessments. Fanciful manipulations of numbers may obscure matters that require attention; may delude us into accepting as improvements changes of no real substance.

The liberties taken with arithmetic are analogous to liberties taken when comparing projects or products. More caveats follow.

Idiosyncratic Comparisons

Project Alpha was developed using the Periclean design method, while the Epidaurean method was used for project Omega. In its first six months of operation, the Alpha software produced 120 customer reports of failure. In contrast, Omega users reported only 12 failures during the first six months of operation. The two software systems are of similar size, and both were released to approximately the same number of customers. A case for declaring the Epidaurean method superior to that of Pericles seems to be made, provisional on further investigation, of course. Investigation, however, quickly invalidates the conclusion. Alpha is a transaction-oriented system, while Omega is a compiler system, and the Epidaurean method centers on the use of the Epidaurus compiler-compiler, irrelevant to transaction oriented systems. Also, any user report of difficulties, including interpretation of ambiguous input diagnostics, counted as a failure in the Alpha scheme of things. For Omega, the only incidents classified as failures were those in which the system failed to compile a correct program or, in one fashion or another, compiled a program in violation of language specifications. We could go on and list other differences, but only by belaboring the point: When comparing the results of different technical approaches, management methods, programming languages, or tools, the comparison is simple to make only when all the other variables are held constant.

This is not to say that comparisons cannot be made, only that one has to analyze carefully. The ideal way of evaluating a change to the standard approach is to experiment with a pilot project. Consider, as an example, structural test coverage tools. If the tool in use for the last several projects gave help in selecting test data sufficient to achieve only 85% coverage, and the new tool used on the pilot project helps attain 95% coverage, the new tool looks like a winner—provided the effects of any other differences between the pilot project and other projects can be discounted.

Technical differences are the most obvious examples of comparisons of dubious worth—recall the effect of programming languages on program size, discussed in Section 2.2—but the general scheme of development or maintenance also enters into the picture. Consider the introduction of seeding as a measure of test sufficiency, and then consider trying to compare the test effectiveness of the pilot project, in which all testing was performed by the developers, with another project in which ownership of code passed to an independent test team as soon as a module was logged in the library.

The problems confronting analysts worsen when comparing like projects of two companies, or perhaps of two divisions of the same company. As a starter, the language in which defects and productivity are reported may be different. It helps some to have both projects conform to the same external scheme—say, two projects planned in accordance with IEEE standard P1058 or the DOD data item description DI-MCCR-80030.

If only the most circumspect comparisons between disparate projects can enter into analyses for quality improvement, we find a much more straightforward situation when the comparison is restricted to projects that result in new releases of the same basic product. Examples of such products are computer operating systems, telephone switches, and data base management systems.

As the balance of this chapter demonstrates, most analysis for quality improvement can take place within a single software product line. Comparison attaches mostly to evaluating the results of a change implemented on a pilot project. For improvements of suitably restricted scope, within individual projects a single discrete section of the product or release can serve as the pilot project for changes to the development approaches, further mitigating the problems attending comparison.

Identification of Weak Links

The first step in improving the quality of software processes is determining where improvement is most needed. Everything cannot be changed at once, partly because change costs and partly because chaos would result. The primary tool for identifying the most needed improvement is Pareto analysis, introduced in Section 9.5 as a technique for singling out, for redesign or recoding, software elements that continually harbor a disproportionate number of faults or cause an untoward number of system failures.

As used for improving processes rather than products, Pareto analysis suffers somewhat from smaller statistical populations. For detecting fault-prone modules, we may deal with 1,000 items of data but, as we shall see, the elements isolated for improvement of the process may number fewer than ten. Despite its arguable statistical validity in this context, the method of Pareto analysis remains the primary analytical approach to the improvement of software processes.

Let us assume fault data has been collected and classified according to the following fault modes:

- Static logic.
- Dynamic logic (faults associated with temporal relations).
- Data handling.
- Computational.
- Interface.
- Data definition and data flow.
- Input/output.
- Use of external data base.
- Other.

The taxonomy itself is of little importance, having been introduced for the sole purpose of illustrating an example of Pareto analysis. For a long-lived product repeatedly given new life by a series of feature releases, a fault data taxonomy might well reflect bugs specific to the product. Such a classification scheme, for example, might include "Redundancy in the XYZ data base," or "Initialization after restart" among the types of bugs.

In any case, going with the generic taxonomy, let us further assume that fault data has been collected from all sources, as in Section 9.5, and from various projects, with results as charted in Figure 10.2.

Cursory inspection reveals that two types of faults, dynamic logic bugs and use of external data bases, are prime candidates for investigation. This does not yet mean that they are likely targets for immediate improvement, simply that the causes of their incidence should be analyzed. Analysis might find that the problem with importing data from external data bases has to do with chronically inaccurate or ambiguous data base

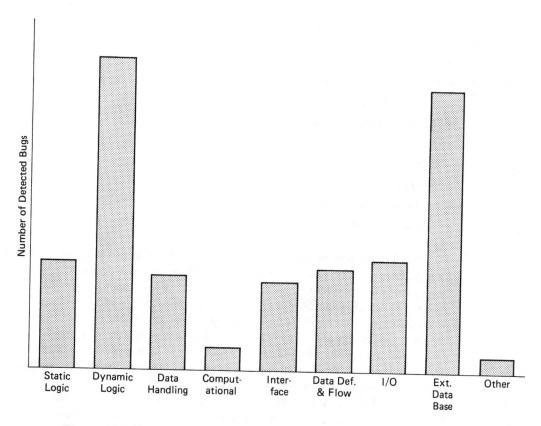

Figure 10.2 Fault Modality for a Hypothetical System

documentation. If the documentation of the data bases cannot be controlled—say, if they are managed and populated by various organizations throughout the world—little can be done about the problem save the lengthy process of proposing and coordinating agreement on an industry standard. On the other hand, analysis of the bugs in the dynamic logic class might reveal that a system for invoking and killing asynchronous tasks is so cumbersome as to be error prone. The solution: Devise a new method made transparent to programmers by a small set of system calls.

Had the Pareto technique illuminated static logic as a worrisome source of faults, the programming language used or the training given programmers in structured programming might have come under question. If data definition bugs were dominant, analysis might have revealed general disuse of the data typing capabilities offered by the programming language. If so, solutions may be found in training, revision of the coding standards handbook, or a new entry in the code review checklist. And so it goes. Pareto analysis tells us what is most worth looking at. The investigation that follows either dismisses the problem or tells us why faults in the investigated class are so numerous. Our experience as software engineers then tells us what to do about it.

Not only can we learn from Pareto analysis of fault specifics, we can also profit from isolating error hazard to steps of the process model. Let us consider one of the waterfall models given in Section 6.1, the one directed to the full development of a

system with embedded computers.

- System specification.
- System design.
- Software requirements.
- Top-level design.
- Detailed design and code.
- Unit test.
- Software integration.
- Software test.
- Hardware/software integration.
- System qualification.

Our interest here is in isolating phases in which faults first enter the system. Obviously, errors can be made in specifying requirements or in designing. But testing' Bug generation during testing, an activity devoted to defect removal, seems anything but obvious. However, removal of a fault implies recoding, and possibly redesign, as well. Any time we design or code, we have the opportunity to generate bugs. As it happens new pieces of design and new code generated during testing are more fault-prone than designs and code produced during the phases that take their names from the work of designing and coding. The reasons for this are several: the haste to get on with testing, the impracticality of scheduling reviews for design and code repairs, and possibly—where the repairers differ from the developers—a restricted view of the material being fixed. All test phases, save qualification, can produce bugs. The term "regression faults" is often applied to bugs produced during testing.*

At any rate, a chart similar to Figure 10.2, attributing the total number of detected bugs to each phase, may point the way to the most vulnerable targets for quality improvement. Let us assume that generation of the software requirements model produce a glaringly high number of defects compared to that of other phases. As with the analysis of fault types, individual requirements model faults are analyzed to detect a pattern. Let us hypothesize that a pattern is found: The documented wording of individual requirements tends to echo the wording of the systems requirements model rather than interpreting the requirements so they will be specific to software. (The hypothesize cause is one I have actually observed several times.) The solution, to establish specific standards for software requirements documentation and to establish means to enforce the standards, is obvious.†

Seeking quality improvement targets by development phase requires the separation of significant bugs from relatively unimportant ones. This means that when we are concerned with the programs themselves, we do not want to consider documentation errors, lapses from standard coding formats, or the like. These should be omitted from the fault counts. On the other hand, if user complaints force us to initiate a quality improvement program for user documentation, our concern is with the sources of documentation errors. For example, the final drafts of guides for the installation of new

---

* The term is also used for bugs produced during maintenance.

† Perhaps the best solution is to do away with voluminous requirements documentation and adopt one the other process models of Chapter 6.

releases may be produced during integration testing, but an inordinate number of the defects found in the guides reaching users have their origins in an earlier phase of preparing the documentation.

This raises another analysis issue: Should we be more concerned with faults—of any kind—that reach users than those that are detected and removed prior to release of the product? The issue is even more germane to the discussion of improving the effectiveness of defect removal operations, which we discuss shortly. If the primary purpose of a quality improvement program is to improve programmer productivity, the answer is no. However, if the primary objective of quality is Quality, the answer is yes.

Pareto analysis of software defects, whether of fault types or the source of faults, is especially productive for products marked by successive releases. Charts, similar to Figure 10.2, are constructed for fault types and sources to show cumulative numbers up to and including the last release. These are compared to charts for the current release. In either of the current charts, any marked change in the ratios of the fault counts compared to the cumulative ratios is a matter of interest. If the software development process has not been changed, the ratios should remain about the same. Suppose, however, that we suddenly see an increase in the number of coding errors when compared to other sources. Investigation might find that code reviews are getting less attention than they had previously received. The industrial model (Figure 10.1) tells us that it is time to "tweak" code reviews, perhaps simply by reminding people of the importance of the reviews.

On the other hand, if the process has been changed, we expect to find a change. If we do not see the change, the improvement failed to do the job we thought it should. Let us hypothesize that Figure 10.2 represents the cumulative fault counts through the fifth product release. Figure 10.3 represents the counts for the sixth release.

Figure 10.3 confirms that the new system of initiating and killing tasks has substantially reduced the relative number of dynamic logic bugs. Now, for heaven's sakes, let's get to work on the usage of external data bases!

Note that the ratios are a more reliable indicator of where quality improvement is needed than are the actual counts. The total number of bugs in release six may be greater than those of any of its predecessors, but that might mean no more than that the sixth release incorporated features inherently more difficult to program.

Figure 10.3 suggests that Pareto analysis will in time be useless for identifying the most likely candidates for quality improvement. As focus is shifted from one fault type to another, all will eventually became approximately equal in hazard; except, of course, the "other" category which will be the largest, requiring that it be replaced by its constituents. (Even so, in the process of dividing it into its parts we shall create another "other"—such is our modesty with regard to the extent of our knowledge of bugs.) In fact, the leveling process is unlikely to occur, if only because we will have adopted new technologies, the product line will have changed, or some other external agent of change will have had an influence.

We should not get the impression that only the familiar waterfall process model, with its seemingly distinct phases, lends itself to the analysis of fault generation. If a composition model employing object-oriented programming is in use, likely fault sources (in the sense of the waterfall's phases) are

- Problem analysis.
- Formulation of classes.

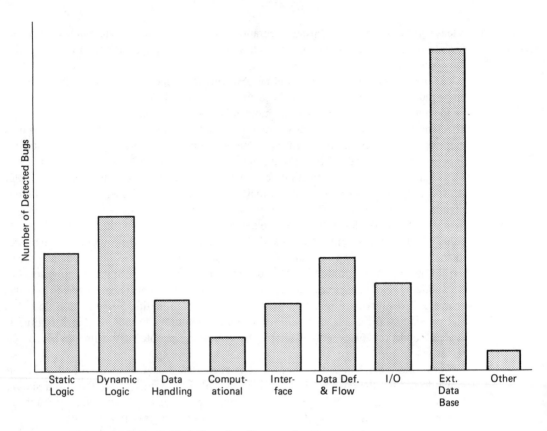

Figure 10.3 Fault Modality after Process Improvement

- Object definition and coding.
- Testing (which may be divided into several phases).

For the operational model, we can identify unique fault sources in the process of developing the executable specification and in the transformation process. For both the operational model and the waterfall modified by rapid prototyping (and the composition model if used also for prototyping), we should consider demonstration of prototype systems to be a source of defects. If the demonstration is not conducted properly, incorrect interpretation of functionality may go unnoticed in the prototype.

Defect Removal Effectiveness

To improve quality we want to know the kinds of faults that have proved the most troublesome, and we want to know the most fault-prone processes. But we need also to know of any processes for removing faults that have proved less effective than they ought to be. Let us hypothesize that our process incorporates the following defect removal procedures:

- Review of requirements documentation.

- Review of system design documentation.

- Review of subsystem design documentation.

- Pseudocode analysis of module designs.

- Static analysis of source code.

- Code reviews.

- Module tests.

- Subsystem integration tests.

- System integration test.

- System functional test.

Each of these should find a number of faults. Reviews of subsystem design documentation, for example, plainly cannot be expected to find coding faults, but they can find defects in the design of the subsystems, the design of the system, and even in the stipulation of requirements. Defects in these classes are all vulnerable to subsystem design reviews, even though the emphasis is on the design of the subsystem itself. Now, let us assume that some time after the system has been released to its users we count all the substantive defects that have been found in the requirements documentation, the system design documentation, and subsystem design documentation. Conceivably, more bugs of these classes are still waiting to be detected, but their number should be so small that for our immediate purpose we assume we have accounted for all the bugs of the three classes.

These bugs are the ones available to have been caught by the subsystem review process. Let us designate their total as D_a. Let D_d represent the number of defects actually detected by the subsystem reviews. The ratio

$$E_{sdr} = \frac{D_d}{D_a}$$

represents the effectiveness of subsystem design reviews.* Similarly, we would calculate E_{rr} for requirements reviews, E_{mt} for module tests and so forth.

Having calculated the various E_i, we now want to use them to determine which defect removal processes need to be strengthened. First, it is useful to know what effectiveness can be expected for each process. Reviews can realistically produce effectiveness ratios roughly between .2 and .8, becoming increasingly effective as the substance of the review becomes less abstract. That is, code reviews are the most effective; reviews of requirements models, the least. The effectiveness of pseudolanguage analyzers and static analyzers is a function of the specific tool used and the fault modality. A reasonable goal for static analyzers is .4, less for design analyzers. The effectiveness of testing has always been a controversial business, but many software engineers believe that individual test phases can achieve effectiveness ratios better than .9.

Consider the faults that we can expect module testing to expose. These include

---

*In an earlier book, I had called a similar ratio the "efficacy of defect removal."[4] My admitted rationale for using a fifty-cent word was to avoid confusing effectiveness with efficiency, which carries with it the connotation of productivity. A colleague subsequently pointed out to me that efficacy looks more like efficiency than does effectiveness. In any case, the ratio has to do only with quality, not cost effectiveness.

- Ambiguities in specifying module external specifications. (Module is designed with one interpretation; test cases designed to another)

- Module design faults not found during design review or by pseudocode analysis.

- Coding errors.

- Data entry errors.

Let us suppose that the ratio calculated for module testing is .40. This means that half again as many of the vulnerable faults (60% of the available ones) went undetected as those that were detected. Not very good. Once again, the evidence of a potential for quality improvement is not the same as knowing what can be done. Further analysis is called for. In our module testing example the acquisition of a dynamic analysis test bed may be indicated. Perhaps the practices for module testing do not involve any test preparation, such as the design of test cases. Alternatively, the standards in use may require such extensive documentation of module test cases that programmers are loath to design many tests. Whatever the reason for the low bug yield of module testing, thoughtful investigation should find a clue.

Apart from comparing one's own defect removal efficiencies with some external standards, potential targets for quality improvement may be found by investigating the fault modes of the bugs each defect removal process successfully uncovers; also of the bugs the processes are unsuccessful in finding. Picking on module testing once again, suppose we find that relatively few of the faults detected by integration testing are interface bugs. In a reasonably perfect world, in which module testing was capable of finding all bugs except those involved in interfaces with other modules, integration testing should produce a harvest of interface bugs only. (That is, module-to-module interfaces.) System testing should find bugs in interfaces to the outside world. When interface bugs become the minority of those found in integration testing, module testing has been fingered. Actually, module testing should be no more suspect than module design reviews, pseudocode analysis of module designs, static analysis of source code, and code reviews, so we would also want to analyze the way these are being performed.

Other examples of the results of analyzing the types of faults found in individual defect removal operations easily come to mind. A much modified system may have many segments of dead code within module structures. (Dead, or unreachable, code may not interfere with processing, but it can interfere with further maintenance, possibly producing future bugs.) A high incidence of dead code immediately suggests that the static analyzer needs improvement. Too many reports of inaccuracies in a user manual probably indicates that its use is not an integral part of system testing. During module testing, a high number of violations of coding standards (substantive ones, like improper use of system calls) is evidence that something has gone wrong with the code review process. Unless such problems aroused the ire of a tester, they are unlikely to be investigated unless corroborated by low defect removal effectiveness ratios. In short, these should be calculated in any case. The calculations do not come easily. We have, after all, to add each detected defect to the number available for detection (D_a) by the preceding processes after confirming its vulnerability to detection by the process. Still, the investigations themselves are time consuming. Without some quantitative help to focus available resources, it is all too tempting to ignore improving the processes of defect removal.

Pareto analysis seems so simple we would like to apply it not only to defect prevention but to defect removal as well. We could produce a chart similar to that of Figure 10.2 showing the number of bugs caught by each defect removal process. However, the height of each column would result as much from the kinds of bugs produced and how they are produced as it would from the effectiveness of the individual defect removal processes.

This section has primarily been concerned with finding, through analysis, areas ripe for improvement. Improvement, itself, comes from applying the precepts of software engineering. Chapter 4 touched upon some of these, but a full treatment of software engineering is plainly beyond the scope of this book. Within our immediate scope, however, is the actual revision of processes once they have been found wanting and once a solution has been found to strengthen them.

10.3 REVISING THE PROCESS

Initiatives to improve quality take several forms. Generic examples of these are

- Revising tools or acquiring new ones.
- Revising techniques (e.g., decomposition strategies).
- Selecting more appropriate programming languages.
- Defining standard practices more explicitly.
- Establishing more effective control mechanisms (e.g., improving criteria for deciding that work can proceed to the next phase).
- Selecting a different process model (see Chapter 6).
- Revamping the testing philosophy.
- Improving the means of recording the artifacts of the development process (e.g., more useful documentation methods or tools).
- Establishing new configuration management policies.

We could continue with the list until every tenet of software engineering has been accounted for, but the above examples serve to make the point that revisions of the development process may be narrow or broad in scope, may be technical or managerial, may primarily be directed at the actions of people or may be automated. There are, however, three constants: proposing and implementing changes, making certain they are correctly followed, and evaluating the effects of the change. The overall scheme of revision is depicted in Figure 10.4, an adaptation of the industrial process control model of Figure 10.1.

Anyone can suggest an improvement. Programmers, programming managers, and software quality engineers are the most likely to make suggestions. Any of these groups—as individuals, as members of task forces, or as members of quality circles—can perform the analyses of Section 10.2 and the subsequent identification of specific improvements. However, installing the improvement will often cross the lines of organizational boundaries and disciplines.

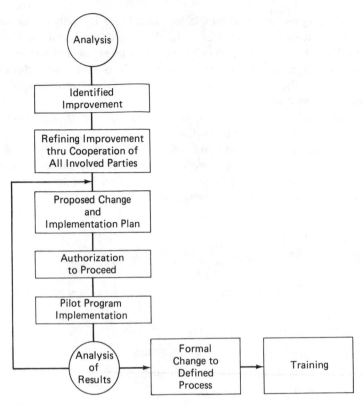

Figure 10.4 Steps Taken in Process Improvement

Proposing and Implementing Process Changes

Reverting to earlier examples, let us assume that a software quality engineer has decided that two problems, the prevalence of problems in coordinating multiple tasks and the number of bugs that could have been prevented by greater use of user-defined data types, call for a revision to the programming practices manual, last updated four years ago. To revise the manual, concurrence will obviously have to be sought from the managers of each of the several programming departments. The manual is actually "owned" by the Director of Software Development, who has a small staff of two to handle administrative affairs. Preparation and promulgation of manuals are administrative affairs.

A general discussion among the managers, the quality engineer, and one of the administrative staff reaches general agreement that a revision of the programming manual would be welcome. The managers, in fact, each know of other parts of the manual that they would like to see updated. No one objects to the specific revisions proposed by the quality engineer.

In short, the prospects for the identified improvement appear promising. However, it is one thing for the quality engineer to suggest that the manual should contain guidelines to solve the identified problems, and another thing to actually produce the guidelines. This is a technical problem, jurisdictionally on someone else's turf and, more important, may be somewhat beyond the expertise of the quality engineer. The technical staff are the only ones to formulate and write the guidelines. Selecting the right people to do the job and finding time for them to do it is left in the hands of the software managers. Finding the funds for the labor is left to the administrator.

The people who will do the work are identified, and one is designated the project leader. A date is established for their common availability for the project, and an estimate is made jointly by the two software managers for whom the implementers are permanently assigned. When out of earshot of anyone but the two managers, the administrator reveals that through creative accounting he can divert some funds, left over from the last release of one of the standard products, to the project. The software director, of course, will have to approve the diversion.

The director comes through and authorizes the implementation plan to be executed.

The new guidelines are issued to the programmers about to start on the design of one of several subsystems of a new product. Some ad hoc instruction in the improvements is given to the programmers by one of the implementers. Early in the coding of the subsystem, the programmers discover difficulty in implementing the new guidelines for user-defined data types. The complaint is universal. The rules are difficult to interpret without examples. Additional ad hoc instruction is given, and at the same time the implementers draft a set of examples.

After the system is released, the quality engineer compares the number of faults involving task handling and data definition in the pilot subsystem with the counts for the other subsystems. No contest. The pilot subsystem has fewer than ten percent of the number found in any of the other subsystems. The quality engineer receives a quality award, publishes a paper on the topic, and is hired by a competitor at a 25% increase in salary.

We have no further need for the quality engineer, anyway. Gathering other revisions to the programming manual, printing them up neatly, getting the software director to sign the cover page, and distributing the manual are all tasks for the administrative staff.

We have been following a simple example of Figure 10.4. The introduction of new tools, new techniques for requirements analysis or for design, or new management methods is inherently more disruptive to the defined practice than the example. To a programming shop that has never had formal configuration control, the notion dies hard that individual programmers do not forever hold all rights to their programs. The shop that never held a design review is unlikely to get the first one right, and perhaps not even the fifth. The staff of the shop that initiates the use of structured analysis techniques and data flow diagrams will have to acclimate themselves to a new view of an old class of problems. First acquaintance with object-oriented programming not only means learning new techniques but unlearning old ones. For changes to the process as these, we can expect that agreement will come harder and the cost of implementation will be greater than in our example. Moreover, far more refinement will usually be required than adding a few examples to a manual. Plainly, though, change does come about. Few programming shops operate as they did even five years ago.

Perhaps we should view a quality improvement program not simply as an agent for change, but as an agent for change in the direction pointed to by measurement.

Training

We left our administrative staff distributing copies of the revised programming practices manual. Actually, they have not yet finished the job. Even had the difficulties that arose in the pilot project not demonstrated that training is essential, we would have thought to conduct training classes to make certain that the staff correctly understands how to use the task control system calls and can make reasonable judgements about structuring data. While our administrators may not provide classroom instruction, we can depend on them to coordinate the training program.

The introduction of new tools usually calls for training, depending on the complexity of the job done by the tool, the effect of its use on other processes, and the engineering of the tool's user interface. New programming languages call for training if the language is sufficiently different from the one currently used. Pascal programmers can pick up C on their own, but should have help in learning C with an object-oriented superstructure. Without training, Pascal programmers can probably learn enough of Ada to do some programming, but to fully exploit the language's potential, training is necessary. No room is left for argument if a rigorous design system or language is instituted. While it is certainly possible for good programmers to learn, say, Anna and VDM (see Section 4.1) on their own, all will learn more quickly and most will learn better if given classroom instruction.

For changes to the process that are unique to the company, instruction must come from within. For example, learning how to live with new home-grown configuration management practices must necessarily be taught by a member of the staff familiar with the policy; usually someone instrumental in formulating the method. With regard to the use of purchased tools, programming languages, and the like, companies have choices. To save costs, companies often decide to have one or more members of their own staff set up the curriculum, often including the use of videotapes, and provide classroom training. The cost savings often are more apparent than real. For one thing, although the color of the money paid for salaries is different and often easier to come by than that distributed by the Accounts Payable department, the time to set up and conduct a training program may cost more than a purchased, off-the-shelf program. More insidiously, the people invariably selected to give such training are among the best programmers on the staff. Time lost to training is taken from the work the employee is valued for.

Training of a different kind is required to overcome either doubts about the value of a newly instituted data collection system, or reticence in having one's programs tested by others. Certain types of quality improvement actions from time to time are sullenly received by the technical staff. Done with sensitivity, explanation to the staff of the change's value to both the company and its personnel should overcome groundless fears and programmer inertia. Of course, we should keep in mind that change carefully conceived by management may correctly be recognized as misbegotten by the people most affected by the change. In response to the statement that an objective of the reviews was compliance to structured programming standards, a training session in conducting code walk-throughs once elicited the comment from a trainee that the company had no such standards.

Training directed as much to motivation as it is to technique is sometimes viewed as *indoctrination*, and in particular, quality indoctrination. The last thing we need is to expect the trainees to uncritically accept the premises of the instruction. Indoctrination, if that is what the training actually amounts to, is in direct contrast to the concept of participatory management that lies behind quality circles. Train and expect that critical questions will help the training process or, even better, make of the training program a crucible for the feasibility of the change.

10.4 IMPROVING THE PRODUCT

Most of this chapter has been devoted to improving the processes by which software is developed and maintained. However, few products cannot stand some improvement, and since the bottom line of quality is drawn at software products, it is time we gave products some attention.

Has the engineer or the programmer yet lived who did not know of some improvements he or she would like to make in the design just released? Programmers often know of components of the program that have grown out of shape through multiple revisions to the external specification of the system or the overall software design. The code seems to work, but the programmers hope that it will never be viewed by peers who had no part in its design or coding. The fondest dream of engineers and programmers is the opportunity to redesign a product. Within reasonable limitations, the opportunity presents itself in the next release of products designed for a long evolutionary life.

Externally, the user interface that seemed so sensible to its designers, and somehow even survived beta testing, proves as popular with real world users as a return to rotary calculators and manual typewriters. Apart from such built-in deficiencies as cumbersome menus, the product, once in the hands of users, may be found to be wanting in features. The owners of a new relational data base system may wish they could view, by a simple command, an ordered list of all domain keys. Shop floor quality inspectors may grumble about the lack of any capability in the new drilling machine software to record manual interventions that alter the feed rates and drill speeds coded by the process control specialists. In a sense, features are to the quality of software as creature comforts and gadgets are to automobiles. Features add quality, not in the sense of reliability or the other "ilities" of Chapter 1 (although usability represents a gray area), but as we understand $30,000 cars to be of greater quality than $10,000 ones.

In short, with the next release of the product we can both improve the "ilities" and increase the product's worthiness. In this section we address the way we can use information to determine the quality improvements most needed.

Back to Pareto

Section 9.5 spoke of the use of Pareto analysis to identify failure-prone modules during development. The word "module" was used to refer to any discrete element of the program sufficiently small to permit having enough of them for statistical purposes. We can perform the analysis at more than one structural level. The "vital few" modules found to have made more than their share of contributions to the failure history of the system under test are singled out for examination. If, in the judgment of the examiners, the modules are bad examples of programming, regardless of cause, the modules are recommended for recoding and, possibly, redesign.

In the first few months of a new release we expect problems to be reported by users. We hope for few failures, but we are not surprised to hear of certain sequences of operations that prevent the completion of processing tasks. Whether few or many failures, we certainly expect to hear of things that do not quite go correctly; compilations occasionally taking 100 times as long to complete as the size of the program seemed to warrant, or terminal emulation software that from time to time clobbers the resident operating system of the microcomputer on which it is installed. The number of these failures—call the less serious ones "glitches" if you will—is often sufficiently high to warrant investigation to determine if the faults in the program are unevenly distributed with respect to the program's structure; that is, if the faults are concentrated in just a few modules. Our tool for dealing with uneven distribution of bugs remains Pareto analysis.

Earlier, this section remarked on the desire of programmers to redesign (or recode) parts of programs they would as soon disown. If we have a mechanism for programmers to raise their misgivings to an appropriate level of management, the redesign of such modules may well enter into the activities of the next release. Mechanisms of this kind tend to work erratically, however. It is one thing for programmers to despise their own work and another to tell the boss about it. Also, management may be reluctant to take the word of the programmer and may want to form their own judgments, but somehow never find the time to do so. Whether or not fingered by conscientious programmers, modules that are failure prone will reliably be identified by Pareto analysis of the failures encountered after release.

Failure is not all. The reason for a programmer wanting a second chance at design or code may have less to do with reliability than with the module's maintainability. Statistics can be kept on the amount of time spent on making changes to modules, and we could perform Pareto analysis to identify the few modules that take an untoward amount of time to revise. The measurements are of arguable value, though, unless there have been so many changes that all modules have a roughly equal history of small revisions and large revisions. Never having seen this situation occur, I doubt that analysis of the effects of poor maintainability can add anything to observations passed up through the maintenance grapevine.

Is Anyone Back There Listening?

Imagine the chagrin of the software customer who regularly calls up to complain about the same problem, who regularly shells out money for the latest software release, and who, with equal regularity, discovers that each release fails to carry with it relief for the problem. In this user's eyes, the software supplier is on a par with the department store that has taken two years thus far to rectify an incorrect debit in the user's account. ("It seems to be a problem with the computer, Ma'am.") The real problem is that no one back there is trying very hard.

When users report failures, or something like failures, software suppliers generally take notice. The problem is assigned a priority, and based on the priority, given a place in the problem-solving queue. Some software or systems suppliers maintain an on-line problem report data base through which the user can view a description of all the problems that have been reported, the status of each (awaiting investigation, under investigation, fix scheduled for release by such-and-such date, deferred for some given reason), and any operational workaround that has been recommended. Other suppliers send out notices to their customers of any reported problems, along with temporary workarounds. Notebooks of these notices grow in thickness between releases. At the other extreme are suppliers who make it their business to fix the problem, but make no effort to inform their customers about it. However they are handled, failures are taken seriously, even to the point of withdrawing products from further distribution until a fix is made.

What should concern us are the problems too mild to be given the attention failures get. These, too, affect the product's quality, if less dramatically. Consider the accounting system in which annual social security withholding percentages and maxima have to be updated in four separate files. The user may complain the procedure requires four times the updating that a proper system would require, but we are more likely to be concerned with the opportunity for error. In any case, the matter is likely to be left uncorrected unless it becomes someone's business to assess the problem, analyze the best way to correct it, and arrange to have it placed somewhere in the product improvement queue.

Making certain that all problems are assessed and disposed of one way or another (leave it alone, fix it with a command file for the next release, and so forth) requires little more than some time and a a data base for correlating like reports. But aggressive improvers of product quality go beyond giving proper attention to gratuitous complaints. Using interviews of randomly selected users and questionnaires, they maintain their own dialogue with users, ferreting out not only unreported grumbles but also suggested feature improvements.

This practice carries with it some risk. If you ask for user feedback, you had better use it. The worst way to keep customer loyalty is to solicit such information and then not use it. I have stayed many nights in hotels but only once returned the card soliciting any comments about the hotel or the service. Ignoring the symptoms I had reported on the card, the response from the hotel chain's Vice President of Quality humphed that the hotel most certainly had not rented the room by the hour before I checked in, since the practice was contrary to the chain's policy. That, of course, was the last time I stayed in a hotel of that chain. Similarly, we have the form found in the back of software user documentation, requesting comment on the documentation. I have mailed such forms to vendors without receiving any response. (A list of these vendors is officially unavailable.) From the hotline of the supplier of an early microcomputer word processor, I once received this response to a telephone inquiry: "Oh yeah, I know we don't list your printer. Yeah, I know it's a popular one. Try the XYZ printer setup—I think that might work. No, I don't know anything about revising the setup menu, that's not my department."

Offering a hotline, while a commendable practice, should be regarded in the same light as inserting a card in each manual asking for comments. If a complaint is legitimate, something should be done about it.

Inviting customers to recommend improvements is fairly common for producers of major systems, but often the invitation comes from the marketing department. There is nothing inherently wrong in this, but marketing should remember that recommended improvements for products should be viewed as a quality matter, not a marketing opportunity to sell the next release. Recommendations for clearer user documentation should be given the same attention as the suggestion that the addition of a particular feature should significantly increase sales.

10.5 SUMMARY

1. Practical limitations on improving the caliber of personnel force quality improvement programs to concentrate on technology and management.

2. Although the fit has weaknesses, within certain constraints the industrial model of process control is a reasonable abstraction of quality improvement programs for software processes.

3. A foundation of measurements underlies the most successful software quality improvement programs.

4. Software engineers must beware of metrics for software that, in trying to fix numbers to inherently nonmeasurable qualities, take liberties with the rules of mathematics.

5. Difficulties attend comparing, between projects, the effects of technical approaches, management methods, programming languages, and tools.

6. Comparison becomes more feasible as the number of variables distinguishing projects decreases. Comparison to determine the effects of improvements is easiest when made between subsequent releases of evolutionary projects.

7. Pareto analysis is a powerful tool for determining the most profitable activities for quality improvement.

8. Pareto analysis can be used to identify suspiciously high incidence of fault modes (static logic, computational, and the like).

9. Pareto analysis can be used also to identify steps in the development or maintenance process that are error prone.

10. Identifying defect removal activities that need improvement is most easily accomplished by calculating the effectiveness of each. An effectiveness metric is basically the ratio of the bugs actually found to those present at the time the activity took place.

11. The above analyses only identify areas to be investigated. Further analysis is required to confirm the existence of problems, to identify specific fault modality, and to arrive at a solution.

12. Despite the diversity of recommended improvements, each revision of a software process encompasses a proposal and implementation stage, subsequent follow-up to ensure that the revised process is correctly followed, and analysis of its effectiveness.

13. Proposal and implementation often involve the concurrence and participation of several disciplines within a company.

14. Personnel training is required after most revisions to the process.

15. Apart from removing latent bugs, product improvements include improving the usability and other quality facets of software and adding to the product's features.

16. Similar to the use of Pareto analysis to find failure-prone modules during testing (Section 9.5), Pareto analysis is used to find failure-prone parts of released software.

17. An aggressive quality improvement program solicits and analyzes feedback from users.

10.6 REFERENCES

[1] G. Weinberg, *The Psychology of Computer Programming* (New York, NY: Van Nostrand Reinhold, 1971), pp. 171–76.

[2] R. Dunn and R. Ullman, "Modularity Is Not A Matter of Size," *Proc. 1979 Annual Reliability and Maintainability Symposium*, IEEE Cat. No. 79CH1429-OR, pp. 342–45.

[3] E. Branyan, L. Thiel, and R. Rambo, "Addendum to Establishment and Validation of Software Metric Factors," presented at the Fourth Annual National Joint Conference on Software Quality and Productivity (Washington, D.C.: NSIA, March 1–3, 1987)

[4] R. Dunn, *Software Defect Removal* (New York, NY: McGraw-Hill Book Co., 1984), pp. 19–20.

Planning the Management of Software Quality

The title of this book carries the promise of material on quality planning, and in this last part we finally arrive at the business of preparing quality plans. This chapter deals with general matters that should be considered when preparing a software quality plan, while the next three chapters each contain a sample quality plan.

11.1 WHAT AND WHY

Section 9.6 defined software quality plans as documentation of activities specific to software quality. As the term is usually used—certainly as it is used here—software quality plans are specific to individual development or maintenance projects. Planning, in the most general sense, applies also to improving the quality of development and maintenance processes and the training and education of staff, but the result of such planning does not appear in the documents we call software quality plans.

Plainly, no sensible managers would undertake a development or maintenance (for simplicity, we henceforth refer only to development) project without planning it, a matter dealt with in Section 5.3. Development plans necessarily emphasize resources, cost, and schedule associated with building software; that is, analyzing requirements, designing, coding, and testing. Although the last can be considered specific to quality, most often—and quite naturally—developers view test successes as demonstrations of successful development. Thus, a development plan may treat testing as another set of tasks required to get the job done, even when the planned test scheme includes ambitious use of defect removal techniques. In contrast, software quality plans consider testing as a set of tasks directed primarily to reducing the risk of delivering a product of poor quality. Accordingly, software quality plans address activities that ensure testing will be performed as planned and will be controlled.

In general, software quality plans are directed to all aspects of ensuring that tasks specific to quality are performed as specified by the defined process and the development plan.

Unless quality assurance is planned, it is unlikely to happen.

From a practical point of view, to ensure the management of quality, software quality plans must specify the quality tasks that will performed, how they will be performed, and who will do them. Software quality plans are working documents, used by project personnel to amplify quality aspects of their task assignments and by managers to determine the scope of the control mechanisms applied to a project. Like other well-written project plans, proper quality plans should be dog-eared by the end of the project.*

Software quality plans can be prepared ab initio for each project. Pretend that one had never been written before, and invent the whole thing. Alternatively, if the software process is a stable one and the emphasis on quality changes little from project to project, a software quality plan, even though specific to a given project, can be an instantiation of a generic plan. After all, if the same kind of tasks are performed from job to job and by the same organizations, writing a software quality plan need be little more than filling in the blanks. (This is not to say that the thought given to planning is any less.)

11.2 RELATIONS TO OTHER DOCUMENTS

A recurring theme of the book has been that software quality derives from the 3-tuple of people, technology, and management. Software quality assurance, the management of software quality programs, is simply one aspect of management. If software projects are to result in quality products, activities other than those specific to quality must also be planned. We have already alluded to project development plans. Documentation, configuration management, and user support plans also are commonly encountered project plans. None of these needs to be a separate document. In principle, all planning may be documented in a single binder. In practice, this is rarely done, partly because the more parts a document has, the longer it takes to find the item you are looking for, but mostly because of the way plans get written. We should expect, for example, technical staff to write development plans, a configuration management or program management group to prepare configuration management plans, and quality engineers to write quality plans. From no more profound a consideration than the logistics of preparation and publishing, it is easier for each responsible organization to do its own thing separately.

Separately in physical form that is, not in concept. Software quality plans must be closely coupled (in the vernacular, "track") to development plans, configuration management plans, and the planning for each test phase. If the development plan calls for

---

* The term "project plans" is used to here to distinguish general plans from plans specific to given tasks (i.e., test plans, installation plans, and the like).

200

Chapter 11:
Planning the
Management
of Software
Quality

reviews of design documentation, the software quality plan should cover control provisions for the same reviews. Continuing with the same example, if the development plan calls for reviews as part of design tasks—indeed, part of the task completion criteria—the software quality plan should specify the manner in which the results of reviews influence the certification of task completions.

Software quality plans define software quality programs; that is, the exact manner of ensuring that quality enters into the activities of producing, maintaining, controlling (in the sense of configuration management), and supporting software projects and products. Plainly, a software quality plan serves no useful purpose unless it closely tracks the other plans. As a result, software quality plans are often the last to be prepared. If the set of project plans derives from a set of generic plans, the interval between the generation of other plans and that of a software quality plan can be short. Beyond the obvious cost savings, we see where schedules benefit from the use of generic plans as templates for project plans.

Whether or not the software quality plan for a given project is produced from a generic software quality plan, the plan can be made fairly concise if reference is made to standard software quality assurance documents. Section 9.1, under the rubric "SQA Documentation," spoke of standards (or procedures, or instructions) for various types of audits, activities related to vendor-supplied software, data collection, and a number of other tasks. Consider, as an example, audits of library control transactions. We can write into a software quality plan the specific editor journal (or whatever) that is examined to see that edition designators are being updated as revisions are made, the method of recording the audits and any discrepancies that are found, and the number of entries examined at each audit. Alternatively, one can refer to, say, SQAProc1296. The efficiency of the alternative is obvious, not to mention the environmental advantage of saving wood pulp.

Less obvious, but perhaps of even greater importance, personnel intimately familiar with quality procedures perform software quality tasks more accurately and thoroughly. The person seeing a reference to SQAProc1296 already knows what it is all about. This is the fifth project on which the procedure has been used, and it is now old hat. On the other hand, if the task description were written bottom-up in the plan, the task may be defined somewhat differently from any way it has previously been performed, possibly confusing the auditors.

Having a library of software quality assurance procedures to draw from implies having an established (even if newly established) and defined software quality program. This should, in any case, precede software quality planning for a given project. Given established standards, software quality planning becomes a top-down process. Too often, a company's first documented introduction to software quality assurance is a software quality plan. Although the plan may be reengineered to fit later projects, an essential basis for evaluating the effectiveness of the selected software quality practices is missing: As with improving the quality of development, improving software quality assurance itself requires definition of the process to be improved.

11.3 SPECIFIC TOPICS REQUIRING PLANNING

The specifics of software quality plans deal with the project at hand: what will be done, how, when, and by whom. The last can involve people from diverse organizations partic-

201

**Section 11.3:
Specific
Topics
Requiring
Planning**

ipating in the project. Even in the presence of a software quality assurance organization, software quality engineers perform only some of the jobs devoted to quality. As a general rule, the players need to be named, if not by their individual names, at least by their positions. We might like to name Cassie Dixon and her colleagues as the authors of integration test cases, but we can settle for "members of the integration test department."

What, how, when, and by whom are the questions that the following topics are all about:

- Measurements.
- Trend analysis.
- Tool certification or calibration.
- Reviews.
- Other passive defect detection.
- Test control.
- Analysis of the product.
- Configuration management.
- Certification of task completions.
- Qualification.
- Other audits (functional and physical).
- Documentation.
- Vendor control.
- Assuring corrective action.
- Quality records.

Each of the topics has been discussed at some length in the preceding pages of the book. Software quality plans translate discussion into brass-tacks actions. Let us see how these topics are tacked down in quality plans.

Measurements

As we have seen in earlier chapters, measurements associated with the development and operation of software figure largely in software quality programs. Not surprisingly, then, we want plans to identify

- The data that will be collected.
- Analyses of the data.
- Use of the analyses (evaluation and reports).
- Who collects, who analyzes and evaluates, and who receives the reports.

Measurements planning does not have to be lumped together in one section of the software quality plan. Indeed, in some cases the usefulness of plans is enhanced by attaching measurement activities to the activities being measured. In this section, for example, measurements of test sufficiency are included under the rubric "Test Control."

202

Chapter 11:
Planning the
Management
of Software
Quality

On the other hand, very ambitious measurements programs have been documented in separate measurements plans (to which the software quality plan should refer).

Beyond the items of the foregoing list, specific matters for the plan to address include

- Forms (paper or mechanized) for collecting data.

- Tools used for analyses (e.g., statistical software packages).

- Analysis models (e.g., model for complexity calculations—see Section 2.3).

- Feedback—making certain that reports get to the people who can take appropriate action or who need the guidance of measurement (e.g., sending analysis reports on customer support problems to the customer service office).

- Evaluation with respect to established criteria—For example, specifying a recommended maximum module complexity, and further specifying the action taken if the maximum is commonly exceeded.

- Connection to quality improvement programs.

The last item reminds us that despite the project-specific character of software quality plans, not all measurements will benefit the subject project. Nevertheless, measurements made for the purpose of improving the quality of processes need to be planned if they are going to be made: The software quality plan is used as a reminder of things that need doing, a warning that things are going to be done, and—frequently—the basis for allocating personnel (read, "costing") to the project's software quality program. Unlike other measurement matters for which the plan should state exactly how the measurement will be used, for measurements related exclusively to improving processes, the plan need specify only the collection and assembly of the data.*   The actual analysis will take place under a quality improvement program. However, unless this is so stated, the disposition of the measurement will appear as a loose thread.

Trend Analysis

Software quality plans should specify the symptomatic analyses planned for the project. Section 7.2 described the use of such analyses in a software quality program. As with measurements, we may not want to have a separate section on trend analysis. Certainly, trends related to testing are best described under testing. Wherever in the plan symptomatic analyses appear, the following should be documented:

- The data analyzed (e.g., estimates of required memory).

- The frequency of analysis—plainly, essential for time trends.

- Who analyzes.

- Analysis tools (e.g., data base software).

- Disposition of the analysis.

With regard to the last, the software quality plan should not attempt to predicate management actions to be taken in response to analysis reports. It is sufficient simply

---

* For example, coalescing defect data from several sources.

203

Section 11.3:
Specific
Topics
Requiring
Planning

to state the form in which the results are to be reported and to whom. Management may, indeed, choose to revise delivery schedules if the staffing rate shows that the current schedules are unrealistic, but this is not the affair of software quality programs. Software quality assurance is a management tool, not the user of the tool.

Tool Certification or Calibration

For software tools, certification and calibration have much the same meaning and we need not dwell on the nuances that distinguish the two. In any case, the exact capabilities of some software tools have a direct bearing on software quality. For example, the kinds of faults that the source code static analyzer can find influence the conduct of code reviews or walk-throughs. For a static analyzer used on earlier projects, the software quality plan can refer to the calibration report. For a new analyzer, the plan should state who is responsible for calibrating the tool's capabilities and how the results will be documented.

We might note that throughout the software quality plan we should expect to find reference to tools. Somewhere, the static analyzer of the preceding paragraph will enter into the plan. Similarly, we might find citations of the use of file comparators, test control tools, a problem data base, and the like. In the view of some, it would seem that all tools used for software development enter into software quality assurance programs. For example, among the "tools, techniques, methodologies and records" that must be identified in plans conforming to MIL-S-52779A,[1] we find "operations research–system analysis techniques" and "software optimization tools." The software development plan certainly should note the way requirements will be analyzed and any tools incident to the analysis process, but we have to question whether software quality plans need to tread so far onto the turf of development.

Reviews

We can scarcely forget to document the reviews planned for the project. Plans need to specify reviewers and the recipients of review reports, the timing of reviews, and—what is perhaps somewhat difficult to plan—the exact material forming the substance of the review. The last requires that the development plan specify all the artifacts of each design task subject to review. Before a project is underway, we are often uncertain of the best way to document the decisions of every design task. We may not even be certain of the character of some of the design tasks that will be undertaken. For example, not until sufficient analysis has been performed, can we define all the existing software elements that will be re-engineered for the current project, so the likelihood is slim of being able to define the kind of documentation appropriate for re-engineering each "reusable" component. Accordingly, quality plans are necessarily vague about some of the material reviewed. It is not unreasonable to include in software quality plans such phrases as "and any other design artifacts of the task."

Plans prepared in accordance with the IEEE Standard for Software Quality Assurance Plans[2] refer to Software Requirements Reviews (SRR), Preliminary Design Reviews (PDR), and Critical Design Reviews (CDR). These terms are borrowed from military usage, where they describe reviews held primarily to satisfy the military customer that the contractor is on the right track (at least with regard to understanding or refining the customer's requirements) and is making real progress. These formal reviews emphasize contractual adequacy or acceptability more than defect removal. They are as much part

204

Chapter 11:
Planning the
Management
of Software
Quality

of a program management plan as they are of a software quality program. If this is the sense of the reviews, and if a productive (in the sense of defect removal) set of internal reviews is not also planned, the software quality plan should emphasize defect removal aspects of the reviews, lest the reviews serve little purpose other than contractual formality. The presence of the customer is likely to dampen the unfettered discussion that attends internal reviews, leading to the unfortunate consequence that formal reviews cannot be counted on to find faults other than those patently traceable to the customer's view of the system requirements.

Of course, we can use the SRR/PDR/CDR terminology of the IEEE standard to refer to internal reviews. In this case, no need to supplement the reviews exists.

Where the reviews take the form of presentations to the customer followed by questions and discussion, many contractors, in an attempt to limit the amount of family laundry hung on the line, elect to hold dry runs of each formal review. Provided they do not degenerate to mere rehearsals run by the marketing department, dry runs can serve the purpose of internal reviews.

Other Passive Defect Detection

Because the use of pseudolanguage processors, static analyzers, formal verification methods, and any other technique or tool for finding defects directly affects quality, the plan should state the subject of the technique or tool, the people using it, and the time at which it is used. For example, "The Faultfinder analyzer will be used on each unit source code file by the author of the code. The programmer must be satisfied with the results—if necessary, annotating any anomaly reported by the analyzer that the programmer considers acceptable—prior to code review." The software quality plan should also state any relationship between the use of the tool or technique and other defect removal methods. Assuming that the subjects of code reviews are unit development folders, which also include compiled source listings and possibly the results of unit testing, we continue the example with, "The programmer will add the analyzer output to the unit development folder."

Test Control

Although the information will likely appear also in software test plan documents or in the development plan, the software quality plan should identify each planned mode of testing (unit, integration, and so forth) and should state for each who designs the test cases, who prepares the test procedures (if any), who conducts the tests, and who prepares the test reports. The duplication serves the purpose of putting the highlights of all defect removal planning information in one place. The actual amount of duplicated information is slim, so this need not be burdensome.

The plan should also state the means used to ensure that the data and code modules used for the test are unambiguously identified. For example, if we use a build tool that accepts a combination of object modules, data modules, and source code modules for linking and binding, it is appropriate to refer to both the build tool and the library control system, and to state how to ensure that tools have been (correctly) used. Ensuring correct use generally takes the form of stipulating on-the-spot test audits or examination of audit trails produced by the tools.

205

Section 11.3:
Specific
Topics
Requiring
Planning

The plan should refer to the documentation of test control systems, test beds for dynamic analysis, and regression control systems if they figure in the test plan.

Test results—whether formally chronicled in reports or, more simply, comprised of collected logs and computer output—should be evaluated to determine if they are satisfactory, outstanding problems notwithstanding. The plan should state who has the responsibility for the judgment. If quantitative criteria are intended as conditions of acceptability, these should be stated in the plan. Typical criteria are those associated with structural coverage or functional coverage.

Similarly, if seeding is used to help determine test sufficiency, the plan should state who plants the seeds, when they are planted, and the criterion for test sufficiency based on seed recapture.

Analysis of the Product

Any plans to analyze failure modes or fault modes and effects (see Section 9.5) should be documented; specifically, who, when, how, and with what tools. Plans for the early identification of fault-prone modules or the identification of failure-prone modules from test data should also be noted. It is crucial that the software quality plan identify who receives these analysis reports. Actions that require substantial redesign will have to be brought to the attention of those offices having the authority to direct design changes.

Configuration Management

Configuration management plans are sometimes included in software quality plans; sometimes only referred to. In one place or another, baseline control (discussed in Section 7.1) needs to be outlined. If, as is the usual case, the configuration management plan is separate from the quality plan, the quality plan should state the means for providing confidence that configuration management is succeeding in its purposes.

Typically, the software quality plan addresses library control audits performed to ensure that material (documentation, other design artifacts, and code) is placed in project libraries at appropriate times, that changes to controlled material are made only with approval, that configuration management decisions are properly recorded, and that obsolete material is deleted from project libraries. (The last does not rule out the use of librarians, such as CMS, capable of reconstructing earlier versions of programs.)

Certifying Task Completions

Section 7.1 spoke of the use of task completion criteria to determine the true status of projects. The software quality plan either should state the completion criteria for each kind of task or should refer to the documents that do (other plans or in-house process standards). In either case, the plan should describe the way objective satisfaction of the criteria is determined.

Objective satisfaction usually takes the form of audits. Assuming the existence of documented quality procedures for each kind of audit, the software quality plan need state only the frequency (or sampling plan) for each kind of audit, who conducts the audit, and to whom the results go. Because the work breakdown structure is unlikely to be complete at the time the plan is written, it may be necessary to speak of certification specifics in terms of the types of tasks that are anticipated.

206

Chapter 11:
Planning the
Management
of Software
Quality

Task certification can overlap with other parts of the plan. For example, test control implies certification of test activities. There is no need to duplicate material found elsewhere in the software quality plan, but pointers to other sections do no harm.

Qualification

The plan should state the basis for qualifying the product and the responsibilities and authority for qualification. Specific matters to be addressed are assurance that library control and corrective action records indicate the product is ready for qualification, the readiness of documentation for delivery, test design, test conduct, and analysis of test results.

Optionally, the quality plan might include the use of alpha testing (see Section 9.3).

Other Audits

Military contractors are familiar with functional configuration audits and physical configuration audits. These terms have appeared from time to time in documents published by the military on software quality, sometimes as contractor requirements treated separately from software quality. Regardless of how the requirements are imposed, contractors for major weapons systems usually have to do them. The audits are also called for by IEEE Std 730-1984[2].

As described in MIL-STD-1521B,[3] functional configuration audits (FCA) are mainly tests of deliverable systems, audited to determine that the system performs according to its external specifications. Test documentation and the use of user manuals enter prominently into FCAs. Except for specific customer documentation of the audit, FCAs are equivalent to product qualification. Well, not quite. Recognizing the realities of software, MIL-STD-1521B also calls for the contractor to brief the military customer on why the software parts of a system did not quite succeed in meeting their requirements, on the incorporation of approved changes to the external specifications (and proposals for more), and on a few more items that need not enter into a software quality plan.

Essentially, for a software quality plan prepared in compliance to an external standard in which FCAs are required, the preparer should rename the section on qualification "FCA" and follow any specifics demanded by the standard. MIL-STD-1521B[4] also covers physical configuration audits (PCA). Essentially, PCAs are inspections performed by the customer to verify that deliverable systems match their documentation (especially their design baselines). Contractors provide design documentation and other paperwork required by the inspectors. The primary emphasis of activities reserved for software is placed on the consistency between documents and between documentation and listings, the compliance of documentation and code annotation with the customer's formats, and the form and marking of media used to deliver the software.

If we want or need to include a PCA in a software quality plan, the easiest approach is to state that relevant material under configuration control will be identified to the customer and that it will be made available for inspection, also that the media will be checked internally before being turned over to the inspectors. Assuming the configuration management system has been working properly, there would seem to be no point in having the contractors perform the equivalent of a PCA in preparation for the customer's inspection.

IEEE Std 730-1984 calls for the inclusion of a separate section on documentation prepared during the course of a project. This conforms to the accepted practice in some quarters, wherein project control and software quality are nearly synonymous with documentation quality. They certainly reflect the belief that the document-driven development model paves the waterfall to software quality. Since, in any case, this model dominates the development of large software systems, there seems justification for a section defining how requirements models and design decisions (and user manuals) will be documented. The development plan, however, is a more suitable place to describe such documentation. Actually, the best practice of all is for both the development plan and the quality plan to refer to company standards for such documentation.

To say that the IEEE standard has a section on technical documentation is not quite correct. The documentation section also covers plans and reports related to a verification and validation program. If we choose to relegate a portion of the quality program to a separate verification and validation program, the quality plan needs to describe the planning of that program and the report produced as its output. In this manner, the Balkanized quality program can, after a fashion, be unified.

Vendor Control

Plans for the project to which the software quality plan applies may include incorporating software developed by other companies. A data management system for tying together geographically distributed corporate divisions may include a commercially available data base system as its central module. For the development of a factory automation system, the vendors of the computer-controlled tools used by the factory may be given contracts to provide software interfaces to the system. Whether vendor-supplied software is off the shelf or developed under contract, we are concerned that the software perform as expected, be usable, be supported, and be delivered on time.

On a number of contracts, the government has demanded that the quality assurance requirements imposed on its prime contractors be propagated (in the vernacular, "flowed-down") to subcontractors. Even where this is inappropriately costly, we would still want the software quality plan to describe no less than

- Checks made on the accuracy and completeness of the technical statement of work given subcontractors.

- Contractual provisions for ensuring the accuracy of vendor progress reports (rather like demanding the vendor conduct internal audits).

- Contractual requirements for the vendor's configuration control of deliverables (we might want to cite something like a PCA).

- Contractual requirements for postdelivery support

- Acceptance criteria for all deliverables—including qualification testing.

All of these, of course, do not apply to off-the-shelf software. On the other hand, for custom software, the contract should require the vendor to supply its own project plans, including one for software quality.

208

Chapter 11:
Planning the
Management
of Software
Quality

Somewhat off the point, the selection of vendors for custom software critical to the success of the project should be based, in part, on an assessment of the development process of each vendor invited to quote on the work. We want to rule out vendors whose process is incompatible with quality. A checklist for a vendor survey should cover

- Process definition—are all activities explained in writing?
- Measurements—especially those for control and quality improvement.
- Staff—especially stability and experience.
- Tools—for development and control.
- Organization—who is responsible and for what?
- Configuration management—who controls and how?
- Defect removal methods.
- Methods for assuring compliance to project plans and the defined process.
- Customer support.
- Tracking of items requiring correction.

The quality aspects of any planned vendor survey activities should be described in the software quality plan. Alternatively, if it does not sit too badly with the legal department, the plan should note that the selection of vendors invited to bid on the contract will be based on historical survey or performance records.

If the development of custom vendor software carries real risk, surveillance beyond the receipt of status reports is required; perhaps meetings with the vendor at logical checkpoints. If so, these additional surveillance activities should also be identified in the quality plan.

Assuring Corrective Action

Two types of discrepancies arise in the course of the contract: technical faults and unapproved deviations from the defined process or plans. Most of the discrepancies are chronicled in reviews, audits, and test reports. Assurance that these be corrected is required.

The software quality plan should describe the method (e.g., maintaining logs of discrepancies) by which one can determine the status of each matter requiring corrective action. The plan should also note the means of drawing the attention of management, at ever-increasing levels of authority if necessary, to delinquent or disputed corrections.

Quality Records

Certain of the records having to do with software quality need to be preserved; perhaps not forever, but for a defined period of time. Qualification reports are prominent among these. Others include the results of surveying customer perceptions of quality, measurements useful for quality improvement programs, and vendor performance information. We have no good rules of thumb to determine what will be useful in the future, but the plan should state the records that will be retained, how they will be retained and for how long, and who has the responsibility for being able to retrieve them.

11.4 SAMPLE SOFTWARE QUALITY PLANS

To lend more substance to the topics of the preceding section, the next three chapters each contain a sample quality plan. Chapter 12 deals with a plan appropriate to a development project of small scale. The plan may, in fact, be an appropriate model for projects of any size if the software development process is mature, well controlled, runs pretty much on its own momentum, and meets management's expectations. Chapters 13 and 14 provide plans more typical of large projects. All three projects are hypothetical. Each chapter has three parts:

- A brief description of what the project is about, salient quality concerns, and relevant organizational matters.
- A brief project development plan—relevant and condensed highlights only.
- The software quality plan.

Although Chapter 4 addressed technologies other than those associated with the disjoint paradigm, and although Chapter 6 discussed alternatives to the waterfall model, all three hypothetical projects conform to the familiar waterfall, deviating from it (in Chapters 12 and 13) only to the extent of using prototyping. The choice of conventional programming practices for all three projects was made in recognition of the need, imposed by the small number of examples, to limit the number of variables. Moreover, the differences in intensity of software quality planning, as appropriate to the size of projects, can best be seen if the basic methods are not too dissimilar. Finally, for the examples to have maximum utility, they need to reflect development practices in use. Despite increasing use of the tools of modern technology and increasing interest in software methodology, it will be a long time before the waterfall, especially when document-driven, loses its hegemony in the world of software development.

The three hypothetical case histories are all projects of Superior Oceanographic Systems,* which has a separate quality assurance department. The QA department is staffed with software quality engineers whose activities are defined by a set of software quality procedures directed to specific quality activities. Appendices contain some of these—not all, but enough to provide examples of what quality procedures look like.

Over the years we have seen documents issued to provide guidelines for improving or controlling software quality. At the level of individual industries, we have the example of Bellcore—the engineering and analysis company serving most of the operating telephone companies in the United States—publishing three separate documents having to do wholly or partly with software quality.[5] At the professional level, we have the myriad of standards published by IEEE. And not suprisingly, some standards, or their equivalents deal primarily or exclusively with software quality plans.

We have already seen reference to IEEE Std 730-1984. MIL-S-52779A was also noted. Although MIL-S-52779A is not accompanied by a "Data Item Description"(DID),[†] the specification itself has been used as a model for preparing software quality plans. The NATO equivalent (really, a paraphrase) of MIL-S-52779A is AQAP-13. An early military standard for software quality plans is DI-R-2174A, used in conjunction with

---

*Now you know who programmed Chapter Two's sailboat computers.

† The name given by the DoD to documentation standards.

210

Chapter 11:
Planning the
Management
of Software
Quality

DOD-STD-1679A. DOD-STD-1679A is a standard, supported by several DIDs, intended to cover all aspects of software development. It has been superseded, first by DOD-STD-2167, and more recently by DOD-STD-2167A.[6] A software quality standard, DOD-STD-2168[7] accompanies DOD-STD-2167A. DOD-STD-2168 can also be used independently of DOD-STD-2167A, as in defining a quality program for software not intended to be embedded in a military system. DOD-STD-2168 is supported by a DID for software quality plans, DI-QCIC-80572.

Two of these standards enter into the three quality plan examples. Given the status of IEEE Std 730-1984 as a voluntary industry standard, a number of readers are likely to find a plan conforming to the standard particularly useful. Therefore, the quality plan of Chapter 13 follows the format of IEEE Std 730-1984. The standard, however, does not explicitly call for measurements, analysis of trends, or analysis of products. These do appear in Chapter 13, with the notation that they are additions to the IEEE Std 730-1984 requirements.

An increasing number of defense contractors are finding themselves required to prepare software quality plans in accordance with DOD-STD-2168, published in April 1988. Therefore, Chapter 14 addresses a hypothetical military project, with DOD-STD-2168 as the basis for the quality plan. The format of the plan follows DI-QCIC-80572.[8]

I have already noted that the software quality plan of Chapter 12 may also be a suitable model for projects of any size. In one sense, the plan conforms more closely to the precepts of this chapter than do the plans of Chapters 13 and 14. Both the IEEE and the current DOD standards remove from the quality plan a significant number of activities belonging to a comprehensive quality program. Except for a review of a separate verification and validation (V&V) plan (IEEE Std. 1012-1986), and a requirement for a functional audit, the IEEE standard for quality plans largely ignores quality activities directed to reducing the likelihood of poor design decisions or poor code. For its part, the government includes within DOD-STD-2167A tasks analogous to the IEEE's V&V, but calls them product evaluations. This leaves DOD-STD-2168 with what amounts to a detached, management, view of a software quality program. These separations should be of little interest to us, since our chief concern is with the planning of reviews and tests, not the document recording the plan. Nevertheless, the reader should bear in mind that the quality plans of Chapters 13 and 14 are not representative of all of the quality planning done. To fill in the gap, Chapter 13 includes a summary of the V&V plan, while the summary of the development plan in Chapter 14 includes plans for product evaluations.

11.5 SUMMARY

1. Software quality plans ensure that activities specific to quality are planned in advance.

2. A software quality plan applies to a single project. However, plans may refer to documented standards and procedures employed on a number of projects. That is, a plan may (indeed, should) refer to the defined process under which the project is carried out.

3. Quality plans should be closely coupled ("track") to other plans: development or maintenance plans, configuration management plans, test plans, and the like.

4. Rather than describing the details of performing quality activities, where possible, software quality plans can refer to documented quality procedures. This offers several advantages.

5. Essentially, quality plans state what, how, when, and by whom.

6. Quality plans cover the following topics: measurements, trend analysis, tool certification or calibration, reviews, other passive defect detection, test control, product quality analysis, configuration management or compliance with CM plans, certification of task completions, qualification, functional and physical configuration audits (if required by customers), documentation, vendor control, corrective action, and quality records.

7. The topics need not be treated in separate sections. For example, measurement activity may enter into several sections of the plan.

8. Several standards calling for or dedicated to software quality plans have been published, mostly military. Two such standards, IEEE Std 730-1984 and DOD-STD-2168 are used as the basis for two of the sample quality plans that follow.

11.6 REFERENCES

[1] MIL-S-52779A, *Software Quality Assurance Program Requirements*, cognizant agency: U.S. Army Computer Systems Command, FT. Belvoir, Virginia, 1979.

[2] *IEEE Standard for Software Quality Plans*, ANSI/IEEE Std 730-1984.

[3] MIL-STD-1521B, *Military Standard: Technical Reviews and Audits for Systems, Equipments, and Computer Programs*, Department of Defense, Washington, D.C., June 4, 1985, pp. 71–74.

[4] MIL-STD-1521B, *Military Standard: Technical Reviews and Audits for Systems, Equipments, and Computer Programs*, Department of Defense, Washington, D.C., June 4, 1985, pp. 75–82.

[5] R. Erickson, "Analysis of Switching System Software for Reliability," Proc. *IEEE International Conference on Communications* (June 1988) pp. 846–851.

[6] DOD-STD-2167A, *Military Standard: Defense System Software Development*, Department of Defense, Washington, D.C., February 29, 1988.

[7] DOD-STD-2168, *Military Standard: Defense System Software Quality Program*, Department of Defense, Washington, D.C., February 29, 1988.

[8] DI-QCIC-80572, *Software Quality Program Plan*, DOD, Washington, D.C., April 29, 1988.

CHAPTER 12

Plan for a Small Project

Superior Oceanographic Systems (SOS) is a noted supplier of electronic systems to the military. For some time the systems have incorporated computers—initially minicomputers, now microprocessors. Some SOS products have as much printed wiring board space given to microprocessor circuitry as to the analog and special purpose digital circuitry with which SOS had established its reputation.

SOS was an early user of computer aided engineering (CAE) for electronic equipments—so early that it had to develop its own CAE systems. These served SOS's purposes so successfully that SOS was soon supplying CAE systems to other companies. Today, the volume of SOS's CAE product line approaches that of its military business.

The engineering directorate handles development for both product lines. Other directorates in the company are the manufacturing, sales, purchasing, quality, and administration directorates. The last includes the Management Information Systems Department (MIS). MIS operates two mainframe computers (Engineering has its own set of computers for use in product development) and supplies the software for them. MIS mostly uses commercial software packages, but a staff of some 20 analysts and programmers produce and maintain custom software, as well. All MIS software and services are for the internal use of SOS. The software quality plan of this chapter applies to a MIS project, one mostly involved with new programs but also requiring the addition of new capability to an existing data base system.

12.1 THE PROJECT

The director of Engineering has requested the MIS department to provide the following:

1. Project scheduling. Given the interdependencies of all the development tasks identified in a work breakdown structure, an estimate of the number of weeks required to perform each task, and any external time constraints tied to calendar dates, return the start and expected completion date of each task. Permit interactive manipulation of all input data including on-line input of arbitrary delays (slack) for the start of tasks.

2. Cost estimating. Based on historical cost data, data descriptive of the size of the project (e.g., number of sensors), and various parameters to define the complexity of the job (e.g., similarity to previous projects, novelty of technology required), estimate the cost of development in labor-months. Allow interactive "what if" experimentation. Further, upon completion of each project, update the historical cost basis with data from the completed project. Statistical techniques (e.g., multiple regression) are to be used for updating.

3. Status tracking. Compare actual task completions with the computed (and stored) schedule. Any deviations should be capable of being used for updating the scheduling function. Also, report scheduled task completions for any future interval (e.g., next week).

4. Common data. All three functions, cost estimating, scheduling, and status tracking, should be computed from common data. Moreover, the common data should be coupled to the existing cost reporting system.

The MIS department responded to the request by performing a cursory analysis of it. They decided that the most straightforward approach would be to modify the data base manager of the current cost reporting system, and to provide the new functions by developing new programs that would operate under the system. Taking an obvious functional approach, they decided that the new work would require the following major tasks:

- Develop a new program, Scheduler, to perform the first requested function.
- Develop a new program, Coster, to perform the second function.
- Develop a new batch program, Update, to update the parameters used for the cost estimating model.
- Develop a new program, Tracker, to report status information.
- Modify the data base manager to provide the necessary additions to the cost reporting data base and to automatically update schedule data with actuals.

The MIS department estimated the cost for the work and the calendar time required (without the benefit they themselves would one day get from the software requested by Engineering) and told the director of Engineering when they would comply with the request. They also advised the director that he or a delegate would be required to participate in the evaluation of the specific software requirements model MIS would develop; specifically, by following MIS's standard practice of prototyping interactive operations and report formats.

213

12.2 THE DEVELOPMENT PLAN

The MIS department divides its development work into the following sequential phases:

1. *Requirements analysis.* The output consists of prototype code, documentation of project-specific use of system calls and other features of the operational environment, and a prose description of required features not covered by the prototype code or for which the prototype code is not explicit. The MIS department also updates its cost and schedule estimates at the conclusion of this phase.

2. *Preliminary design.* The proposed software system is divided into functionally distinct subsystems (in this case, each program is so divided) and the interfaces among them are defined. Interfaces to the outside world, identified in the requirements model, are more exactly specified. Definitive behavioral specifications are prepared for each subsystem. If appropriate, state diagrams are prepared to amplify specifications of both functional requirements and interfaces.

3. *Subsystem design.* Each subsystem is decomposed into a set of hierarchically related logical modules. Each module is described by a behavioral specification. These are generally brief, often no more than a paragraph of text accompanied by external data specifications.

4. *Physical design.* The logical modules are combined into physical modules, either by coalescing logical modules having analogous functions or by "assimilation." By the latter term, MIS means that the functions of logical modules of very small scope (e.g., a module whose only job is to move a field from one record to another) are better realized by in-line code. Specifications are then written for each physical module.

5. *Code and module test.* Each module is tested by the programmer who coded it. Programmers test according to their own lights, keeping no formal records. Programmers turn over tested modules to the MIS librarian.

6. *Integration.* The modules comprising each subsystem (in our example, program) are integrated in top-down fashion. Test specifications detail the test cases used for integration. The test cases derive from the behavioral specifications for each subsystem. No test report is prepared, but the testers keep a log of tests successfully passed and the symptoms of all failures.

7. *System test.* The subsystems are linked and the program(s) installed on the mainframe computer. Tests directed to the interfaces between subsystems and programs (if more than one) are performed. The phase ends with a demonstration to users, who are encouraged to generate test cases of their own. Any planned user documentation enters into the tests. The demonstration is the basis for user acceptance.

8. *Introduction and documentation.* Announcements are made to all potential users of the new system's availability. If the MIS department believes they are necessary, it gives classes in the use of the system. Design documentation is cleaned up and codified for subsequent use during maintenance programming.

Within the MIS department, "analysts" handle the first phase of requirements analysis. One analyst continues through phase 8 in the role of project manager. Programmers are responsible for phases 2 through 6, although, when other project demands permit, programmers assigned to other projects perform the integration tests. Even then, however, project programmers design the integration test cases. The analysts return to run the system tests, using test cases of their own design. An analyst has responsibility for phase 8 also, except that a programmer usually assists in the documentation effort.

Although the same analysts and programmers perform maintenance, they do not necessarily follow the same steps. SOS defines maintenance as fixing bugs in delivered software, adapting software to new operational environments (e.g., changing some system calls to accommodate new terminal hardware), and changing software to reflect modifications or additions to the behavioral specifications of existing systems.

One of the analysts is assigned to manage each maintenance project. In many cases, the project is a one-person effort, erasing the line that distinguishes managers from workers. The manager has the responsibility of determining the point of entry in the sequence of development phases for the maintenance project. Cursory analysis of a bug, for example, may reveal that only steps 5 through 7 need to be performed. Our case, however, poses a major maintenance effort, and will go through all the phases. (Phases 7 and 8, of course, apply to the combination of new programs and the data base modification.) The handling of configuration management represents the most significant difference between the maintenance part of the project and the development of the new programs. The MIS librarian will not copy either documents or code into the private libraries of the people who will work on the project until the librarian has received signed authorization by the MIS manager.

The output of preliminary design is mostly documented by text, supplemented by state diagrams, screen layouts, a data dictionary, and graphical depictions of data structures. Except for module external data specifications and further development of the data dictionary, program design language in the format accepted by a pseudocode analyzer documents the rest of the design effort. The programming language for the example project will be PL1, and will follow prescribed standards that limit nesting levels, define the annotation scheme, and so forth.

Each member of the MIS department has a copy of the three-inch thick looseleaf notebook (SP Notebook) that documents the software process. From time-to-time, programmers go directly to the notebook for specific information (e.g., the distribution lists for reports), but mostly, programmers are directed to the notebook by pointers in development plans. The development plan specific to the example makes numerous references to specific pages of the notebook. The plan also names the manager of the project and sets forth a schedule for each of the defined tasks. The tasks defined in the plan include the first phase (as a single task), preliminary design for each of the four new programs and the data base modification, and place holders (that is, dates for the stipulation of additional tasks and schedules) for the further design, code, and integration activities. The plan establishes the starting dates for system test and the introduction phase. Although many tasks await definition, the plan estimates the labor load by calendar month.

MIS estimated that the work will result in about 8,000 noncomment lines of new source code. The modification work will involve interfaces with approximately 60,000 lines of existing code. The development plan calls for an average nonclerical staff of eight people. SOS leaves it up to the MIS manager to decide whether a project will be served by the quality directorate's software quality engineers. The MIS manager uses a rule of thumb: If a project is planned to last more than four months or cost more than 25 labor-months, the software quality engineers will be called in. Of course, this is only a rule of thumb, and the manager's decision is affected by such subjective considerations as the visibility of the project to higher management. In our example, both the estimated cost and the size of the project meet the criteria for calling on Quality.

Once assigned (full or part time), an SOS software quality engineer starts off by learning about the project and preparing a software quality plan. MIS projects not served by Quality still follow the MIS procedures for reviews, test planning, and the like. However, any planning for these is included in the development plan. Quality, however, feels that a separate quality plan is necessary if the quality engineers are to take full advantage of the quality discipline. Which brings us to the software quality plan.

12.3 THE QUALITY PLAN

As an editorial nicety, the section numbering system will be continued. Plainly, the numbering for a real quality plan would start, not with *12.3.1*, but with *1*. Also, references to appendices, which normally would not be part of the plan, are bracketed. The references to fictitious SOS documents are included only to lend verisimilitude to the plan.

Software Quality Plan
for
Project A12B34

12.3.1 Scope

This plan covers software quality activities applied to the subject project, from requirements analysis through introduction and final documentation.

12.3.2 References

1.   SOS Doc. 987654, Software Development Plan (SDP) for Project A12B34.
2.   SOS Standard Practices for the Development and Maintenance of MIS Computer Software (SP Notebook)
3.   Memo for File (J. Salomon, Jan 6): Configuration Management Responsibilities for Project A12B34
4.   Memo for File (G. Handel, Jan 2): Project Management Responsibilities for Project A12B34
5.   SOS Doc. 300100, Software Quality Assurance Operating Procedures (SQAOP)

12.3.3 Tools

The following tools, planned for use on the project, have previously been certified for project use.

• Quicklook Compiler—certified by Report V1234 for prototype development.
• Design rule Offense Generator (DOG)—certified by Report V3456 for pseudocode analysis.

- NBM PL1 Compiler V3.12—certified by grandfather rule for compilation under Operating Systems V1.0 through V2.11.

- NBM Operating System V2.11—certified by grandfather rule.

- PL1 Unit Preprocessor (PUP)—certified by Report V5678 for preprocessing external load references prior to linking.

The use of Code Auditor Tool (CAT) to ensure compliance with the SOS standard practices for PL1 code will be certified by the quality directorate prior to the tool's use. Specific features certified will be annotation standards, restrictions on loop and branching nesting depths, and indentation levels. CAT's accuracy at counting total statements, non-comment source statements, and branch instructions will be certified. CAT's capability to list external references will be certified. All certification tasks will be accomplished by use of the tool on actual source code files in the current SOS library.

12.3.4 Reviews

Reference: SQAOP Section 3.1 for specifics of preparing for and conducting reviews.

Requirements Model. Within one week of the engineering directorate's approval of all prototype code and the completion of all requirements documentation for the project, hard copy output of the requirements analyses will be reviewed for (1) compliance with Section 2.3 of the SP Notebook, (2) technical feasibility, and (3) clarity. A single review will cover the requirements models for the programs Scheduler, Coster, Update, Tracker, and the modifications to Manager. Review participants will include the liaison person from Engineering, the project manager and each analyst directly responsible for requirements documentation, at least two programmers, and the software quality engineer assigned to the project. The project manager will designate the analysts and programmers at least two weeks before the review takes place. The software quality engineer will chair the review and will record any corrective actions that are required.

Preliminary Design. Within one week of the completion of all preliminary design documentation for each program (and the modification to Manager), the documentation will be reviewed for (1) compliance with Section 2.4 of the SP Notebook, (2) compliance with the applicable requirements model, (3) technical feasibility, and (4) clarity. Coster and Update will be reviewed at the same meeting. Review participants will include at least one analyst designated by the project manager, each programmer contributing to the design documentation, and the software quality engineer assigned to the project. The software quality engineer will chair each review and will record any corrective actions that are required.

Physical Design. The physical design of each of the new programs will be reviewed by the lead programmer assigned to the program. The objective of the review will be to ascertain responsiveness to the preliminary design of the program and compliance with Sections 2.7, 2.8, and 2.9 of the SP Notebook. For Manager, the physical design for new modules and the revised physical design for modified modules will be reviewed by C. P. E. Bach, who is responsible for the cost reporting data base. Each reviewer will record any corrective actions that are required and will copy the record to the assigned software quality engineer. The physical design reviews will be held within one week of the completion of the design documentation and pseudocode, the substance of the reviews.

Test Specifications for Integration Testing. The software quality engineer assigned to the project will review the test specifications for subsystem integration of each program for compliance with Section 3.3 of the SP Notebook and for traceability to the behavioral specifications of each subsystem. Update, and possibly other programs as well, may not be divided into subsystems. In these cases, the integration test specifications will be reviewed with respect to the behavioral specifications of the program itself. Any items requiring corrective action will be logged and reported to the project manager. The review will be held no less than 30 days prior to the start of integration testing.

Test Specifications for System Test. The software quality engineer will review these for compliance with Section 3.4 of the SP Notebook and, at the program level, for traceability through the preliminary design specifications to the requirements model of the program. At the full system level—that is, for tests directed to the operation in concert of all the programs involved in the project—traceability will be with respect to the stipulated interfaces among the programs. Any items requiring corrective action will be logged and reported to the project manager. The review will be held no less than 30 days prior to the start of system test.

Test Report. The software quality engineer will review the report of system testing for compliance with Section 3.9 of the SP Notebook.

12.3.5 Audits

The software quality engineer assigned to the project will conduct audits as follows:

Library Control. For all software, SQAOP 4.1 [Appendix A-1] will be applied at weekly intervals for each program from integration testing through the completion of system testing. In addition, the procedure will be used at the completion of physical design for Manager modifications. Discrepancies will be logged and reported to the project manager and to the configuration manager.

Subsystem Logical Design. At the conclusion of each subsystem design phase, approximately 20% of the behavioral specifications of the defined modules will be examined for compliance with Section 2.7 of the SP Notebook. Discrepancies will be logged and reported to the responsible programmer. Following advice from the responsible programmer that discrepant specifications have been corrected, the specifications will be reaudited. If more than one quarter of the examined specifications for a single program are found discrepant, the audit will be extended to include 100% of the logical modules. The audits will be conducted per SQAOP 4.4.

Code. For approximately 20% of the modules in each program, the reports output by Code Auditor Tool will be examined and any discrepancies will be logged and reported to the responsible programmer. Programmers are not to provide CAT reports until they (the programmers) are satisfied with the results. If more than one quarter of the examined

CAT reports for a single program are found discrepant, the audit will be extended to include 100% of the physical modules.

Integration Test. As time permits, but no less than once a week during periods of integration testing, test logs will be examined for compliance with Section 3.8.4 of the SP Notebook. Special attention will be given to ensuring that planned test cases are performed as specified and on program builds comprised of logic and data modules drawn only from the project's BUILD.DSK library. Discrepancies will be logged and reported to the programmers responsible for test activities.

System Test. Prior to qualification exercises, audits during system test will be identical to those during integration testing, except that the tested material will be drawn from the project's COMPO.DSK library.

Final Documentation. The logic documentation manual for each new program and the modified manual for the cost accounting data base will be audited per SQAOP 4.9 for compliance with Section 5.1 of the SP Notebook. The system user manual will be audited per SQAOP 4.10 [Appendix A-2] for compliance with Section 6.1 of the SP Notebook. Discrepancies will be logged and reported to the project manager.

12.3.6 Qualification

The system, comprising all programs, will be considered as qualified for use by the engineering directorate when the following criteria are met:

- Analysis by the quality engineer that test cases have been documented to demonstrate all functions defined in the requirements model. Such documentation will include purpose, input conditions, expected results, and operational conditions, as specified in Section 3.4 of the SP Notebook. (Test cases used during demonstration of the prototype may be included without further documentation.)
- Completion of all planned system test cases.
- Signature approval by the Engineering representative witnessing or participating in system test.
- Sufficient operation of the system, using the preliminary or final user manual, by the software quality engineer to satisfy the engineer that the system can be correctly used by all Engineering managers. These exercises will use a copy of the actual SOS cost accounting data base.
- No known defects that prevent correct completion of stipulated operations.
- Fewer than 80 known problems (total of all programs) of minor severity (e.g., awkward data entry operations).
- All corrective actions dealing directly with the software have been closed.

The assigned software quality engineer will complete form SQAOP-F14 when these criteria have been met or waived. Waivers will require the signatures of both the project manager and the software quality engineer.

12.3.7 Certification of Task Completions

Weekly summaries of reviews and audits will be prepared by the software quality engineer and copied to the project manager. These summaries will highlight any discrepancies that compromise the completion of tasks as specified by the SP notebook. Further, although most individual tasks will not be subject to audit, the summaries will highlight any trends that reveal that sets of similar tasks are not being completed according to the stipulated standards.

12.3.8 Corrective Action

The software quality engineer will merge all logs of required corrective actions into a composite log. The composite log will have two parts, one for corrections specific to the software (e.g., defects) and one for procedural discrepancies. Each part will contain the following information:

- Description
- How problem was found and when
- Name of person assigned to correct the problem
- Date of assigned correction
- Date of verified correction
- Key to method of verifying correction (see SQAOP 5.2)

Weekly, the software quality engineer will query the logs to determine any corrective actions that are overdue. In concert with the person assigned an overdue correction, the quality engineer will reschedule correction. In the event that the responsible person cannot commit to a revised date or disagrees on the need for the correction, the quality engineer will report the matter, by memorandum, to the project manager. If the project manager does not resolve the issue to the satisfaction of the quality engineer, the quality engineer will report the issue to the SOS quality director.

12.3.9 Defect Data Collection

Daily during periods of integration and system testing, the quality engineer will distribute copies of Form SQAOP-F12 to the test team and will collect completed forms. These data will be used for product analysis (see 12.3.10).

12.3.10 Product Analysis

Following the completion of integration testing for each program, the following measurements will be made by the quality engineer:

- Average module fan-in/fan-out ratio, using PUP. The measurement will be placed in the project summary file.
- Number of bugs found in each module. The quality engineer will employ Pareto analysis per SQAOP procedure 9.0 [Appendix A-3] to identify any modules that appear

to have contributed an untoward number of bugs to the total. The quality engineer will present his or her findings by memorandum to the project manager.

At the completion of qualification (signoff of SQAOP-F14), the following measurements [for later use when considering improvements or the additions of new features] will be made by the quality engineer:

- For each program, percentage of processor time utilized by each module.
- For defects found during integration and system testing, the total number attributed to each of the categories of SQAOP 10.0. This will be added to the MIS quality data pool.
- Number of NCSS per module per program. Total per program.
- Average number of parameters per procedure call per program.
- Elapsed time for the quality engineer to perform each of the interactive operations specified in the requirements model. The quality engineer will use his or her discretion to limit the number of options for each operation. Where the elapsed time is sensitive to data volume or other environmental conditions, the conditions under which the measurement was made will be recorded.

Except for the second of these, the quality engineer will place the measurements in the project summary file.

12.3.11 Trend Analysis

Weekly during integration and system testing, the quality engineer will examine test logs and update the following charts:

- (Cumulative) tests planned and tests executed (first time) vs. calendar time.
- (Cumulative) tests passed and tests attempted (first time) vs. calendar time.
- (Cumulative) defects detected and fixes verified vs. calendar time.

Each week, the quality engineer will analyze these data and prepare written evaluations in memo form for distribution to the project manager.

Weekly during system testing the quality engineer will also update a chart of discrete functions successfully tested. Again weekly, the quality engineer will analyze the data and present a written evaluation to the project manager.

12.3.12 System Release

Upon completion of Form SOS98765, the MIS department may announce the system's availability. The signatories for the form are

- Configuration Management (TBD).
- Project Manager (TBD).
- Engineering (TBD).
- Quality Assurance (TBD).

Before signing the form, the quality engineer will witness the installation of the software on the MIS mainframe to make certain that the load modules are identical to those qualified.

12.3.13 User Feedback

Form SQAOP-F17 will be affixed to the back cover of each copy of the user manual. User comments received by the quality directorate via this form will be coalesced on a monthly basis for the first year of operation, and will be forwarded to the project manager.

12.3.14 Record Retention

For one year from the date of the system's release, all quality records will be retained in the "current activities fileroom." At the conclusion of the period, all records except trend charts and evaluations, which will be destroyed, will be sent to the quality records archives. For one year after completion of Form SOS98765, the project summary file will be maintained by the project manager. Following the period, the file will be relocated to the MIS project archives.

Plan Following an Industrial Model

We continue with the adventures of Superior Oceanogragphic Systems (SOS), the subject of Chapter 12. For a software project larger than the MIS project of Chapter 12, we turn to SOS's computer aided engineering (CAE) business. Software for CAE products is developed and maintained by SOS's engineering directorate. Engineering follows a document-driven waterfall model. For CAE projects, it has adopted the documentation and planning standards of the IEEE.

13.1 THE PROJECT

The people who manage CAE software development had been disgruntled about the amount of new design that went into each new product. In particular, despite great similarities between products, even between products of different lines, few software components ever seemed to be used in a second application. Some attempts had been made to design components that would lend themselves to later reuse, but somehow few were ever used again. One likely reason was that the techniques for designing for reuse were not well established, but even if they were, SOS had no mechanized way of helping programmers match existing components to the needs of new applications.

After considerable study, engineering management decided that the best approach to software reusability was to replace its top-down decomposition design methodology with a composition model; specifically, one based on object-oriented programming. A group of programmers, experimenting with object-oriented programming for a few months, had generated enough enthusiasm to capture management's attention. To throw over old (and tested) methods for a dramatically different approach to software development was a matter quite different from a limited experiment with new technology. At the least, installation of a composition model would require a healthy investment in software tools, which brings us to the project for this chapter.

Management decided that if its expectations were realized the investment in tool development would pay off in only three years. The full payoff would have to be within the CAE product line; application of a composition model to the development of software for military systems (also under Engineering) would require too tough a struggle in trying to bend regulations such as DOD-STD-2167A to the needs of bottom-up design.

Part of the investment in tools had already been made: SOS had an object-oriented compiler, OooC (Object-orientation on C) and a run-time environment named Dynamic. Both had been purchased for the experiments noted earlier. To support a composition model and to make production use of object-oriented programming practical, further tools would be required:

- Ooditor, a context-sensitive editor for creating and rewriting classes and objects. The editor would have both textual and graphic capabilities.

- Canvasser, to permit programmers to interactively browse inheritance trees and class descriptors, with extension to objects, in the search for existing components suitable for a current application.

- Boss, a tool coordinator with windows, pull-down menus, and other graphic delights, under which Ooditor and Canvasser would run. Boss would also provide the mechanism for saving new or rewritten components in libraries, copying components for editing into new components, and similar basic programming functions.

Additional software was also identified, but management felt that this short list was enough to prove feasibility of an object-oriented composition model. The other stuff would have to wait, at least until first use of the model and tools on a pilot project (more about this shortly) was complete.

SOS would have liked to write all three programs in OooC, but funding arrangements required that the job be completed within the fiscal year, and management decided that it would be stretching its object-oriented skills too thin to attempt all three in OooC. Accordingly, management decided that only Boss would be written in OooC. Ooditor and Canvasser would be written in ordinary C. However, one or the other would subsequently be rewritten in OooC using the new tools. This would be Engineering's way of alpha testing the tools.

Over the course of several years, engineering management had developed faith in the document-driven* waterfall model; this despite continuing high costs for software development and maintenance (leading to the investment in tools for a composition model). The current project was to be no exception, especially since the investment would consume all of the internal development funds (those not provided by Marketing for new products or enhancements) for the balance of the year. Relative to most engineering projects, the project's size was expected to be modest, totaling about 30,000 NCSS. However, the project would get as much attention as more typical engineering software

---

* We'll see SOS take some liberties with the word "document."

225

Section 13.2:
The
Development
And V&V
Plans

projects, since it represented the first significant extension of SOS's CAE effort into CASE (Computer Aided Software Engineering). As a concomitant to the choice of a document-driven software development model, management called for the customary use of the IEEE documentation standards, including the ones for V&V and software quality plans.

13.2 THE DEVELOPMENT AND V&V PLANS

Since the Software Quality Plan prepared to IEEE standards refers to a V&V plan, this section summarizes not only the development plan, but also the V&V plan.

13.2.1 Development Plan

Document-driven models emphasize tangible output from each phase until testing is able to start. The phases of the engineering department waterfall model and the output of each entering into the software quality plan follow:

1. Concept (essentially, the substance of Section 13.1)
2. Requirements
    *   Software Requirements Specification (SRS)—Note that as used here and in the titles of other documents, following IEEE practice, "specification" means "document," not a detail found in a document. We see this again in the next chapter. The SRS for our project will evolve into complete sets of external specifications starting from a point marked by natural language descriptions of the most basic behavioral specifications. Some diagrams and sketches supplement the text. The basic specifications were documented in the feature set definition produced during the concept phase. The completed SRS will follow the spirit of the IEEE standard for SRSs,[1] but not the form, especially since prototype code will replace a great deal of text.
    *   Interface requirements documentation—This will address the interfaces among the new programs and between them and OooC and Dynamic.
    *   User documentation—Specifically, the preliminary manual for the three programs, used in concert.
3. Design
    *   Software Design Description (SDD)—"A translation of requirements into a description of the software structure, software components, interfaces, and data necessary for the implementation phase."[2] SOS actually divides the design phase into two stages, preliminary and detailed design. The output of the preliminary design stage is a preliminary SDD, while the complete SDD represents the output of the detailed design stage.
    *   Test Plan—"To prescribe the scope, approach, resources, and schedule of the testing activities. To identify the items being tested, the features to be tested, the testing tasks to be performed, the personnel responsible for each task, and the risks associated with this plan."[3]
    *   Test Design Specification—"To specify refinements of the test approach and to identify the features to be tested by this design and its associated tests."[4]

- Preliminary Test Case Specification—"To define a test case identified by a test design specification."[4] Actually, SOS plans to prepare test case specifications for integration tests of each of the programs and for the system test of the three working together. The last item may be viewed as a system integration test. Many of the test case designs will be no more than copies of the exercises used to evaluate prototypes of the three programs. Accordingly, in one of SOS's customary deviations from the IEEE documentation set, they do not follow the IEEE standard for test case specifications.

4. Implementation
   - Source code listings.
   - Executable code.
   - Final Test Case Specification documents.
   - Test scripts—SOS uses test scripts, rather than the test procedures called for in the IEEE Standard for Test Documentation (see Design phase, above), and then only for tests that call for specific sequences of operations not implied by user manuals. SOS test scripts define the exact step-by-step operations required during a test—enter this, record that, and so on.
   - Unit test logs (Note: IEEE V&V Standard calls for unit testing during testing phase.)

5. Testing
   - Integration test logs—One for each of the three programs.
   - System test logs
   - Anomaly reports resulting from integration and system test

6. Installation and Checkout—For the subject software, installation and checkout amount to alpha testing as noted in Section 13.1.
   - Evaluation reports prepared by programmers selected for alpha testing.

7. Operation and Maintenance—Although the software is for SOS's internal use, if the new development model proves successful, engineering management expects to see anomaly reports, removal of latent defects, and proposals for modifications and additions handled no differently than if the software were for a CAE system destined for SOS's customers. For the operation and maintenance phase, SOS also plans to have classes in object-oriented programming, composition design approaches, and, of course, use of the new tools. Initially, the entire CAE programming staff will be trained in groups of 20. Later, to provide classes for new hires, the courses will be repeated twice a year.

Development of each of the three programs is led by a section head, the first line of programming management. A separate test group, also led by a section head, will handle integration and system testing. With the project manager, the four section heads form the systems management group, meeting weekly to discuss the project's technical direction. The project manager, also a section head, is the person who conceived, sold, and led the experiments in object-oriented programming. For this project, the project manager will report directly to the manager of CAE software development. The manager of CAE software development will report to the director of CAE engineering, who will report to the director of engineering.

Although SOS has a separate software maintenance department for CAE software, the novelty of the subject project led management to the decision to leave maintenance

227
Section 13.2:
The
Development
And V&V
Plans

to the development programmers—at least until enough of the maintenance staff had received training in the new disciplines.

As noted in Section 13.1, the requirements of all three programs will evolve with rapid prototyping. The proposed behavior of Canvasser and Ooditor will be prototyped in Lisp, while Boss will be prototyped in OooC. The Boss prototype will start with the execution of newly created classes, stubbed with objects to provide static demonstrations of menus and the like. The systems management group augmented by two of the programmers working on Boss will evaluate all three prototypes at each demonstration. After each evaluation they will prepare a memorandum delineating required changes and any greater specificity required for the next round. In the case of Canvasser and Ooditor, the final Lisp code will represent most of the requirements model for translating the prototype into C. The balance of the requirements documentation will constitute the SRS: natural language to describe features, state diagrams to illustrate the many and diverse combinations of states the three programs can assume (and the purpose of each), and information flow diagrams to describe the interaction of all three programs and their user.

For Canvasser and Ooditor, once the prototypes and SRS are baselined, functional decomposition will proceed according to conventional practices. In the document-driven approach used by SOS Engineering, design decisions are recorded in natural language, supplemented by state diagrams and data flow diagrams, all eventually recorded in the SDD. Detailed design of each defined module is mostly done in the language of the Program Design Statement Language System (PDSLS). As it gets baselined, the pseudocode will be added to the SDD.

As noted earlier, design of Boss will proceed with the definition and instantiations of classes to ever-increasing levels of specificity, along with concomitant demonstrations of the evolving capabilities, thus forming a continuum of programming activity. As they are coded, classes and objects will be added to a special library, which will later serve as the data base for testing Canvasser.

The information contained in this section is released, more formally and with much detail, in the development plan prepared by SOS for the project. At about the same time as the development plan, SOS prepared configuration management, verification and validation, and software quality plans. The last, prepared by the quality directorate, is found in Section 13.3. Both the configuration management and V&V plans have obvious connection to the software quality plan. Because of the number of intersections between it and the software quality plan, the V&V plan is summarized below.

13.2.2 Verification and Validation Plan

SOS prepared the V&V plan along the lines of ANSI/IEEE Std 1012–1986. A software verification and validation plan (SVVP) includes "V&V tasks to:

1. Verify that the products of each software life cycle phase:
   (a) Comply with previous life cycle phase requirements and products (for example, for correctness, completeness, consistency, accuracy)
   (b) Satisfy the standards, practices, and conventions of the phase.
   (c) Establish the proper basis for initiating the next life cycle phase activities

2. Validate that the completed end product complies with established software and system requirements."[5]

For what the IEEE standard calls "noncritical" software, the category into which the subject project falls, the standard tells its readers that the V&V tasks described therein are not mandatory, although recommended. The V&V tasks SOS intends to pursue for the project are largely a subset of those in the IEEE standard with some interpretations peculiar to SOS.

The project's SVVP names the members of the engineering staff who have specific V&V responsibilities, defines QA responsibilities, provides a schedule of V&V activities keyed to events identified in the development plan, defines the intended V&V tasks and reports, and describes the procedures that will be followed. The tasks, reports, and procedures are summarized below. QA assignments are indicated by the notation [QA]. Assignments to the test group (comprised of programmers) are indicated by the notation [T].

Tasks

- Evaluation of prototype performance with respect to project objectives.
- Review SRS from user perspective.
- Evaluation of SRS with respect to SOS standards. [QA]
- Review software interface document with respect to correctness and consistency.
- Review software interface document with respect to SOS standards. [QA]
- Prepare test plan for Canvassar and Ooditor integration and for system testing. [T]
- For Canvasser and Ooditor, prepare traceability table to trace design artifacts and tests to specific sections of prototype code or to specific textual or diagrammatic items in the SRS.
- Prepare system qualification plan. [QA]
- At several stages of design, review design artifacts or prototype performance (for Boss) for correctness and consistency with the requirements model as indicated by the traceability table.
- Review design artifacts and demonstrations of prototypes for compliance with SOS standards. [QA]
- Prepare test specification for Canvasser and Ooditor integration and for system testing. [T]
- Prepare test case specifications and test scripts for Canvasser and Ooditor integration and for system testing. [T]
- Conduct code reviews on logically related groups of source code files.
- Evaluate source code with respect to SOS standards. [QA]
- Perform unit testing.
- Perform Canvasser and Ooditer integration testing [T].
- Perform system test [T].
- System qualification. [QA]
- Alpha testing—using the system to redesign and rewrite either Canvasser or Ooditor in OooC.

229

Section 13.2:
The
Development
And V&V
Plans

- System test performed with the rewritten Canvasser or Ooditor, but using the same test cases. [T]

- System qualification using the rewritten Canvasser or Ooditor. [QA]

Reports

- For each review, minutes emphasizing detected faults.

- For each prototype demonstration, minutes delineating satisfactory feature demonstrations and inadequacies or deficiencies in features unsatisfactorily demonstrated.

- Memoranda delineating discrepancies in conformance to applicable standards and project plans. [QA]

- Anomaly reports for each problem encountered in integration, system, qualification, and alpha testing. Anomaly reports are prepared, also, for problems encountered after the system is released for general use. These reports describe the problem, its effect on operation and its most probable cause; assign one of three severity levels; and recommend future action on the anomaly. (Note: this is a subset of the anomaly reports called for in the IEEE standard.) [T]

- At initial baselining of each requirements model and SDD, a phase summary report, summarizing the results of V&V tasks conducted during the phase preceding the new baseline. At the conclusion of all module level testing for each program, a report summarizing the results of V&V tasks conducted during the implementation phase. The emphasis of these reports is placed on an overview of anomalies and their resolution, assessments of software quality, and recommendations for improvements.

- Phase reports summarizing integration and system testing. These are similar to the phase reports for the preceding phases of the waterfall cycle. [T]

- Qualification report. [QA]

- Installation and Checkout phase report, summarizing the results of alpha testing.

- Requalification report following reprogramming of Ooditor or Canvasser. [QA]

- Final V&V report. This report, coauthored by all personnel involved with V&V, will provide an assessment of the quality of the system from the various facets of software quality. It will also contain recommendations for improvements in the product.

Procedures

- Anomaly reporting and resolution—Provides the criteria for deciding that an anomaly needs to be reported. The V&V plan defines the distribution of anomaly reports, and provides criteria, based on severity levels, for the resolution of anomalies reported during system and subsequent testing. The three severity levels are defined in terms of effects on system operation.

- Task iteration policy—Recognizing that development will be iterative, necessarily so in the case of Boss and inevitably so for Canvasser and Ooditor, the V&V plan provides criteria for repeating V&V tasks tied to phase or event milestones. Mostly, the criteria are linked to configuration control. For example, if a change to a baselined SRS is approved, affected parts of the revised SRS will be reviewed before the change is incorporated into the requirements baseline.

- Deviation policy—The V&V plan defines the form and distribution of memoranda delineating discrepancies from project plans and SOS standards. The policy also calls for QA's pursuit of responses to such memoranda and QA's responsibility to escalate deviations to ever-higher levels of authority until matters are finally put to rest.

- Cross references—For assurance that V&V policies will not be jeopardized by an inability to control the project, the V&V plan refers to the SOS standards for engineering software, and to the project's configuration management, development, and quality plans. Moreover, many items in the V&V plan simply point to relevant sections of the SQA plan, where the specifics are given. Note that the SOS standards describe the V&V practices from which the project's V&V plan is drawn, and to which the actual V&V plan (recall, this is just a précis) refers.

13.3 THE QUALITY PLAN

The one document this chapter presents in the form specified by an IEEE standard, rather than summarizing, is the quality plan, which follows IEEE Standard for Software Quality Assurance Plans.[6] The standard is supplemented by IEEE Guide for Software Quality Planning.[7] In the section numbers that appear below, Sections 13.3.x through 13.3.13 correspond to Sections 3.x of the IEEE Standard. Plainly, the numbering for a real quality plan would start, not with *13.3.1*, but with *1*. In another deviation from an authentic plan, the plan that follows contains some notes and references to the appendices that follow Chapter 14. These are bracketed. Note, also, that Sections 13.3.14 and 13.3.15 are not included in the IEEE standard.

The IEEE Standard for SQA Plans calls for the inclusion of many standards governing development (e.g., documentation standards). The standard also calls for the plan to state how reviews and audits are conducted and other procedural matters. A premise of this book is that the best environment for quality is a stable one, one in which programming and managerial practices differ little from one project to another. Accordingly, the plan refers to SOS's standard practices wherever possible. As with Chapter 12, some of the practices referred to can be found as appendices to provide the flavor of how they may be documented. In the majority of cases, where no appendix is provided, it is unnecessary to speculate on the substance of the practice; every matter referred to is explained elsewhere in the book.

Software Quality Assurance Plan
for
Project CASE001

13.3.1 Purpose

This Software Quality Assurance Plan (SQAP) covers development of the Canvasser, Ooditor, and Boss computer programs, components of the SOS object-oriented software development environment. With appropriate changes of name, the plan will be used for other, yet unidentified, components of the environment. Development of the development environment is funded as an internal Engineering project. Members of the engineering programming staff will use the environment for the development of future CAE products and CASE tools. Possibly, the environment, when completed, will be offered to the

CASE marketplace. Accordingly, the project requires the quality attention given all SOS CAE products.

The environment will permit the future use of development methods based on object-oriented programming. The success of the new methods of software development depends on the quality of the software developed under Project CASE001. Accordingly, and apart from future marketing possibilities, the project is important to the future course of the CAE product line.

The SQAP conforms to ANSI/IEEE Std 730-1984, except that, following SOS engineering programming practices, the ANSI/IEEE standard is supplemented by sections on measurements and trend analysis. Also, tool certification is included. Also, the IEEE standard's functional audit is replaced by qualification, which subsumes the purposes of a functional audit.

13.3.2 References

1. SOS Doc. 234567, Software Development Plan (SQP) for Project CASE001.
2. SOS Doc. 100100, Standard Practices for the Development and Maintenance of Engineering Software.
3. SOS Doc. 234568, Configuration Management Plan (CMP) for Project CASE001.
4. SOS Doc. 234569, Verification and Validation Plan (V&V Plan) for Project CASE001.
5. SOS Doc. 300100, Software Quality Assurance Operating Procedures (SQAOP).
6. Memo for File (F. J. Haydn, April 4): Project Management Responsibilities for Project CASE001.

13.3.3 Management

13.3.3.1 Organization. The attached organization chart [Figure 13.1], extracted from the SOS four-level organization chart, supplemented by the functions pertinent to Project CASE001, depicts the organizations (elements) responsible for prosecuting the subject project. Responsibilities of elements (e.g., CAE Engineering) not specific to the subject project are given by the SOS corporate policy guidebook. CASE001 responsibilities are

- Project CASE001 Systems Management—Responsible for assuring compatibility of Boss, Canvasser, and Ooditor (and all three with OooC and Dynamic), and evaluating technical decisions affecting overall behavior of evolving environment for object-oriented programming. The last includes evaluation of all prototype code demonstrations. The group is headed by the project manager, who has the following additional responsibilities: overall coordination and direction of technical tasks from requirements analysis through alpha testing and coordination of V&V tasks other than those for which Quality is responsible. (See V&V Plan.)
- Ooditor Group—Development of Ooditor through unit testing. The group is divided into two teams, one for requirements modeling and one for design and implementation. The head of the group is also a member of the systems management group. At the conclusion of the requirements phase, the members of the requirements modeling team will be reassigned to the test group and the Ooditor design and implementation team.
- Canvasser Group—identical to above.

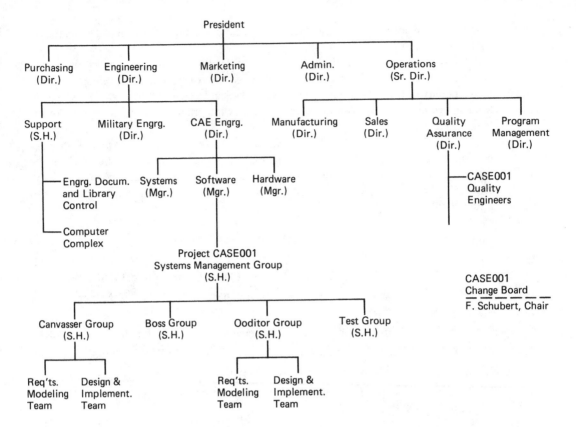

Figure 13.1 EIEI/CASE001 Organization

- Boss Group—Development of Boss through production code and execution. The head of the group is also a member of the systems management group.

- Test Group—Preparation of integration and system test documentation; performance of those tests; preparation of test reports and anomaly reports; limited problem diagnosis; liaison with Boss, Canvasser, and Ooditor groups for debugging. Head of group is a member of the systems management group.

- Engineering Documentation and Library Control Group— Repository for all approved documentation and computer library components. Entry of changes to all approved library components. Dissemination of change information. Physical release of controlled software for test or distribution.

- Change Board—See Configuration Management Plan. The change board has the only authority for release of CASE001 software for general distribution. However, no release is permitted without the recommendation of the project manager.

- Quality Engineering—Management of CASE001 quality program; qualification; various audits as described in subsequent sections; participation in V&V activities as described in subsequent sections.

Conflicts among the elements reporting to the CASE001 systems management group are resolved by that group or by the project manager alone. Conflicts between the change management board or the engineering support department and any of the elements reporting to the project manager will be resolved by the director of engineering if agreement cannot be reached at lower levels. Conflicts between quality engineers and CASE001 programmers will, if possible, be resolved by the lead quality engineer and either the head of the applicable programming group or the project manager. If necessary, such conflicts will escalate to

1. CAE engineering director and quality director.
2. Engineering director and operations senior director.
3. The agenda of the weekly senior staff meeting.

Conflicts between quality engineers and the engineering support department will, if possible, be resolved by the lead quality engineer and the head of the engineering documentation and library control group. If necessary, such conflicts will escalate to

1. Support manager and quality director.
2. Quality director and engineering director.
3. Engineering director and operations senior director.
4. The agenda of the weekly senior staff meeting.

13.3.3.2 Tasks. The primary tasks (not including reports, measurements, trend analysis, product analysis, and tool calibration) follow:

Concept Phase (in progress)

1. Return on Investment analysis, CAE Memo for File #8881.
2. Identification of major system components and assignment of features to each, CAE Memo for File #8872.
3. Feasibility Study and Report, CAE memo for File #8879.
4. Feature Set Definition, CAE Memo for File #8868.
5. Software Development Plan (SDP).
6. Software Configuration Management Plan (SCMP).
7. Software Verification and Validation Plan (SVVP).
8. Software Quality Assurance Plan (SQAP).
9. Reviews per Table 1. [Table 13.1]

Requirements Phase

1. Development and demonstration of Boss prototype, iterated as necessary.
2. Evaluations of Boss prototypes and preparation of evaluation reports.
3. Development of Boss SRS.
4. Review of Boss SRS.
5. Development and demonstration of Canvasser prototype, iterated as necessary.
6. Evaluation of Canvasser prototypes and preparation of evaluation reports.

Concept Phase Task	Reviewed by				
	CAE Eng. Dir.	Software Mgr.	Case001 Proj. Mgr.	Change Board Chair.	QA Dir.
1	X*	X*			
2		X			
3	X	X*			X
4		X			
5		X*		X	
6			X*		X
7			X*		X
8			X		X*

* May not be delegated.

Table 13.1 Concept Phase Reviews

7. Development of Canvasser SRS.

8. Review of Canvasser SRS.

9. Development and demonstration of Ooditor prototype, iterated as necessary.

10. Evaluation of Ooditor prototypes and preparation of evaluation reports.

11. Development of Ooditor SRS.

12. Review of Ooditor SRS.

13. Development of Systems Interface Documentation—intrasystem interfaces and interfaces to OooC and Dynamic.

14. Review of interface documentation.

15. Prepare preliminary User Manual.

16. Review of preliminary User Manual.

17. Audits for conformance to SOS standards and the SDP of evaluation reports, SRSs, interface documentation, and preliminary User Manual.

18. Preparation of Measurements Plan (MP). [Not required by IEEE Std.]

19. Documentation of test cases used to evaluate prototypes.

Design Stage of Design and Implementation Phase

1. Develop and incrementally evaluate Boss structure.

2. Design and document test cases for incremental Boss executions.

3. Prepare SDD for Boss.

4. Review Boss SDD.

5. Prepare preliminary SDD for Canvasser.

6. Review preliminary Canvasser SDD.

7. Complete SDD for Canvasser.

8. Produce PDSLS design language analysis report for Canvasser.

9. Review Canvasser SDD.

10. Prepare preliminary SDD for Ooditor.

11. Review preliminary Ooditor SDD.

12. Complete SDD for Ooditor.

13. Produce PDSLS design language analysis report for Ooditor.

14. Review Ooditor SDD.

15. Prepare Test Plan for integration and systems testing.

16. Review Test Plan.

17. Prepare preliminary Test Design Specification.

18. Prepare traceability table for Canvasser and Ooditor

19. Prepare qualification plan.

Implementation Stage of Design and Implementation Phase

1. Complete data design of Boss.

2. Review completed Boss.

3. Code Canvasser.

4. Generate static analysis report for Canvasser.

5. Review Canvasser code.

6. Unit test Canvasser code.

7. Code Ooditor.

8. Generate static analysis report for Ooditor.

9. Review Ooditor code.

10. Unit test Ooditor code.

11. Complete Test Design Specification document.

12. Review Test Design Specification.

13. Prepare Test Case Specification Document.

14. Review Test Case Specification Document.

15. Prepare test scripts as necessary.

16. Complete User Manual.

17. Review User Manual.

Testing Phase

1. Incrementally integrate Canvasser components and test.

2. Incrementally integrate Ooditor components and test.

3. Test Ooditor operating under Boss.

4. Test Canvasser operating under Boss.

5. Execute tests of Ooditor operating in concert with Canvasser, both under Boss.

6. Perform qualification testing.

1. Limited release to a CAE programming group for alpha testing. The group will be identified during the test phase.

2. Perform alpha testing—Redevelop either Canvasser or Ooditor in OooC using CASE00 software.

3. Modify software as necessary per alpha test evaluations.

4. Regression testing as necessary following changes.

5. Repeat system tests with revised Canvasser or Ooditor.

6. Requalify system.

Operation and Maintenance Phase

1. Removal of latent defects.

2. Change Board action on recommended improvements or additions of new features.

3. Regression testing following any change.

4. Analysis of reported anomalies.

5. Training of CAE programming staff.

13.3.3.3 Responsibilities. Tables 2 through 5 [Tables 13.2 through 13.5] give the primary and supporting functional responsibilities for each of the life cycle tasks, starting with the requirements phase.

13.3.4 Documentation

13.3.4.1 Purpose. The following documents govern the development, verification, validation, use, and maintenance of the subject software. Unless noted, Engineering is responsible for the origination, verification (with participation from QA), maintenance, and control of each. Until the software is released for general availability, CASE001 project personnel are responsible for maintenance and control. After release, maintenance and control will pass to a yet unformed CASE maintenance group and to CAE Engineering Support, respectively.

1. Software Requirements Specifications for each program.

2. Software Design Descriptions for each program.

3. Software Verification and Validation Plan.

4. Software Verification and Validation Report.

5. User Manual.

6. Test Plans and Specifications.

7. Software Development Plan.

8. Software Configuration Management Plan.

9. System Qualification Plan (QA has all responsibilities). [Note: this is not required by IEEE standards.]

10. Qualification Report (QA has all responsibilities). [Note: this is not required by IEEE standards.]

				Requirements Phase					
Task	*Syst. Mgmt.*	*Canv. Rqmts.*	*Canv D&I*	*Boss Group*	*Oodit. Rqmts.*	*Oodit. D&I*	*QA*	*Test Group*	*Change Board*
1				P					
2	P			P					
3				P					
4	P			S			P	P	
5		P							
6	P	S		P					
7		P							
8	P	S	P				P	P	
9									
10	P				S	P			
11					P				
12	P				S	P	P	P	
13		P		P	P				
14	P								
15		P		P	P				
16	P							P	
17							P		
18							P		
19		P		P	P				

Note: P indicates primary responsibility
     S indicates support role

Table 13.2 Responsibilities for Requirements Phase

13.3.4.2 Minimum Documentation Requirements. Minimum requirements for the above documents are found in SOS Doc. 100100, Reference #2.

13.3.5 Standards, Practices, and Conventions

13.3.5.1 Purpose. SOS Doc. 100100, Reference 2, specifies the technical tasks and the manner in which they are to be performed for each life cycle phase of CAE software. CASE001 software is included under the category CAE software. The document establishes primary and secondary responsibilities for all generic tasks. These may be matched with the task descriptions of Section 3 to determine responsibilities. Generic software quality assurance tasks are defined in SOS Doc. 300100, Software Quality Assurance Operating Procedures (SQAOP), Reference 5.

13.3.5.2 Content. The following extract from the SOS 100100 table of contents identifies the relevant standards, conventions, and practices governing documents and other artifacts of the development of the subject software.

- Section 2.1—Design of test cases for prototype evaluation.
- Section 2.2—Prototype demonstration and evaluation.

Design and Implementation Phase Design Tasks

Task	Syst. Mgmt.	Canv. Rqmts.	Canv D&I	Boss Group	Oodit. Rqmts.	Oodit. D&I	QA	Test Group	Change Board
1				P					
2				P					
3				P					
4	P		P	S		P	P	P	
5			P						
6	P	P¹	S				P	P	
7			P						
8			P						
9		P¹	S	P		P	P	P	
10						P			
11	P				P¹	S	P	P	
12						P			
13						P			
14			P	P	P¹	S	P	P	
15			S	S		S		P	
16	P						P	P	
17			S	S		S		P	
18		P			P			S	
19							P		

Note: P indicates primary responsibility.
S indicates support role.

¹Designated team leader, only.

Table 13.3 Responsibilities for Design

- Section 2.3—Prototype evaluation reports.
- Section 2.4—SRS and interface documentation.
- Section 3.2—SDD. Note: The SDD for Boss will necessarily be different from the stipulations of Section 3.2. In particular, emphasis will be placed on the natural language definitions of classes and objects and their relations to the features identified in the Boss SRS.
- Section 3.3—Problem decomposition.
- Section 3.7—Use of Program Design Statement Language System (PDSLS).
- Section 4.1—Coding standards for structure, labeling, and annotation.
- Section 4.2—Unit test practices and reporting.
- Section 5.1—Integration and system test documentation.
- Section 5.2—Release of source code to integration libraries.
- Section 5.3—Control of test materials.
- Section 5.4—Regression test policies.
- Section 6—Product release and change control.

Design and Implementation Phase Implementation Tasks

Task	Syst. Mgmt.	Canv. Rqmts.	Canv. D&I	Boss Group	Oodit. Rqmts.	Oodit. D&I	QA	Test Group	Change Board
1				P					
2			P	S		P	P	P	
3			P						
4			P						
5			S	P		P	P	P	
6			P						
7						P			
8						P			
9			P	P		S	P	P	
10						P			
11		S		S	S			P	
12[2]	P	P[1]	P	P	P[1]	P	P	S	
13			S	S		S		P	
14[2]	P	P[1]	P	P	P[1]	P	P	S	
15								P	
16		P		P	P			S	
17	P						P	P	

Note: P indicates primary responsibility.
S indicates support role.

[1] Designated team leader, only
[2] All groups indicated not required for each subtask. See Section 6.4 [Section 13.3.6.4]

Table 13.4 Responsibilities for Implementation

- Section 6.4—Problem reporting.
- Section 7.1—User documentation.
- Section 7.2—User training.
- Section 8—Software Verification and Validation.

The following sections of SOS 300100 (SQAOP) define the operating procedures used for software quality assurance. Note that all procedures concerning software reviews are contained therein.

- Section 1—Introduction.
- Section 2—Tool certification.
- Section 3—Reviews.
  3.1 Preparation and conduct.
  3.2 Reports.
- Section 4—Audits.
  4.1 Library control. [See Appendix A-1]
  4.2 Unit folders. (not applicable to CASE001)
  4.3 Requirements documentation.
  4.4 Design documentation.

Testing Phase

TASK	Syst. Mgmt.	Canv. Rqmts.	Canv D&I	Boss Group	Oodit. Rqmts.	Oodit. D&I	QA	Test Group	Change Board
1			S					P	
2						S		P	
3				S		S		P	
4			S	S				P	
5			S	S		S		P	
6							P	S	

Installation and Checkout Phase

TASK	Syst. Mgmt.	Canv. Rqmts.	Canv D&I	Boss Group	Oodit. Rqmts.	Oodit D&I	QA	Test Group	Change Board
1									P
2	Staff for alpha testing to be determined								
3		P	P	P	P	P			
4		S	S	S	S	S		P	
5								P	
6							P	S	

Operation and Maintenance Phase

TASK	Syst. Mgmt.	Canv. Rqmts.	Canv D&I	Boss Group	Oodit. Rqmts.	Oodit. D&I	QA	Test Group	Change Board
1			P	P		P			
2	S								P
3								P	
4	P						P		
5	Training Staff to be determined								

Note: P indicates primary responsibility
S indicates support role

Table 13.5 Responsibilites for Testing and Later Phases

 4.5 Source code.
 4.6 Unit testing.
 4.7 Integration testing.
 4.8 System testing.
 4.9 Final logic documentation.
 4.10 User documentation.
 4.11 Distribution of audit reports.

- Section 5—Tracking of corrective actions.

- Section 6—Defect severity levels. [See Appendix A-4]

- Section 7—Qualification.
 7.1 Qualification plan.
 7.2 Qualification specification.
 7.3 Qualification audit.
 7.4 Qualification test operations.
 7.5 Qualification report.

- Section 8—Defect data collection.

- Section 9 – Module fault incidence analysis. [See Appendix A-3]

- Section 10—Analysis of fault aging.

- Section 11—Analysis of defect removal effectiveness.

- Section 12—Product measurements and analysis.

- Section 13—Trend analyses.

- Section 14—Vendor surveys.

- Section 15—Vendor surveillance.

Section 4 is designed to ensure compliance to SOS 100100 [and also to MIS programming standard practices]. References to the procedures are found in the following sections.

13.3.6 Reviews and Audits

13.3.6.1 Software Requirements Review (SRR). See Reference 5, Sections 3 and 4.3. Three SRRs will be held, one each for Ooditor, Canvasser, and Boss. Inputs to each SRR will consist of the evaluation reports pertaining to the final prototype demonstration (in the case of Boss, the demonstration resulting in an approved user interface), the applicable SRS, documentation of the test cases used in the final prototype demonstrations, and the software interface specification. The SRR will be held within two weeks of the delivery of draft SRSs to Engineering Documentation and Library Control.

The SRRs will be held to ensure technical feasibility and traceability to the feature set definition, clarity of documentation, and compliance with Sections 2.3 and 2.4 of Reference 2. Review participants will include the entire applicable requirements modeling team, the team leader of the applicable design and implementation team, all members of the systems management group, a member of the test group, and at least one QA engineer. Names will be provided by appropriate supervision at least two weeks before the review takes place. The software quality engineer will chair the review and will record any corrective actions that are required.

13.3.6.2 Preliminary Design Review (PDR). See Reference 5, Sections 3 and 4.4. A PDR will be held for each of the three programs within one week after the draft preliminary SDD is submitted to Engineering Documentation and Library Control. For Canvasser and Ooditor, the SDD is expected to contain a definition of software structures down to each functional compilation unit and global data structure (see Section 3.2 of Reference 2). For Boss, the SDD is expected to describe the classes, their hierarchical structure, and their instantiations used in the final prototype of the requirements phase.

The PDRs address continuing technical feasibility, clarity of documentation, and compliance with Section 3.2 of Reference 2. Review participants will include the entire applicable design and implementation team, the team leader of the pertinent requirements modeling team, the systems management group, one member of the test group, and at least one QA engineer. Appropriate supervision will designate participants at least two weeks prior to the scheduled reviews. The QA engineer will chair the review and document the findings.

13.3.6.3 Test Plan Review. See Reference 5, Section 3. The plan for integration and system testing will be reviewed within two weeks of submittal of the plan to Engineering Documentation and Library Control. The review will address the feasibility of the planned test process (including assurance that necessary resources will be available), clarity, and conformance to Section 5.1 of reference 2.

   Review participants include the plan author, the systems management group, and a QA engineer. The last will chair the review and document the findings.

13.3.6.4 Test Specifications. See Reference 5, Section 3. Test design and test case specifications will be reviewed at least 30 days before the start of the applicable tests. The reviews will address assurance that all system features and discrete functions of the SRSs will be tested, tests are feasible, and documentation conforms to Section 5.1 of reference 2. Reviewers will be provided traceability tables to help them ensure that testing will be complete with regard to system and program requirements. However, in off-line reviews, QA will check to make certain that for each table entry, at least one test at each of the integration and systems levels has been designed.

   The reviews will also serve the purpose of making certain that, to the fullest extent possible, test designs used for prototype evaluation are used again for testing the production versions.

   For integration test documentation, review participants will include the author of the work reviewed and—at the discretion of the head of the test group—other members of the group in addition to the author, the team leader for requirements modeling of the applicable program, at least two members of the applicable design and implementation team, and a QA engineer. For system test documentation, the only difference is that the full systems management group will participate. All test documentation reviews will be chaired by the QA engineer, who will also document the findings.

13.3.6.5 Critical Design Reviews (CDRs). See Reference 5, Section 3. CDRs will be held for groups of closely related software structural elements: the module level for Canvasser and Ooditor, and classes for Boss. The CDRs will determine the acceptability of the detailed software designs as found in the SDD, traceability to the preliminary design sections of the SDD, and, except for Boss, conformance to the requirements of Section 3.2 of Reference 2. For Boss, the basis for conformance will be the standards of the OooC language specification and annotation standards still to be defined.

   For Canvasser and Ooditor, input to each CDR will also include a report from the PDSLS pseudocode processor.

   The software elements entering into each review will be determined at the conclusion of the preliminary stage of the design phase. The reviews will be held within one week of the submittal of the relevant SDD sections to Engineering Documentation and Library Control. Participants will include the author(s), at least one member of the corresponding requirements modeling team (presumably, the team leader), one member of each of the other two design and implementation teams, a member of the test group, and from time to time a QA engineer. QA will attend three-tenths the total number of CDRs, randomly selected. If QA finds consistent discrepancy between the way CDRs are conducted and Section 3 of Reference 5, QA will attend all subsequent CDRs. CDRs will be chaired by the test group representative, who will also record the findings.

13.3.6.6 Software V&V (Plan) Review (SVVPR). [Note that IEEE Standard for SQA Plans calls for a V&V Review, while the Guide to SQA Plans calls for a review of the plan, as described here.]

See Reference 5, Section 3. The Software V&V Plan (SVVP) is reviewed to make certain that it is feasible, that the schedule of V&V activities is consistent with the development schedule, that it conforms with the requirements of Section 8 of Reference 2, and that all necessary V&V assignments have been made. Since several of the specifics of the V&V Plan are carried out as specifics of the SQA program (e.g., standard practices for reviews are documented in Reference 5 rather than Reference 2), the review of the SVVP also ensures conformance to applicable QA standards. Since the V&V Plan contains exit criteria for all work packages, the review will emphasize the plan's documentation of assessable (quantifiable wherever practicable) exit criteria.

The review is held within two weeks of submittal of the draft plan to Engineering Documentation and Library Control. Review participants include the author(s), all members of the CASE001 systems management group, the head of the test group (and other members at the head's discretion), the chairperson of the change board, one member of the CAE Engineering Systems Department, a member of the engineering documentation and library control section, and the lead quality engineer assigned to the project. The review will be chaired by the chairperson of the change board, who will document the findings.

13.3.6.7 Code Reviews. See Reference 5, Section 3. Code reviews will emphasize traceability to applicable SDD sections, good design practice, defect detection, and—for Canvasser and Ooditor—conformance to Section 4.1 of Reference 2.

For Canvasser and Ooditor, code reviews will be conducted for each compilation unit. Compilation units generally will correspond to the design structures of individual CDRs. Before system testing starts, reviews will be conducted on complete Boss code structures corresponding to the structures reviewed in individual Boss CDRs.

Input to Canvasser and Ooditor code reviews will include the code listings generated by the compiler and the reports of the static analyzer, CLASS. Listings produced by the OooC compiler and the reports generated by CLASSIER, a modified version of CLASS, will constitute the input for Boss code reviews.

The participants in each review will be the author(s) of the code, one programmer from each of the other two implementation and design teams, one member of the test group, and from time to time, a QA engineer. The basis for QA participation will be random sampling, with a median attendance at three tenths of the total number of code reviews. If QA finds consistent discrepancy between the way reviews are conducted and Section 3 of Reference 5, QA will attend all subsequent code reviews. The reviews will be chaired by the test group representative, who will also record the findings.

13.3.6.8 Qualification. See Reference 5, Section 7. Qualification will have two main parts: audits and testing. Audits will make certain that all technical problems have been closed out (or, if sufficiently minor, have an acceptable plan for solution), and that final user documentation is ready for use during testing. (See Section 4.10 of Reference 5.) [Appendix A-2]

Entry to qualification testing requires that the software have no level 1 defects (defects that prevent correct completion of documented features), fewer than three known level 2 defects per thousand noncomment source lines (NCSS), and fewer than five known level 2 defects per thousand NCSS. Section 6 of Reference 5 defines the three severity levels. Patches will not be permitted in the program loads submitted for test.

Qualification testing, conducted by QA, will include planned tests to check basic feature performance and arbitrary operation of the system over a total of 40 operating hours. The planned test cases will be drawn from those used for system testing. System test cases are rerun to increase confidence, apart from that provided by library control, that the software about to be released for alpha testing is identical to the version used at the conclusion of system testing. The arbitrary operation will make certain that the user manual is adequate—or can be made so with suitable inserts—for alpha testing.

Successful qualification testing requires that the software be free of level 1 defects, have fewer than 90 level 2 defects, and have fewer than 300 level 3 defects. The known level 2 and 3 defects include those discovered during system testing, regardless of whether they appeared again during qualification testing. Following the successful conclusion of testing, the lead software engineer and the project manager will complete and sign form SQAOP-F14. The signed form will be forwarded to the change board to enable limited release (for alpha testing) of the software package.

QA will issue a qualification report, documenting its findings.

13.3.6.9 Physical Audit. See Reference 5, Section 4.9. Concurrently with qualification, QA will examine the SDD for consistency with source code. Ten percent of the SDD will be so inspected. Also, to ensure that all code elements are described in the SDD, 20% of the entries in the load maps will be selected and the SDD examined to ensure that the entries are found therein under the same name.

13.3.6.10 In-Process Audits. [Note that the audits described here do not include technical audits of interface specifications, design, and code as required by the IEEE SQA Plan Standard. Such evaluations are left for the reviews described above.]

See Reference 5, Sections 4.3, 4.4, and 4.5. As part of its participation in SRRs, PDRs, and test documentation reviews, and as part of its limited participation in CDRs and code reviews, QA will examine material constituting the substance of the reviews for conformance to applicable sections of Reference 2. For CDRs and code reviews, QA will also audit for conformance to Section 3 of Reference 5.

QA will audit the traceability table prepared by Engineering to make certain that all functional requirements are accounted for.

QA will sample 25% of all prototype demonstrations and 25% of prototype evaluation reports during the requirements phase to determine conformance to Section 2.2 and 2.3 of Reference 2. If, in the auditor's opinion, either the demonstrations or the reports consistently and substantially deviate from the standard, sampling will be increased to 100%.

During the design and implementation phases of Boss, QA will sample 20% of all prototype evaluations and evaluation reports for conformance to Sections 2.2 and 2.3 of Reference 2, as tailored for suitability to design refinement rather than requirements modeling. Apart from the normal reporting of discrepancies, if, in the auditor's opinion, either the demonstrations or the reports consistently and substantially deviate from the tailored standard, the auditor will immediately attempt to resolve the matter with the leader of the Boss design and implementation team. Failing this, the lead software quality engineer will, in turn, escalate the problem to the Boss section head and the project manager to get an expedient resolution. If none is possible, the matter will be referred to the director of quality assurance for the conflict procedures outlined in Section 3.1. [Section 13.3.3.1 of this chapter]

For Canvasser and Ooditor, QA will examine 10% of the unit test reports for conformance to Section 4.2 of Reference 2. See Reference 5, Section 4.6. If, in the auditor's opinion, the reports consistently and substantially deviate from the standard, procedures will be initiated analogous to those for resolving problems in Boss demonstrations during the design phase.

During periods of integration testing, QA will witness 20% of all integration test operations. The auditor will focus on the test group's adherence to verification of correct versions of components, adherence to test case specifications or applicable test scripts, accurate logging of test results, and correct completion of defect data forms. See Reference 5, Section 4.7. If, in the auditor's opinion, the test operations consistently and substantially deviate from standards, sampling will be increased to 50%.

During system testing, QA will witness all test operations. The audit purposes will be the same as those for integration testing. However, all code changes will require formal baseline change approval, and the basis for success criteria will derive exclusively from the SRSs and the Feature Set Definition, CAE Memo for File #8868, authored by W. Mozart and H. Purcell. See Reference 5, Section 4.8.

Code control audits are described in Section 3.10.

Following each audit, the auditor will prepare a memo record of the audit, containing date, specific items or activities examined, results, and—if appropriate—conclusions. Distribution of audit reports will be as specified in Section 4.11.1 of Reference 5. The lead software quality engineer will prepare monthly summaries of audit activity, emphasizing conclusions documented in audit reports and discrepancy counts classified by audit category. Distribution of the reports will be as specified in Section 4.11.2 of Reference 5. Also, all discrepancies will be recorded in the composite log of required corrections.

13.3.6.11 Managerial Reviews. At the end of each life cycle phase, managerial reviews will be held to determine if phase exit criteria have been sufficiently satisfied to recommend transition to the succeeding phase. Compliance with phase exit criteria will be based, as applicable, on V&V reports, audit report monthly summaries, the composite log of correction items, measurements reports, trend analysis, product analysis, and test results. The reviews will be held within one week of completing all the documentation required to establish a new baseline.

No format for the minutes is specified. However, the minutes must plainly record the basis for judging whether transition to the next phase is justified.

The review at the end of the requirements phase will require completion of the SRSs for all three programs and the interface documentation. Participants in this review will include the project manager, the three program section heads, the head of the test group, and the lead software quality engineer. The project manager will chair the review and the quality engineer will record the minutes.

Since it is unlikely that the SRSs for all three programs will be completed simultaneously, design may proceed on any program for which the SRS has been completed while awaiting the completion of others. However, immediately upon completion of the requirements phase managerial review, the designers of any design work so accomplished must informally review the work for consistency with the applicable SRS.

Managerial reviews will be held at the end of the design and implementation phases and at the end of integration testing. These reviews will be similar to the one at the end of the requirements phase, except that reviews will be held individually for each of the programs, without the need for simultaneity.

Managerial reviews will be held at the end of the testing phase and at the end of the installation and checkout phase. These, too, will follow the format of the requirements phase review, except that alpha test evaluation reports and product analysis reports will govern the judgments to be made at the end of the installation and checkout phase.

Managerial reviews will be held quarterly during the operation and maintenance phase. Participation and input for the reviews remains to be determined.

To avoid a potentially unstable product, at all managerial reviews consideration will be given to the need for formal regression to an earlier phase. Such consideration will be given to the individual programs and to the entire system. Anomaly measurements and trend analysis reports will form the primary basis for deciding if regression is advisable.

13.3.7 Software Configuration Management

The configuration management plan can be found in Reference 3. G. Telemann of QA is a member of the change board, and he or his delegate will attend all change board meetings. The change board is empowered as the sole authority to release CASE001 software and to authorize changes to baselined materials.

13.3.8 Problem Reporting and Corrective Action

See Reference 5, Section 5. QA will maintain a composite log for tracking items requiring corrective action. The log is divided into two parts: one for technical problems and the other for deviations from project plans or engineering or quality standards. The sources for the log entries include anomaly reports, review minutes, audit reports, test logs and reports, and evaluation reports prepared during alpha testing. Problems found during prototype evaluations will *not* be included in the log. Problems found by integration testing will *not* be included in the log if they are fixed the same day they are detected. (They will, however, be entered on defect collection forms.)

Each item will be given a unique identifier, the date of entry, the name of the person entering the item, a brief description of the problem with a reference to its documented source, the name of the person (if necessary, organization) responsible for correction, the date assigned for correction, the status of the correction (pending, active, completed, completion verified), the date the item is closed (verified completion), and a reference for the closing of the item.

Verification of correction will depend on the nature of the problem. Generally, the correction of technical problems found during reviews will be considered verified when the reviewed document or artifact is updated. Problems of sufficient scope to warrent a second review will be considered verified only upon successful completion of the review. The correction of problems found during testing or use will be considered verified by successful testing. Generally, verification that procedural problems have been corrected will require a memo from the person who had reported the problem. Details on the methods of verifying correction are given in Section 5.2 of Reference 5.

The log will be maintained in Account QACASE on the Engineering Mainframe Complex. Details for reading the log will be provided to all CASE001 project management personnel and to the chairperson of the change board.

During qualification testing and alpha testing and during the operation and maintenance phase, reported problems will be screened before entry into the correction log. Such problems, reported on Form S-7890 [Appendix A-5], will be stored in an interim log (also in Account QACASE) until confirmed by change board action. The SCMP states that the change board will assign analysis of reported problems to Engineering or QA for confirmation. The interim log format will be identical to that of the correction log, except that assignments will be for analysis, not correction, and that "verification" should be interpreted as confirmation that a real problem exists.

13.3.9 Tools, Techniques, and Methodologies

[Note: the IEEE Standard addresses only *SQA* tools, techniques, and methods.]

Reference 5 describes the techniques and methods that are used for software quality assurance. With regard to tools, see Section 2 of Reference 5 for tool certification procedures.

The tools directly entering into software quality assurance that are planned for use on CASE001 software follow:

1. PDSLS pseudocode processor. Used on Canvasser and Ooditor to detect certain classes of errors in the detailed design of software components and inconsistencies among components. PDSLS also provides structural reports of the relations among components. PDSLS will be used by the designer of each component before the CDR pertaining to the component. PDSLS will be used by the design and implementation team leaders at their discretion on aggregates of components. Certified by Report V4567 for files of up to 1,200 source statements. [Certification not required by IEEE standard.]

2. C Language Analysis Standard System (CLASS). Used on source code files to report unreachable code, patently infinite loops, language specification violations, uninitialized variables, loop and branch nests exceeding specified depths, certain data flow anomalies, and inconsistencies among files. CLASS will be used on source code files by their programmers after compilation but before unit testing. At the discretion of the leader of the design and implementation team, CLASS will be used on aggregates of source files. Certified by report V7890 for source code files up to 10,000 statements.

3. C Language Analyzer Standard System Incorporating Enhanced Reporting (CLASS-IER). Similar to CLASS, but capable of dealing with functions required to implement object-oriented programming. CLASSIER, which is still under development (see Section 3.12), will report all class instantiations within the same source file as the class. CLASSIER will be used on source code files by their programmers after each compilation. At the discretion of the head of the Boss group, CLASSIER will be used on aggregates of source files totalling no more than 10,000 statements. QA will certify the capabilities of CLASSIER at the vendor's facility prior to delivery to SOS.

4. Infobank data base system. Used for correction action logs, defect data bases, and library control records. Certification not required, since tool does not directly affect product.

5. ERECT—Program load binder. Accepts logic and data components in binary or C source code and builds an executable program load. Checks component edition identifiers against those on link list. Automatically loads patch files after other files have been linked. Used to assist code library control during testing and for final release. Certified by grandfather rule.

13.3.10 Code Control

Until releasing source code files for integration testing, programmers will create and modify code through the QSM librarian system. No external control mechanism will be imposed.

Source code and data modules will be loaded onto the CASE001 system disk for integration. A disk entry journal will capture the entry. The disk entry journal is "owned" by Engineering Documentation and Library Control (EDLC), which has read access and which also maintains hard copy of the journal. If compiled, the object version of each source code module will automatically be placed on the system disk and a journal entry will be made. Program loads will be generated by ERECT from link lists prepared by the test group for integration testing. The link lists will be prepared by EDLC for system, qualification, and alpha testing, and for general releases. See Reference 2, Section 5.2 for edition labeling practices.

Integration testing baselines will be established each time a new group of compilation units has been successfully tested in the evolving system. Once baselined, source code for the units may be changed only on the system disk and only by the EDLC librarian. Library control audits by QA (see Section 4.1 of Reference 5) will be held at random intervals during integration and subsequent testing, but no less than once a week. The audits will examine the system disk journal to determine the author of changes to baselined materials, will compare selected code file versions with the EDLC records, and will compare edition designation on link maps with the EDLC record of authorized editions.

During integration and subsequent testing, if the test group deems it advisable to return a changed module for unit testing, the EDLC librarian will be advised to release the module to its programmer, and will record the release. On returning the module to the CASE001 system disk, the procedures for initial release will be repeated.

At the conclusion of each day of integration testing, the librarian will back up the system disk on tape. From system testing on, backup will occur at the end of each day during which a change to the product (as distinct from test harness) code or data was made. Mother and daughter backup tapes will be stored in the EDLC file room.

13.3.11 Media Control

Following the usual practice of the engineering computer center, when not on-line for testing or production purposes, disk packs containing CASE001 software in any form will be stored in closed cabinets in the "ready area" of the computer room. For security purposes, from qualification testing on, the EDLC librarian assigned to CASE001 will request the operator to copy all backup tapes and will arrange to have the copies, after verification, removed to the archives center on Sibelius Street. As is the usual practice, the librarian will add the CASE001 archive tapes to the tickler file used to schedule refreshing of any tape archived for more than six months.

Access to the computer room, the EDLC file room, and the archive center is gained only by magnetic card readers. No SOS employee is enabled access to all three areas. The security system central computer maintains a file of all door openings gained through card reading. For each opening, a record is stored containing employee number, date, time of day, and door identification. Records are destroyed when 30 days old.

Labeling of media, whether disk pack or tape reel, will follow the usual practice of volume number, creation date, and identification of all libraries therein. The disk pack and tape locator records maintained by the CASE001 librarian will carry information identical to the media labels.

13.3.12 Supplier Control

SOS has contracted with Rameau-Couperin Industries (RCI) to produce the CLASSIER static analyzer from a base consisting of the CLASS static analyzer. No other vendors were considered, since RCI holds the rights to CLASS, and, given the familiarity of the SOS staff with CLASS, the interests of quality dictated that CLASS methods of code analysis be continued.

Since CLASSIER will not be incorporated in the CASE001 production software, RCI was not required to comply with the IEEE standard for SQA plans. RCI has its own software quality program. Internal auditors monitor the program and prepare monthly audit reports for each project. RCI agreed to have the CLASSIER statement of work include SOS's right to review the audit reports for CLASSIER on demand. An SOS quality engineer will review these reports monthly per the applicable provisions of Section 15 of Reference 5.

The statement of work stipulates RCI's delivery of an acceptance test procedure 30 days prior to testing and SOS acceptance testing at RCI's facilities. Acceptance testing may not start until the test procedure itself has been accepted by SOS. An SOS quality engineer will review the procedure for general conformance with Section 7.2 (Qualification Test Specifications) of Reference 5, which has been furnished to RCI, and for specific traceability to the technical specifications prepared by SOS for CLASSIER. The quality engineer will witness the acceptance tests. Acceptance will constitute tool certification.

13.3.13 Records Collection, Maintenance, and Retention

The measurements of Sections 14 and 15, along with reports of analysis and evaluation results, will be retained in hard copy form in the quality assurance records room for a period of three years. Hard copy audit reports will be kept in the room for one year. Hard copy test case specifications, test scripts, and test reports will be kept for the earlier of five years or six feature releases.

Documents and other artifacts of CASE001 development will be maintained by the EDLC according to engineering standards.

13.3.14 Measurements

Defect Data Collection. Defect data will be collected from the following sources:

1. SRRs, PDRs, CDRs, and code reviews.

2. Anomaly reports produced during system, qualification, and alpha testing, and during operation.

3. Diagnostic logs produced during integration, system, qualification, and alpha testing, and during operation.

A composite defect data base will be maintained by QA on an Infobank data base. The fields in the data base will be as follows:

1. Identification number. Where applicable, the number will be the same as that of corresponding records in the corrections log. This will permit filling in certain fields by conjoining defect records with those of the corrections log.

2. Method of detection (SRR, system test, and so forth).

3. Category of fault (logic, input/output, and so forth, as given in Section 8 of Reference 5).

4. Attributed origin (requirements phase, system test regression, and so forth, as given in Section 8 of Reference 5).

5. Module(s) in error.

6. Severity level per Section 6 of Reference 5.

7. Date of detection.

8. Date of verified fix.

Data related to documentation errors will not be collected. However, reported problems in user documentation, from qualification testing on, will be collected separately. QA will grade these reports by severity (major or minor). QA will also date the receipt of each report and the date (if any) of the release of a corresponding fix.

Unfiltered Reports. Following qualification, QA will report the number of defects attributed to each origin class. Three reports will be generated, one for each severity level. At the same time, QA will report the total number of defects by fault category. QA will distribute the reports per Section 10 of Reference 5. Also following qualification, QA will report the number of faults found by each defect removal operation (review type, test series, and so forth). Three reports will be generated, one for each severity level. QA will distribute the reports per Section 10 of Reference 5.

Process Analysis. Per Section 11 of Reference 5, at the conclusion of qualification testing QA will calculate and report the effectiveness of each method of defect removal. Since the calculation assumes that all defects will have been found at the time of the calculation, the accuracy of the report will be reduced to the extent that defects are found after release. The report will also compare the results with those of past projects.

Structural Measurements. See Section 12 of Reference 5. QA will collect the complexity measurements produced by the CLASS and CLASSIER analyzers and will calculate and report the mean and standard deviation of complexity for each program. QA will also identify and report modules having complexities exceeding twice the standard deviation and two and a half times the standard deviation. For each program, QA will calculate and report the mean and standard deviation of the number of parameters in function dummy argument lists. QA will also report those functions having twice and two and a half times the standard deviation. For the reported functions, QA will also report the number (if any) of control variables in the argument lists. QA will calculate and report the mean and standard deviation of module fan-outs (number of subordinate modules). QA will also report the modules having fan-outs twice and two and a half times the standard deviation. QA will generate the reports for each program within two weeks of the last module's release to integration testing.

The measurements are expected to be useful in early identification of some of the modules likely to prove troublesome during testing. QA will compare all calculated means and standard deviations to similar measurements made on earlier programs to detect the potential for testing and reliability problems greater than had been anticipated.

All reports will be distributed to the project manager and all CASE001 section heads.

Failure-Prone Modules. See Section 9 of Reference 5. At the conclusion of integration testing for each program, QA will prepare three histograms, one for each severity level, depicting the number of modules falling into class intervals of detected faults. Only faults found during testing will be included. At the conclusion of system testing, QA will prepare three similar histograms applicable to the aggregate of the three programs. QA will use Pareto methods to identify and report any modules contributing an unusually large number of faults to the histogram.

The histograms and the evaluations reports will be distributed to the project manager and all four section heads.

13.3.15 Trend Analysis

See Sections 10 and 13 of Reference 5.

Memory Utilization. QA will plot estimates or measurements of the amounts of central computer real memory and disk storage of data required by each program. Estimates plotted will be those from the feasibility study report, the SRR, the preliminary SDD, and the completed SDD. At biweekly intervals during the implementation stage, QA will calculate the sums of actual module real memory requirements (for modules released to integration testing) and SDD estimates (for modules not yet so released). The calculations will be added to the real memory plot.

Once all modules are loaded into the integration test load, QA biweekly will update the real memory plots with information provided by the load maps. The updates will continue until the conclusion of system testing.

Biweekly during integration, QA will update the disk storage data requirement plot from file directory data.

All updated plots will be distributed to the project manager and the three program section heads starting with the preliminary SDD. Any disquieting trends will be noted directly on the plots.

Prototype Progress. Weekly during the requirements phase, QA will plot the cumulative percentage of features successfully prototyped for each of the programs. Criteria for success will be drawn from the prototype demonstration evaluation reports. Any disquieting trends will be noted directly on the plots. QA will distribute the plots to the project manager and the three program section heads.

Design Progress. Weekly during the detailed design stage of the design and implementation phase for each program, QA will plot the cumulative percentage of designed components. The components will be those identified in the preliminary SDD, updated as necessary. The criterion for determining when a component has been designed will be the release for implementation of all detailed design associated with the component. The plot, bearing notations of any disquieting trends, will be distributed to the project manager and the three program section heads.

Implementation Progress. Weekly during the implementation stage, for modules released for implementation, QA will plot the cumulative percentage that has been coded. This plot will be drawn on the same chart as that for design progress. The criterion for determining when a module has been implemented will be its release to the test group for integration.

Integration Test Progress. Weekly, for each program during integration, QA will plot the cumulative number of test cases planned to have been attempted, those actually attempted, and those that have succeeded. QA will distribute the plot to the project manager, the head of the test group, and the applicable programming section head.

System Test Progress. Weekly during system testing, QA will plot the cumulative number of test cases planned to have been attempted, those actually attempted, and those that have succeeded. QA will distribute the plot to the project manager and the four section heads.

Known Defects. Monthly during the integration and checkout phase and the operation and maintenance phase, QA will plot the cumulative number of known defects remaining in the system. The plot will continue through successive software releases. QA will distribute the plot to the project manager and the CAE engineering software director.

Fault Reports and Fault Aging. Monthly during the integration and checkout phase and the operation and maintenance phase, QA will plot the cumulative number of fault reports, the number of unanswered fault reports, and the number of fault reports closed. The criteria for closure will be either (1) documented analysis that the report was erroneous, or (2) release of a fix. QA will distribute the plot to the project manager and the CAE engineering software director.

13.4 REFERENCES

[1] *IEEE Guide to Software Requirements Specifications*, ANSI/IEEE Std 830-1984.

[2] *IEEE Recommended Practice for Software Design Descriptions*, IEEE Std 1016-1987, p. 10.

[3] *IEEE Standard for Software Test Documentation*, ANSI/IEEE Std 829-1983, p. 10.

[4] *IEEE Standard for Software Test Documentation*, ANSI/IEEE Std 829-1983, p. 12.

253
Section 13.4:
References

[5] *IEEE Standard for Software Verification and Validation Plans*, ANSI/IEEE Std 1012-1986, p. 10.

[6] *IEEE Standard for Software Quality Plans*, ANSI/IEEE Std 730-1984.

[7] *IEEE Guide for Software Quality Assurance Planning*, ANSI/IEEE Std 983-1986.

CHAPTER 14

Plan Following a Military Model

We come now to the original core business of Superior Oceanographic Systems (SOS), military systems. SOS has considerable freedom in the way it goes about systems engineering and hardware design. Such is not the case for the software embedded in SOS's systems. The military's early history of software projects that were completed too late, at too great a cost, and in a state that made maintenance difficult led to a series of government standards and specifications that prescribe the software development practices of its contractors.

Since 1988, SOS has hewn to the top-down, document-driven philosophy of DOD-STD-2167A,[1] augmented by MIL-STD-483A[2] for configuration management, MIL-STD-490A[3] for specification practices, MIL-STD-1521B[4] for formal reviews, DOD-STD-2168,[5] which defines the requirements for contractor software quality programs, and the host of data item descriptions (DIDs) cited by DOD-STD-2167A and DOD-STD-2168.

We might note, at the outset, that claims have been made that DOD-STD-2167A does not require defense contractors to adhere to a top-down, document-driven, software design model. However, the sequence of formal reviews found in the standard lends itself only to top-down approaches, at least until one gets to the phase that the standard calls "detailed design." Moreover, only an appendix entitled "Evaluation Criteria" refutes the implication that the standard's many references to "documents" are to natural language text. In paragraph 10.2 of the appendix we read that "document," when referring to an item being evaluated, may sometimes be something "other than a document." Taking back even this grudging concession to modern software engineering, paragraph 10.2.2 then tells us that "understandability" derives from the rules specified in the U.S. Government Printing Office Style Manual, and—unless defined in the document under evaluation—from the definitions of terms found in the manual, in a designated dictionary, and in MIL-STD-12. From this we must infer either that a state diagram can never be understandable, or that it is understandable as long as the right labels are used.

We should also observe that what appear in DOD-STD-2167A to be phases— requirements analysis, preliminary design, detailed design, etc.—are carefully defined in

Section 4.1.1 of the standard as *activities*. Indeed, we are told that the activities may overlap and may be iterative. This clause has caused advocates of the standard to declare that the standard does not mandate a top-down waterfall; that no temporal dependencies attend the planning of the activities. Nevertheless, few managers will take advantage of the clause to precede preliminary design with detailed design or coding.

In any case, DOD-STD-2167A is less doctrinaire on the issue of development methods than is the set of IEEE standards. This doesn't make SOS much the happier, though. The IEEE standards are voluntary; SOS can pick, choose, and interpret as it sees fit. The military standards are mandatory, and interpretations run the risk of failing approval. SOS did take some liberties with the government in formulating its internal standards for the tangible output of development tasks, but not so many as to make government inspectors suspicious that the company is snookering them.

Now that we have returned to the fortunes of SOS, let us recall from Chapter 13 that the engineering software department is split into two parts, one to develop software for CAE products and the other for military systems.

14.1 THE PROJECT

Several years of improving relations between the Soviet Union and the United States were interrupted by a developing trade war. It seems that the United States decided to place a high tariff on beluga caviar, and the U.S.S.R. retaliated with an increased tariff on imported prewashed jeans. Or maybe it was the other way around. In any case, the primary antagonists, the U.S. Secretary of Commerce and the Soviet Trade Minister, were quick to add other imports to the burgeoning trade war. In short order the incendiary issue threatened to envelop not only the people of both nations, but the rest of the world as well. The United Nations, with the concordance of the ambassadors of the two quarreling countries, passed a resolution to have the matter put to rest by a single-handed, round-the-world sailboat race between the U.S. Secretary of Commerce and the Soviet's Trade Minister. To give both skippers time to acquire boats and to practice, the race was scheduled to take place in approximately one year. In the meantime, no new tariffs were permitted. Although the resolution was not clear on the terms for the denouement following declaration of a winner, those voting in favor were attracted to the idea of putting both gentlemen to sea for a year—perhaps forever. At an urgently called cabinet meeting, Commerce asked the other departments for any help they could offer for the race. Defense came up with a proposal. Given that the boat that takes best advantage of air and water currents is the one more likely to win, the American boat should be provided with sensor inputs and computational capabilities to keep its skipper apprised of the optimum course to steer. Meteorological information from satellites and shipboard observation stations can be relayed to the boat anywhere at sea via digital, very low frequency (VLF), transmissions. Combined with the sailboat's own measurement of relative wind and boat speed, these data are all that are needed for an onboard computer to produce optimum steering information. A senior DOD official, given to thoughts of water nymphs when his frenetic schedule so permits, code-named the project NAIADS. His staff backed into the name with "Naval Assist to Insure Against Defeat of the Secretary."

As it happens, the computational problem has considerable commonality with weather modeling problems normally given to supercomputers to solve. We cannot consider sailboats appropriate "platforms"—to use the military locution—for supercomputers. Nevertheless, in witness of its faith in American industry to respond to seemingly intractable problems, DOD prepared a technical specification document for the system and invited a number of contractors to quote. SOS, coupling its previous experience in oceanography to a low price, won the contract.

The SOS system had the following major subsystems:

- VLF antenna and receiver.
- Demodulator.
- Microcomputer, hard disk, and video display unit.
- Battery pack, water-powered generator, and DC to AC converter.

In line with the precepts of DOD-STD-2167A, design of the software could not officially begin until after a formal review of the software requirements specification (SRS). Nevertheless, during preparation of the proposal SOS submitted to the government, well before an SRS would be prepared, SOS found it could scarcely estimate the programming cost without accomplishing some design work. Although no more design was accomplished than necessary for a credible cost basis, one design decision was to configure the microcomputer software as a single program, or Computer Software Configuration Item (CSCI). The program would be divided into foreground tasks and overlaid background tasks. Each task (more precisely, the package enveloping it) would be regarded as a subsystem, or top level Computer Software Component (CSC). The only foreground tasks were those for task control, input, and output; although two tasks required a bit of input processing:

- Data logging—accepting system inputs and arranging them in a time-ordered data base.
- Skipper interface—accepting and interpreting keyboard requests for new output and refreshing the last requested output.

The primary background tasks were

- Resolving diverse water current data into a composite set of vectors.
- Resolving diverse air current data into a composite set of vectors.
- Updating the previous recommended course, based on the latest composite water current input.
- Updating the previous recommended course, based on the latest composite air current input.
- Optimally combining the two recommended courses.
- Computing present position.
- Adjusting the recommended course according to local boat speed and wind measurements.
- Given the computed water currents and estimated leeway, computing the compass course to steer to make good the recommended course.
- Recommending the sails to set before the skipper retires for the night.

A group of utility packages would be memory resident at all times. The utilities included a digital filter for computing optimum updates and course combinations, routines for interpolation and extrapolation, coordinate conversion, and the like. The group would be a top level CSC, with each of the packages a subsidiary CSC. Indeed, the digital filter package would have CSCs nested to a considerable depth.

Some further design was accomplished on each of the top level CSCs, including identification of lower-level CSCs, as in the case of the digital filter. A matrix of interfaces among the CSCs was developed, with some analysis given to each. The sum cost was the estimated cost of developing each of the identified CSCs, their interfaces, and some minor modifications to the multi-tasking operating system, SOD. To the sum, SOS added 20% for meetings and other diversions from development work, and a not inconsiderable cost for each of the formal reviews with the customer. In chronological order, the reviews are

- SRR—System Requirements Review (applies to full system, not just software).
- SDR—System Design Review (applies to full system, not just software).
- SSR—Software Specification Review.
- PDR—Preliminary Design Review.
- CDR—Critical Design Review (several of these, at different stages of design).
- TRR—Test Readiness Review.
- FQR—Formal Qualification Review, following FCA (Functional Configuration Audit) and PCA (Physical Configuration Audit).

Some of these reviews and audits were seen also in Chapter 13, which followed the IEEE software management standards.

For projects this large (SOS would have to greatly expand its programming force to complete the job within the allocated year), the government would normally appoint an Independent Verification and Validation (IV&V) contractor to examine the copious documentation produced and to participate in formal tests. However, the Secretary of Defense, while willing to help Commerce, was not about to take more of a hit on his budget than was necessary.

The project would not only be the largest software development effort yet under-taken by SOS, it would be SOS's first large-scale use of Ada. However, SOS had used Ada on a few small projects in the past, and a fairly capable set of Ada tools were on hand. Except for the capability to respond to the keyboard, output to the VDU, and accept input messages from the VLF demodulator, concurrency would be a minor issue. In any case, SOS had a multi-tasking operating system, SOD, to handle the run-time management of (Ada) tasks. The elemental software entity that would be managed, the Computer Software Unit (CSU), would be the (Ada) package. Packages would cor-respond to library entries, and wherever possible would be traceable to some testable aspect of the SRS. Traceability would not always be possible, of course. For example, nothing in the SRS would stipulate *how* new data were optimally to update old solutions, so traceability of packages in the digital filters would have to be implied, rather than explicit.

Structurally, the lower level CSCs of DOD-STD-2167A would be packages of CSUs. (That is, the CSUs would be packages contained within CSC packages.) In the specifications and bodies constituting the packages of higher level CSCs, one would find the lower level CSCs declared. The foreground and background tasks loosely referred to earlier as top-level CSCs would actually be packages containing computation tasks. All this was to ensure correspondence with library control methods, as well as to take advantage of Ada's capabilities for data abstraction and information hiding. Separate libraries would be maintained for the specification and body parts of packages and tasks.

In short, SOS planned to map the nomenclature of DOD-STD-2167A onto the structure of the programming language, thereby providing a structural foundation for the management requirements of DOD-STD-2167A.

To ensure security of radio transmissions, the government's request for proposal had stated that the VLF demodulator would be government furnished equipment (GFE); specifically, a cryptographic unit used by the Navy on its ships. The demodulator had yet to be used with the microprocessor proposed by SOS. Since the software-intensive demodulator had a tricky output protocol, SOS proposed to contract with the supplier of the demodulator to develop a driver for the unit. SOS would take responsibility to integrate the driver into the software system. Development of the small driver program would be the sole software subcontract.

Although DOD-STD-2168[5] is entitled "Defense System Software Quality Program," it really defines the requirements for ensuring that such a program is planned and carried out. Most of what we would require of a software quality program is specified by DOD-STD-2167A.[1] Contractors define their plans for these quality activities within a development plan conforming to data item description (DID) DI-MCCR-80030A.[6] As Section 11.1 noted, no doctrine prevents us from embedding quality plans embedded in development plans. However, we should understand that the external quality plan (Section 14.3) required by the government contains only a subset of the quality activities of Section 11.3.* Since, in any case, our interest in planning for software quality is greater than our interest in the exact way we document the plans, the following synopsis of relevant parts of the development plan emphasizes the elements of quality planning required by DI-MCCR-80030A. This is similar to the approach taken in Chapter 13, where an application of the IEEE's verification and validation plan required summarizing.

14.2 THE DEVELOPMENT PLAN

The NAIADS development plan describes the SOS organization analogously to Figure 13.1. The hardware and software of the central engineering computer system is described in the manner of a parts list. The plan defines the several types of computer workstations used by SOS and gives the number of each allocated to the project. The plan also specifies the number of project personnel falling into such categories as project management, programming, testing, library control, and QA. An activity chart depicts the interrelations among the many planned tasks and the planned start and finish date of each. The descriptions of most of the tasks scheduled to occur during the design and subsequent phases note that the tasks will be divided into tasks of lesser scope at an appropriate time.

The development plan states that the schedule will be jeopardized if SOS does not get information, including algorithms, from the National Oceanographic and Atmospheric

---

* DOD-STD-2168 is intended to stand alone if, for whatever reason, DOD-STD-2167A is not applied to a contract. Accordingly, in the absence of the latter standard, we would lay out the entire quality plan under the DOD-STD-2168 umbrella.

Administration (NOAA) according to the schedule provided by the government in its request for quotation. The plan identifies this as a risk area.

The software development library and the procedures for controlling it are stipulated in considerable detail. The most conspicuous libraries are the source libraries for Ada package specifications, Ada package bodies, Ada subprograms used in more than one package, the extensive library of packages containing global physical data (meteorological, geodesic, and oceanographic), and the production library into which compiled packages are linked. Other than unit testing, all testing takes place from the production library. The key to the most critical library control procedures is the software that builds CSCs of any level of structure from subordinate packages.

With reference to SOS form S-7890 [Appendix A-5], the plan describes the manner in which problems are formally reported and their disposition documented. SOS uses S-7890 for problems encountered during system and subsequent testing, and also for any changes, other than the addition of new features, requested by either customers or SOS personnel. Whether such changes (e.g., enhancing a display) can properly be considered problems is immaterial.

Elaborating on the overall organization chart provided earlier, the plan describes the way the NAIADS programmers (called "software engineers" by the military) will be organized. Using the chart of Figure 14.1 as a reference, the plan tells not only of the organizations directly involved in development, but also of the role of each in evaluating quality.

Correspondence between the functional responsibilities of most of the groups shown in Figure 14.1 and the top level CSCs of Section 14.1 is plain. However, Figure 14.1 also shows a test group independent of development and a system analysis group. The responsibilities of the former are similar to those of Chapter 13's test group. The system analysis group, however, is different in kind. First, this group, along with the project manager, B. Bartok, J. Brahms, and G. F. Handel, form the requirements analysis team. Their job will start with preparing the Software Requirements Specification (SRS), and continue with the preparation of external specification documents for each of the top-level CSCs. The group will also prepare interface documentation. Once design of the CSCs starts, the system analysis group will be at the core of evaluating the tangible output of each stage of design. Primarily, the members of the group will be concerned with coordinating the design efforts to ensure the compatibility of the CSCs. However, the system analysis group will have the further responsibility of evaluating the goodness of design with respect to the precepts of software engineering, the SOS design guidelines (SOS document 100100, outlined in Section 13.3.5), and the capabilities offered by Ada. Here is an example of the multitude of items looked at: To expand the use of private types, the system analysis group will take note—if only a quick look—of all visible type declarations. Some of these analyses will take place within the review process, but also, especially at higher CSC levels, in independent study.

The development plan identifies the software tools (called "software items") planned for use—everything from compilers to test tools. The ones specific to the quality plan are

- Sadie—A pseudocode analyzer incorporating Ada constructs. Unlike code written in Anna (Section 4.1), Sadie code is not provable. Sadie can handle up to 10,000 lines of pseudocode and 100 packages.

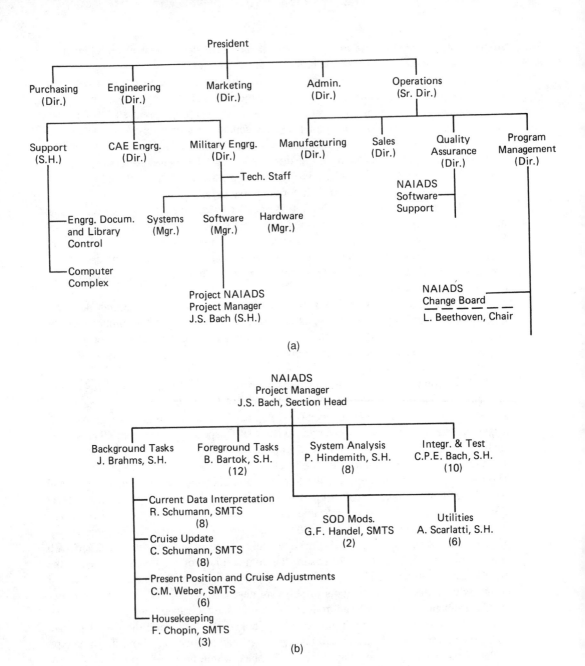

Figure 14.1 Organization

- Addie—A static analyzer for Ada code. Addie audits Ada code for violations of nesting depth constraints, certain data flow anomalies, and inconsistencies among files. Addie also instruments Ada code for test coverage analysis.

- Edie—A dynamic test coverage analyzer. Edie reports percentage of statements, decision-to-decision paths, and paths incorporating three branch points, including the entry and terminal branch statements.

• Revert—Used in testing with simulated input. Input to Revert includes test case number and run number, identification of script files, and identification of files for storing output. Revert also compares the output files with those output from a previous test specified by run number.

The plan defines the phases planned for NAIADS development as in Figure 14.2. As we would expect, each phase is defined primarily with respect to the documents it produces. However, maintaining consistency with DOD-STD-2167A (and especially with Figure 2 of the standard), the definition of the phases includes the formal reviews associated with each.

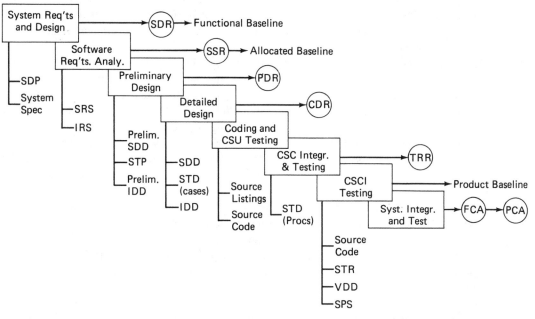

Key to Reviews and Audits:
SDR System Design Review
SSR Software Spec. Review
PDR Preliminary Design Review
CDR Critical Design Review
FCA Functional Config. Audit
PCA Physical Config. Audit

Key to Documents:
SRS Software Requirements Spec.
SDP Software Development Plan
IRS Interface Requirements Spec.
SDD Software Design Document
STP Software Test Plan
IDD Interface Design Document

STD Software Test Description
VDD Version Description Document
SPS Software Product Specification

Figure 14.2 Development Phases for NAIADS

Most people whose work revolves about military documentation standards refer to all but a few by the initials of the documents. SOS personnel are no exception. Translations of the initials, some of which we saw in Chapter 13, follow:

• SDP—Software development plan (the subject of this section).

• SRS—Software Requirements Specification.

• IRS—Interface Requirements Specification.

• SDD—Software Design Document.

- IDD—Interface Design Document.

- STP—Software Test Plan.

- STD—Software Test Description.

- VDD—Version Description Document (contains information capable of distinguishing one version of a software system from all other versions).

- SPS—Software Product Specification (actually, the sum of the updated SDD and source listings at the time of product release).

The NAIADS system specification had been written by the time the SDP was prepared. From a functional perspective, nearly all the system external specifications were embedded in the software. The few exceptions—VLF receiver sensitivity, weight, screen brightness, and the like—were taken directly from the government's technical specification and from SOS's proposal.

The plan notes who will support the formal reviews listed in Section 13.1. (These are formal in the sense that they provide opportunities for the government to take discretionary management actions, not unlike the opportunities internal reviews offer SOS's own management.) The plan also states how SOS will prepare for and conduct the reviews. SOS's discretion in the substance of the agenda for each review is limited, since MIL-STD-1521B willy-nilly establishes the framework for holding formal reviews.

Skipping to the system integration and test phase (we get back to the early phases shortly), the SDP has little to say. Activities involving the full system are planned elsewhere. Nevertheless, the SDP does say that the system analysis group would remain intact to support system integration and test, and that required software changes would be handled through the formal problem report mechanism.

For the phases from Software Requirements Analysis through CSCI testing, the plan describes the artifacts (apart from the formal documents) produced in each phase, the group responsible for each artifact or formal document, and the technical approaches to all development tasks.

The government was so specific in its requirements for NAIADS that SOS planned to forego its usual practice of refining requirements models through prototyping. Instead, the SRS would be developed by mapping functional groupings found in the system specification into conventional software-oriented procedures. To take an especially simple example, the function of converting the computed best magnetic course to an actual compass heading, compensated for current and leeway, resolves to a problem in vector analysis. That is, the SRS restates the system problem in terms of the requirement that the software solve a problem in vector analysis within some stipulated error.

Given the Balkanization of software development inherent in a document-driven waterfall, we look for common threads to lend coherence to the process. For projects conforming to DOD-STD-2167A, at least for the phases from Preliminary Design through CSCI Testing, Software Development Files (SDFs) provide one such thread. SDFs contain material not formally documented. By the time development is completed, NAIADS SDFs will document design constraints, the results of simulations and the algorithms simulated at each step of design; schedule and status information; detailed test preparation information; and test results. (DOD-STD-2167A does not mention simulations, but talks of "Design considerations ... Design documentation and data.")

As early as preliminary design, test requirements for integrating each top-level CSC will be dropped into its SDF. As the CSCs are further decomposed during the detailed design phase, test requirements will be inserted into subordinate SDFs established at appropriate CSC levels. During the detailed design phase, CSC integration test cases descriptions will be placed in CSC SDFs. All pretest documentation for CSU testing will go into the CSU SDFs. During CSC integration, test data will get added to appropriate SDFs. By the time top-level CSC integration is reached, the SDFs for the CSC will be coalesced into a composite CSC SDF. Moreover, results of tests of the CSC in anticipation of Formal Qualification Testing (FQT) will go into an SDF for the CSCI.

FQT activities spin another common thread. The SRS will contain requirements for qualification. The plan for FQT, the STP, will be generated during Preliminary Design. The STP will identify the tests required to comply with the SRS's qualification requirements. Detailed Design will see test cases documented in the STD to implement the STP test requirements. During CSC Integration and Testing, the STDs will be expanded to include procedures (like Chapter 13's test scripts, but wordier) for running the test cases and analyzing the results. Also, as noted earlier, FQT test cases will be "dry run" to check out the test procedures. Apart from updating documentation, actual qualification testing is the substance of the CSCI testing phase. The plan states that FQT is primarily the responsibility of QA. QA defines the test requirements, although Engineering designs the actual test cases and procedures and runs the tests. QA reviews the STD, compares the test cases to a traceability table of its own making, witnesses the qualification tests, analyzes the results, and in conjunction with the system analysis group prepares the test report.

Perhaps the strongest thread connecting the discrete phases, and next to FQT the activities most pertinent to the quality program, is the set of product evaluations. By phase, the evaluations (all quoted from DOD-STD-2167A) are

System Requirements Analysis and Design

- SDP.
- System Specification.
- Preliminary SRS.
- Preliminary IRS.

Software Requirements Analysis

- SRS.
- IRS.

Preliminary Design

- Preliminary SDD.
- Preliminary IDD.
- STP.
- CSC test requirements (found in SDFs).

- Completed SDD.
- Completed IDD.
- CSC test cases (found in SDFs).
- CSU test requirements and test cases (found in SDFs).
- STD.

Coding and CSU Testing

- Source code.
- CSC test procedures (found in SDFs).
- CSU test procedures and test results (found in SDFs).
- 30% (DOD-STD-1267A does not specify the percentage) of all SDFs, evaluated for compliance with the SDP.

CSC Integration and Testing

- CSC test results (found in SDFs).
- Updated STD.
- Updated source code and design documents.
- 30% of all SDFs.

CSCI Testing

- STR.
- Updated source code and design documentation.

System Integration and Testing

- Updated source code and design documentation.

For all of the product evaluations, the plan stipulates evaluation criteria and procedures by referencing specific sections of SOS document 300100, introduced in Chapters 12 and 13. Although the document is entitled Software Quality Assurance Operating Procedures (SQAOP), many of the evaluations will be performed by Engineering staff. The development plan states who, whether programmers or quality engineers, is involved in each evaluation and the person's responsibilities. With reference to the names and organizations of Figures 13.1 and 14.1, the responsibilities for product evaluation follow these guidelines:

- Plans—Quality Assurance, except that the system analysis group evaluates the software test plan (essentially, a qualification plan) prepared by Quality Assurance.
- System Specification—J. S. Bach and the technical staff (not shown on Figure 13.1) reporting to the director of military engineering.

- SRS and IRS—For technical matters, J. S. Bach, B. Bartok, J. Brahms, G. F. Handel, C. P. E. Bach, and A. Scarlatti. For compliance with relevant DIDs, Quality Assurance.

- Design documentation—For technical matters, the system analysis group, except that peer reviews of detailed design and code will also be held. For compliance with relevant DIDs, Quality Assurance.

- CSU and CSC test documentation—Quality Assurance and (CSC only) the system analysis group.

- SDFs—Quality Assurance.

- Test reports—Quality Assurance, except that problems will be brought to the attention of the system analysis group.

- Source code listings—20% will be reviewed by system analysis group; all will be subject to peer review. Quality Assurance will review 30% for compliance with standards.

Ordinarily, the requirements of DOD-STD-2167A would have been passed on to Harmonic Modulation Inc., the supplier of the VLF demodulator. In name, they were. However, the small scope of Harmonic's software work warranted harsh tailoring, defined by the standard as the deletion of nonapplicable requirements. Actually, other than subcontractor control and activities at the system and CSCI levels, all the requirements would seem to apply to Harmonic. However, by defining the subcontracted driver program as a CSU, only CSU level requirements had to be laid on Harmonic. Nevertheless, the development plan also called for QA to evaluate the technical specifications attached to the Harmonic subcontract.

The NAIADS configuration management plan is included in the SDP. Among other particulars, the plan names L. Beethoven of Program Management as the chairman of the change board (corresponding to the "review board" of DOD-STD-2167A). Other standing members of the board, named in Figure 14.1, include J. Brahms, P. Hindemith, and C. P. E. Bach. Hardware Engineering is also represented.

With reference to the CSU/CSC/CSCI structural levels and Section 6 of SOS Document 100100, the plan states the method for attaching unique identifers to the NAIADS documentation and software files. Apart from the formal baselines (see Figure 14.2) for documentation and code, SOS established development configuration control procedures for the project, again with reference to Section 6 of Document 100100. These are no less definitive, but do not require government approval for changes, as do the formal baselines. Essentially, once a document has been reviewed and accepted, it enters the development baseline and cannot be changed without authorization of the change board.

The review and approval process is initiated by a problem/change report (Appendix A-5). Recall that the report form is used both for problems and for changes having nothing to do with problems in software behavior. For example, during coding a programmer may conceive of a much faster algorithm than that documented in the design. (At the moment, the programmer is acting as a coder, not a designer, but we cannot stop good programmers from being good programmers—nor would we want to.) The board will meet weekly during the development period, but emergency meetings can be arranged, even if doing so requires the majority of the attendees to be delegates of the standing members. Once testing starts, problems encountered in testing, from outright failures to cosmetic matters, instigate most change requests. Change requests are expected to identify code and documentation affected by the change. One of the jobs of the board will be to question whether all of the affected documentation has been identified. Upon approving a request, the change board will issue change authorization orders to Engineering for implementing the change. In actual practice, many of the changes will have been tried out informally, but the change authorization order will still be required to authorize the Engineering Documentation and Library Control (EDLC) people to update controlled code and documentation files.

SOS will maintain a data base of all change requests and authorizations, permitting them to trace a given request to specific editions of each affected code file and document. Backwards tracing will also be possible.

Code and media control will be similar to that planned for the CASE100 project (see Sections 13.3.10 and 13.3.11), except, of course, the libraries and system disk will be different. As in Section 13.3.10, QA will audit system disk journals, code files, EDLC records (primarily the data base of releases and changes), and link lists for correspondence. As an example, QA will check to see if a recent change to a document is reflected in the data base and if it has been disseminated, whether by electronic mail or hard copy, to appropriate personnel. In this example, evidence of the recent change would be found in the journal of the documentation library.

QA will audit most frequently during integration testing, less frequently during the paper design stages and CSCI testing. The audits during CSC integration, CSCI testing, and system testing will lead to the physical configuration audit (PCA). That is, additional audits for ensuring consistency of delivered code and documentation will mostly be checks to make certain that discrepancies from earlier audits have been corrected.

DOD-STD-2167A calls for a planned corrective action process only for material under configuration control. Since SOS does not place a document under control until after its review, the company plans to maintain informal corrective action logs similar to those of Section 13.3.8 for items arising before material is internally baselined. A second log will be maintained for controlled material. The source of entries for the second log will be problem reports. Each entry will be assigned one of five severity levels. As outlined in Appendix C of DOD-STD-2167A, three of these are substantive and two are sufficiently minor to suggest that problems at these levels will be corrected only as an adjunct to some other change.

A third corrective action log will deal with deviations from the SDP ("discrepancy reports," in the language of DOD-STD-2167A). Typically, discrepancy reports will cite the failure of documents to adhere to documentation standards. Most of these will be picked up by QA in its participation in product evaluations, while others will come from audit reports prepared by QA.

QA will maintain all three corrective action logs, using a date tickler to flag overdue corrections.

The plan to support NAIADS software after delivery to the government is documented, not in the SDP, but in a separate Computer Resources Integrated Support Document (CRISD). In any case, SOS's plans for support were subsequently turned down by the government. Taking a strict interpretation of the terms of the race, the Attorney General ruled that on-site installation of changes by people other than the skipper would violate the requirement that the boat be sailed solo. One could conceive of downloading new program loads via the VLF link, but VLF data rate capabilities make the idea impractical. As for downloading patches, the Secretary of Commerce himself said he would have no part in it. "I hear that playing around with binary patches can only get one into trouble," he said.

14.3 THE QUALITY PLAN

The quality plan for NAIADS software bears the title "Software Quality Program Plan" (SQPP). The NAIADS SQPP follows the format of DID DI-QCIC-80572.[7]

The quality plan does not embody a measurements program. SOS plans one, of course. To do otherwise would contravene SOS's precepts of software management. However, the contract with the government calls for delivery of a software quality program plan compliant with DOD-STD-2168. Since the standard says nothing about measurement plans, SOS prepared a separate, nondeliverable, one. This chapter does not include the measurements plan, which is similar to Sections 13.3.14 and 13.3.15.

As in Sections 12.3 and 13.3, asides to the reader and references to appendices are bracketed. Continuing to follow the practice of Chapters 12 and 13, subsections are numbered for sequence with the rest of the chapter. However, the subsection numbers of the SQPP itself are given in brackets directly after the 13.3.x number. Again following the practice of Chapter 13, references are made to existing quality procedures; specifically SOS Document 100100, Standard Practices for the Development and Maintenance of Engineering Software, and SOS Document 300100, Software Quality Assurance Operating Procedures (SQAOP). Consistent with the fairly enlightened view of software engineering it takes, DOD-STD-2168 actually makes reference to the contractor's standard operating procedures mandatory. Nevertheless, to avoid vitiating the usefulness of the sample software quality plan, the references to SOS standards are used only as substitutes for necessarily wordy descriptions of routine procedures. We can infer these procedures from earlier chapters of the book. In describing the essence of quality activities appropriate to large software projects, each subsection remains self-sufficient despite the references to SOS standards. Here is the plan:

SOFTWARE QUALITY PROGRAM PLAN
FOR THE
NAIADS SYSTEM

[Several lines follow this giving contract number, deliverable data item number, date, and contracting agency name and code.]

Prepared by:
Superior Oceanographic Systems
1 Research Campus
Growthtown, TR
Approved by I. Stravinsky

Table of Contents:

14.3.1 [1] Scope

14.3.1.1 [1.1] Identification. This SQPP applies to the software of the system entitled, "Naval Assist to Insure Against Defeat of the Secretary," code-named NAIADS. There is no approved system identification number.

14.3.1.2 [1.2] System Overview. NAIADS will be installed on a sail-powered naval platform intended for use by the U.S. Secretary of Commerce in settling trade barrier disagreements with a classified foreign power. The system will provide the secretary with timely navigational advice computed from interfaced oceanographic and meteorological observations made by systems other than NAIADS.

14.3.1.3 [1.3] Document Overview. This document defines the planned software quality program the contractor intends to apply to the development and installation of the computer software portions of the NAIADS system. Throughout the life of the subject contract, the document will be used by the contractor to ensure that a quality program compliant with DOD-STD-2167A and DOD-STD-2168 is effected.

14.3.1.4 [1.4] Relationship to Other Plans. Problem reporting, product evaluations, qualification, corrective action, subcontractor control, and control of program materials, all elements of the NAIADS quality program, are defined by the NAIADS SDP. The SQPP identifies the procedures and quality tools that will be used in the software quality program. The SQPP also identifies the personnel and resources that will be used to implement the quality program.

14.3.2 [2] Referenced Documents

Doc. No.	Title
1. 123456(N)	NAIADS Technical Specification
2. SOS-112233	NAIADS System Specification
3. SOS-445566	NAIADS Software Development Plan
4. DOD-STD-2167A	Defense System Software Development
5. DOD-STD-2168	Defense System Software Quality Program
6. DOD-STD-480	Configuration Control, Engineering Changes, Deviations, and Waivers
7. SOS-100100 revH	Standard Practices for the Development and Maintenance of Engineering Software
8. SOS-300100 revD	Software Quality Assurance Operating Procedures

14.3.3 [3] Organization and Resources

14.3.3.1 [3.1] Organization. SOS organizations (See Figure 14.1) involved with the software quality program are

a) Engineering—Responsible for technical product evaluations and test activities. Specifically, as follows:
   - J. S. Bach and the Engineering Technical Staff—Evaluate System Specification
   - J. S. Bach, B. Bartok, J. Brahms, G. F. Handel, C. P. E. Bach, and A. Scarlatti—Evaluate SRS and IRS.
   - System Analysis Group—Evaluate STD, IDD and SDD, CSC test documentation, and source code listings (partial); coauthor STP; prepare STR.
   - Test Group—Generate documentation for and perform top-level CSC testing; document FQT test case and procedures; perform CSCI testing.
   - Foreground and Background task groups—Document and perform CSU testing; document and perform CSC testing short of top-level CSC testing.

b) Quality Assurance—Evaluate SDP for compliance with the SOW and CDRL. Coauthor STP. Provide input to STR. Evaluate STD for consistency with predecessor documents, CSU and CSC test requirements for consistency with SDDs and the IDD, CSU source code listings for compliance with the SDP (partial), CSU and CSC test procedures for compliance with the SDP, SDFs for compliance with the SDP and traceability to predecessor SDFs, test reports for compliance with the SDP and—in the case of CSC tests—conformance with expected results. Audit library control and configuration management procedures. Inspect deliverable data for compliance with the CDRL and applicable DIDs. Audit test activities.

c) Program Management—Configuration management, through the instrument of the change board, which Program Management chairs.

14.3.3.2 [3.2] Resources.

14.3.3.2.1 [3.2.1] Contractor Facilities and Equipment. The software will be developed at the SOS main offices at Research Campus. Backups of all software media will be maintained at the SOS building on Sibelius Street. Configuration control records, logs of correction items, text for all deliverable data, audit reports, and all other text will be entered, stored, and modified using the central engineering computer complex in the main offices.

14.3.3.2.2 [3.2.2] Government Furnished Facilities, Equipment, Software, and Services. None are required for the software quality program.

13.3.3.2.2 [3.2.3] Personnel. Software project manager (J. S. Bach)—Section Head, 10 years management of weapon systems programming.

Group heads—6 required; Section Head or Senior Member of Technical Staff (SMTS); minimum of seven years weapon system programming.

Engineering Technical Staff assigned to NAIADS—3 required (part time); minimum 15 years weapon system design. At least one such person shall have a minimum of five years of experience in handling oceanographic and meteorological data.

System Analysis Group (not including group leader)—-8 required; SMTS or Member of Technical Staff (MTS); minimum of five years' experience in development of software systems of no less than 100,000 NCSS; at least four people shall have a minimum of eight years of such experience.

Test Group (not including C. P. E. Bach)—4 SMTS, 4 MTS, and 2 Associate Members of Technical Staff (AMTS); total experience in integration and testing of weapon systems software shall be no less than 50 years.

Chairperson of Change Board (L. Beethoven)—Senior Program Manager—15 years integrating the work products of diverse functional organizations and complying with contractual requirements.

Quality Assurance—One group leader, Quality Section Head, minimum 10 years of programming and five years of software quality engineering experience; 6 Quality Engineers as follows: three Senior Software Quality Engineers (SSQE), two Software Quality Engineers (SQE) and one Associate Software Quality Engineer (ASQE) having an aggregate of no less than 35 years of computer programming and 10 years of software quality assurance experience. For the SSQE, SQE, and ASQE personnel, equivalent levels (SMTS, MTS, AMTS) of engineering personnel may be substituted provided the experience requirements are met and the substitutes are temporarily assigned to the Quality Assurance Directorate for a period of at least one year.

14.3.3.2.4 [3.2.4] Other Resources. No other resources are required for the software quality program.

14.3.3.3 [3.3] Schedule. Since the activities of the software quality program are interwoven with system development activities, the schedule found in Section 3.2 of the SDP includes the activities of the software quality program. This schedule indicates the initiation of each activity, its dependence on other events, the completion times for each activity, and other key development milestones (such as formal reviews). Activities specific to the software quality program are indicated by the symbol {Q}. [The chapter does not actually contain the schedule, which in book format would run for more pages than anyone would want to read. Readers unfamiliar with the depiction of dependencies will find dependency networks illustrated in Figures 7.1 and 7.2.]

14.3.4 [4] Software Quality Program Procedures, Tools, Records

14.3.4.1 [4.1] Procedures.

Reviews. Evaluation of the SDP, STP, System Specification, SRS, IRS, IDD, SDD, and other artifacts of development will be performed according to the review procedures of Section 3 of Reference 8. Section 3.1 defines the preparation and conduct of reviews. The reviews share the objectives of evaluating internal consistency, understandability, and—for documents—compliance with applicable DIDs. The specific objectives* of each review follow:

- SDP: Traceability to the Statement of Work (SOW) and the Contractor Data Requirements List (CDRL).

---

* Readers familiar with DOD-STD-2167A will note that the evaluation criteria in this section are largely taken directly from the standard. The reader should be cautioned, however, that there are differences. For example, DOD-STD-2167A lists no specific evaluation criteria for CSC test requirements, but calls for traceability to the SRS and IRS—listed below as criteria for CSC test requirements—in the evaluation of CSC test cases.

- STP: Traceability to the System Specification, IRS, SRS, consistency with the SDP, and feasibility.

- System Specification: Technical feasibility and traceability to the technical specification appended to the SOW and the SOS NAIADS proposal.

- SRS: Traceability to the System Specification, consistency with the IRS, testability of discrete requirements, adherence to Section 2.4 of Reference 7, and reasonable allocation of system resources among critical functions.

- IRS: Traceability to the System Specification, compatibility with the GFE demodulator, and testability of discrete requirements.

- IDD: Traceability to the SRS and IRS, and consistency with the SDD.

- SDDs: Traceability to the SRS and IRS, consistency with the IDD, and consonance with SOS design principles.

- CSC test requirements: Traceability to the SRS and IRS, and—at all but the highest CSC level—consistency with the IDD and SDD.

- CSC test cases: Traceability to the CSC test requirements and consistency with the SDDs and IDD.

- CSC test procedures: Traceability to the CSC test cases and adequacy of detail.

- CSU test requirements: Complete and accurate consistency with IDD and SDDs.

- CSU test cases: Traceability to the CSU test requirements.

- CSU test procedures: Traceability to the CSU test cases and adequacy of detail.

- STDs: Test cases and evaluation criteria traceable to the IRS and SRS. Test procedures traceable to test cases.

- SDFs: Consistency with the SDP and SOS standards.

- Source code: Traceability to the SDDs and IDD and consistency with the SDDs. Also compliance with SOS design standards for maintainable code. Groups of package specifications may be evaluated separately from the package bodies.

- CSC test results: Conformance with expected results, completion of test procedures, documentation of outstanding problems, and fitness for further CSC integration or CSCI integration.

- Results of CSCI integration (integration of top-level CSCs): Conformance with expected results, completion of test procedures, documentation of outstanding problems, and fitness for FQT.

- STP: Traceability to the STD, completeness of testing, adequacy of analysis of deviations from expected results, adequacy of the report's assessment of NAIADS performance, and documentation of outstanding problems.

Other Product Analysis. Staff of the System Analysis Group will analyze selected, detailed portions of the SDD and selected CSU source files for conformance with SOS design and code software engineering guidelines and for advantageous use of the Ada language. These analyses will take place before the material is placed under configuration control.

Phase Transition Decisions. The project manager will hold meetings at appropriate times to determine whether the state of the developing product is adequate to support entry to the next scheduled phase of development. For each such meeting, the project manager will determine the meeting's participants.

The criteria appearing in the following list will be considered for phase transition determinations. QA will prepare summaries of the application of the criteria at least three days before scheduled phase transition meetings. However, relevant evaluation reports and similar items will be presented at the meetings. The project manager will designate a participant at each meeting to prepare and distribute a memorandum delineating the results of the meeting.

Note that transitions to the phases falling between Detailed Design and CSCI testing may require several meetings, as different areas of the NAIADS software progress at different rates. Note also, that several CDRs may be required.

- Transition to Software Requirements Analysis—System specification evaluation complete and satisfactory; outstanding areas of uncertainty documented; SDP evaluated, judged satisfactory, and under configuration control; readiness for SDR.

- Transition to Preliminary Design—SRS and IRS evaluations complete and satisfactory; zero outstanding areas of uncertainty in system specification; outstanding uncertainties in SRS and IRS documented and completion of solutions scheduled; SRS and IRS under configuration control and judged 95% compliant with requirements; readiness for SSR.

- Transition to Detailed Design—Zero outstanding uncertainties or problems in SRS and IRS; preliminary SDD and IDD evaluations complete and satisfactory and documents under configuration control; STP evaluation complete and satisfactory; all documents judged 95% compliant with requirements; outstanding SRS and IRS problems documented and solutions scheduled; readiness for PDR.

- Transition to Coding and CSU Testing—Detailed SDD and IDD evaluations complete, satisfactory, and with outstanding problems documented and scheduled for solution; SDD and IDD under configuration control; CSU test designs complete; SDFs judged 90% compliant with requirements; STD test cases prepared; readiness for CDR.

- Transition to CSC Integration and Testing—CSU source code and test reports evaluated and judged satisfactory, material under configuration control, and all outstanding problems documented and scheduled for fix; CSU source code and test reports judged 95% compliant with requirements; CSU source code in Ada libraries under configuration control; CSC test cases and procedures evaluated and judged satisfactory; SDFs judged 90% compliant with requirements; readiness for TRR.

- Transition to CSCI Testing—CSC test reports evaluated and found satisfactory with all outstanding problems documented and scheduled for fix; CSC regression tests conducted as necessary and the test reports found satisfactory; CSC source code in Ada libraries under configuration control; CSCI test cases and procedures documented in the STD, evaluated, and judged satisfactory and 100% compliant with requirements; CSC SDFs judged 90% compliant with requirements.

- Transition to System Integration and Test—CSCI test results evaluated and found satisfactory with zero major problems (top three severity levels) and all minor problems documented; CSCI test reports judged 98% compliant with requirements; all software components resident in the production library and under configuration control; VDD and SPS evaluated and found satisfactory with outstanding problems scheduled for fix; STD test procedures revised as necessary in light of CSCI test experience; readiness for FCA and PCA.

- Transition to Delivery—FQT test results evaluated and judged sufficient for the purposes of system deployment; zero major problems; all minor problems documented; FCA and PCA complete and successful.

In-Process Audits. In-process audits are the procedures used to determine compliance with the SDP and Reference 7. The procedures will be performed by QA as follows:

- Documentation—All deliverable documentation will be audited for compliance with applicable DIDs. The procedures for documentation audits are found in Reference 8. Application of the procedures follows:
  ☐ System Specification, SRS, and IRS—Section 4.3. 100% audit coverage.
  ☐ SDD and IDD—Section 4.4. 100% coverage of preliminary documents and 50% coverage of completed documents.
  ☐ CSU SDFs—Section 4.2. 30% coverage.
  ☐ CSC SDFs—Section 4.2. 50% coverage.
  ☐ CSCI SDF—Section 4.2. 100% coverage.
  ☐ CSU test documentation—Section 4.6. 30% coverage.
  ☐ CSC test documentation—Section 4.7. 50% coverage.
  ☐ STD—Section 7.2. 100% coverage.
  ☐ VDD—Section 4.12.1. 100% coverage.
  ☐ SPS—Section 4.12.2 100
  ☐ STP—Section 7.5. 100% coverage. Note: although jointly prepared by QA and Engineering, the auditor will not be one of the authors.
- Code Library control—Section 4.1 of Reference 8
  ☐ CSU testing—Following testing of CSUs, QA will examine the controlled source listings and the code files entered onto the Ada libraries for consistency. 30% of all CSU source code will be so audited.
  ☐ CSC testing—During CSC testing, QA will examine the edition numbers of source code files entering into test program loads for consistency with the edition numbers found in the controlled Ada libraries. Ten percent of the source code files in 30% of the program loads will be examined each week.
  ☐ CSCI testing—Identical to CSC testing, except that edition numbers of binary modules in the production library will also be correlated with source code files. Twenty percent of the binary modules will be examined
  ☐ System Test and Integration—Identical to CSCI testing.
- Configuration Management
  ☐ Baselines—Since the material entering into the functional and allocated baselines will be forwarded to the government on magnetic media, QA will witness the

copying of the documents to ensure that they are copied from the correct document library.

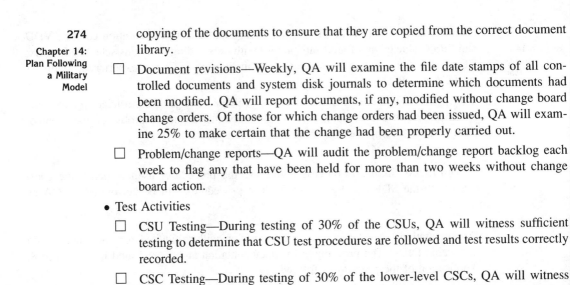

☐ Document revisions—Weekly, QA will examine the file date stamps of all controlled documents and system disk journals to determine which documents had been modified. QA will report documents, if any, modified without change board change orders. Of those for which change orders had been issued, QA will examine 25% to make certain that the change had been properly carried out.

☐ Problem/change reports—QA will audit the problem/change report backlog each week to flag any that have been held for more than two weeks without change board action.

- Test Activities

☐ CSU Testing—During testing of 30% of the CSUs, QA will witness sufficient testing to determine that CSU test procedures are followed and test results correctly recorded.

☐ CSC Testing—During testing of 30% of the lower-level CSCs, QA will witness sufficient testing to determine that CSU test procedures are followed and test results correctly recorded. During testing of the top-level CSCs, QA will witness 30% (by time) of the test activities to determine that CSC test procedures are followed and test results correctly recorded.

☐ CSCI and System Testing—QA will witness 100% of the testing to determine that STD test procedures are followed and test results correctly recorded.

Corrective Action Tracking. QA will maintain three logs of items requiring correction. The first will derive from reviews and analyses of material not yet under configuration control. The second will derive from problem reports and formal review action items. The third will derive from audit reports and QA's participation in documentation reviews.

The first log, which addresses matters beyond the scope of pertinent government standards, is described, along with its use, in Section 5 of Reference 8. The log derived from problem reports will have the following fields for each entry: problem/change report number, date of problem, date of change board action, severity level, date of fix assignment, group assigned to fix, person assigned to fix, date assigned fix, date fix is ready for rereview (if problem initially found in a review) or date fix is ready for test, identification of tests (with respect to test case documentation) fix was tested on, date problem was closed. If more than one problem is reported on the same report form, suffixes will be applied to the report number to distinguish the problems from each other. The log will be maintained in account QANAIDAS on the central computer. Scheduled dates will be coded as such until replaced by the dates of assignment completions. Daily, the Tick utility will be applied to the log to report all overdue scheduled dates. Daily, persons who have failed to achieve their scheduled dates will be notified, except that an overdue action will not be reported twice in the same week. At the discretion of QA, supervision will be advised of assignments that have slipped significantly.

The log resulting from audit reports will contain the following fields for each entry: audit report number, person to whom audit report was forwarded for action, date of report, date requirement for action was responded to, memorandum number outlining negotiated action, negotiated date for completion of action, completion of action. The

Tick utility will be applied as above. Also, the Tick utility will report any audit reports for which one week or more has passed without a response.

Weekly, QA will plot the number of delinquent corrective actions and the number of open items. These plots, and any pertinent conclusions that can be drawn from them, will be reported to the project manager.

Evaluation of Software Management. Weekly, the NAIADS project manager and his direct reports will meet to discuss the status of the project. The minutes of these meetings will remark any trend to deviate from contractual compliance or adherence to the SDP. The minutes are copied to the software manager for Military Engineering. The agenda for these meetings will include discussion of the reports generated by QA from the corrective action logs.

Media Control. As part of the PCA, QA will audit the records of the Engineering Documentation and Library Control (EDLC) center to ensure that the program load on the production library is backed up and the backup shipped to Sibelius Street. QA will also witness comparison of the program load and the delivery tape using the FILECOM utility to ensure that the version delivered is that tested during CSCI and system integration and testing. Since source code tapes are also required to be delivered, QA will audit the EDLC records to ensure that the controlled source code files have been backed up and shipped to Sibelius Street. QA will audit the EDLC records to confirm that the checksums of the Ada library source code files and those of the delivered tape are identical. QA will examine the delivered tapes, after packaging, to ensure that they have been properly marked and enclosed in magnetic proof containers. QA will make certain that the package contains hard copy of the checksums of all files. QA will stamp the outer covers of the packages to authorize shipment.

QA will also inventory the contents of the documentation shipment to ensure that it contains only the controlled, current editions of deliverable documentation.

Subcontractor Management. QA will inspect the SRS provided to Harmonic Modulation to ensure that it complies with DI-MCCR-80025. Technical review will follow Section 3 of Reference 8. QA will witness acceptance testing (CSU testing, only) at the subcontractor's facilities. Shipment of the CSU and associated documentation will be authorized using form QA8877. Visits to the subcontractor prior to acceptance testing are not anticipated. However, the subcontract terms provide for such visits at the discretion of SOS. Visits will be made in accordance with Section 15 of Reference 8 if the Program Management Directorate, based on its interpretation of monthly status reports, requests them. No specific allocation for such on-site surveillance has been made, since the subcontract is not expected to take more than three months to complete.

Formal Reviews. All formal reviews will be held at the SOS VIP Conference Center and Lounge. These reviews are the SDR, SSR, PDR, CDR, and TRR. Prior to each review, a package of documentation relevant to the review will be prepared for each government participant. QA will examine a sample package to ensure that each required document is included and that it is of the current, controlled, edition.

An SOS employee will be designated to prepare action item minutes for each break-out and plenary session. Prior to concluding the review, Program Management will compile a composite list of action items. The list will be distributed to all attendees at the final plenary session, to permit them to comment on omissions or inaccuracies.

The action items will be added to the correction action item logs in account QANAIDAS and will be tracked by QA.

SOD Certification and Control. As is planned for application CSUs, CSU design and code reviews and CSU tests will be performed for the update of SOD 1.4 to SOD 2.0. Following CSU testing, all SOD 2.0 testing procedures will be subsumed by the testing of application CSCs and the NAIADS CSCI. Revised SOD documentation, in SOS format, will be inspected per Section 4.9 of Reference 8.

14.3.4.2 [4.2] Tools. All tools planned for use in the software quality program are in current use at SOS.

Sadie. EDCL number: T6010. Version 1.3. Sadie analyzes design language statements for inconsistencies between Ada package specifications and Ada package bodies, and with respect to individual package bodies, violations of design rules. Sadie is used on portions of the SDD written in design language pseudocode prior to product evaluation (review) of the SDD.

Addie. EDCL number: T6013. Version 2.1. Addie analyzes Ada production source code for inconsistencies between package specifications and package bodies, inconsistencies among coded package specifications, inconsistencies between subprogram declarations and bodies, inconsistencies between subprogram calls and declarations, and, with respect to individual subprograms, violations of certain coding standards and processing conventions. Addie also analyzes and instruments Ada code for test coverage analysis. Addie is used on source code files prior to product evaluation (review) of the code, but after the code has been compiled.

Edie. EDCL number: T6014. Version 2.1. Edie analyzes Ada code instrumented by Addie. Edie reports the percentage of certain structural classes exercised in a given test; specifically (a) statements, (b) decision-to-decision paths, and (c) paths incorporating three successive branch points including the entry and terminal branch statements. Edie maintains a history of coverage, and for designated test case numbers reports cumulative percentages of coverage. Edie is used during CSU testing. Testing of a CSU is not considered complete until the following criteria are attained for the three coverages:

(a) 100%.

(b) 95%.

(c) 90%.

Revert. EDCL number: T6101. No version number. Revert is used to control testing when input can be provided from script files. The script must contain all input data for the test. Test output must be directed to disk. Tests are invoked by manual input of test case number, run number, script file name, and output file name. Revert maintains a log of output file names specified for preceding tests, and will compare the content of the current run with the earliest (or any other specified) output file. Revert is optionally used to control CSC testing, when such testing can be completely defined by script files. For applicable test cases, use of Revert is mandatory following a change to a CSC, to ensure that correct operation evinced by previously successful test cases has not been adversely affected by the change. Such regression testing may take place during any test phase.

Infobank. EDCL number: T1001. Version 3.0. The Infobank data management system permits users to configure data bases for the storage and retrieval of information having multiple attributes. Stored information may be queried manually or retrieved by preset parameterized report forms. All correction action items will be stored on Infobank.

Central Engineering Computer Complex. The central engineering computer complex is subject to continuous change as hardware and software needs evolve and as new software and hardware technology reaches the industrial marketplace. The January facilities brochure, appended to the SQPP, describes the complex, except that the operating system on Processor #1 has been updated to COW 6.2 and that an additional three Ray Microsystem workstations have been installed.

Tick. EDCL number: T1113. No version number. Tick, a programmed report generator for the Infobank operating system, operates on data files to report data associated with specified dates or sets of dates. Tick will be used to query correction action logs for overdue action points.

FILECOM. No EDCL number; FILECOM is a utility provided by the COW operating system. COW 6.2 is in current use. FILECOM is used to compare files of any format located on any readable media. If the files are identical, FILECOM reports no difference. If the files are alphanumeric, and two files are not identical, FILECOM reports the number of lines different. For differing files of other formats, FILECOM reports the sequence number of the first byte of the first specified file that is different from its equivalent in the second file. FILECOM is used to ensure that delivered program files are identical to the authorized versions under configuration control.

14.3.4.3 [4.3] Software Quality Records.

Audit Reports. In-process audit reports are prepared directly upon completion of an audit. The reports for the NAIADS project will be stored in account QANAIADS on the central engineering computer complex. One printed copy of each report will be stored in the QA current activities file room in a conventional letter-size file cabinet. Resident government inspectors may have access to any of these reports at any time upon verbal request to the NAIADS software quality assurance group leader. The formats of the reports and their generic contents are prescribed by Section 4 of Reference 8.

Reviews. Minutes of all product evaluation reviews are prepared directly upon completion of the review. The minutes, or review reports, for the NAIADS project will be stored in account QANAIADS on the central engineering computer complex. One printed copy of each report will be stored in the QA current activities file room in a conventional letter-size file cabinet, and also in the project management office. Resident government inspectors may have access to any of these reports at any time upon verbal request to the NAIADS software quality assurance group leader. The formats of the reports and their generic contents (with respect to evaluation date, participants, criteria, results, and recommended corrections) are prescribed by Section 3.2 of Reference 8. Problem reports resulting from product evaluations are referred to in the evaluation reports, but documented separately.

Problem Reports. Problem reports, whether generated by evaluation review or testing, are prepared per SOS form S-7890, appended to this SQPP. [See Appendix A-5.]

Reports of open problems, if any, at the time of FQT are available to the government upon verbal request to the NAIADS software quality assurance group leader.

Test Reports. Upon their completion, hard copy CSU and CSC test reports will be added to applicable SDFs. The reports will comprise the following parts:

- Test log—Identification of test case number and run number, brief statement of results, reference to problem/change report numbers (if any). The test log is cumulative for the testing performed on each CSU or CSC.
- Problem reports—See above.
- For each test case, comparison between expected results and actual results. Only the last run of each test case will go into the SDF.
- Analysis of the cumulative results. The analysis report will have the following format:
  - CSU or CSC part number and name.
  - Report date, identification of tester(s), and identification of report author(s).
  - List of outstanding problems, if any, with corresponding problem report numbers.
  - Qualitative summary and evaluation of demonstrated product characteristics.

Resident government inspectors may have access to any of these reports at any time upon verbal request to the NAIADS software quality assurance group leader.

STR. The results of formal qualification testing of the CSCI will be recorded per DI-MCCR-80017A. The STR is deliverable under the NAIADS contract.

Acceptance Test Results for Subcontracted Software. The results of the acceptance testing performed on the VLF demodulator software driver, subcontracted to Harmonic Modulation, will be recorded the same as SOS CSU tests. However, the original copy of the test report will be placed, not in an SDF, but in the Purchasing Department files. A duplicate will be retained in the QA current activities file room, where it may be viewed by resident government inspectors at any time upon verbal request to the NAIADS software quality assurance group leader.

14.3.5 [5] Notes. Owing to the compressed schedule under which NAIADS software is being developed, certain activities described in foregoing sections are likely to be complete by the time this document is approved. Product evaluation of the system specification is certain to be among these activities. Nevertheless, the procedures described in Section 4.1 derive from standard SOS practices for military software, and will have been carried out in anticipation of the preparation and approval of the SQPP.

SOD 1.4, the proprietary multi-tasking operating system upon which the NAIADS CSCs will be built, has been used in two other systems developed by SOS. It is controlled by the EDLC under the same procedures as developmental software. Minor modifications required for the NAIADS application will result in delivery of version 2.0. The modifications remove the capability of operator alteration of configuration parameters, substituting load-balancing logic. Design and code of the modifications are restricted to nine CSUs.

This SQPP does not include provisions for nondeliverable software [defined by DOD-STD-2168 as software used for manufacturing or the qualification or acceptance of hardware or software], since none is intended to be used for the NAIADS project.

[A glossary of all acronyms and abbreviations is normally included in this section. However, the glossary is combined with that for Chapter 13, and can be found in Appendix B-1.]

14.3.6 Appendixes

References 7 and 8 are appended as Appendixes A and B. [In fact, none of reference 7, the engineering software standards, is appended. Five representative sections of reference 8, the SQAOP, can be found in Appendixes A-1 through A-5.]

[Epilogue: Bon voyage, Mr. Secretary, and don't let the documentation become moving ballast!]

14.4 REFERENCES

[1] DOD-STD-2167A, *Defense System Software Development*, Department of Defense, Washington, D.C., February 29, 1988.

[2] MIL-STD-483B, *Configuration Management Practices for Systems, Equipment, Munitions, and Computer Software*, Department of Defense, Washington, D.C., June 4, 1985.

[3] MIL-STD-490A, *Specification Practices*, Department of Defense, Washington, D.C., June 4, 1985.

[4] MIL-STD-1521B, *Technical Reviews and Audits for Systems, Equipments, and Computer Software*, Department of Defense, Washington, D.C., June 4, 1985.

[5] DOD-STD-2168, *Defense System Software Quality Program*, Department of Defense, Washington, D.C., February 29, 1988.

[6] DI-MCCR-80030A, *Software Development Plan*, Department of Defense, Washington, D.C., February 29, 1988.

[7] DI-QCIC-80572, *Software Quality Program Plan*, DOD, Washington, D.C., April 29, 1988.

APPENDIX A-1

Library Control Audits

A-1.1 SYSTEM JOURNALS

To determine if controlled materials, code or documentation, have been modified, auditors shall examine project editor journals for evidence of alteration of controlled files. Journals are maintained on the central engineering computer complex for each disk containing controlled project files. The auditor shall note any files modified since the last audit, the date of modification, and the author of the modification.

The auditor shall compare evidence of change found on system journals with authorizations for change found on change orders. The auditor shall record (1) any unauthorized changes and (2) any authorized changes that have not been implemented by the date assigned by the change order.

A-1.2 FILE DATE STAMPS

Auditors shall examine the date stamps of randomly selected files of controlled material to identify files changed since the last audit. The auditor shall then compare evidence of change with authorizations for change found on change orders, as above. The number of selected files shall be approximately 10% of the total number of controlled files.

A-1.3 SOURCE CODE EDITIONS

For controlled code, auditors shall examine EDLC project records to determine the authorized current edition of randomly selected source code files. The auditor shall then examine the project source code disk(s) and compare the editions found therein with those of the EDLC records. The auditor shall record any discrepancies. The number of selected source code files shall be approximately 10% of the total number.

A-1.4 CODE SUBMITTED FOR TEST OR DELIVERY

The auditor shall compare edition numbers of source code files (if accommodated by the build tool), binary files, and data files identified on the build list with the authorized editions listed in the EDLC records. The editions of binary files shall be compared with the editions of equivalent authorized source code files. The number of files examined shall be approximately 10% of the total number, randomly selected, except that for qualification testing or delivery all shall be examined. Discrepancies shall be recorded. As an alternative to this procedure, procedure 5 may be used once testing has progressed to the use of a production library.

A–1.5 AUDIT OF PRODUCTION LIBRARY

This procedure is an alternative to procedure 4. The auditor shall examine the edition numbers of randomly selected files, source code, binary, or data, in the production library for correspondence with the source code editions identified in the EDLC records. Ten percent of the total number of files shall be examined, except that for qualification testing or delivery, all shall be examined if the test or delivery build is generated from the production library. Any discrepancies shall be recorded.

A–1.6 LINK MAPS

For CAE or military software, link maps generated by the build tool shall be examined following qualification testing or delivery preparation. The edition numbers of external references on the link maps shall be compared to the authorized editions of source code and data files found in the EDLC records. Discrepancies shall be recorded.

A–1.7 SUMMARY AUDIT REPORT

Descriptions of all discrepancies shall be attached to the summary. The format of the summary follows:

Date: *Auditor:*   *Project Name:*
Method for random selections:

Procedure 1
   Journal #1 –
      Files changed:

   Journal #2 –
      Files changed:
         .

         .

         .

   Journal #n –
      Files changed:

(Note: Listings may be appended to the report in lieu of recording the data on this form.)
Discrepancies: List journal no. and file name:

Procedure 2 (note: repeat for each applicable library)
   Library:
   Total number of files:
   Files examined:

(Note: Listings may be appended to the report in lieu of recording the data on this form.)
Discrepancies: List library, file name, date stamp, and edition on disk:

Procedure 3 (note: repeat for each library)
   Library:
   Total number of files:
   Files examined:

(Note: Listings may be appended to the report in lieu of recording the data on this form.)
Discrepancies: List file names and editions on disk.

Procedure 4
   Build number:
   Total number of files:
   Files examined:

(Note: Listings may be appended to the report in lieu of recording the data on this form.)
Discrepancies: List file names and editions on disk.

Procedure 5
   Production library identification:
   Total number of files:
   Files examined:

(Note: Listings may be appended to the report in lieu of recording the data on this form.)
Discrepancies: List file names and editions on disk.

Procedure 6
   Load identification:
   Discrepancies: (List external references.)

Audits of Final User Documentation

A–2.1 COMPLIANCE WITH STANDARDS AND PLANS

The auditor shall examine user documentation to make certain that it complies with Section 7.1 of SOS 100100 or with the SP Notebook and with the general requirements for user guidance outlined in the software development plan. The auditor shall record any deviations from the information content specified in the applicable standard. The auditor shall also record any seemingly arbitrary deviations from the format guidelines recommended in the applicable standard.

A–2.2 COVERAGE

The auditor shall examine the documentation to make certain that it provides guidance for all modes of installation, initialization, or user interaction. The auditor shall record any modes not covered.

A–2.3 UNDERSTANDABILITY

The auditor shall read the entire document and shall note any parts inapproriately difficult to understand. The auditor shall note also where organization of the material *requires* improvement. However, the auditor is not expected to proofread the material expressly to find areas in which organization *can* be improved.

A–2.4 EDITORIAL

The auditor shall record any misspellings, gross misuse of language, typographical errors, or similar editorial problems that are noticed. However, the auditor is not expected to proofread the material expressly to find such errors.

A–2.5 SUMMARY AUDIT REPORT

As necessary, descriptions of all discrepancies shall be attached to the summary. The format of the summary follows:

284

**Appendix
A–2:
Audits
of Final
User Docu-
mentation**

Date: _____ Auditor: _____ Project Name: _____

Document Name: _____

	Yes	*No*
Procedure 1 Document is compliant*	☐	☐
Procedure 2 Coverage is 100%*	☐	☐
Procedure 3 Document is completely understandable*	☐	☐
Procedure 4 Editorial comments are attached	☐	☐

* Describe any problems on separate sheets attached to the summary.

APPENDIX A–3

Analysis of Module Fault Incidence

A separate analysis should be performed for each level of severity.

A–3.1 DEFINITIONS

Module: A unit of code representing the lowest structural level for which fault data has been collected. Typical modules are procedures, CSUs, compilation units.

Fault: Anything wrong with code that should be corrected.

A–3.2 STEP 1

Tabulate the number of faults found in each module and order by increasing number of faults.

A–3.3 STEP 2

Determine the point in the tabulation dividing the modules into two groups: the 80% least faulty modules and the 20% most faulty modules (approximately).

A–3.4 STEP 3

If the total number of faults in the faulty group is greater than 80% of the total number of faults, tentatively identify the modules as candidates for fault analysis. If not, go on to step 5.

A–3.5 STEP 4

Revise the dividing point in the tabulation by a small number, delta, to divide the modules into two new groups: those accounting for 80 + delta percent of all faults and those accounting for 15 - delta percent. If the number of modules in the 80 + delta percent group is less than 20 - delta percent, the 20 - delta percent group replaces the tentative list of candidates for fault analysis. Continue iterating until no further diminution of the tentative group is possible.

A–3.6 STEP 5

Prepare a memo reporting the findings. State the applicable severity level. Report the fault/module distribution of Step 2, either by histogram or in tabular form. If the criterion of Step 3 was not met, report that fault history incidence reveals no modules as candidates for further fault analysis. Otherwise report the names of the modules in the tentative group of candidates identified in Step 4. Distribute the report to the manager of the software project and to any other management levels defined in the quality plan.

Defect Severity Levels

Note: CAE software level 1 comprises priorities 1 and 2.
        CAE software level 2 is identical to priority 3.
        CAE software level 3 comprises priorities 4 and 5.

Note: The following classification guidelines are based on DOD-STD-2167A.

A–4.1 PRIORITY 1

A priority 1 defect will affect the behavior of a software system such that

• The essential functions of the system can not be completed, or

• An operator can not complete essential operations, or

• Personnel safety can be jeopardized.

A–4.2 PRIORITY 2

A priority 1 defect will affect the behavior of a software system such that essential performance can be degraded with no feasible workaround to compensate for the defect's effect. This definition applies also to degradation of performance caused by constraints defects may place on operators.

A–4.3 PRIORITY 3

Priority 3 defects are the same as those of priority 2, except that workaround solutions can be established.

A–4.4 PRIORITY 4

Priority 4 defects do not affect essential capabilities of the software system, but result in operator inconvenience or annoyance.

A–4.5 PRIORITY 5

All other defects. For example, a defect that requires an operation to take one more
memory location than necessary to perform a function.

Form S-7890, Software Problem/Change Report

This report is used to report problems or request changes to material under configuration control. This form is intended to be compatible with Section 10.2.5.10 of DI-MCCR-80030A. All fields are to be filled in. If the required information is not applicable, write "N/A"; if not yet available, write "TBD."

System or project name: _____

Originator: _____

Name _____Tel. _____Dept. _____

Problem/change report number (get from EDLC librarian):
Single sentence description of problem or reason or change:

Software to which problem or change pertains (List all structural levels known, in descending order from highest to lowest):

Applicable documentation (List all documents):

Date form was submitted:
Priority or severity level:
Conditions prompting report (e.g.: test case no., run no., and date; operational site and date; production no.):

Description of problem or reason for change (Include conditions under which problem occurs or is believed potentially to occur):

Relation to other problem/change reports (List report numbers and single sentence descriptions):

Analyst assigned to problem or change:

Name _____Tel. No. _____Dept _____

Date assigned _____Scheduled completion date _____

Completion date of analysis _____Labor hours used _____

Discussion of solution or change, with emphasis on recommendation (attach any applicable simulation results or other data):

Quantified effect of recommended solution or change on cost and schedule:

Effect, if any, of recommended solution or change on other software elements, systems, equipments, field support, training, and so forth:

Status assigned by change board
Signature if recommended solution/request is approved:

_____

Assignment to implement solution or change request:
Name _____Tel. No. _____Dept. _____
Date assigned _____Scheduled completion date _____
Date of final approval of change _____

Edition numbers in which change first appears (Provide full software or documentation number and edition for each item changed):

Glossary of Acronyms and Abbreviations for Chapters 13 and 14

AMTS	Associate Member of Technical Staff
CAE	Computer Aided Engineering
CASE	Computer Aided Software Engineering
CDR	Critical Design Review
CDRL	Contract Data Requirements List
CLASS*	A static analyzer. CLASSIER* is a modified version.
CMP	Configuration Management Plan
CSC	Computer Software Component
CSCI	Computer Software Configuration Item
CSU	Computer Software Unit
DID	Data Item Description
DOD	Department of Defense
EDLC*	Engineering Documentation and Library Control
ERECT*	Software load binder or linker
FCA	Functional Configuration Audit
FQR	Formal Qualification Review
FQT	Formal Qualification Testing
GFE	Government-Furnished Equipment
IDD	Interface Design Document
IEEE	Institute of Electrical and Electronic Engineers
IRS	Interface Requirements Specification
IV&V	Independent Verification and Validation
MP	Measurements Plan
MTS	Member of Technical Staff

* Made-up name

NAIADS*	Name of project for Chapter 14
NCSS	Noncomment Source Statements
OooC*	Object-orientation on C, a compiler
PCA	Physical Configuration Audit
PDR	Preliminary Design Review
PDSLS*	Program Design Statement Language System
QA	Quality Assurance
RCI*	Rameau-Couperin Industries
rev	revision
SCMP	Software Configuration Management Plan
SDD	Software Design Description (Chap. 13)
SDD	Software Design Document (Chap. 14)
SDF	Software Development Folder
SDP	Software Development Plan
SDR	Software Design Review
SMTS	Senior Member of Technical Staff
SOD*	A multi-tasking operating system
SOS*	Superior Oceanographic Systems
SOW	Statement of Work
SPS	Software Product Specification
SQA	Software Quality Assurance
SQAOP	Software Quality Assurance Operating Procedures
SQAP	Software Quality Assurance Plan
SQPP	Software Quality Program Plan
SRR	Software Requirements Review (Chap. 13)
SRR	System Requirements Review (Chap. 14)
SRS	Software Requirements Specification
SSR	Software Specification Review
STD	Software Test Description
STP	Software Test Plan
SVVP	Software Verification and Validation Plan
SVVPR	Software Verification and Validation Plan Review
TRR	Test Readiness Review
V&V	Verification and Validation
VDD	Version Description Document
VDU	Visual Display Unit (commonly, a screen monitor)
VLF	Very Low Frequency

Index